Digital Audio Explained

For the Audio Engineer

Second Edition

Digital Audio Explained

For the Audio Engineer

by Nika Aldrich

Second Edition

Sweetwater®
music technology direct™

Published by Sweetwater Sound, Fort Wayne, Indiana.

Printed in the United States of America

Design by Mike Waskiewicz

Library of Congress Control Number: 2005902744

ISBN 1-4196-0001-X

Second Edition

Dedicated to Avery

And all others who seek to learn about and understand the world around them.

Acknowledgements

I wish to extend a special "thank you" to those who have helped me understand digital audio well enough that I can be helpful to others: David Stewart, Dick Pierce, Paul Frindle, Glenn Zelniker, Jim Johnston, Richard Kulavik, Stan Cotey, Erik Lovell, and Keith Evans. Your time and energy is greatly appreciated. Thank you also to the many editors who have contributed to this book, including David Stewart of Sweetwater Sound, Glenn Zelniker of Z-Systems, Dick Pierce of Professional Audio Development, Joe Bryan of Universal Audio, Richard Kulavik of AKM Semiconductor, Dennis Tabuena, and Paul Frindle.

TABLE OF CONTENTS

Foreword

By Dr. Glenn Zelniker

Each passing year brings new proclamations about the pervasiveness of digital audio technology. Each year also brings new books and articles on digital audio technology, each one promising to endow the reader with newfound clarity and a depth of understanding he/she had heretofore not imagined possible. In many respects, these writings can be viewed as successes, in some cases chronicling the latest and greatest research and development and providing researchers with new starting-points for discovery, in other cases educating degreed engineers who merely need to learn the vocabulary of an unfamiliar field. It is safe to say that digital audio is now a mature discipline that is not merely pervasive; omnipresent might be a better description. As yet, there have not been many texts that attempt to educate the far broader demographic who also needs to know how digital audio really works: the practitioners who actually use digital audio equipment to make recordings. This book is for those people.

Other than mere intellectual curiosity, why should the end-user care about the theory behind the technology? (I should emphasize that there is nothing wrong with mere intellectual curiosity and that this book will certainly be satisfying to the "knowledge collector.") Armed with the knowledge in this book, the digital recordist will be endowed with two exciting capabilities:

- The ability to make better digital recordings

- The ability to make informed technological choices, see through the haze of marketing hype, and spend equipment and media dollars more effectively

Would you like to have these capabilities? It is easier said than done; it will require a bit of discipline and mental investment on the part of you, the reader. I urge you to read the material with an open mind, commit to reading manageable chunks of material at a time (it could be a few pages or it could be a chapter), and resist the temptation to move forward until you understand what you have read. Things that are worth learning often demand some effort, and understanding digital audio may actually require you to do a bit of "unlearning," for the field of digital audio has long been fraught with misinformation and superstition. Diligent reader who stays the course will be rewarded with a newfound clarity as well as the capacity to grow with the field itself – in addition to being a better recordist and a better consumer!

Digital Audio Explained fills a long-standing gap in the body of literature on digital audio by presenting much of the underlying theory of digital audio without presuming that the reader has any advanced mathematical skills or an understanding of physics. The book is far more than a mere user's guide that explains which knob to turn or which setting to use; rather, it teaches the principles that form the basis of digital audio from the ground up: acoustics, human hearing, waveform analysis, sampling theory, data conversion, and digital processing. The exposition of these topics is assisted and enhanced by a rich collection of graphics that complement the text at every step.

By necessity these principles sometimes need to be presented heuristically rather than rigorously. Approaching digital audio through the more traditionally rigorous route, usually taken by researchers and designers, is likely to leave you "cold" and bogged down in a morass of mathematical details that will seem irrelevant to the end goal of being a better digital recordist or a smarter consumer. In the fields of research and design, however, there is a vast body of literature available, much of which will be within your mental grasp once you complete this book. Armed with the knowledge you have gleaned from this book, you will find that you will know

1. What questions to ask

2. Where to go for the answers

I have long felt that these two things are the most important side effects of an education in any field.

In closing, I urge you to go ahead and invest the time and mental energy in reading this book. Keep at it. Do not let it become yet another book you have glanced at, put up on your bookshelf and forgotten about. It contains the requisite material for you to become a knowledgeable digital audio practitioner and a smarter person, each of which carries its own rewards. The pedagogical style is friendly and approachable and asks very little of the reader with regard to formal background. Your investment will reap dividends in short order. I have yet to see a quicker path to such a depth of understanding of the subject than this book. So open your mind, take your shoes off, put your feet up, and get busy. Most of all, though, remember why you are reading this book and enjoy the process.

— September 2004

Dr. Glenn Zelniker is President of Z-Systems Audio Engineering and is co-author of Advanced Digital Signal Processing: Theory and Applications.

Introduction

"Audio Engineer" is a lofty title. In any other field an "engineer" brings to mind an academian with an intense scholastic background, a slide rule or calculator with "the big screen" in pocket, and a manner of talking that always seemed a foreign language to those who were not intimately familiar with their field. In the audio industry, "engineer" is often a self-appointed title indicating some level of proficiency in the recording arts. Often "audio engineers" or "recording engineers" can become "engineers" with no advanced schooling at all, but rather with a stint in "the school of hard knocks."

The term "audio engineer" was born from the days when such a person practically had to build their own equipment. The engineers of the 50s and 60s would have to understand electrical engineering well enough to construct what did not otherwise exist for their specific recording needs. Today's audio engineer tends to be more of an artist than a scientist. Certainly there is still a lot to engineer in today's studio, but few would disagree that the "engineers" of today have it easy compared to those in years past.

Because the role of the engineer has changed, what he has needed to know has changed precipitously. No longer is a graduate education required to learn how to combine audio signals. For that matter, secondary education is not really required at all. Those who do attend school in music technology fields often find that the courses more closely align with the arts department than the math and sciences departments.

It seems that, with the vast amount of information available through media, a bit of internship at a recording studio, reading through the manuals of various pieces of equipment, and some hands-on experience, is all that is necessary to know about producing the best audio recordings and can be learned independently. So much of the information seems intuitive enough that it is difficult to understand where any confusion would possibly exist. Most people who have been introduced to a loose paraphrasing of the Nyquist theory think it is so obvious that they have a hard time determining why it took so long to formulate and further wonder why, as obvious as the premise is, it is even worth naming after someone.

Throughout the last several years I have served in the capacity of being a consultant for recording studios, recording engineers, mastering engineers, and recording artists. I am confronted on a daily basis with the realization that misinformation in the audio industry is increasing to the point of being damaging. The misinformation does not only thrive at the consumer level, but in the project studios and major studios, and by some of the best names in the recording industry (remember, there is no degree required to be a world famous "audio engineer"). Before long, myths stemming from intuitive deductions based on incomplete information run rampant and the media and manufacturers tend to further compound the problem. I have also been confronted with the reality that poor understanding of how the recording systems really work is leading to lesser quality results, and clearly the proliferation of digital recording has been the instigator of the general lack of understanding in our industry.

I have observed three things that led me to write this book:

1. That the average audio engineer has an understanding in very specific aspects of digital theory but a very poor understanding of the foundational math and science that is the backbone of acoustics, audibility, and recording technology. Without the foundational knowledge in place, any variance from a known set of parameters either leads to confusion or incorrect "intuitive" conclusions being drawn.

2. That the information and knowledge are readily available, BUT, that the resources and people that harness that knowledge speak in the foreign language of "calculus" or "physics" or the above mentioned "engineer's speak," making the information essentially unavailable to the recording engineers that populate the audio industry at this time.

3. That there are several books written for the audio engineer, and several books written about the advanced concepts that really provide the foundation for an understanding of digital audio, but these two types of books do not intersect.

This book will take the advanced concepts that are really the basis of our industry that are so often misunderstood and will present them in a comprehensive fashion for the audio engineer who does not know the language of "engineer's speak."

Because of this, however, it is crucially important that the book be read in a linear fashion, from cover to cover. Any attempts at skipping around from chapter to chapter as the information is needed will provide the same, incomplete foundation and will allow incorrect conclusions to be drawn and confusion to arise and will completely undermine the intent of this book. So much of the information on any given topic is presented in a fashion that expects that the reader has accomplished complete comprehension of previous points. I cannot stress this enough. I literally wrote this entire book in a few weeks, linearly, from beginning to end, working to ensure that one point fed into the next and that there was little opportunity for incorrect conclusions to be drawn. Missing one, minor detail may have a tremendous effect on the understanding of a later section where that one detail is the foundation for a larger issue.

If the book is approached as intended the reader will, by the end of the book, not only have a new, better sounding approach to digital recording and not only have a comprehensive understanding of major issues like IIR and FIR filters, dither, jitter, 1-bit converters, Fourier analysis and convolution reverbs, but will also be able to dispel some of the most prevalent myths of the audio recording industry. Namely:

1. Higher sample rate digital recordings inherently sound better than lower sample rate recordings, all things being equal

2. More bits inherently sound better than fewer bits, all things being equal

3. Recording the signal "hotter" will yield better digital recording results

4. Clock quality makes no audible difference in a recording studio

5. Clock quality is important to every box in a recording studio

6. Digital recording or mixing can never sound as good as analog recording or mixing

7. DSD is better than PCM, all things being equal

Digital Audio Explained

For the Audio Engineer

Part One

Sound and Hearing

Chapter One

Understanding Sound

A comprehensive understanding of digital audio must begin with a thorough awareness of the recording process unto itself. Understanding the recording process requires reconciling several areas of potential confusion including what sound is, how it is generated and propagated, how it is heard and interpreted by the ear, what the key components of sound are and how differences in sounds are identifiable and interpreted. These areas may seem rather mundane and redundant for most readers, but it is only with an agreement on several foundational elements that we can ensure that digital audio will be explainable using the terms and premises that we have established early on when we get to more advanced sections of this book.

DEFINING SOUND

"Sound" is the term used to describe any change in air pressure that triggers neural reactions in the human auditory system in a manner that we call "hearing". Speaking in a traditional sense, sound is simply changes in air pressure. These changes in air pressure, however, have to fall into a realm that we can hear. Air pressure changes can occur on many levels, from the type that the meteorologist tells us about on the evening news to the pressure that builds up in a soda can while it is shaken. Each of these examples constitute changes in air pressure, but sound, specifically, requires that the changes in air pressure fall into a range that can be sensed by the ear.

The changes in air pressure have to happen within a certain, very specific range of speeds and at certain, very specific amounts. This is the reason that a drop in barometric pressure announced by the weatherman on the evening news does not get manifested by the human ear as an audible occurrence: it does not fit into that very specific set of requirements that is required of the air pressure changes in order to qualify as "sound".

Very shortly we will learn more about the human ear, but for now we will have to simply accept a few principles in order to move forward, but with the understanding that more information later will help to explain how this all works. In the meantime, we must accept that the ear can only hear changes in air pressure if they change from one amount of pressure to another amount and then change back, and it must do that within a certain amount of time (no longer than about 1/40th of a second).

HOW SOUND IS CREATED

These very fast changes in air pressure are created by any item that can pressurize and then depressurize the air in a short amount of time. One example of this would be a speaker cone, which can move out, pressurizing the air in front of it, and then move back, depressurizing that air, all within a very short amount of time. Other examples would include the skin on a drum, which functions very similarly to a speaker cone when struck, a piece of wood when struck or anything else that would very quickly move back and forth, pressurizing and then depressurizing the air very quickly. We could also say that sound is created by anything that quickly vibrates when some form of energy is applied to it. A scientific term that defines the degree to which an item vibrates when energy is applied to it is "elasticity". Any item that is non-elastic will not vibrate when struck but will rather simply move and stop. Since all devices vibrate to some degree, and therefore completely "non-elastic" items exist only in science textbooks, nearly every item generates "sound" when energy is applied to it (such as when the item gets struck), with the only caveat being those items whose elasticity is such that the air pressure changes that result when energy is applied are either too small, too slow, or too fast to be recognized by the human auditory system.

On very elastic devices, such as rubber bands and springs, the physics involved is fairly obvious. When a rubber band, for example, is stretched away from its resting position and released, the initiating energy causes it to change shape. As the middle of the rubber band stretches outward, its momentum from the initial energy causes it to expand and the fact that it is very elastic allows this to happen. Eventually, however, the tension overcomes the inertia that moves it outwards and the middle of the rubber band reaches a maximum displacement from its resting position. At this point the tension starts to move the rubber band backwards, continually accelerating its movement. Inertia from its backwards movement causes it to move again past the resting position, and the same cycle starts the other direction.

Physicists have studied this movement and have come up with mathematical formulas that can indicate how much and what type of movement will occur in a given elastic device. "Hooke's Law" is used to tell us that if we plot on a graph the displacement of a perfectly

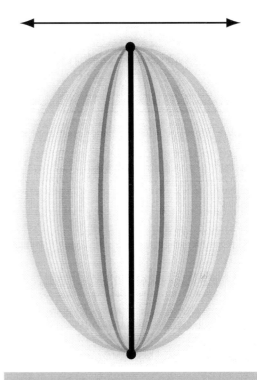

FIGURE 1.1A: The Movement of an Elastic Device, Such as a Rubber Band

The movement of an elastic band is shown, captured at even intervals of time. If one were to plot, on graph paper, the distance that the middle of the device (or any other point on the device) moves over time this would yield a sine wave.

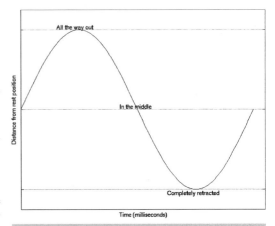

FIGURE 1.1B: Plotting of the Movement of the Middle of the Elastic Device Over Time

If the movement of the middle of the rubber band is graphed over time the result is a "sine wave."

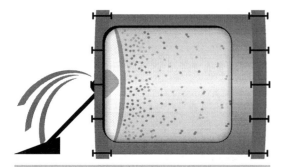

FIGURE 1.2A: **A Kick Drum After Hit, Compressing the Air in Front of it.**

As the drumhead is forced inwards, the air molecules in front of it compress.

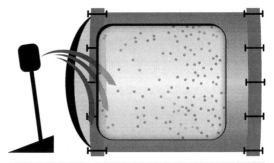

FIGURE 1.2B: **The Kick Drumhead Retracting**

The movement of the drumhead outwards creates an area of low pressure in front of the drumhead.

elastic device (such as our theoretical rubber band) over time (Figure 1.1), that the result will yield a shape called a "sine wave."

All objects have some degree of elasticity but the size of the item, the shape of the item, the thickness of the item, the density of the item and many other properties of any given object yield that when a "less than ideal" object is struck, the movement it yields produces a multitude of sinusoidal waves. For now, however, we will continue to explore nearly perfect devices that move in very neat and organized sinusoidal fashions. Moving away from rubber bands, we will pretend that we have a drum, and said drum has a head that is "science textbook quality" and yields very simple movements and responds like a simple sine wave.

As the drumhead moves out, the air in front of the drumhead compresses, causing an area of higher air pressure immediately in front of the head. When the drumhead retracts, an area of low pressure is created in front of the drumhead. This is demonstrated in Figure 1.2.

As the drumhead moves in a perfect sinusoidal fashion the changes in air pressure that result occur in a perfect sinusoidal shape: the maximum displacement outward occurs and thus causes the greatest compression of the air molecules in front of it. This represents the peak of the sine wave. As the drumhead reverts back to its resting position the air pressure in front of it is normal (not greater than nor less than the normal atmospheric pressure in the room), but it is at this moment that the drumhead is moving the fastest. This is represented by fact that the angle of the sine wave as it passes through the "resting position" is the steepest. As the drumhead reaches the furthest distance

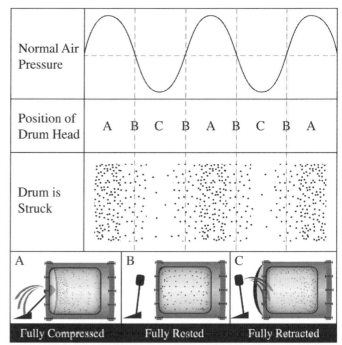

FIGURE 1.3: **Air Pressure in Front of the Drumhead**

As the drumhead moves outward (A) the air pressure in front of the head increases. When the drumhead is at its normal resting position (B) the air pressure in front of the drum is the same pressure as the nominal pressure in the air. When the drumhead is fully retracted (C) the air pressure in front of the drum is lower than room air pressure.

in the other direction the greatest change in air pressure occurs in the negative direction. In a perfect situation (science textbook) the amount of displacement of our drumhead in the backward direction would be the same as the amount of displacement in the forward direction. In real life this does not occur because friction causes the drumhead to slow down, preventing it from reaching the same displacement in the negative direction that it does in the positive direction. Figure 1.3 shows the simplified behavior of the drumhead.

THE TRANSMISSION OF SOUND

The movement of the drumhead outwards causes a wave of pressure to be "pushed," or "propagated" through the air. The molecules in the air transfer their energy to adjacent air molecules, which transfer their energy to the next air molecules, and so on and so on, causing the area of high pressure to move forward. As this area of high pressure moves forward, however, the air molecules fill the void left behind them and move backward. This movement of the air molecules forward and backward causes the wave of high pressure to move forward subsequently followed by the wave of low pressure. The net effect of this back and forth motion is that the air molecules themselves do not actually change position when all the motion ceases. The air molecules essentially stay in roughly the same place but the pressure wave moves forward, caused by the movement of the air molecules forward and backward.

An easy way to visualize this is to think of a child's slinky. If we take that slinky while it is compressed and draw a line across it then we will end up with a dot on the slinky at each of the tops of the "spirals" of the slinky when it is laid out. These dots represent individual air molecules. If we stretch the slinky out to about ten feet long and let it settle we will notice that all of the "dots" come to rest at an equal distance from each other. When one end of the slinky is pushed forward, a wave of pressure "propagates" through the slinky as the dots move closer to each other and then retract from each other. Notice that the net effect is that each individual "air molecule" does not actually move much distance at all. Each individual "air molecule" ends up at the same place that it started, though the wave of pressure propagates at a high speed through the slinky. This is very similar to what happens in the air. The air molecules, in trying to maintain a certain distance from each other (constant air pressure) move back and forth, pushing a wave of air pressure forward through the air. The air as a whole does not change location. An example of this is shown in Figure 1.4.

Another way to visualize this is by imagining a swimming pool with a ping-pong ball floating on it. If a stone is thrown into the pool creating waves on the pool's surface, the ping-pong ball will bob up and down with the waves but will not move much in a "lateral" direction (forward or backwards) at all. It certainly will not move toward the edge of the pool at the speed that the

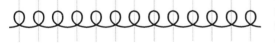

FIGURE 1.4A: **Examples of Wave Propagation**

A spring stretched out but in a state of rest. The "top" of each loop in the spring is an equal distance from the surrounding spring loops.

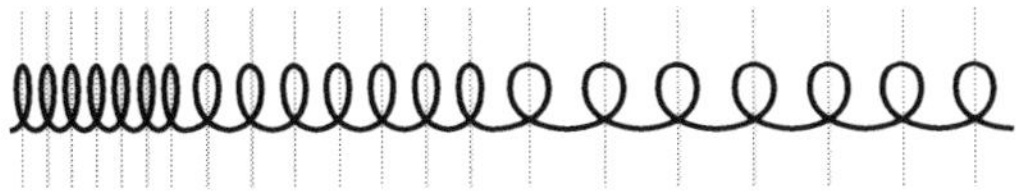

FIGURE 1.4B

If the left side of the spring is quickly pushed inwards the left side of the spring is momentarily compressed. The distance between the "tops" of each loop are no longer a fixed distance apart.

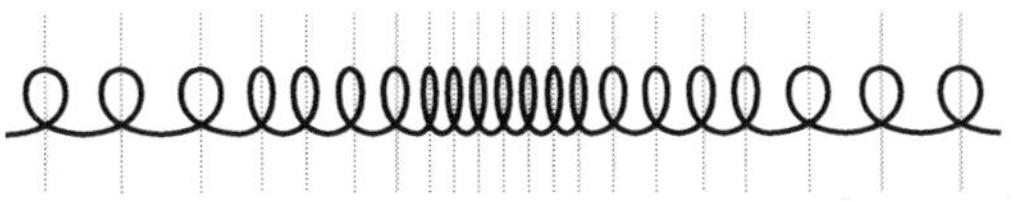

FIGURE 1.4C

The area of "compression" propagates through the spring. Notice that each loop in the spring does not travel particularly far, but the "compression wave" travels all the way through the spring. This compression wave is created as each loop in the spring moves back and forth in an organized fashion, one after the other, each one effectively "pushing" the other loops to move forward and then subsequently "pulling" them back to rest.

waves move. The reason is that the ping-pong ball has friction with the water directly underneath it, and since that water underneath the ball does not change location or move in a lateral direction, the ping-pong ball will not change location either. The ping-pong ball's lateral movement shows us fairly accurately what the movement of the water immediately below it is.

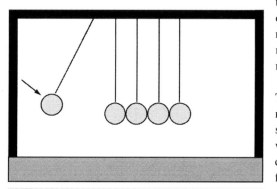

FIGURE 1.5A: **Energy Passing Through Newton's Cradle**

The speed at which the drumhead moves in our original analogy is NOT the speed at which the air pressure wave will move through space. The air pressure wave moves forward at the speed in which the air molecules bounce off of each other and transfer the energy forward through space. The speed that the drumhead moves is only the speed at which the stick hit the drumhead (maybe 100mph or so). The pressure wave that leaves the drumhead leaves at the speed that the energy from the drumhead transmits through air molecules.

The best example used to describe this is the typical set of hanging balls called "Newton's cradle", as in the diagrams given in Figure 1.5. As the ball on the left is raised and released it only moves at a relatively slow speed through the air. As soon as it hits the next ball, however, the energy is transmitted to it, and to all of the subsequent balls through the chain very quickly. By the time the energy is transmitted to the last ball and it moves forward it appears that no time has elapsed. In actuality, it takes some time for the energy to transmit through all of the balls, but because the balls are so dense and so close together, that energy transmits in what appears to be no time at all.

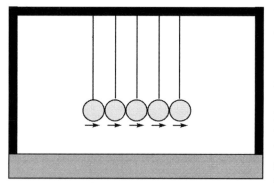

FIGURE 1.5B

The energy passes first from the first ball to the second ball, then from the second ball to the third ball, and continuing through all of the balls. This "appears" to happen instantaneously because the balls are made of a dense material (metal) and because the balls are close together, making the transfer of energy very fast.

If the balls were either less dense, like bean bags, or if they were further apart from each other it would take noticeably longer for the energy to transmit through the balls, as shown in Figure 1.6.

A similar thing occurs with pressure waves: sound waves pass through the environment independent of the speed of the vibrating device. Sound pressure waves move faster through metal than water and faster through water than air. High air pressure or low humidity causes slower air pressure movement than does wet or low atmospheric pressure conditions. Sound waves at high altitudes where the air is less dense, therefore, move faster than sound waves at sea level. Most often the "speed of sound" is figured for the speed of the wave propagation at sea level and has been calculated to be 776 mph, or about 1138 feet per second. Often times the audio industry approximates this to be "about 1 foot per millisecond," or about one foot per thousandth of a second.

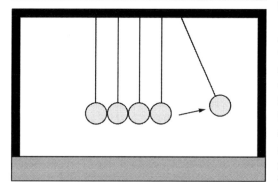

FIGURE 1.5C

Nearly all of the energy is passed through each of the balls, through to the last one, starting the cycle over again in reverse.

It is fairly important to understand a couple of key details at this point that are often areas of confusion. First, due to diagrams in many textbooks and other informative materials of waves being created or propagated, many people are under the impression that the air itself moves, and that the air itself moves in a sinusoidal capacity (air molecules move up and then down, etc.), such as Figure 1.7 would indicate.

It is important to understand that, overall, the air itself does not move. Individual molecules move back and forth at any given moment in time, but in the end, each molecule ends up approximately where it started. Further, the air itself does not move in the shape of sine waves like light does. Instead, there are areas of high and low pressure, and the pressure itself moves. This is represented in waves on paper, but the waves on paper really represent areas of high and low pressure and not the direction of the movement of the individual air molecules.

Second, it is important to understand that the air pressure waves are the same "shape" as the movement in time of the device that creates them. An extremely elastic device moves in a sinusoidal fashion and the results yield sinusoidally shaped areas of high and low pressure. A device that does not move sinusoidally produces air pressure changes that are congruous with the shape of the movement of the device. For example, a device that moves triangularly when struck creates triangularly shaped waves of air pressure (Figure 1.8).

Back to our drumhead: as our perfect, very elastic device moves forward it will reach its maximum point of displacement and then return back to where it started. It will return back to where it started with some new momentum and this energy will carry it past its starting point and to an equal point on the other side. Then, once again, the tension will overcome its inertia and pull it back to its original position at which point the cycle will begin again. In our perfect environment this will continue forever.

In a more realistic environment, the drumhead will lose some of its energy over time due to air resistance and friction. As this happens, each subsequent movement of the drumhead back and forth will instead result in less and less displacement until the drumhead eventually comes to rest back at its starting position. Figure 1.9 displays the decreasing energy in the drumhead's movements.

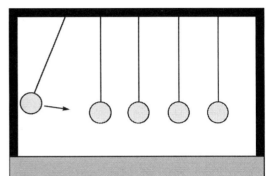

FIGURE 1.6A: Energy Passing Through A Less Efficient Newton's Triangle

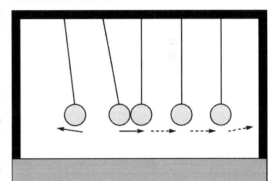

FIGURE 1.6B

Energy still passes through all of the balls, but the process does not appear to happen instantaneously because of the added space between each of the balls.

FIGURE 1.7: A Diagram Showing How Sound Waves Do Not Move Through the Air

A commonly misinformed belief has the air molecules traveling through the air in a sort of sinusoidal fashion. This more closely relates to explanations of how light waves move but is inaccurate with respect to the way in which sound waves travel.

FIGURE 1.8: Triangular Air Pressure Waves

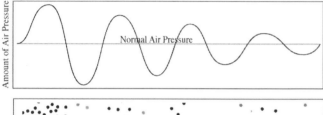

FIGURE 1.9: Air Pressure Waves Decreasing in Pressure Change Over Time

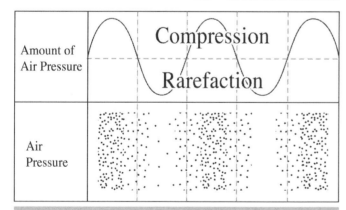

FIGURE 1.10: The Identification of the Compression and Rarefaction Portions of Waves

On a plot of the changes in air pressure that yield sound, the portions of the plot that represent higher air pressure, or "compressed" air are said to show "compression." The portions of the plot that represent air pressure lower than the nominal air pressure in the environment are said to show "rarefaction."

Every time the drumhead moves outward it sends away a wave of high pressure at the speed of sound. Every time that it moves backwards it sends away a wave of low pressure at the speed of sound. The amount of pressure is related to how far out or back the drumhead moves. As it moves less and less far out it creates waves of less and less pressure. As it moves less and less far back it creates waves of low pressure that are closer and closer to the pressure of the air when the drumhead is at rest.

The waves of high pressure are called areas of "compression." The waves of low pressure are called areas of "rarefaction."

We already defined earlier that sound can be created by any item that has elasticity and that all physical, non-science-textbook items have elasticity. We can infer from this that when an object is struck, causing it to change shape, and the object changes back to its original position, that the momentum that it carries will force it to move in the opposite direction. It is impossible for an item to be struck, move outward, and then return to rest without some swing past neutral in the opposite direction. For this reason, it is impossible to have a high-pressure wave, or compression wave, that is not followed by a rarefaction wave of some form. One necessarily requires the other due to the simple physical reality of inertia.

The entire period of time, from the initial movement, past the peak of compression, through a return to its original position, past its peak of rarefaction, and back to its original position again is called a "cycle." The compression wave and the ensuing rarefaction wave are treated as a single wave and that wave's shape is called a "waveform."

This shape is called a "waveform" and a "complete cycle" whether it is a sine wave or not. Any compression followed by its ensuing rarefaction qualifies as a cycle.

A few more details should be clarified before we continue. First, we have been discussing wave propagation as a "two-dimensional" event, in that the waves move out along a straight line, such as down the length of a slinky. In actuality the waves move more in a circular pattern, akin to how pressure waves of water move when a stone is thrown in a pool. As such, the amount of air pressure in the waves decreases because the energy spreads wider and wider apart as the circle at the leading edge of the wave continues to expand. The amount of energy used to create the pressure wave cannot yield more than the total amount of energy that the pressure wave carries. As the pressure wave increases in size (the circumference of it increases) the energy at any given point of it decreases. A more accurate diagram of the radial movement and decreasing energy of a wave is shown in Figure 1.12.

It should be noted that the length of the wave does not change, but the amount of air pressure change does decrease as the pressure wave moves away from the source. It should also be pointed out that the movement is really not entirely "circular", but more "spherical," as the pressure wave moves in all directions, including vertically.

Finally, we should clarify that our examples above were mostly using devices that have very "ideal" elasticity and move in sinusoidal fashions only. In reality, the devices that create sound are going to create much more complex waveforms because multiple parts of the elastic device move at the same time (Figure 1.13). We will look more closely at these situations later.

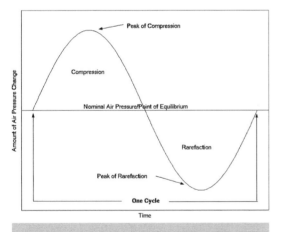

FIGURE 1.11: Labeling the Parts of a Waveform

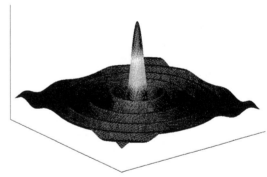

FIGURE 1.12: Sound Propagates in All Directions

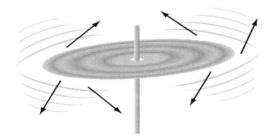

FIGURE 1.13A: The Creation and Propagation of Complex Waveforms

FIGURE 1.13B: A Waveform Created By a Cymbal

Chapter Two

Parts of a Waveform

The primary focus of studying audio in this context is to be able to reproduce it. In order to reproduce a waveform it is necessary to understand what it is that makes a particular audio waveform unique. There are four identifying characteristics of a sound wave that are important to identify and understand. These four characteristics fully describe and define the waveform. If all four of these characteristics can be accurately recorded and duplicated then it will be possible to completely re-create the waveform. The objective of the science and the art of "recording" is specifically to be able to re-create waveforms and duplicate the sound that originally occurred. These defining characteristics of the waveform are the *amount* of air pressure change, *how fast* the waveform occurs, the *time* at which the wave occurs, and the *amount of random variation* in the waveform. These will be referred to as amplitude, frequency, relative phase, and dynamic range. We will address these characteristics in detail in that respective order.

AMPLITUDE

The amount of variation in air pressure from the normal atmospheric pressure in the area to either the highest pressure at compression or the lowest pressure at rarefaction is termed the "amplitude" of the waveform. When discussing amplitude we are only discussing the maximum variation from the normal pressure in the area, so the normal pressure in the area (the room in which the sound is made) is irrelevant to the amplitude.

We will be discussing later more about how sensitive the ear is to changes in amplitude, but suffice it to say for now that it is extremely sensitive to changes in air pressure and that the difference between the smallest change and the largest change it can detect is tremendous.

Although we are still a ways from describing how the ear works, the amount of pressure change needed to trigger a reaction in the ear is measured in terms of bars, the same unit used to measure barometric pressure. The amplitude of air pressure change necessary for the ear to recognize it is generally accepted as being .0000000002 bars, or .0002 microbars. This is based on studies done at Bell Labs in the early 1900s. The maximum amplitude of air pressure change the ear can hear before pain is experienced in the average human is around .0002 bars, or 200 microbars. The range between the loudest and the quietest sound that a human could hear is so large that it became impractical for scientists to represent sound levels in traditional numerical means. Imagine trying to plot on a piece of graph paper the quietest amplitude that the human could hear and the loudest amplitude we could stand. The graph paper would have to be tall enough that the largest identifiable amplitude could be 1,000,000 times larger than the smallest one!

In order to make the numbers more practical to handle, the scientists at Bell labs put the human hearing range on a logarithmic scale, as is shown in Figure 2.1.

By doing this they made it possible to put the entire amplitude range of human hearing on a more workable scale. At the time that the studies were done, the range of human hearing was divided into 10 large units that, as a tribute to Alexander Graham Bell, the engineers at Bell labs called the Bel. The Bel represents too wide a difference in amplitude for most practical use in sound situations, so the decibel (one tenth of a Bel) is more often used to describe sound pressure level changes. The Bel is signified as "B" whereas the

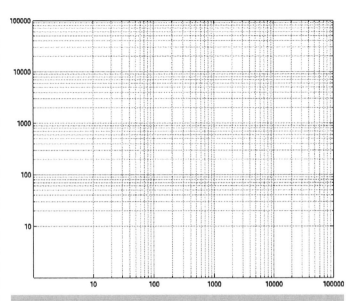

FIGURE 2.1: **The Logarithmic Scale**

decibel is signified as "dB." It is important at this point to note that the Bel and the decibel are merely ways to measure the relationship between two different amounts of air pressure change. In this particular situation we are using it to measure the relationship between the smallest and the largest changes in air pressure that the human auditory system responds to. It can also, however, be used to measure the relationship between any two changes in air pressure levels. If a stereo system is playing at a certain level and we turn the stereo system up some amount we would describe the amount it was turned up in terms of decibels. If a shotgun blast creates a certain amount of air pressure change then we could measure the difference between the quiescent air pressure and the change created by a rifle in terms of decibels.

Note that we could not say that the shotgun blast "is," or "produces" a certain number of decibels. Since the decibel is a way to measure the relationship between two different amplitudes, we could not discuss a shotgun blast in terms of decibels because there is no other amplitude to which to compare it. We could, however, say that it is a certain number of decibels of amplitude larger or smaller than another level, such as a rifle shot, a rock concert, the quietest amplitude we can hear, etc.

It is crucially important to remember that a decibel is not a measure of a single amplitude level – it is a measurement of the relationship between any two amplitudes. A decibel is a relative term used for comparing one waveform's amplitude with that of another.

One other useful thing that the engineers at Bell Labs did, however, was attempt to quantify the quietest amount of air pressure change (amplitude) that humans could hear. They determined that the portion of the population with the most sensitive low-level hearing was black women from age 18-22. With very sensitive equipment it was determined, using that portion of the population, the smallest air pressure change that was detectable at a specific given frequency was .0002 microbars. This amount of air pressure change was prescribed as an absolute reference level and defined as 0dB SPL (Sound Pressure Level).

By creating a reference level of 0dB SPL it would now be possible to indicate how loud a shotgun blast was without referencing it to another event. It would now be possible to reference it to simply the quietest sound that humans can hear, or .0002 microbars. A shotgun blast could now be said to be 140dB SPL at a six-inch distance, in that the relationship between the air pressure level of the shotgun blast and .0002 microbars is 140dB. There is, however, a fine difference between saying that a shotgun blast is 140dB SPL and saying that it is 140dB. The latter does not actually indicate anything useful, as it does not compare the shotgun blast to

220dB SPL - Inside a Diesel Engine

200dB SPL - Jet Engine at Takeoff

170dB SPL - Ear Drum Disintegrates

120dB SPL - Threshold of Pain
105dB SPL - Rock Concert
90dB SPL - Downtown Urban Traffic from Curbside
85dB SPL - Typical Music Listening Level
80dB SPL - Noisy Office Environment
70dB SPL - Small Orchestra
60dB SPL - Typical Conversation Between Two People
50dB SPL - Background Office Noise
40dB SPL - Quiet House at Night
30dB SPL - Typical Recording Studio

0dB SPL - Threshold of Hearing

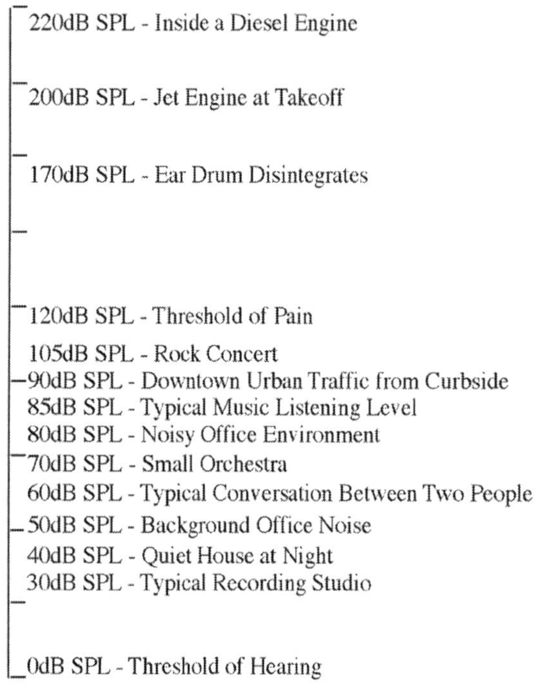

FIGURE 2.2: Sound Pressure Levels of Some Common Sounds

anything, which the use of the decibel measurement must inherently do.

It is also important to note that 0dB SPL does not represent a complete absence of air pressure fluctuations. It is merely the quietest air pressure change that we humans are capable of hearing.[1] Based on the logarithmic scale we could determine that an air pressure change of an amplitude of .0001 microbars would be equal to –6dB SPL, and air pressure changes can get quieter than that. 0dB SPL is merely a convenient reference level.

Now that we have established a reference level we can give some perspective for some common sounds in daily life and how much sound pressure they yield (Figure 2.2).

We should also further clarify that using the decibel is not only a matter of convenience in reducing a large variation to a small variation (the difference between .0002 microbars to 200 microbars now gets reduced to 120dB) but it actually more closely represents the way in which we hear. Looking again at the logarithmic chart, the visual representation shows that ten times the values only accounts for a doubling of the physical space on the graph, as indicated in Figure 2.3.

We should probably further clarify that there are several different measurements that use some form of the decibel. For example, the decibel can just as easily be used to compare changes in amplitudes of other things besides air pressure. It can be used to compare changes in voltage and wattage. On the following page is a reference list of other measurements for which the decibel is used. Note that in every one of the examples the unit shows a reference point. This is because a decibel is always a comparison between two amplitudes. If one unit is assigned by a given standard measurement or protocol then there is a constant value available for the comparison.

With respect to amplitude representing the maximum air pressure change, it also represents the maximum amount that the elastic device that generated it had to move. A drumhead's movement away from its normal resting position is directly related to the amplitude of the air pressure change it generates. The drumhead, being an elastic device, does not require the same amount of energy to move equal distances. For example, if it takes a certain amount of energy for the drumhead to move one centimeter from its resting position it does not require the same amount of additional energy to move an additional centimeter from its resting position. The further it has to move the more the device must stretch and the more energy it takes to accomplish that. This energy is transferred from the drumhead into the air, so as the amplitude of the air pressure changes increase at a constant rate the amount of potential energy represented by the waves changes at a much faster rate.

As the amplitude of a waveform increases, the power in it increases exponentially. If the amplitude is doubled then the power is quadrupled. The formula is $P \sim A^2$ where P is the power and A is the amplitude. This means

---

1 At a given frequency that humans are predisposed to be very sensitive to. Further studies have indicated that at other frequencies some humans can hear as low as –8dB SPL.

Unit of Measure	What it Measures	Definition
dBA		The dB SPL figure with a weighting curve applied to it
dBC		The same as dBA but with a different weighting curve
dBc		dB referenced to a carrier (voltage or power)
dB FS		dB referenced to the maximum amplitude capable of being represented in a digital system
dBm	power	dB referenced to a milliwatt
dBmV	voltage	dB referenced to 1 mVrms across 75 ohms
dB SPL	power	dB referenced to .0002 microbars
dBu	voltage	dB refenced to 0.775 Vrms across 600 ohms Sometimes dB referenced to 1 uVrms, hence the alternate terminology below to avoid confusion
dBv	voltage	Alternate for terminology for dBu (referenced to 0.775 Vrms)
dBV	voltage	dB referenced to 1 Vrms
dBW	power	dB referenced to 1 Watt

that if the amplitude of a waveform increases 6dB (doubles) then the power in it quadruples. If the power in a waveform doubles then the waveform's amplitude only increases by 3dB.

To recap our understanding of the first characteristic of a waveform and how we describe it:

• Amplitude is measured in bars of atmospheric pressure.

• Because the changes in bars can be so large, we use a logarithmic scale to denote changes in amplitude.

• The decibel is the unit used to denote a relationship between amplitudes of different waveforms.

• The decibel is always a comparison between two different amplitudes.

• We use dB SPL as a way of comparing amplitudes to a reference amplitude of .0002 microbars.

• Doubling the "perceived loudness" of an event is equivalent to approximately a change of 6dB SPL.

• As the amplitude increases the power increases quadratically.

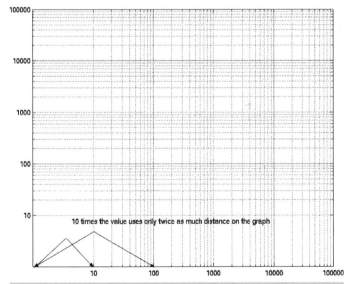

FIGURE 2.3: **Observations of the Logarithmic Scale**

This scale is much more closely aligned with our hearing. We tend to perceive a sound pressure level increase of about 6dB SPL in amplitude as only a doubling of the "loudness." This means that 90dB SPL seems to us to be about twice as loud as 84dB SPL, just as 16dB SPL seems to us to be about twice as loud as 10dB SPL. We can infer from this that if we take the quietest thing that is audible and double its air pressure change that it should be around 6dB SPL, and if we double it 19 more times that will be loud enough to cause us pain. (19 x 6dB SPL = 114dB SPL). It is therefore evident that while the logarithmic method of noting amplitude may seem to distort the very wide range of signals that we can hear, it presents them in a way that is more akin to the way we actually hear.

FREQUENCY

The second identifying characteristic of a waveform is how fast the waveform completes a cycle. This is the

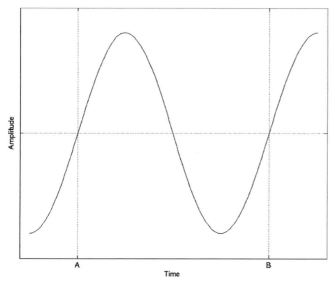

FIGURE 2.4: Understanding Frequency

amount of time it takes for an elastic device to flex one direction, flex back the other direction, and then return to its initial starting place again (though it would not stop at this point – it would be on its way to another period of compression). The frequency of a waveform is identified in Figure 2.4.

The difference in time between (A) and (B) defines the period of a waveform. The units of the period are seconds. The frequency of a wave is the number of full cycles the wave makes every second. So, the frequency is just 1/period. For example, a sinusoid with period of 1/100 of a second would have a frequency of 1/1/100 = 100 Hz.

The "frequency" of a waveform is the speed at which a complete cycle occurs. Frequency is measured in cycles per second, or Hertz. We know from Newtonian physics that while the amplitude changes over time, a device that is freely vibrating (oscillating) will continue to vibrate at the same frequency. This means that if a drumhead (or any "transducer") is struck, that the waves of pressure that follow will decrease in amplitude, but will continue to propagate at the same frequency. Therefore, if a transducer with energy applied to it creates an air pressure wave that takes 1/50th

of a second to complete a cycle, it will continue to put out decreasing amplitude waveform cycles that take 1/50th of a second to complete. This waveform would be a 50Hz waveform (50 cycles per second) though the amplitude would decay over time.

When discussing audio it is common to refer to frequencies in Hz or in kHz (kiloHertz, or thousands of cycles per second) because the total range of human hearing falls into the Hz and kHz range. When discussing digital audio and audio recording there are applications wherein frequencies in the MHz (MegaHertz, or millions of cycles per second) need to be discussed.

We generally represent frequencies in music as "notes." A given "note" is a representation of a particular frequency. This makes the writing and reading of music much easier and more organized than writing music in terms of which frequencies are supposed to be played.

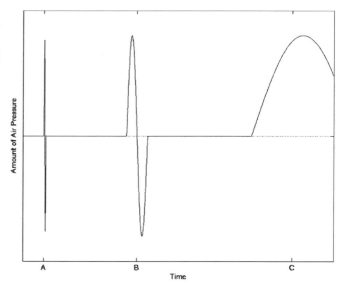

FIGURE 2.5: Relationship Between Wavelength, Period, and Frequency.

Waveform (A) is a 1000Hz waveform. A single cycle of it is .001 seconds and it is 1.138' long.

Waveform (B) is a 100Hz waveform. A single cycle of it is .01 seconds and it is 11.38' long.

Waveform (C) is a 10Hz waveform. A single cycle of it is .1 seconds and it is 113.8' long.

The musical notes that are used all have frequency values that are associated with them. Most of the time the A above middle C is tuned so that it puts out 440Hz waveforms. In another (rather counterintuitive) situation, the frequencies of waveforms are not perceived by the human auditory system as "linear." We humans hear the musical "octave" as a doubling of the frequency. Therefore, the note A an octave above 440Hz is 880Hz. All of the note 'A's across the keyboard are as follows: 27.5Hz, 55Hz, 110Hz, 220Hz, 440Hz, 880Hz, 1.76kHz and 3.52kHz. Notice that the bottom octave on the keyboard only covers a range of 27.5Hz, but the octave between the top two 'A's covers 1,760Hz. To figure the frequency of any note we can multiply the frequency of the note below it times

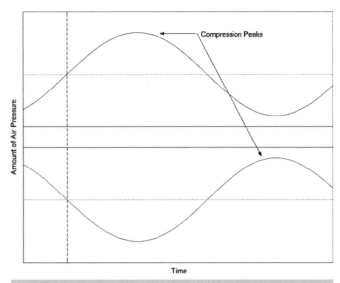

FIGURE 2.6: Two Waveforms in Opposite Phase

1.059462. Thus, to figure out the frequency of note middle C, multiply 220Hz (the frequency of A below middle C) times 1.059462 to get the frequency of Bb (below middle C), again to get the value of B (below middle C), and again to learn that middle C is about 262Hz.

We do not often need to know the wavelength of a waveform when working with recording audio, but since it is so closely related to frequency it seems appropriate to cover. Understanding wavelengths is important in the art of acoustical design, such as designing recording studios.

Since we already know the speed of sound, if we learn the frequency of a waveform we can also determine the physical length of the air pressure wave's cycle. The math is simple: we know that air travels roughly 1138 feet per second. If we have a 1Hz wave it would take an entire second for a complete cycle, so the length of the pressure wave must be 1138 feet long. If, however, we had a 2Hz wave then each waveform could only be half as long, or 569 feet. We can derive from this a very simple formula:

$$Wavelength\ (in\ feet) = \frac{Speed\ of\ sound\ (in\ feet/second)}{Frequency\ (in\ cycles/second)}$$

Since the speed of sound is a constant value, we can write the formula out like this instead:

$$Wavelength\ (in\ feet) = 1138\ /\ Frequency\ (in\ Hz)$$

Or

$$Wavelength\ (in\ feet) = Frequency\ (in\ Hz)\ x\ 0.000879$$

PHASE

The third characteristic of a waveform is phase. This refers to what time the waveform occurs in comparison to other events. "Phase" is a word used to refer to when, exactly, a cycle starts in time.

In Figure 2.6, the amplitude and the frequency of the two waves are the same but the time that the first wave starts is different than the second. These two waveforms are said to be "180° out of phase" with each other. If the peak of the waveforms occurred at the same time the waveforms would be said to be "in phase" with each other.

Just as with amplitude, the phase of a waveform is always compared to the phase of another waveform. A waveform by itself cannot be "out of phase," but in comparison to another waveform it can be. Therefore waveform A above is not out of phase with anything until it is compared to waveform B.

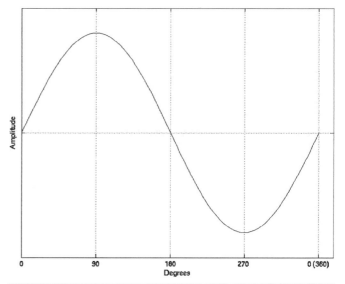

FIGURE 2.7: **Degrees and Waveforms**

Phase of waveforms is measured in degrees with 0° being the beginning of the waveform, where it crosses the nominal level and begins its compression peak, and 180° being the beginning of the rarefaction peak.

Phase is measured in degrees. If a sine wave is divided into degrees, then the compression peak occurs at 90°, the rarefaction peak occurs at 270°, the beginning of the waveform is both at 0° and at 360°, and the "zero crossing" in the middle is at 180° (Figure 2.7).

If we compare two waveforms of differing phase then we can tell how far out of phase they are simply by looking at 0° on one waveform and then observing when (in degrees) in relation to that waveform the second waveform passes 0° (Figure 2.8).

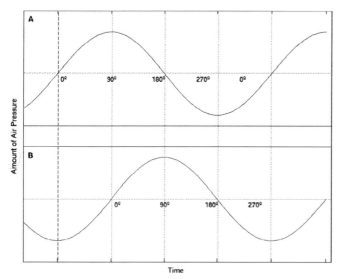

FIGURE 2.8: **Comparison of Phase of Two Waveforms**

Waveform (A) and waveform (B) are of the same frequency, but they are out of phase with each other by 90°.

DYNAMIC RANGE

The final identifying characteristic of an audio waveform is the relationship between the amplitude of the waveform itself and the amplitude of the random variations within it. This characteristic of waveforms is often ignored or misunderstood partially because "textbook" waveforms often show "perfect" waveforms that do not appear to have any error in them. The amount of "noise" or "random variation" is a real part of any real (non-textbook) waveform, and something that needs to be kept into account. The topic of noise, however, will require a chapter of its own and more groundwork needs to be laid before we can understand why and how the level of the noise (the low level random variations in the signal) as it relates to the amplitude of the "intended" part of the waveform is an identifying characteristic of audio waveforms. A lack of understanding of the importance of this characteristic, however, is probably one of the greatest sources of confusion and misunderstanding of digital audio.

SUMMARY

In summary, there are four identifying characteristics of waveforms. If all four are recorded and duplicated then the waveform can be perfectly accurately reproduced. Amplitude is the height of the waveform. Frequency is the speed at which the waveform oscillates and is directly related to the waveform's wavelength. Phase is only pertinent if more than one waveform is involved and is a comparison of the timing of the two waveforms. Dynamic range we do not know anything about, yet, but has to do with the amount of error in the waveform.

Chapter Three

Complex Waveforms

So far we have been primarily discussing sine waves. This is based on the physical principle we laid out earlier that showed that elastic devices tend to vibrate in a sinusoidal fashion, increasingly so the more elastic the devices get. The less elasticity an item has the less ability it has to vibrate in a perfect sinusoidal fashion. It should be no surprise to us that a speaker's cone is very elastic: we need it to be very elastic if we intend for it to be able to reproduce all waveforms that we desire for it to be able to reproduce, including pure sine waves.

Not all waveforms, however, are sinusoidal. In fact, the vast majority of musical waveforms are not. This chapter is about all waveforms that are not sinusoidal, thus "complex" waveforms.

Most devices are not as ideally elastic as our examples in the previous chapter. One situation in which we might encounter this might be a piece of wood that is struck, not in the center, but toward the outside edge. When this piece of wood vibrates, two different movements happen simultaneously. The entire piece of wood moves up and down in a sinusoidal fashion, but smaller portions of the wood also move in a sinusoidal fashion, with "nodes" created where no movement happens, or where the multiple movements meet. The nodes on a piece of resonating wood are shown in Figure 3.1.

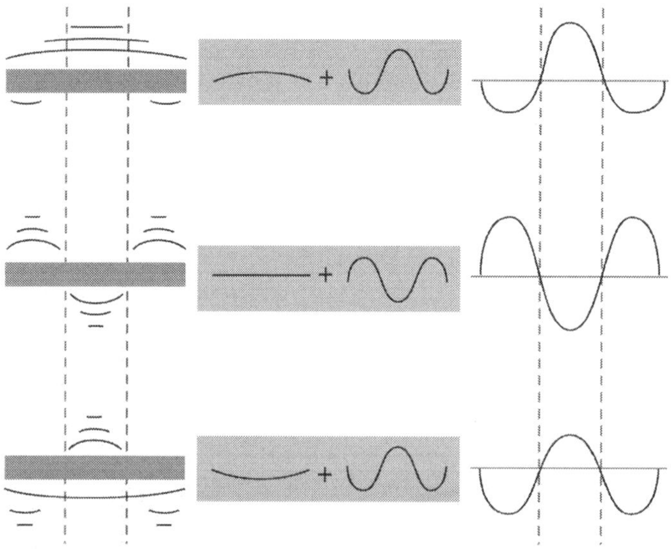

Each of these individual movements is sinusoidal, but the overall movement of the wood and the overall air pressure waveforms that are created are no longer sinusoidal.

FIGURE 3.1: Vibrations on a Theoretical Block of Wood

The block of wood does not vibrate like a perfectly elastic device but is rather more complicated. In this simplified example, the wood vibrates in two, combined patterns yielding a complex waveform.

The waveform produced is the result of adding the two waveforms together. When waveforms are added together the result is the same as adding the amplitude of each of the waveforms together at each, individual, infinitely small moment in time (Figure 3.2).

The result is no longer a sine wave but it is still a waveform that is composed of multiple sine waves. If one of the sine waves were to be subtracted (attenuated) back out of this resultant waveform (using a filter, for example) all that would be left would be the other sine wave.

In 1801, a French mathematician and physicist by the name of Baron Jean Baptiste Joseph Fourier was studying heat waves and their propagation. He authored a paper in 1822 entitled *Théorie Analytique de la Chaleur* in which he proposed that all waveforms can be represented as a sum of various sine waves. Seven years later a mathematician by the name of Jacques

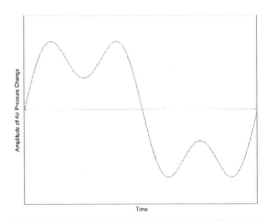

FIGURE 3.2: **The Waveform Produced by the Block of Wood in Diagram 3.1.**

Charles François Sturm provided a mathematical proof for this, which is the foundation for waveform analysis still today. This mathematical result is known as The Fourier Theorem (FOR'ee-ay).

One can look at the Fourier Theorem through either a construction or a deconstruction approach. One can either use Fourier Analysis to show that any given waveform is actually a compilation of multiple sine waves (deconstruction), or they can show that any desired waveform can be created simply by summing various sine waves together. When looking at the elasticity of various devices and determining their specific movements we are really talking about creating complex waveforms by means of adding together multiple sine waves of varying frequency, amplitude and phase. Once we accept, however, that all waveforms that occur are the summation of multiple sine waves, and once we understand why that is the case, it might be more practical to take the latter approach and try to figure out, based on some common waveform shapes, which sine waves must be added together to create them.

The lowest frequency that an elastic object creates is called the "fundamental." Each whole number multiple of that frequency is called a "harmonic." If the fundamental frequency (also called the "first harmonic") is 100Hz, the additional harmonics would be 200Hz, 300Hz, 400Hz, 500Hz and so on. The "even harmonics" are all of those harmonics wherein the fundamental frequency is multiplied by an even number. The odd harmonics are all of those in which the fundamental is multiplied by an odd number. Therefore, if 100Hz is a fundamental, 200Hz, 400Hz, 600Hz, etc. would be the even harmonics and 300Hz, 500Hz, 700Hz, etc would be the odd harmonics.

These harmonics are also called "overtones." To add confusion, the first "over"tone is actually the second harmonic. The fundamental, or the first harmonic, is not considered an overtone. Any overtone that is an integer harmonic (such as the first, second, third, fourth harmonics, etc) is called a "harmonic overtone." Any overtone that is not an integer harmonic is called a "non-harmonic overtone". If the fundamental frequen-

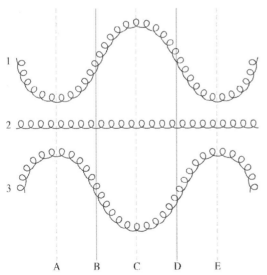

FIGURE 3.3: **Nodes and Antinodes in a Spring**

A vibrating spring is shown at three different moments in time. Regions (A), (C), and (E) represent "nodes" in the spring's movement. Regions (B) and (D) represent antinodes where the spring does not move at all.

cy is 100Hz then 200Hz would be the first harmonic overtone whereas if a 211Hz overtone happened to be present it would be considered a non-harmonic overtone.

Visualizing harmonics is fairly simple with the elastic slinky analogy. If a slinky vibrates at the fundamental frequency then the entire slinky moves in a single wave. If one end of the slinky vibrates faster the slinky will end up with a "node" in the middle and two complete waveforms will be created, one on each half of the slinky. This creates the first harmonic overtone of the fundamental (the first harmonic overtone being the second harmonic). If the slinky vibrates as a whole at 10Hz, and since we know that when the wavelength gets cut in half the frequency doubles, the first harmonic overtone is 20Hz. If we vibrate the slinky faster we end up with two nodes and the third harmonic overtone at 30Hz. This is shown in Figure 3.3.

What happens in the slinky happens in most elastic objects to varying degrees, though in most objects these various vibrations all happen at the same time because of the complexity of the elasticity of the object. As the different parts of the device vibrate in various, combining ways, multiple harmonics are created. The amount of harmonic content is responsible for the tonal difference between different musical instruments and is known as "timbre." The timbre (TAM'ber) of an instrument is the makeup of its harmonic content. Different instruments inherently yield more of some harmonics and fewer of others. The relationship between these is how we audibly identify individual types of instruments versus others. Examples of this are shown in Figure 3.4.

As a general rule, when a particular instrument plays a note its harmonic content is going to be the same regardless of what note it is playing. All of the harmonics overtones shift up or down the frequency scale in correspondence with the note played, but for the most part the relationship between all of the frequencies it produces are approximately the same. Note that the relationships of the harmonics does actually change to some degree as the notes change on an instrument, and

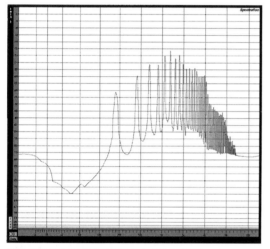

FIGURE 3.4A: **The Spectral Content of a Trumpet**

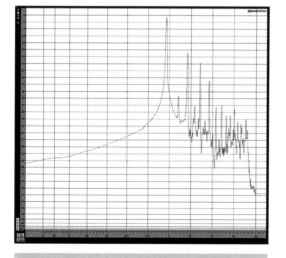

FIGURE 3.4B: **The Spectral Content of a Flute**

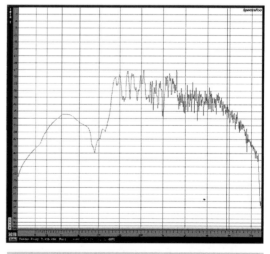

FIGURE 3.4C: **The Spectral Content of a Piano**

that change also contributes to the character of the instrument, but in a broad sense the arrangement of the overtones present when a note is played is unique to the instrument and makes the instrument audibly identifiable.

SUMMING SINES

Analyzing several simple waveforms will help to give us an idea of exactly how it is that complex waveforms are created. If, for example, we start with a sine wave of a particular frequency, and add to it all of its related harmonics we can generate a waveform called a "sawtooth" wave, as is shown in Figure 3.5.

There is a specific ratio of the amplitude of the various frequencies that create a sawtooth wave. Each harmonic is added with the amplitude of the inverse of the number of harmonic that it is. For example, the fundamental is used at an amplitude of 1, whereas the second harmonic is added at the amplitude of 1/2, the third

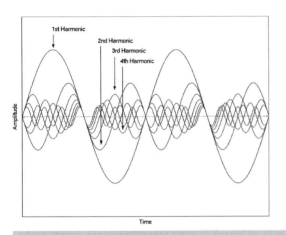
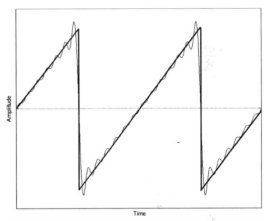

FIGURE 3.5: **Creating a Sawtooth Wave**

A sawtooth wave is the result of summing all of the harmonic overtones of a fundamental together with a particular relationship between the overtones.

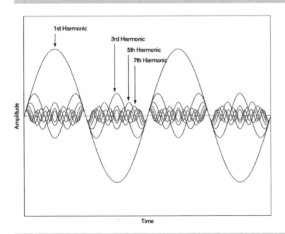
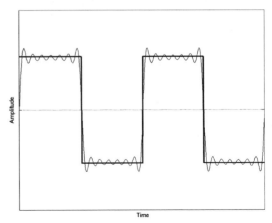

FIGURE 3.6: **Creating a Square Wave**

A square wave is the result of summing all of the odd harmonic overtones of a fundamental together with a particular relationship between the overtones.

at 1/3, etc. A true sawtooth wave requires an infinite amount of harmonics and at amplitudes that get infinitely smaller the higher they get. The highest harmonic present in a sawtooth wave is infinitely high, but is present at an amplitude of 1/infinity. The waveform in Figure 3.5 only shows the first seven harmonics.

By using the same formula used to create a sawtooth wave but only using the odd harmonics one can create a "square wave." The square wave uses the fundamental with an amplitude of 1, the third harmonic at an amplitude of 1/3, the fifth harmonic at an amplitude of 1/5, and all of the other odd harmonics at the equivalent ratios, *ad infinitum*. The composition of a square wave is shown in Figure 3.6.

A "triangle wave" is created using the same frequencies as a square wave but with a different ratio of amplitudes between all of the harmonics. A triangle waveform is created by using the fundamental at an amplitude of 1, the third harmonic at an amplitude of 1/9, the fifth harmonic at an amplitude of 1/25, and all additional odd harmonics with an amplitude of 1/(harmonic number)^2. The composition of a triangle wave is shown in Figure 3.7.

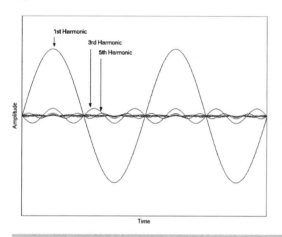 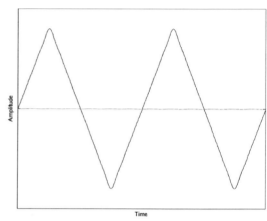

FIGURE 3.7: Creating a Triangle Wave
A triangle wave is the result of summing all of the odd harmonic overtones of a fundamental together with a particular relationship between the overtones.

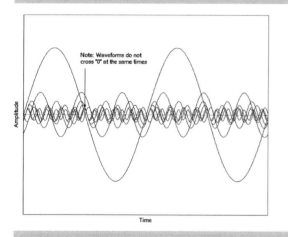 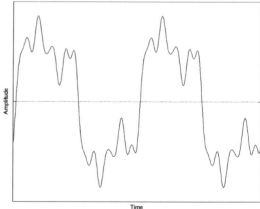

FIGURE 3.8: Square Wave Frequencies Summed With a Different Phase Relationship
Simply summing specific frequencies with specific amplitudes does not yield a square wave. The phase relationship between the original waveforms must be formulaic as well.

As was mentioned above, the Fourier Theorem can be looked at in two different ways. One way (construction) would be that any waveform can be created simply by summing various sine waves. This is the approach that we have used in the above three examples. The practical application of this is not very apparent and is, to some degree, oversimplified. In reality one cannot merely sum those frequencies together and anticipate that said waveforms will be created. In reality, they have to be summed together with phase as a contributing characteristic. If we use the same frequencies and the same amplitudes but did not align the phase at specific points and in certain ways we might still have a waveform that sounds the same because the ear is not particularly sensitive to the phase of each, individual harmonic in a repeating waveform, but this waveform would be different than the waveforms shown above.[1] The waveform in Figure 3.8 has the same frequency and amplitude content as a square wave, and if it repeats as indicated the ear will not be able to decipher it from a square wave, yet it very clearly is not square. This is an example of a situation where the ear is not sensitive to phase. As was discussed in Chapter Two, there are only specific situations wherein the phase of a waveform is consequential to the audibility of the waveform.

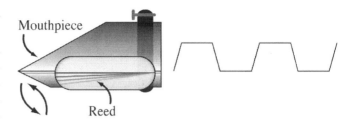

FIGURE 3.9: **The Movement of a Clarinet Reed Producing a Waveform**

The clarinet reed "slaps" back and forth between its maximum positions up and down, much like a flag in a stiff wind. The resulting waveform is very close to a square wave.

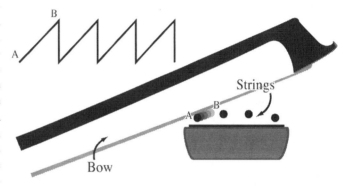

FIGURE 3.10: **The Movement of a Violin Producing a Waveform**

As a violin bow is applied to the string the friction of it "pulls" (A) the string until the tension gets great enough that the string breaks free of it (B) and returns to the beginning position. The cycle then starts over, several hundred or thousand times per second.

The reason for understanding the makeup of a square wave is not for the purpose of creating square waves, but rather because they (and sawtooths and triangles) are to some degree naturally occurring waveforms. Understanding how to create a square wave tells us more about how naturally occurring waveforms are actually constructed and gives testament to the Fourier Theorem – that all waveforms are composed of sine waves.

The square wave, for example, naturally occurs in an instrument like the clarinet. The reed on a clarinet's mouthpiece, when blown across, slaps up and down very quickly to the point of its maximum tension (Figure 3.9). This movement is similar to that of a flag blowing in a stiff wind. The end of the flag whips back and forth in the wind, quickly changing direction much like a square wave. If the clarinet reed was made of a material with different elasticity it might flutter back

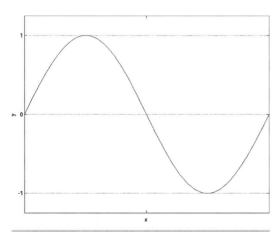

FIGURE 3.11: **A Figure of a y=sin(x) Sine Wave**

and forth in more of a sine wave pattern. It does not, however, thus we have the clarinet as a good example of what square waves sound like.

The sawtooth, on the other hand, is more similar to the sound of a violin. The reason is that the heavily rosined bow catches the string and pulls it with constant force causing the upward angle of the sawtooth wave. Once the tension of the string gets too strong for the friction of the rosin and bow it quickly snaps back to its original position where the rosin on the bow catches it again and the cycle repeats (Figure 3.10). This, obviously, happens several times per second. To be precise, if the violinist is playing the note "A" above middle C, it happens exactly 440 times per second. As the violinist reduces the length of the strings with their fingers' pressure on the string against the neck, the string has more tension so the cycle happens more frequently. At the highest notes that a violinist can play this happens around 3500 times per second.

These examples show us that a sawtooth wave and a square wave are naturally occurring waveforms for certain types of elastic devices. The Fourier theorem tells us that they are comprised of sine waves. Our exercise earlier showed us that indeed these waveforms are made up of various sine waves so that when we see examples of these waveforms, or other waveforms in the real world, we know that they are merely complex

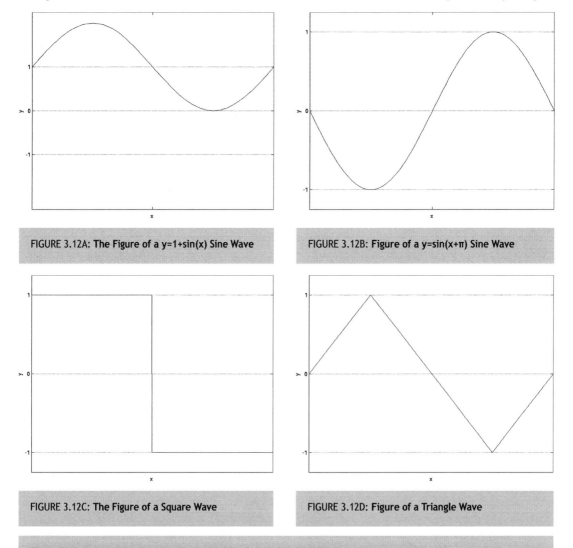

FIGURE 3.12A: **The Figure of a y=1+sin(x) Sine Wave**   FIGURE 3.12B: **Figure of a y=sin(x+π) Sine Wave**

FIGURE 3.12C: **The Figure of a Square Wave**   FIGURE 3.12D: **Figure of a Triangle Wave**

Figure 3.12 shows some other waveforms resulting from other formulas.

additions of multiple sine waves at differing frequencies and amplitudes.

TRANSFORMS

All waveforms are capable of being described by a mathematical formula called an "equation." A sine wave, for example, can be written by the formula $y = \sin(x)$. A sine wave is shown in Figure 3.11.

It is not the intent of this book to get particularly mathematically involved, so we will not be discussing exactly why that equation is the one that represents that waveform, but it is important that we all simply accept that that is the case and that all waveforms can be described by means of an equation, albeit not always such a concise one.

The formulas are not always neat and orderly. The more complicated the waveform the more involved the formula. Even the waveform comprising a 5 minute song, though it is 5 minutes long, can be expressed by a single, very long and complex mathematical formula.

A mathematical equation describing a waveform indicates the amplitude of the waveform at various points in time. The description of the amplitude at certain points in time in a waveform is called a function. Therefore, whenever we discuss "functions" we are discussing the equation that describes a waveform. We might as well substitute the word "function" for the word "waveform" for the sake of discussion, because they are essentially interchangeable in their usage for the sake of the discussion herein. Since a particular equation defines a particular waveform and since a function is just another way of saying "equation," a function could be

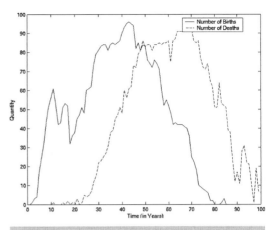

FIGURE 3.13A: **Figure of Births and Deaths of a Population Over Time**

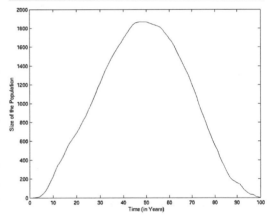

FIGURE 3.13B: **A "Transform" of Figure 3.13A**

Figure 3.13A above shows the births and deaths in a population of people over a one hundred year time span. Assuming that this is a new population of people, Figure 3.13B "transforms" this same data to a plot of the size of the population over the same period of time.

thought of as representative of a waveform. If we read the phrase, for example, "the frequency of a function can be determined by certain means," we can understand this to mean that "the frequency of a waveform can be determined by certain means."

A transform is a mathematical formula that takes one function and turns it into a function that tells us something different. In other words, it is a mathematical formula that takes one waveform that represents one thing and gives us a function that tells us something else that is somehow related. Let us look at a couple of examples.

If we had a graph that showed us the birth and death rates of a certain population over a period of time, that graph would represent some kind of a waveform. That graph, however, could actually be used to extrapolate all kinds of other data. For instance, a careful analysis of this graph could also be used to show us the total population of that area. Of course the birth and death rates chart would have to start when the first person lived in that area. If that was the case then, knowing the birth and death rates, we could indeed determine the total population of that area throughout that period of time. If we chart the total population on a graph (changing over time) then it will also give us some sort of a waveform, and that waveform will be related to but not identical to the original waveform representing the birth and death rates over time. The mathematical formula that takes the birth/death function (waveform) and turns it into the population function (waveform) is called a "transform." This particular example is shown in Figure 3.13.

A more abstract look at transforms will show that our birth and death graph could also yield a plot of the average age of the population over the same period of time. A different transform (mathematical formula) would need to be used in this situation, but again, there would be a mathematical formula that would allow us to take the first graph (function, waveform, equation) and create an "average age" graph from it. Because the births and deaths graph could be transformed to give us a graph of the size of the population with one transform (mathematical formula) and the average age of the population with another transform, there would also be a transform that could give us the age of the population from just knowing the size of the population over time. In most situations, if there is a relationship between A and B and between A and C then there must also be a direct relationship between B and C, though there are mathematical exceptions to this principle when it comes to transforms.

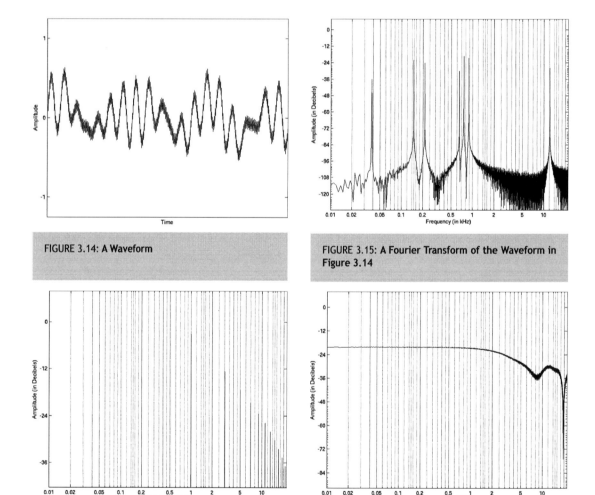

FIGURE 3.14: A Waveform

FIGURE 3.15: A Fourier Transform of the Waveform in Figure 3.14

FIGURE 3.16: Figure of the Fourier Transform of a 1kHz Square Wave

FIGURE 3.17: A Figure of the Fourier Transform of a Snare Drum Hit

A transform is, to reiterate, simply a mathematical formula. A transform is a mathematical formula that takes one mathematical function that tells us one thing and turns it into a function that tells us something else.

FOURIER TRANSFORM

The Fourier Transform is the mathematical formula that can take a waveform representing air pressure changes and transform it into a function describing the waveform's frequency content: the amplitudes of those frequencies and the phase of those frequencies that are present within that waveform. At this point it is understood that all waveforms are composed of merely a multitude of sine waves. The Fourier Transform tells us the distribution of sine waves in a function by indicating the amplitude and phase of sine waves comprising a given function. When this information is graphed we can visually see exactly what frequencies and at what amplitudes and corresponding phases they would have to have been "added" together in order to create the original waveform.

The Fourier Transform gives us two pieces of information that can each be graphed separately. First is a graph of which frequencies were present in a waveform and at what amplitudes. Second is a graph of the phase at which said sine waves were present. Generally, the latter is ignored and the Fourier Transform graph is thought of only as the graph that yields the amplitude of the various frequencies that are present. In actuality, however, the Fourier Transform does give two sets of data: the amplitudes at the various frequencies present, which can be plotted, and the relative phase of the frequencies present, which can be plotted. The graph of the amplitude of the sine waves present is called an "amplitude spectrum graph," as it shows us the frequency spectrum of the waveform in question. Keeping the terminology straight is important. The Fourier Transform is merely the formula that analyzes a waveform and yields its frequency content. It is often, however, used to denote the very function that it creates. For example, one might say, "apply the Fourier Transform to that waveform to see which frequencies were present." In this context it is referring to the formula. They might also say, however, "the Fourier Transform of a square wave indicates that it is composed of frequencies of many different waveforms." In this context it is referring to the result of applying the formula to the original function. The actual plot of the Fourier Transform as a graph is the amplitude spectrum graph. Although we will not be figuring out the math, the Fourier Transform is given as:

$$f(x) = \int_{-\infty}^{\infty} F(k)e^{2\pi i k x} dk$$

If we are given a waveform, as in Figure 3.14, then the Fourier Transform of this is plotted on an amplitude spectrum graph (a spectrograph) as in Figure 3.15.

The peaks on this graph represent the frequencies in that waveform where the energy is the strongest. The amplitude spectrum graph above shows that .038kHz, .158kHz, .24kHz, 11kHz and other frequencies were very prominent in the creation of the waveform in Figure 3.14. If we knew the phase of each of the frequencies involved we would be able to completely recreate the waveform from knowing which frequencies were present according to the amplitude spectrum graph plot.

From what we know about square waves, we can already anticipate what a square wave's Fourier Transform yields. The amplitude spectrum graph plot (spectrograph plot) of the Fourier Transform of a 1kHz square wave is given in Figure 3.16.

One weakness of a Fourier Transform's spectrograph plot is that it analyzes the entire waveform and calculates the result of all of the energy at all of the frequencies within it. This means that over a long period of time on a typical piece of audio, every frequency will likely be present and very few frequencies will show any more energy than other frequencies. One example is shown in Figure 3.18.

This spectrograph plot tells us very little information about the waveform in question other than the fact that over the entirety of the waveform, all frequencies seem to be fairly equally represented. In actuality, this spectrograph plot could have come from either of the waveforms in Figure 3.19.

Both of these waveforms contain all frequencies, but the waveforms are obviously very different. Because of the difficulty in easily utilizing the information that a Fourier Transform yields, another method is often used for analyzing waveforms. Rather than looking at the entire waveform and performing a transform on it, we can instead look at the amplitude in short slices of time, doing separate Fourier Transforms on small pieces of the waveform rather than the waveform as a whole. By doing this we can see not only which frequencies were present and how much amplitude they had, but we can more visually observe *when* the frequencies occurred. We already know that a Fourier Transform itself tells us when frequencies occur because it tells us the frequency vs. phase information. On a lengthy and complex waveform, however, it is difficult to process and use the information. Therefore, looking at Fourier Transforms of short pieces of the waveform makes the information more readily available and easier to visually comprehend and utilize.

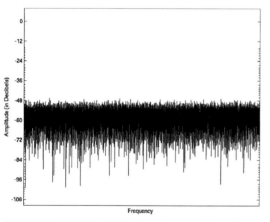

FIGURE 3.18: **Figure of the Fourier Transform of a Particular, Long Waveform**

Multiple, small Fourier Transforms can be graphed on an amplitude spectrum graph that changes over time. Another way to graph these multiple Fourier Transforms would be using a chart called a "Short Time Fourier Transform," or "STFT." This takes the multi-

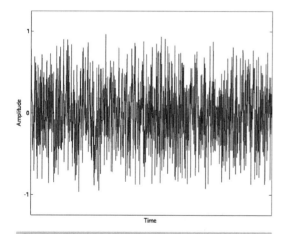

FIGURE 3.19A: **White Noise**

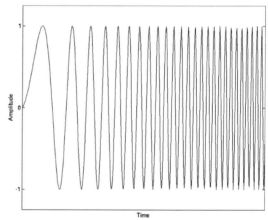

FIGURE 3.19B: **A Frequency Sweep**

Both the waveform in Figure 3.20A and the waveform in Figure 3.20B would produce the same spectrograph plot from a Fourier analysis, as both waveforms contain all frequencies at equal amplitudes, though the waveforms are clearly different.

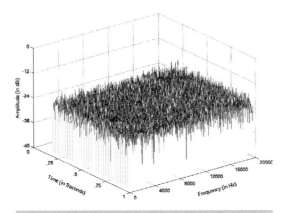 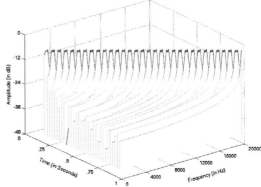

FIGURE 3.20A: STFT Figure of the Waveform in Figure 3.19A

FIGURE 3.20B: An STFT Figure of the Waveform in Figure 3.19B

After looking at the Short Time Fourier Transform Figures of the waveforms in Figures 3.20A and 3.20B one can clearly see that the two waveforms are indeed different, as their Fourier Transform Figures change over time.

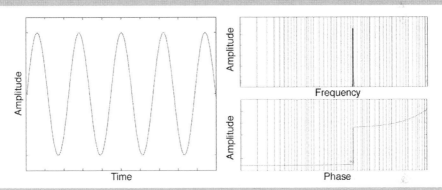

FIGURE 3.21A: A Waveform and Figures of its Fourier Transform for Phase and Frequency

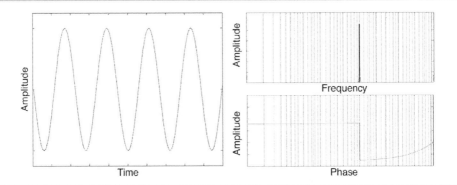

FIGURE 3.21B: A different Waveform and Figures of its Fourier Transform for Phase and Frequency

Although the waveforms in Figure 3.21A and 3.21B look to be the same, they have different Fourier Transforms because the phase of the two waveforms is different. Although two waveforms can have the same spectrograph plots, the spectrograph plot only shows half of the information that a Fourier Transform yields. The crucial phase plots of these two waveforms indicate that indeed the two waveforms are different. Though the frequency and amplitude information is the same, the time, or phase of the waveforms is different, thus the two waveforms are unique and different.

ple, individual, short time Fourier Transforms and plots the results on a three dimensional graph such that the "z," or 3rd dimension represents the changes in time. Fourier Transforms of the audio are done in short periods of time and then plotted as layer upon layer on a three dimensional field. The STFT plots from the two waveforms in Figure 3.19 show us that, while the overall energy of the frequencies present in the waveforms is the same, the time at which those frequencies occurred was different. These plots are shown in Figure 3.20.

This type of chart, often called a "waterfall plot," is an effective way of viewing Fourier Transforms over time. The chart above shows us that in the second plot, the waveform was really a sweep of a sine wave that started at 5Hz and stopped at 20kHz, whereas the first plot seems to yield all frequencies present at an equal amount from the beginning to the end of the waveform.

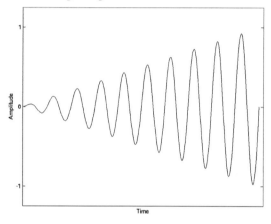

FIGURE 3.22: **A Waveform that Changes Amplitude**

This waveform, which changes amplitude over time, is not a sine wave. Though it may appear to be sinusoidal, at all places in its plot in which it changes amplitude it is slightly deviating from actually being sinusoidal, meaning that it is a complex waveform.

An inverse Fourier Transform is the mathematical tool for recreating a waveform starting with its Fourier Transform. This mathematical formula takes into account both parts of a Fourier Transform (the amplitude vs. frequency analysis and the phase vs. frequency analysis) and recreates the original waveform. A single waveform can only yield one possible Fourier Transform result, and a given Fourier Transform can only yield one possible waveform. For this reason, two waveforms that are only different in their phase relationship will yield differing Fourier Transforms. Clearly the amplitude analysis of them will be the same, but the phase analysis will be different. When each part of the Fourier Transform is taken into regard, the original waveform, and only the original waveform, can be reconstructed. Again, it is important to remember that any given waveform, regardless of how short or how

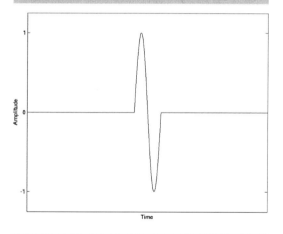

FIGURE 3.23A: **A Waveform that Appears to be Sinusoidal**

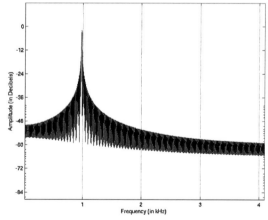

FIGURE 3.23B: **Spectrograph Plot of the Waveform in Figure 3.23A**

The waveform in Figure 3.23A appears to be sinusoidal, but in actuality it is not, as its Fourier analysis shows in the spectrograph plot shown in Figure 3.23B above. The fact that the waveform "started" and "stopped" requires that additional harmonic information is present.

long it is, has a unique Fourier Transform that it yields. Just the same, any Fourier Transform is representative of a unique waveform (Figure 3.21).

As a sidebar and for further clarification, when a particular function is plotted with the x-axis indicating time (as in a normal plot of audio waveforms, where the y-axis is amplitude of the wave and the x-axis is time) the function is said to be "in the time domain." When the x-axis is frequency (as in a amplitude spectrum graph plot) the function is said to be "in the frequency domain." What "domain" a function is in is merely what its "x" values represent. In mathematical jargon, the Fourier Transform is a mathematical formula used for taking functions in the time domain and mapping them to the frequency domain.

Although we are not going to be computing any Fourier Transforms, they teach us a lot about the information contained within a waveform. As we get closer to discussing digital audio we will need to discuss the frequency content of what is trying to be recorded in order to ensure that the digital systems are capable of recording and reproducing the proper frequency content. Further, transforms in various capacities are the building blocks of digital signal processing, which we will be covering later in this book. Finally, understanding Fourier Transforms gives us the groundwork to understand that all waveforms are composed of multiple sine waves of various frequencies with varying levels of amplitude. If every waveform can be transformed from the time domain to the frequency domain then every waveform must indeed be the combination of multiple sine waves, as the frequency domain represents specifically the sine waves present in the waveform. Understanding and appreciating this is a key to understanding how audio really works.

Another variation on the Fourier Transform is the Fast Fourier Transform, or "FFT." The FFT is a specific way of doing a Fourier Transform that makes the calculation much more efficient. Oftentimes the term FFT is used interchangeably with Fourier Transform as the difference is essentially just the methodology. In this book we use the terms "Fourier Transform" "FFT" and "spectrograph plot" nearly interchangeably. A spectrograph plot refers specifically to just the frequency content, whereas "FFT" and "Fourier Transform" supposedly refer to a complete Fourier Analysis, which yields both the spectral content and the phase content of the waveform in question.

SINE WAVES LAST FOREVER

A common area of misunderstanding, and a topic related to complex waveforms that is crucial to thoroughly cover is that of waveforms that "change shape." A sine wave has a very specific shape and follows a very specific mathematical formula: $y = A \sin(x)$, wherein A is the amplitude. Any variation from that formula or from that shape yields a waveform that is not truly a sine wave. The same is true of square waves, sawtooth waves, and any other kind of waveform, in that a specific formula represents the waveform and any variation from that formula means it is no longer the same, simple waveform. A repeating sine wave can exist at a particular amplitude, but any change in amplitude yields a waveform that no longer has the same shape.

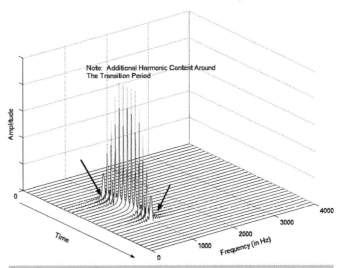

FIGURE 3.24: **The STFT Figure of the Waveform in Figure 3.23A**

The Figure above shows that the existence of additional harmonic information primarily occurs at the transition stages when the waveform appears to start and stop.

This means that a repeating sine wave that changes amplitude is no longer a simple sine wave but, *ipso facto*, becomes a complex waveform! Such a waveform would not fit the formula y = A sin (x) because A would have to change over time and would not be a constant value (Figure 3.22).

The additional frequency content present in this waveform that changes amplitude over time is a byproduct of the changing of the amplitude. That additional frequency content is necessarily added when the waveform changes shape. This also means that a sine wave cannot ever begin because at the moment that the sine wave "starts" it is greatly increasing in amplitude in a short period of time. At that moment in time, a tremendous amount of harmonic content is included in the waveform. The same would be true of a sine wave that ends abruptly; harmonic content would be added to the sine wave at that time, as any sine wave cannot change in amplitude without its function changing. The Fourier Transform of a supposed "sine wave" that starts and stops shows that there is a lot more frequency content present than just the implied frequency itself. The Fourier Transform of this waveform is shown in Figure 3.23.

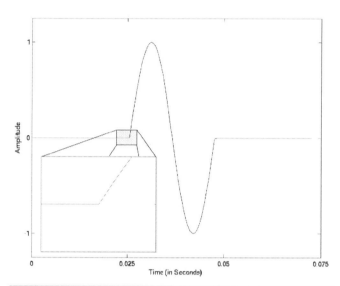

FIGURE 3.25A: A Waveform that Appears to be Sinusoidal

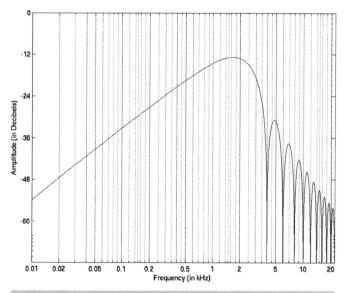

Figure 3.25B: Indication of the Frequencies Present in the Waveform in Figure 3.25A

Figure 3.25A shows a waveform that appears to be sinusoidal except for the fact that it starts and stops at fixed moments in time. Because it does this we know that the waveform is not actually a sine wave, as sine waves do not start and stop. In actuality, the "starting" portion of the waveform contains several frequencies that, when summed together, yield the resulting waveform shown in Figure 3.25A.

An STFT analysis of this waveform shows that indeed the additional harmonic content occurs primarily at the time when the drastic change in amplitude occurs.

These additional harmonics are not lost on the ear, nor is this just a mathematical exercise. The audible effects of this can be heard simply by turning on any audible source. At the moment that it is turned on an audible "click" or "blur" can often be heard. This "click" is the sound of all of the harmonic content that was present in the beginning of that waveform that caused it to rapidly increase in amplitude. In the example in Figure 3.25, the portion of the waveform shown is not, in any way, a portion of a sine wave. That portion of the waveform does not fit into the y = A sin (x) formula in any capacity, and therefore must be a more complex waveform. Figure 3.25 shows the frequencies that are actually present in that waveform, and thus are actually present if a supposed "sine wave" increases in amplitude instantaneously.

The slower the change in amplitude the closer the harmonics present are to the original waveform. To very slowly change a 100Hz sine wave in amplitude might require the additional frequencies of 99 Hz and 101Hz. Since these additional frequencies are so close to the fundamental this does not register to our auditory systems as a change in timbre but merely as a change in amplitude for reasons that we will discover later.

It is extremely important to understand that a waveform that changes amplitude over many cycles inherently implies that additional harmonic content is present. Therefore, a sine wave can only truly exist if it lasts forever. A Fourier Transform will only yield a single spike on an amplitude spectrum graph if the waveform that it transforms never starts and never ends. Otherwise, additional content is necessarily present. True sine waves can only last forever.

FOOTNOTES

[1.] In actuality, various studies have recently concluded that we humans *can* hear the difference between the phase of the various components of a waveform, such that a square wave will actually sound different than the waveform in Plot 3.8. The reasons provided for this, however, are beyond the scope of this book. As a general principle this issue is still hotly debated.

Chapter Four

Band-Limited Waveforms

Each waveform has a minimum and maximum frequency. In general, frequencies range from 0Hz to infinity. In any case, the range of frequencies in a given waveform is called its 'bandwidth'. Most waveforms of interest have restricted bandwidths—they do not go on to infinity. A "band" refers to any group of frequencies in a restricted range. A waveform is 'band-limited' when it contains only frequencies in a given band. Band-limited waveforms occur when a filter of some form does not allow certain frequencies to pass. These filters can be analog devices made of capacitors, resistors, and/or inductors. They can also be digital devices that prevent certain frequencies from passing, numerically. They can be undesirable, as in the action of a bad electrical wire, or intentional in the form of a high pass filter on a microphone that reduces rumble or a low pass filter on a mixing board that rolls off unnaturally occurring frequencies at the top of the audible range. Any device that affects the frequencies present in a waveform functions as a filter or a band-limiter. This includes a microphone that has steep roll-off above 20kHz, a speaker that does the same, the human ear, or any device that has a frequency response that is not completely flat from 0Hz to infinity. In other words, everything, including air, is a filter to some degree. Confusingly, not all filters are inherently band-limiters, as some filters do not change frequency content but instead merely change the phase of a waveform. All band-limiters, however, are inherently filters.

Filters cannot actually completely remove any frequencies. They can at best only attenuate them severely. Therefore, we are not saying that a filter has to completely remove frequencies to create a "band-limited" waveform. The fact that we are calling the waveform "band-limited" implies, however, that we are attenuating frequencies rather than either boosting them or allowing them to pass unaffected. A band-limited waveform could simply be a signal that has been run through a notch EQ, eliminating some of the frequencies from the middle of the spectrum. In this situation the "band" to which the waveform is limited is the combination of the frequencies above and below the notch EQ. Most of the time, a "band-limited" waveform refers to one that has attenuated high frequencies and/or low frequencies. The vast majority of the time a "band-limited waveform" is discussed in this industry it is understood to be a waveform that has an upper boundary of its frequency content.

When certain bands in a waveform are removed, the waveform inherently changes shape. For example, when high frequencies are removed from a waveform the waveform will be restricted to having less sharp transitions, as seen in Figure 4.1.

We can already start to ascertain what will happen to a square wave when all of the high frequency content is removed from it: the very steep corners on the square wave will not be able to exist, as that sharp movement indicates the presence of extremely high frequencies. The "corners" on a square wave are created by the very highest frequencies. The fewer the higher frequencies the more rounded the corners on the square wave become. The same is true of a triangle wave, a sawtooth wave and any other waveform. Without all of the frequencies present the waveform must inherently change shape. Without all of the frequencies present its Fourier Transform changes and, as we know, a different Fourier Transform necessarily indicates a different corresponding waveform in the time domain. An illustration of this is shown in Figure 4.2.

Recognizing the fact that any medium acts as a filter to some degree we can now see that square waves, triangle waves and sawtooth waves do not truly exist anywhere other than in textbooks. As we already know, the frequency content of those waveforms requires an infinite amount of bandwidth (based on the formulas showing the frequency content they contain), and since it is impossible to ever have an infinite amount of bandwidth (because of the band-limiting effects of any transmission medium, such as the air), it is therefore impossible for such waveforms to actually ever exist in a pure sense. Therefore, when a clarinet makes the sound of a square wave, we know that it is not completely square, but rather simply resembles a square wave. In order for it to be truly square the reed from the mouthpiece on the clarinet would have to move from one extreme to the other without any time passing. In order for a violin to yield a true sawtooth wave, the string would have to move back to its resting position without any time passing.

As the pass-band, or the range of frequencies that is not affected, shrinks, the waveforms tend more and more toward the shape of sine waves. For a square wave, if a low pass filter is put in and it attenuates all frequencies including the third harmonic and above, the waveform that remains is simply the sine wave at the fundamental frequency. This is shown in Figure 4.3.

As the square wave gets filtered so that it contains fewer and fewer of the harmonics present within it it becomes more and more sinusoidal. Figure 4.3C shows a square wave that has been filtered to only contain few of the harmonics, making the waveform notably not-square. Eventually, as is shown in Figure 4.3F, if the band becomes narrowed enough the waveform is limited to only being a sine wave.

A square wave provides an ideal example for observing what happens when band limiting a waveform because there is a wide frequency range where there is a complete lack of frequency content (such as the large gap between the first and second harmonics where no frequency content exists). More realistic waveforms are a bit more involved, as frequency content generally exists throughout the entire frequency spectrum. This is complicated by the fact that filters are not infinitely steep, but rather "roll off" over a range of frequencies. Frequencies within the transition band are capable of existing within the waveform but at reduced amplitudes.

A transient is a fast, non-repeating waveform, often containing a very wide range of frequency content. A perfect, "textbook" transient (or "impulse") actually contains all frequencies, as shown in Figure 4.4.

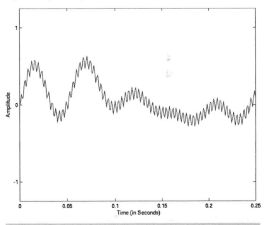

FIGURE 4.1A: A Complex Waveform

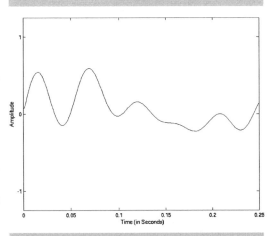

FIGURE 4.1B: A Band Limited Version of the Waveform in Figure 4.1A

The waveform in Figure 4.1A has high frequencies in it. When those high frequencies are removed and the waveform becomes "band limited" its shape changes accordingly.

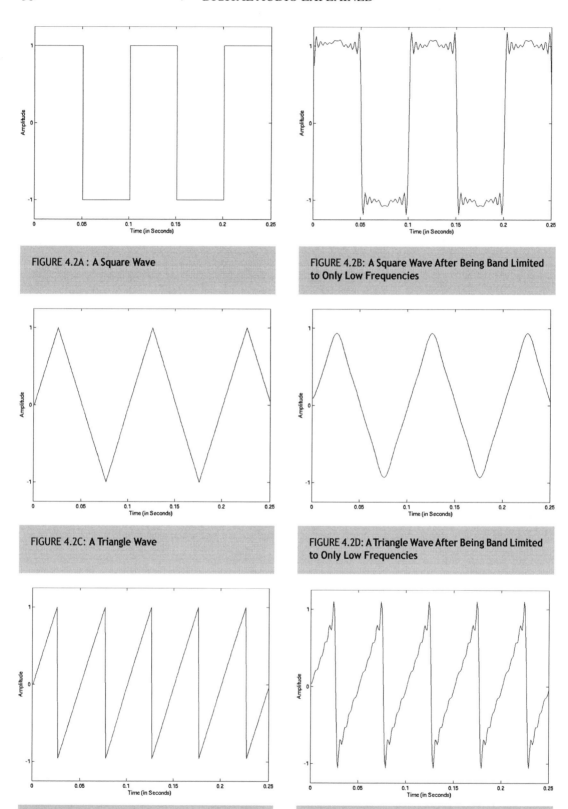

FIGURE 4.2A : A Square Wave

FIGURE 4.2B: A Square Wave After Being Band Limited to Only Low Frequencies

FIGURE 4.2C: A Triangle Wave

FIGURE 4.2D: A Triangle Wave After Being Band Limited to Only Low Frequencies

FIGURE 4.2E: A Sawtooth Wave

FIGURE 4.2F: A Sawtooth Wave After Being Band Limited to Only Low Frequencies

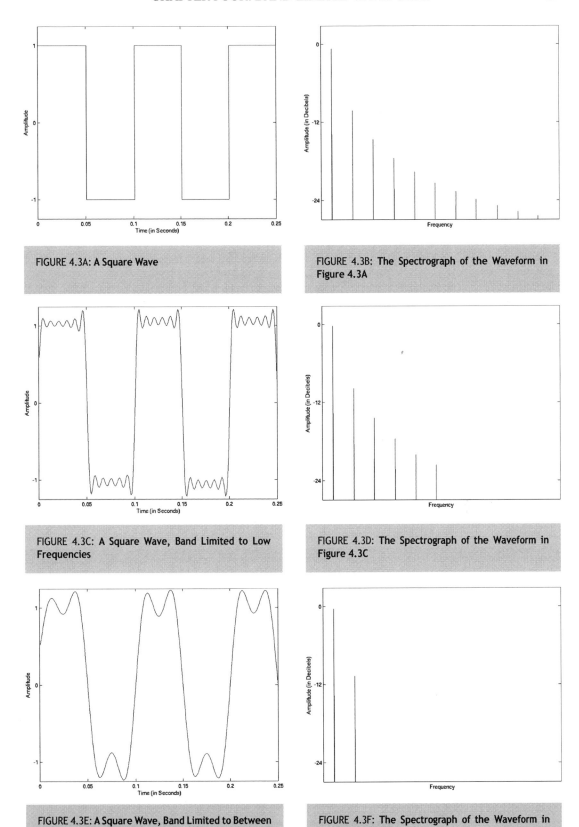

FIGURE 4.3A: A Square Wave

FIGURE 4.3B: The Spectrograph of the Waveform in Figure 4.3A

FIGURE 4.3C: A Square Wave, Band Limited to Low Frequencies

FIGURE 4.3D: The Spectrograph of the Waveform in Figure 4.3C

FIGURE 4.3E: A Square Wave, Band Limited to Between the 2nd and 3rd Harmonics

FIGURE 4.3F: The Spectrograph of the Waveform in Figure 4.3E

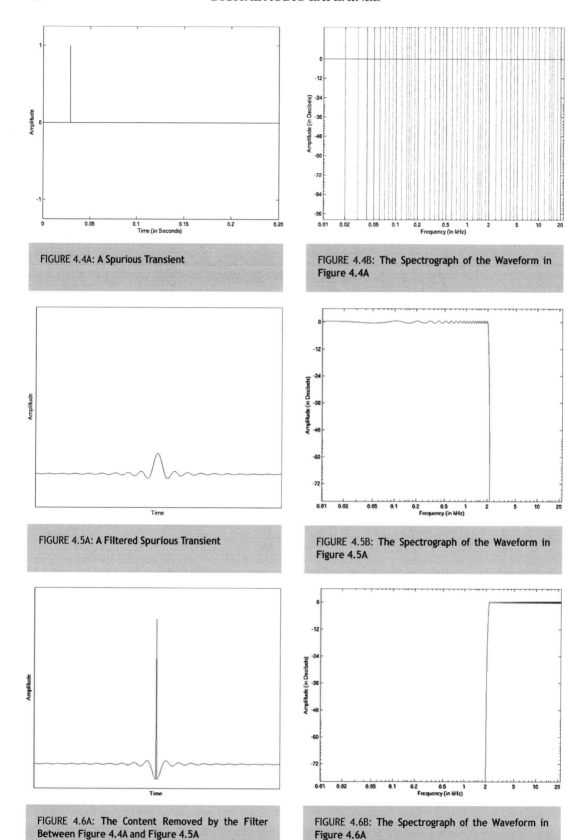

FIGURE 4.4A: A Spurious Transient

FIGURE 4.4B: The Spectrograph of the Waveform in Figure 4.4A

FIGURE 4.5A: A Filtered Spurious Transient

FIGURE 4.5B: The Spectrograph of the Waveform in Figure 4.5A

FIGURE 4.6A: The Content Removed by the Filter Between Figure 4.4A and Figure 4.5A

FIGURE 4.6B: The Spectrograph of the Waveform in Figure 4.6A

We know that the lower the frequency the longer the wavelength, so it seems somewhat counterintuitive that a wavelength of infinitely short wavelength is comprised of sine waves of much longer wavelengths. Indeed it is, however. When a low-pass (high-cut) filter is applied to this waveform it shows us what the content is within its pass-band (Figure 4.5). Figure 4.6 is a spectrograph plot of the material that was filtered out of the transient by the filter.

We can see in Figure 4.7 that if we overlay the frequencies in the stop-band (the frequencies that were filtered out) with the frequencies in the pass-band, indeed a summing of the two together yields the original spurious transient. This shows us that the impulse is indeed a combination of a series of sine waves that each all a wavelength longer than the transient itself.

Figure 4.5A showed what happens when a spurious transient is filtered to contain only its low frequency material. Figure 4.6A showed the material that was filtered out. Figure 4.7A shows that if the material that got through the filter and the material that was filtered are summed together that the result is indeed the same as the original waveform - the spurious transient.

Continuing with our understanding of band-limited waveforms, we can also deduce (for the mental exercise only) that if the pass-band is infinitely narrow then the only waveform that can exist in that realm is a sine wave at that specified frequency. More abstractly, the sine wave at that frequency would never be able to increase or decrease in amplitude overall because to do so would require other frequencies to be present, as was discussed in the preceding chapter.

There are many types of filters with many types of slopes and other affects. Much more will be covered on how filters are actually implemented in Part 3 on signal processing. Some degree of an understanding of filters will be crucial to understanding how digital audio works. There are a few points within this chapter that bode repeating, as they relate to specific examples that we will be visiting in later chapters:

• A "square" wave becomes much less square as the fundamental frequency of the square wave approaches the end of the pass band.

• Complex waveforms of all shapes and sizes become much more sinusoidal as the fundamental approaches the end of the pass band.

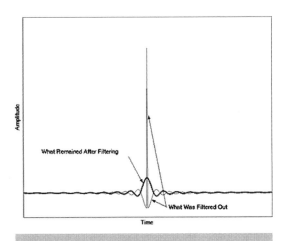

FIGURE 4.7A: The Waveforms in Figures 4.5A and 4.6A

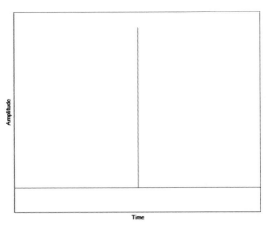

FIGURE 4.7B : The Result of Summing Together the Material in Figures 4.5A and 4.6A

Chapter Five

Noise

We know that sound is very simply changes in air pressure. A brief study of physics tells us that the air is in constant movement; air molecules are constantly colliding with each other at a high rate of speed. Anytime an air molecule collides with another air molecule energy is transmitted between them and both molecules end up moving. These molecules end up colliding with other molecules, continuing the pattern until all air molecules end up in motion (Figure 5.1).

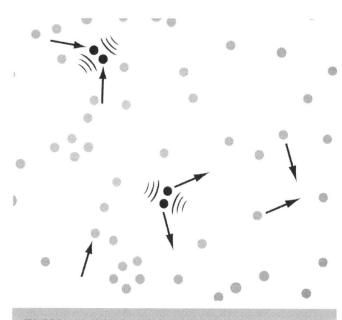

FIGURE 5.1: Air Molecules Colliding With Each Other

All that "sound" accomplishes is getting the air molecules to bounce off of each other in organized ways. As we know, however, the air molecules do not all move forward but it is rather their colliding that moves a pressure wave forward. Any time the air molecules move, however, the air pressure at any single point in space changes. It changes because that space is filled with multiple air molecules colliding and causing an area of compression. Then, when the molecules vacate that space after colliding, an area of low pressure remains (Figure 5.2).

The third law of thermodynamics indicates to us that the motion of the air molecules slows down as the temperature cools (and, conversely, speeds up as the temperature raises). As the air heats up collisions happen more often, essentially spreading the air molecules further apart. As the air cools down fewer collisions happen such that more air molecules can fit in the same space. This can be thought of like a dance floor in a club during a slow dance where not much movement is happening: many people can fit on the floor at a time. If people were to start dancing the tango, far fewer people could be on the floor at once because of the amount of collisions that would happen; the group of people on the floor would spread themselves out in a hurry after a few collisions.

The only times when there would not be a constant movement of the air molecules would be in one of two situations: either when the temperature is at absolute zero degrees or when there is no air (a vacuum), meaning there are no molecules to collide. In either of these situations there will subsequently not be any sound, either.

A complex mathematical analysis of the actual movement of the molecules present in the air indicates that the level of these *atmospheric* fluctuations is approximately –6dB SPL. This means that air has a very low-level sound on its own, and this atmospheric noise is half the amplitude of the quietest level that the ear can hear, or around .0001 microbars.[12]

Because of this constant energy and air movement there is a consistent amount of very low level "sound" occurring at all times. Constant, random sound is called "noise." Noise also occurs in electrical environments and any other medium where a signal (whether electrical, air pressure, light, or otherwise) gets transmitted. The noise is the random amount of variation that occurs in any medium simply from physical properties of the medium itself. This means that noise is

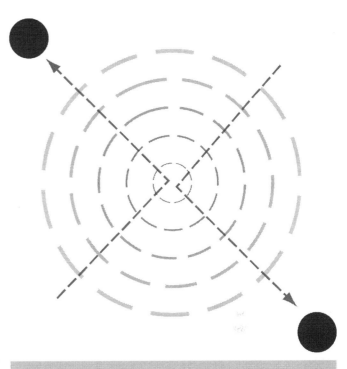

FIGURE 5.2: Low Pressure After Two Air Molecules Collide

Two air molecules collide and then vacate that space. While both air molecules are in that space that particular space has high air pressure. After they have vacated that space that area has low pressure.

inherently present in any electrical wire and any other transmission medium. It is impossible to have any information transmitted in any capacity that does not somehow contain noise since noise is random behavior and all particles in the universe yield certain amounts of random activity in their behavior. This means that any transmission system comprised of anything in the universe (including metal, water and air) yields some noise.

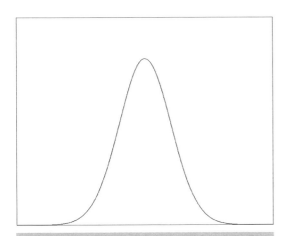

FIGURE 5.3A: The Gaussian or "Bell Shaped" Distribution Curve

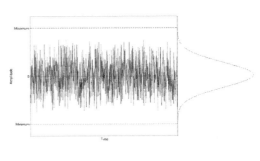

FIGURE 5.3B: Noise Amplitude Follows Gaussian Distribution

The amplitude of the noise follows the Gaussian distribution curve in that, at any given amplitude, the probability of the amplitude of the noise can be determined by Gaussian distribution.

Noise is completely random sound and can be plotted as a waveform just like any other waveform. The randomness of this sound ironically has certain, identifiable behaviors.

The first identifying characteristic of atmospheric noise is that the distribution of the amplitude follows a Gaussian (or "bell shaped") curve centered on no air pressure change, or the *zero crossing*. An observation of the waveform will show that the majority of the air pressure levels over the course of time fall in an area around the zero crossing in a statistically identifiable pattern. The very least amount of time the air pressure is at the highest level or the lowest level, and most of the time it is near the zero crossing. The amount of time that the air pressure is at any particular level is determinable from the same Gaussian distribution that is often used for setting grades for students. The odds that the air pressure will be at any particular level at any given moment in time are shown on the graph in Figure 5.3.

Any noise that exhibits this type of distribution is called "Gaussian Probability Density Function" noise. Completely random, unfiltered, natural noise is Gaussian in nature, though not all noise is completely random or unfiltered.

The second identifying characteristic of pure noise is that the waveform of the noise is the combination of all frequencies at equal amplitudes. Over a long enough period of time, a Fourier Transform of the waveform of the noise shows us that all frequencies are present with an equal amount of overall energy. This means that the same energy is present at 20Hz that is present at 21Hz, 10.422kHz, and 157.349322MHz. All frequencies are present at the same amplitude over time.

This also means that the total energy in the 20Hz to 40Hz octave will be much lower than the total energy in the 10kHz to 20kHz octave. If we look at a series of frequency bands wherein each band covers a 1Hz range, then the 20Hz to 40Hz range might have 20 "units" of energy, or 1 unit per frequency (20-21Hz, 21-22Hz, 22-23Hz, etc.). The 10,000Hz to 20,000Hz octave, on the other hand, would have 10,000 units of energy for the same 1 unit of energy per band. This occurs because the random energy creates equal energy at all frequencies, but higher musical octaves spread across more frequencies than lower octaves. This is because every octave represents a doubling of the frequencies within it. The graph in Figure 5.4 shows that the amplitude at all *frequencies* is the same. The graph in Figure 5.5 shows that the amplitude at all *musical octaves* is different.

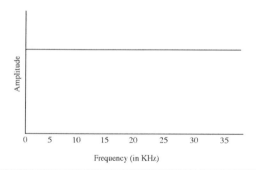

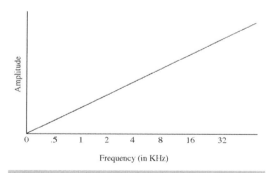

FIGURE 5.4: **Fourier Transform of White Noise on a Linear Frequency Graph**

White noise has equal amounts of noise at all frequencies, so a spectrograph plot will show white noise as a straight and horizontal line if the graph has each frequency representing an equal amount of space on the x-axis.

FIGURE 5.5: **Fourier Transform of White Noise on a Linear Octave Graph**

While white noise has equal amplitude of noise at all frequencies, our ear does not hear frequencies linearly. When looking at a plot of white noise on a graph that has each octave (instead of individual frequency) taking equal amounts of space on the x-axis, the plot looks different. As indicated above, white noise sounds to our ears as though it has a lot of high frequency content for this reason.

Because of the fact that our ears do not hear frequency ranges linearly, atmospheric noise seemingly has much more high frequency content than low frequency content. The sound of this noise is similar to that of tape "hiss;" low frequency content is still there but at a much lower amplitude to our ears than the high frequency content. Any noise that is random and has equal power per equal sized frequency band is called "white noise." Pure, random, natural noise is white noise. It is important to note that noise being Gaussian in distribution and being "white" are not completely interrelated. Gaussian noise can be non-white and white noise can be non-Gaussian. Noise can have Gaussian probability of the amplitude at any given moment in time and

can be something other than equal amplitude at all frequencies. Just the same, noise can be white, in that it is equal amplitude at all frequencies, and not have Gaussian probability of its amplitude at given moments in time. It just happens that pure, natural noise is both Gaussian AND white.

Another type of noise is "pink noise." This type of noise is used to represent, more closely, the way in which we humans hear. Pink noise contains equal energy at all *musical octaves,* which means less energy in the individual higher frequencies than in the low frequencies. Pink noise has just as much total energy between 20Hz and 40Hz as it does between 10kHz and 20kHz. Pink noise is demonstrated in Figure 5.6.

There are other types of noise as well, some of which will be covered in later chapters.

When a waveform is propagated in the presence of noise, the noise is added to the waveform in the same manner that any other two waveforms are added together: the value of the two waveforms (the noise waveform and the original waveform) are added together at each, infinitely small moment in time. This is shown in Figure 5.7.

So far we have only talked about the noise present in the air due to the constant state of air movement, even when at a steady state. Noise can also be created in the air due to the ongoing reverberation of sound in that acoustical space. Various, more determinable waves of air pressure are going to be moving around any acoustical space at all times due to sound that leaks into that space or just the actions of people, nature, or machinery present. Even in a very quiet room there is a constant level of sound that can be heard, many of the sources of which are miles away. Traffic, air traffic, ventilation systems, electrical sounds such as the squealing of televisions or the buzzing of lights all create sound that can be heard at low levels in a room. As these waves of small amounts of air pressure reflect off of the walls of an acoustical space, various collisions of air waves happen, continuing to dissipate the energy throughout a room and continuing to degrade the sound into less

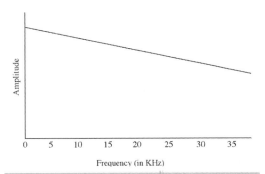

FIGURE 5.6A: Fourier Transform of Pink Noise on a Linear Frequency Graph

Pink noise has equal amounts of noise at all octaves, so a spectrograph plot shows that pink noise has decreasing energy in the higher frequencies since each octave in the higher frequencies covers a greater amount of bandwidth.

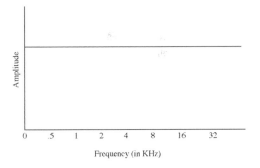

FIGURE 5.6B: Fourier Transform of Pink Noise on a Linear Octave Graph

Pink noise is designed and filtered to sound "flat" to our ears, as the plot above indicates. Between each octave the same amount of noise is present with pink noise. White noise sounds more like "tape hiss" whereas pink noise sounds more like a jet engine roar.

Pink noise sounds to us like it has equal energy across the audible spectrum because it has just as much low frequency noise as high frequency noise per octave. The sound of pink noise is more similar to a jet engine or a running vacuum cleaner. Pink noise is simply white noise that has been filtered to attenuate the higher frequencies with a slope of 3dB per octave. Pink noise can be Gaussian or non-Gaussian in distribution, just like white noise.

and less coherent and recognizable sources and turning it into a background level of sound that we also call "noise."

This *background noise* is present in any acoustical space to a consequential degree. A loud factory with heavy machinery obviously has a high amount of background noise. A business office with the ongoing din of commotion has a noise level of around 35-45dB SPL. A typical empty concert hall can have a noise level of 25-30dB SPL. A quiet recording studio might get its noise floor down to 15dB SPL. Rooms with less than 10dB of "self noise" are very rare. The self-noise of acoustical environments is not inherently Gaussian nor white in nature, but it certainly may tend toward either.

Noise is also induced into a signal from other means. Any form of electrical resistance also creates white noise. This means that any signal that is transmitted electronically is not only subject to the noise present in the signal to start with, but also has additional noise added to it by various electrical components in the signal path. Even wire itself adds noise. Not dissimilar to the random behavior of air molecules, all electronic devices add noise simply due to random behavior of electrons in the components. Further, any form of amplification amplifies the noise present and adds its own noise from the components used to build the amplifier.

In addition to atmospheric, environmental and electrical noise, the diaphragm on any microphone is in a constant state of flux. This *transducer* can never be at complete rest (unless it is in a vacuum), so the result, even in silence, is that the microphone capsule sends out a certain amount of low level noise. This low-level microphone noise is then increased by the microphone's internal amplifier, which also adds its own inherent noise to the cacophony.

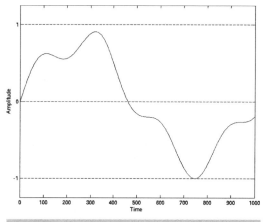

FIGURE 5.7A: A Waveform

Finally, there are the very obvious methods of inducing noise onto a signal, such as putting the signal through a noisy tube amplifier.

By the time any waveform gets to its destination it has been subjected to several means of noise production and amplification, as demonstrated in Figure 5.8. Note the difference between Figure 5.8A and Figure 5.81, and the difference between the spectrograph plots in Figures 5.8B and 5.8J.

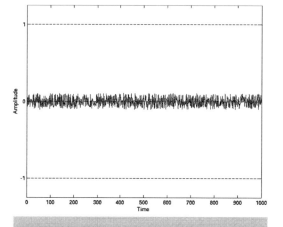

FIGURE 5.7B: White Noise

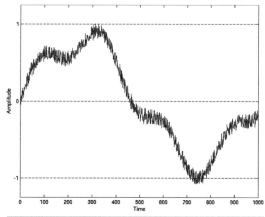

Figure 5.7C: The Waveform With White Noise Added

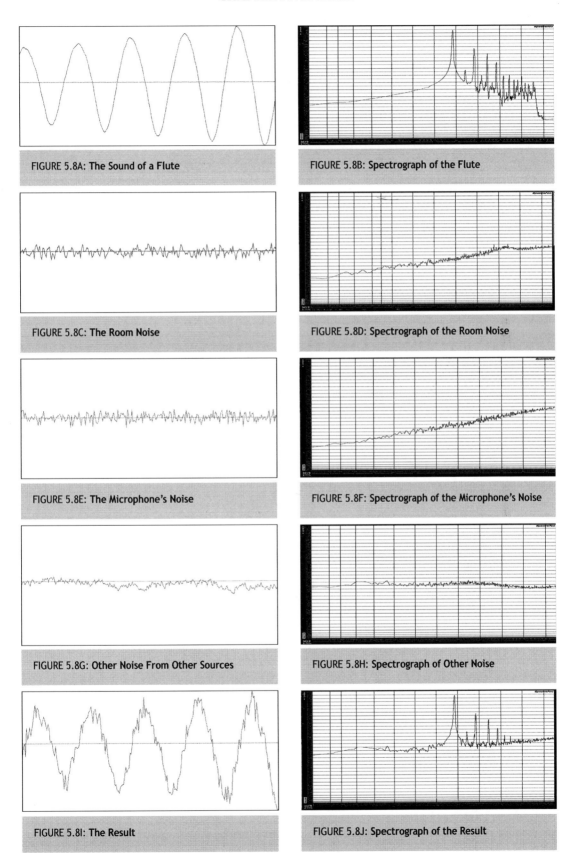

FIGURE 5.8A: **The Sound of a Flute**

FIGURE 5.8B: **Spectrograph of the Flute**

FIGURE 5.8C: **The Room Noise**

FIGURE 5.8D: **Spectrograph of the Room Noise**

FIGURE 5.8E: **The Microphone's Noise**

FIGURE 5.8F: **Spectrograph of the Microphone's Noise**

FIGURE 5.8G: **Other Noise From Other Sources**

FIGURE 5.8H: **Spectrograph of Other Noise**

FIGURE 5.8I: **The Result**

FIGURE 5.8J: **Spectrograph of the Result**

The waveform is now far removed from the pure waveform that it started out as. A pure sine wave is no longer pure once the random variations of noise are added to the waveform. Since it is impossible to have a waveform without any noise added to it we know that it is therefore impossible to have a pure waveform of any capacity. The noise level may be so quiet that when added to the "signal" waveform it is unapparent and does not show up on graphs, charts or plots. Noise, however, is always present on any waveform. We now know that not only can a pure sine wave not exist unless it can last forever, but we also know that a pure sine wave cannot exist in any capacity because it is impossible to have a sine wave without any noise. The concept that a pure waveform of any variety cannot exist without noise is another critical barrier to understanding digital audio for a lot of people.

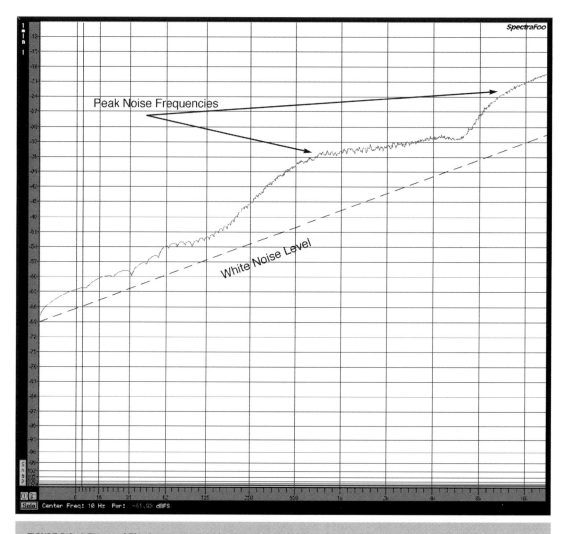

FIGURE 5.9: A Figure of The Spectrograph of More Common Noise

DYNAMIC RANGE

We can infer from the fact that not all noise is white that not all noise is truly flat (equal amplitude at all frequencies). Most noise has a particular sonic identity. The cumulative noise from all noise adding devices likely yields a noise floor that is different than the noise represented in Figure 5.4.

The relationship between the amplitude of the original signal and the amplitude of the lowest discernable signal is called "dynamic range." Since dynamic range is a relationship between two different amplitudes it is measured in decibels. The dynamic range of a waveform can be found by taking the amplitude of the highest peak in the waveform (in decibels) and subtracting from that the amplitude of the lowest discernable signal within the waveform. If the amplitude of the signal at its highest point is 6dB higher than the amplitude of the lowest discernable part of the signal then the signal is said to have 6dB of dynamic range.

Dynamic range is often confused with *signal to noise ratio* or "SNR," a measurement of the ratio between the signal's peak amplitude and the amplitude of the noise floor.

Typically, SNR is calculated only between the peak of the waveform and the *peak* frequency of the noise floor. This measurement is useful especially when observing the effect of a particular box on the signal. It is essentially a way of noting the highest amplitude of any random variations that are added to the signal. At this point we are not concerned with the signal to noise ratio of a waveform. For the time being we are most interested in a relationship between the peak of the waveform and the level of the white noise floor within it for reasons that will be evident upon understanding how the ear works. In Figure 5.9 the peak frequency shown is very

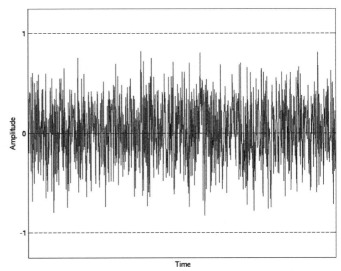

FIGURE 5.10A: A Spectrograph plot of What Appears to be White Noise

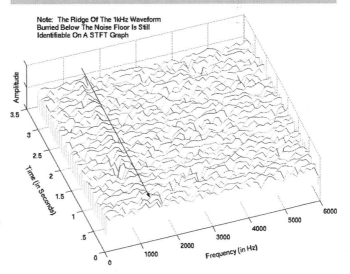

FIGURE 5.10B: A Spectrograph Plot of the Waveform Shown in Figure 5.10A Plotted Over Time

Figure 5.10B shows that the waveform shown in Figure 5.10A has a 1kHz sine wave buried beneath it at a lower amplitude than the amplitude of the noise.

much noise induced by the electrical equipment that transmitted a given signal. In most situations, the signal to noise ratio of this signal would be measured from the highest peak of the audio down to the cumulative amplitude of the noise at all frequencies, which is heavily determined by the peak indicated. In other words, the amplitude of the noise used to measure SNR is inherently higher than the noise at the peak indicated, yielding a dynamic range of no greater than –18dB (FS).

For practical purposes, however, there is a lot of usable and clearly identifiable material below the peak frequency of the noise indicated. The noise floor that represents natural, white noise is well below the peak noise floor. The high peak at 1kHz does define the signal to noise ratio of the signal represented by the graphic but does not necessarily define the dynamic range of the signal, as material would be easily identified at much lower amplitudes at 125Hz. The dynamic range is the range between the amplitude of the highest peak and the amplitude of the lowest identifiable material represented. This leaves some room for conjecture, as the lowest "identifiable" material is not clearly defined. One might assume that "identifiable material" might be any material above the white noise floor, as white noise represents random, naturally occurring noise. White noise might be seen as the "bottom line" or "floor" for audio - the level below which no identifiable material can exist. This is notably not the case. Even if the noise floor is white, in that it has equal power at all equal sized frequency bands, this does not indicate that it is truly random nor that there is not a level of some degree of organization within it. In other words, signals can still exist at lower amplitudes than the noise, within the noise, that are still identifiable.

The waveform in Figure 5.10 is white noise, as a Fourier Transform analysis reveals. In reality, however, the noise is not completely random. A Fourier analysis of this waveform, presented as an STFT, shows that there is a repeating sine wave with a peak amplitude 6dB below the level of the noise. This sine wave indicates that this noise floor is very clearly not entirely random.

Figure 5.10B shows that the waveform shown in Figure 5.10A has a 1kHz sine wave buried beneath it at a lower amplitude than the amplitude of the noise. This sine wave is barely visibly discernable in this graphic, but due to the sensitivity of the ear, this sine wave would be easily recognized.

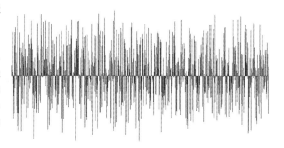

FIGURE 5.11A: A Noise Signal

What this actually indicates is that while the signal appears to be a "noise floor" it is actually not the actual "floor," as valid signals still exist within it, partially organizing what would otherwise be a random signal. A noise floor of any amplitude can still have valid signals well below it. Even though naturally occurring atmospheric noise exists at –6dB SPL, this does not mean that audio cannot exist below that. Anything that causes movement of the air molecules with less energy than the air molecules already have still causes movement in air molecules that cause air pressure changes. This energy simply re-directs the air molecules from their original path, in essence "organizing" the molecules and continuing to create sound.

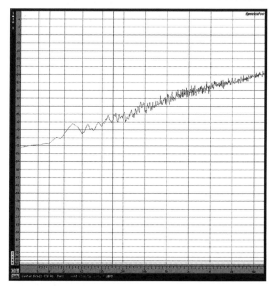

FIGURE 5.11B: A Spectrograph Plot of the Waveform Shown in Figure 5.11A

The noise signal shown in Figure 5.11A is essentially white noise as can be surmised by Figure 5.11B

If, in a perfectly anechoic chamber, a speaker plays some tones that measure 6dB SPL at one meter, then at two meters the pressure has spread over a broad enough area that the sound level is at 0dB SPL. At four meters the sound is at –6dB SPL and the amplitude of the sound is exactly the same amplitude as the atmospheric noise present. At eight meters the sound is at –12dB SPL and is therefore below the amplitude of the atmospheric noise. This does not mean that the force exerted by the speaker no longer has an effect on the air molecules at that distance; it is just that its effect is no longer as consequential, and is to some degree outweighed by the natural motion of the air molecules. An analogy to this might be taking an electric fan outside and turning it on. At a few feet back the effect of the fan can be felt. At a few feet back farther it will not be felt as much. The effect of the fan dissipates over distance, so that at some distance back it cannot be felt at all, especially if there are mild breezes present that seem stronger than the fan's breeze. This is not to say, however, that it does not still have an effect on the air at those distances. Even if in a windstorm, that fan will still have *some* sort of effect on the air around it. This effect becomes increasingly less significant and increasingly harder to measure but its effect never actually wears off. Even hundreds of miles away the actions of that small electric fan still have some sort of effect, but that effect becomes practically impossible to quantify in light of all of the other air movement that is more powerful than it.

It is important to clarify that sound literally continues getting quieter forever and that at some level the other air pressure influences that are also present, such as various contributors of noise, dwarfs it. Sound never completely dissipates. This also holds true in other noise inducing environments. Analog tape, for example, adds a lot of noise to a signal. When one records a decreasing amplitude waveform onto analog tape, the noise induced by the analog tape eventually becomes much higher than the amplitude of the original waveform. The waveform of the noise gets added to the original waveform and yields the original waveform with a certain amount of random variation. The original waveform is still there and present at a decreasing level. At some point, the amplitude of the noise dwarfs the amplitude of the original signal, but since the noise got *added to* the original waveform, the original waveform is still completely present all the way down to an infinitely low amplitude. At some amplitude, the original waveform simply becomes too difficult to recognize due to the high amplitude of the noise. The signal does not ever completely dissipate. The noise that gets added to it simply overwhelms it to the point that it is no longer discernable. The same occurs through any other source of noise: microphones, microphone amplifiers, amplifiers, speakers and more. The original signal is always still present, but some of it may be buried deep beneath the noise and therefore not identifiable.

FIGURE 5.11C: **A Different Noise Signal**

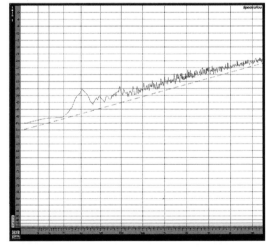

FIGURE 5.11D: **A Spectrograph Plot of the Waveform Shown in Figure 5.11C**

The noise signal shown in Figure 5.11C is not pure white noise. The peak amplitude of the noise in Figure 5.11C is the same as the noise in Figure 5.11A, but the white noise floor within it is much lower in amplitude, as is identified by the dashed line.

We discussed earlier that atmospheric noise is white in nature. It therefore makes sense to measure the amplitude of the signal that occurs above a white noise floor. We now know, however, that we should not dismiss everything below the white noise floor as inconsequential. Even the material below the white noise floor is consequential to some degree. Once we are dealing with white noise, however, the rate at which the signal dissipates into that noise to the point of indeterminacy becomes predictable. We can measure, for example, how far below the (white) noise floor a signal is detectable in particular situations with particular tools and this would be a fixed amount. We cannot determine, however, how far below the *peak* frequency in a non-white noise floor a signal can still be identifiable, since simply knowing the peak tells us little about the amplitude of the noise at other frequencies. The most important use of this is measuring how far below the *white* noise floor is detectable by the human auditory system. If we quantify the SNR of a signal by the amplitude above the *peak frequency* in a noise floor then there will be too much variation on what the impact will be of the material below that peak frequency. The example given above in Figure 5.10 clearly shows that a tremendous amount of consequential material can be present below the peak noise floor, and this then becomes less predictable than the signal below a *white* noise floor. If we only use the *peak* noise floor to compare waveforms there can be a great difference between two waveforms that will be said to share that same specification. See Figure 5.11.

For the sake of comparing waveforms, the "dynamic range" of an audio signal needs to reflect the difference in amplitude between its highest peak and the lowest discernable part of the signal. We will soon learn about the human ear that the lowest discernable part of a signal is readily identifiable and predictable if the amplitude of the white noise floor in a waveform is established.

DYNAMIC RANGE: IDENTIFYING CHARACTERISTIC OF AN AUDIO WAVEFORM

It is clear and evident that complete silence does not exist where it is possible to have sound (in other words where any air exists). Noise is a part of any environment that can transmit waveforms. Because of this, the noise gets added to every waveform that is transmitted. Some degree of random variation is therefore present in every analog waveform. Most textbooks simply ignore the random variations in a signal, as textbooks are the only place where pure waveforms can exist anyway. Conventional wisdom says that the noise in any waveform can be described by the other characteristics of a waveform. Since the noise is really a complex waveform of its own, it can theoretically be represented by a combination of amplitude, frequency, and phase information. The characteristics of the noise can then be added to the characteristics of the signal, yielding a comprehensive description of any waveform. In traditional waveform analysis this approach would be appropriate. In audio, however, a more appropriate approach exists. This is because the audio waveforms are heard by the human auditory system. The human auditory system has a finite dynamic range it is capable of hearing, as will be discussed in the following chapter. The dynamic range that the ear is capable of hearing is very much defined by the amplitude of the white noise floor of a signal. Below that noise floor, a signal is only capable of being heard down to a specific, determinable amplitude. Below that amplitude, the human auditory system will not recognize the signal in any capacity. Although "dynamic range" is the actual specification of the waveform that we are concerned with, measuring this is very difficult because the ear's ability to discern signals changes dependant upon many signal characteristics. More prudent is to simply measure the amplitude difference between the peak amplitude of a waveform and its white noise floor. The dynamic range of a waveform is going to be a relatively fixed amount greater than the difference between the peak and the white noise floor, since we can only discern signals a certain, predictable amount below the (white) noise floor. This is precisely the reason that, while discussing "dynamic range" in this chapter, we have also been discussing noise: the amplitude of a flat frequency distributed noise such as white noise *defines* dynamic range in the case of human audibility. The white noise floor is not the bottom of the dynamic range, but it determines and defines where the bottom is. This is also the reason that so much of the audio industry focuses on the amplitude of noise, either through signal to noise ratio capability specifications on equipment or "THD+noise" specifications on equipment, or other noise based specifications.

The purpose of deriving identifying characteristics of waveforms in the first place is to ensure that the waveforms can be reproduced. This reproduction can either happen after transmission or after recording and playback. Both are examples of "communicating" the waveforms. It can be of little surprise that one of the most consequential papers in the field of digital audio was entitled "Communication in the Presence of Noise" (by Claude E. Shannon, 1949). The title of the paper itself identifies that, as a valid and characteristic part of the signal, a complete recognition of the presence of noise was crucial to the further development of the technology of waveform communication (in his case, audio transmission). The purpose of the exercise of determining defining characteristics of a waveform is to be able to somehow describe the waveform for later reproduction.

The dynamic range of a waveform, identifying the lowest amplitude discernable, is a pertinent specification of a waveform. Signals present in a waveform that are lower than the lowest discernable part of the signal are inconsequential and not necessary to accurately reproduce.

For these reasons it is not only necessary to understand the frequency and phase and amplitude portions of a waveform, but also the minimum discernable amplitude characteristics of a waveform. Without this final characteristic of a waveform the waveform can be reconstructed accurately, but since any waveform that is audible has a limit to the discernability of low-level components within it, accurately recording or transmitting that low-level information is excessive and not beneficial to the process of audio waveform reconstruction. *Knowing* the amplitude of the lowest discernable signal, however, is crucially important, because all parts of the waveform that are present at an amplitude *higher* than this minimum amount are necessary to accurately record and thus must all be considered.

In short, knowing the minimum identifiable amplitude is not a *requirement* of audio waveform representation in the way that frequency, amplitude, and phase are. Since, however, perfect waveform recording or transmitting can never happen because of the random variations discussed above, identifying exactly *how* accurately a waveform needs to be recorded is important. When analyzing how accurately a waveform needs to be recorded we need to know the minimum discernable level of any part of the waveform. Therefore, in real world conditions, where a certain amount of random variation or noise will permeate any recording or playback situation, ensuring that those variations are below the amplitude of the lowest discernable part of a waveform is crucially important. As such, the dynamic range of a waveform is a necessary characteristic of an audio waveform to identify if the waveform is to be accurately recreated.

ADDING NOISE

So far we have studied what happens when waveforms get added together in terms of the resultant, complex waveform. We have also studied that adding two identical waveforms together results in doubling the amplitude, or an increase in the signal by 6dB. We have not studied the amplitude change that results from summing together two signals that are not identical. When two waveforms are "related" to each other they are said to be "correlated," and when two signals are completely unrelated to each other they are said to be "uncorrelated." Two random noise signals are said to be "uncorrelated" to each other because if each is random then they have no relation to each other.

When two uncorrelated signals of equal amplitude are summed together the overall amplitude does not double. The only thing that doubles in this situation is the power of the new waveform. This is a logical conclusion to draw: if we have two speakers next to each other, each playing signals that are unrelated to each other then the resulting noise does require twice the power to produce that each individual waveform required. The power of the resulting waveform, then, is doubled.

We remember from Chapter Two that if a waveform has double the power that the amplitude only increases by 3dB. This is precisely what happens when two equal amplitude, uncorrelated signals get added together: the result is 3dB louder. Since random noise is uncorrelated to itself, adding together two noise signals of equal amplitude yields a resulting waveform with an amplitude that is 3dB louder. If four equal-amplitude random noise signals are summed together then the resulting amplitude would be 6dB louder, or twice as loud as one of the individual signals.

Let us analyze a situation for practical implementation of this information. We have two identical waveforms and each has random noise on it (Figure 5.12). What happens if we add these two waveforms together? Perhaps the two waveforms have an amplitude of 20dB SPL and the noise present in the waveforms has an amplitude of 6dB SPL, so the signal to noise ratio of each waveform is 14dB.

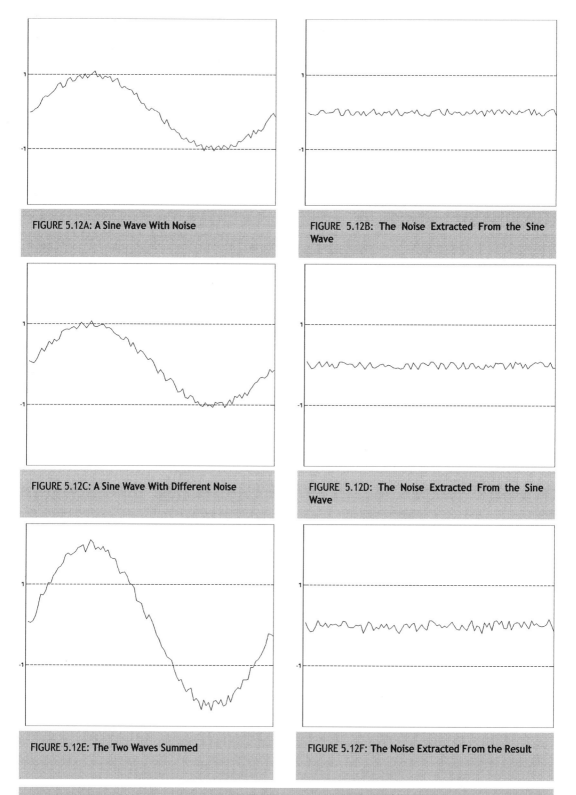

FIGURE 5.12A: A Sine Wave With Noise

FIGURE 5.12B: The Noise Extracted From the Sine Wave

FIGURE 5.12C: A Sine Wave With Different Noise

FIGURE 5.12D: The Noise Extracted From the Sine Wave

FIGURE 5.12E: The Two Waves Summed

FIGURE 5.12F: The Noise Extracted From the Result

Point 1 to point -1 represents 20dB SPL. The noise is 6dB SPL in B and D. When the two waveforms are summed the amplitude of the result is 26dB SPL. The amplitude of the noise within the waveform only increases, however, to 9dB SPL, so the dynamic range of the signal increases.

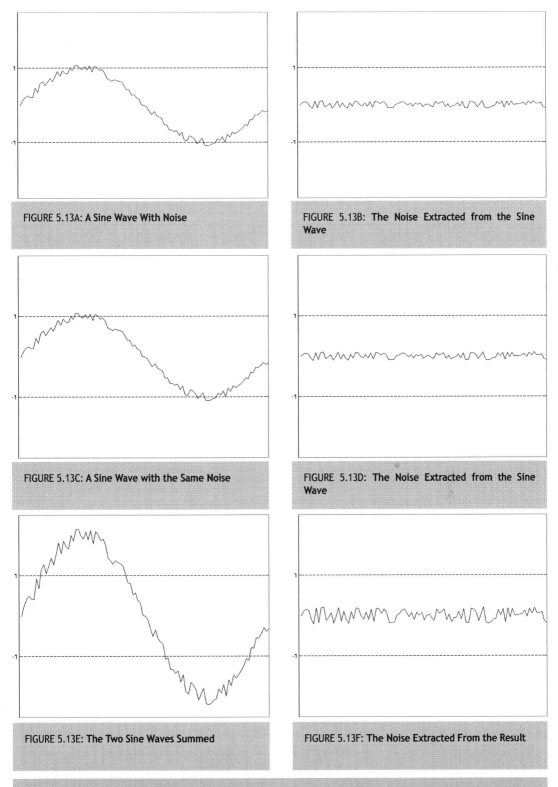

FIGURE 5.13A: A Sine Wave With Noise

FIGURE 5.13B: **The Noise Extracted from the Sine Wave**

FIGURE 5.13C: **A Sine Wave with the Same Noise**

FIGURE 5.13D: **The Noise Extracted from the Sine Wave**

FIGURE 5.13E: **The Two Sine Waves Summed**

FIGURE 5.13F: **The Noise Extracted From the Result**

Point 1 to point -1 represents 20dB SPL. The noise is 6dB SPL in B and D. When the two waveforms are summed the amplitude of the result is 26dB SPL. The amplitude of the noise within the waveform increases to 12dB SPL, so the dynamic range of the signal stays the same.

The two waveforms will sum together to create a new waveform with twice the amplitude, or 26dB SPL. The noise, however, will sum together and only double the power, causing an increase in amplitude of 3dB. The overall noise will increase from 6dB SPL to 9dB SPL (Figure 5.12F). The result is a waveform with a peak amplitude of 26dB SPL and a noise floor of 9dB SPL (Figure 5.12E), or an overall signal to noise ratio of 17dB. By summing two waveforms together that each had unrelated random noise, the signal to noise ratio improved by 3dB. This premise is commonly used to improve the signal to noise ratio of a noisy but repeatable source.

We can look at another example. Let us sum together two waveforms that have identical noise (Figure 5.13). The noise on the two waveforms is no longer random because it is the same in each waveform. What happens when we double the amplitude of this signal? Does the signal to noise ratio of the signal improve? The answer is no. If we double the amplitude of the signal then the signal increases by 6dB and the noise increases by 6dB along with it.

In this situation we are not adding two random noise signals together because the noise in each waveform is not random with respect to each other. Because of this, the noise becomes 6dB greater, as any signal does upon doubling its amplitude. In this situation, the signal to noise ratio stays the same and does not improve by 6dB. This is what happens when a signal with noise on it is amplified. The signal is amplified and the noise is amplified and the signal to noise ratio between them can do no better than stay the same; often it gets a little worse since the amplifier adds its own noise.

For a final example let us sum together two waveforms that are distinct but have equal amplitudes, each, however, with the same noise (Figure 5.14).

What would happen in this situation? The two waveforms that get added together create a new waveform that has twice the power of the individual ones. The amplitude does not double in this situation, but only increases overall by 3dB since the waveforms are different and unrelated. The noise, on the other hand, sums together and does double in amplitude because the noise waveforms are identical. If each waveform was a 20dB SPL waveform and each noise floor was present at 6dB SPL then the result of summing them together would produce a 23dB SPL waveform and noise of 12dB SPL. In this situation, since the noise was identical but the waveforms were different the signal to noise ratio decreased by 3dB so that the result is no longer 14dB of signal to noise ratio but rather 11dB.

This happens quite frequently when noise is induced into multiple signals by a common source. For example, on an analog mixing board the power supply might generate noise that infiltrates all of the channels so that noise on each channel is identical, or "correlated." When multiple channels are summed together the noise increases by 6dB for every doubling of the number of channels but the signal only increases by 3dB for every doubling of the channels because the signals passing through each of the channels on the mixer are generally different, or uncorrelated. This is a common way in which poorly designed analog mixing boards can cause a decrease in the signal to noise ratio of signals passing through them.

The increase in signal to noise ratio resulting from summing two waveforms together only occurs if the two waveforms are correlated and the noise waveforms within them are uncorrelated. If the opposite occurs then the signal to noise ratio decreases.

Since dynamic range is directly related to the amplitude of the noise floor, in each of the examples above where the signal to noise ratio increased or decreased the dynamic range of the signal did the same. However, if the signal to noise ratio of a waveform is 14dB the dynamic range of the waveform can be much greater because humans can discern signals well into the noise floor of a given signal. This is because "dynamic range" is based on perceptual quantities. In the realm of audio waveforms the dynamic range is based on the human ability to hear below the noise floor a certain amount. In other fields, such as RADAR, video, or other areas where waveforms are used, the dynamic range may be different because the ability to perceive signals below the noise floor may be greater or weaker than that of the human ear. In audio, however, certain characteristics

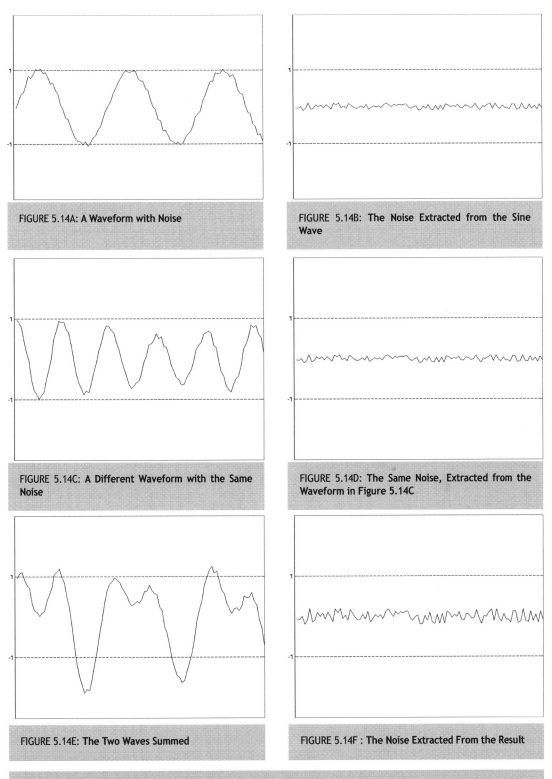

FIGURE 5.14A: A Waveform with Noise

FIGURE 5.14B: The Noise Extracted from the Sine Wave

FIGURE 5.14C: A Different Waveform with the Same Noise

FIGURE 5.14D: The Same Noise, Extracted from the Waveform in Figure 5.14C

FIGURE 5.14E: The Two Waves Summed

FIGURE 5.14F : The Noise Extracted From the Result

Point 1 to point -1 represents 20dB SPL. The noise is 6dB SPL in B and D. When the two waveforms are summed the amplitude of the result is 23dB SPL. The amplitude of the noise within the signal increases to 12dB SPL because the noise signal was simply doubled. The dynamic range decreases by 3dB because the noise simply doubles (6dB) whereas the signal itself only increases by 3dB.

of the ear define how far below the noise floor we can discern signals, so the ear itself is a determining factor of the dynamic range of signals. The crux of this is that "dynamic range" is a valid characteristic when looking specifically at "audio waveforms" because the perceptual abilities of the ear to detect signals below a flat noise floor are definable. In the greater science of waveform analysis, "dynamic range" could not be considered a definable characteristic of waveforms because the limits of our ability to detect signals below the noise floor is not as clearly defined.

SUMMARY

In summary, any unique waveform can be transmitted, recorded, and reproduced if four unique factors of the waveform are identified. Frequency identifies the specific sine waves used to create the waveform. Amplitude represents the level of each of the sine waves at the various frequencies that compose the waveform. Phase is a measurement of the time that the individual sine waves occurred in relation to each other. Finally, dynamic range is an indication of the difference between the highest amplitude of the waveform and the lowest discernable amplitude of a waveform, essentially defining the minimum amplitude that need be identified within a waveform. In the case of audio waveforms, this is essentially determined by the amplitude of the white noise floor of a given waveform. Each of the four of these characteristics is necessary to describe an audio waveform accurately, and any waveform can be completely accurately described with only these four measurements. With accurate identification of these four characteristics, any audio waveform can be accurately recreated, recognizing again that the purpose of recreating the waveform is for the sake of human hearing.

FOOTNOTES

[1] Ludwig, Art. The Physics of Sound. 9 January 2003. <http://www.silcom.com/~aludwig/Physics/Main/Physics_of_sound.html>.

[2] Note that the 0dB SPL threshold of hearing coincides with 1kHz signals. Humans can hear lower than 0dB SPL at other frequencies.

NOTES:

Chapter Six

The Ear

This book is specifically written for audio engineers. As such, understanding the eventual recipient of the audio to be reproduced is pertinent and appropriate. In the case of audio engineers the eventual recipient of the audio is assumed to be the auditory system of human beings.

The study of the human auditory system has been the focus of an intense amount of research for hundreds of years. There are a litany of sciences that are related to the study of the ear, including anatomy, audiology, otology, and neurology. Observations of behaviors of the ear date back to the sixteenth century, and several of the parts of the inner ear's anatomy have etymological roots dating to the seventeenth century. The majority of the work in determining the physiology of the human auditory system dates to the late nineteenth century. The science of audiology was not recognized until the 1920s, though the science of otology dates back hundreds of years. Much of the research on the physiology of the inner ear and the relationship between the ear and the brain has been done in the past hundred years.

The human ear can be divided into three consequential portions as identified in Figure 6.1. The three sections are known as the outer ear, the middle ear, and the inner ear. The outer ear deals specifically with air pressure

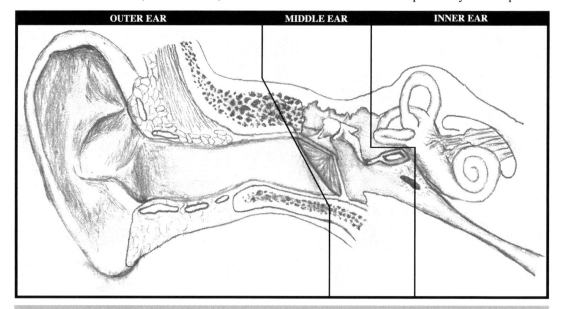

FIGURE 6.1: **The Human Ear.** *The human ear is divided into three regions, the outer ear, the middle ear, and the inner ear.*

changes. The middle ear converts the air pressure changes from the outer ear to fluid pressure changes in the inner ear using a mechanical system. The inner ear converts the waves of fluid pressure change into neural pulses that travel to the brain via the VIIIth cranial nerve.

THE OUTER EAR

The outer ear consists of the piece of exterior skin-covered cartilage called the "pinna" and the external auditory canal. The pinna serves two primary functions: the first is to provide an acoustical "bowl," functioning as the opposite of a megaphone, funneling the sound into the ear. The second function is accomplished by the shape of the pinna, which causes the sound waves to have to "bend", or "refract" around it such that not all frequencies from all directions end up in the ear canal at the same amplitude or at the same time. Higher frequencies approaching the pinna from the rear of the head become attenuated more than higher frequencies approaching the ear from off center and are fractionally delayed as well. This characteristic aids us in determining the location of a sound source.

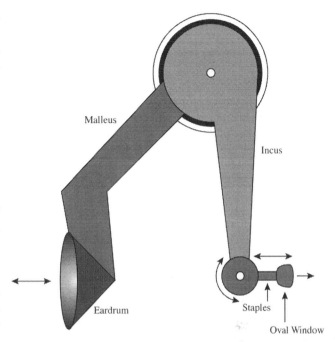

Malleus

Incus

Eardrum

Staples

Oval Window

FIGURE 6.2: The Movement of the Ossicles

The three bones in the middle ear, called the "ossicles," move in a sophisticated type of lever action. The eardrum, connected to the malleus, causes the malleus to rock about the pivot created by the incus. The subsequent rocking of the incus causes the stapes to move accordingly.

The motion is not dissimilar to how a piano key strikes a string on an upright piano: several mechanical components all work as levers and pivots against each other until the downward force on the piano key causes an upward force of a hammer against the string.

The external auditory canal is the opening in the ear that extends toward the eardrum, or "tympanic membrane." The external auditory canal opens into the *concha*, or the deepest part of the pinna, which has a diameter of 1 to 2 cm. The canal itself has a diameter of just over a half centimeter, but extends 2 to 3 cm into the ear before terminating at the tympanic membrane. The canal acts like any resonant cavity does: certain frequencies become amplified to some degree within the canal. Between the shape of the pinna and the resonance of the external auditory canal, the sound hitting the ear is amplified 10 to 15dB in a frequency range extending from about 1.5kHz to 7kHz. Some scientists put forth the theory that this amplification of certain frequencies implies another purpose to the outer ear: a baby's cry generally centers around 2kHz to 3kHz, right in line with the 2.5kHz resonant frequency of the external auditory canal. Perhaps the outer ear serves as an evolutionary trait for the survival of the species and protection of the young.

THE MIDDLE EAR

The middle ear starts with the tympanic membrane, a cone shaped, very thin transducer that is approximately a centimeter in diameter. Inside the middle ear is a cavity called the "middle ear cavity," or "tympanum." The volume of the tympanum is about 2 cubic centimeters, thus not as large as the external auditory canal. The "oval window" is at the opposite side of the middle ear, and is the entrance of the inner ear. Through the middle ear are positioned three small bones called "ossicles," which serve the purpose of converting vibrations of the tympanic membrane to fluid vibrations in the inner ear. The first of the bones (the *malleus*) is attached to the tympanic membrane itself by means of a lengthy piece of bone that extends out to the middle of the tympanic membrane. As the tympanic membrane vibrates the malleus vibrates with it. The malleus is connected to the *incus*, which, in turn, is connected to the *stapes*. The chain of the three ossicles is called the "ossicular chain," and terminates where the stapes attaches to the *oval window membrane*. As the tympanic membrane vibrates with air pressure changes the oval window membrane vibrates respectively. A simplified diagram of the movement of the ossicular chain is given in Figure 6.2.

Because the outer ear is completely separated from the middle ear by the tympanic membrane, air pressure changes outside of the ear (such as large changes in barometric pressure) need to be balanced with changes in the middle ear or else the tympanic membrane would be pulled in or out of its nominal position. As with any elastic device, when the eardrum is stretched to its maximum position its ability to vibrate is heavily dampened. The ear compensates for this by means of the "Eustachian tube," a tube that allows air to flow from the nose into the middle ear, keeping the air in the middle ear at the same pressure as the outside air. If the Eustachian tube did not exist then every time the air pressure changed outside our hearing ability would decrease. This is precisely why our hearing ability *does* decrease when we get a cold and our Eustachian tubes fill with fluid and the middle ear cannot depressurize. We also notice a decrease in hearing ability when we change altitudes quickly before our ears "pop." The "popping" occurs as the middle ear either releases air or takes in air from the Eustachian tubes, once again bringing the middle ear's air pressure to a point of equilibrium with the air in the outer ear, allowing the ear drum to come to rest at its natural position.

In Chapter One we discussed that in order for air pressure changes to constitute "sound" they had to be recognizable by the human auditory system. Not all changes in air pressure qualify as sound. The fact that the Eustachian tubes constantly equalize the air pressure between the outer and middle ears shows us that slow changes in air pressure will never manifest themselves at the inner ear, and thus will not be detected and will not qualify as "sound," per se. If the Eustachian tubes depressurize quickly a "pop" is heard due to the eardrum moving to a position of equilibrium.

THE INNER EAR

The inner ear is really where the "hearing" takes place. The outer ear and middle ear only take the vibrations in the outside world and transfer them to the inner ear, while also providing protection from drastic changes in air pressure and foreign objects. The inner ear contains three sections: the vestibule, the semicircular canals, and the cochlea.

The *vestibule* is the chamber of the inner ear - the "meeting place" of the semicircular canals and the opening to the cochlea. The stapes, the last in the chain of the ossicles, connects to the vestibule by means of the oval window membrane, to which it is attached. As the tympanic membrane moves back and forth the ossicles transfer those movements to the oval window, which, in turn, moves back and forth in parallel with the tympanic membrane. The entire inner ear is filled with fluid. Since the tympanic membrane and the oval window membrane are virtually connected (through the ossicles) the situation raises an interesting question of how efficiently the motion of the tympanic membrane is able to vibrate the fluid filled chamber of the inner ear, fluid being much more dense than air. The loss of energy would appear to be great, causing a reduction in amplitude and distortion in the inner ear. This is compensated for by the fact that the surface area of the tympanic membrane is much larger than the surface area of the "footplate" at the end of the stapes. This allows the pressure provided at the tympanic membrane by the air to be equivalent to the pressure provided to the inner ear by the stapes. This is not too dissimilar than the reason that one's hand does not make a dent in a piece of wood when it is slapped, but when the same force is applied holding a hammer and hitting a nail, the nail is able to indent the wood. The large amount of force is more effective when concentrated, and by the footplate of the stapes being approximately 1/18th the size of the tympanic membrane, the force applied to the inner ear is enough to compensate for the fact that the inner ear is filled with a fluid that is much more dense than air. The result is that the transfer of energy from the tympanic membrane into the inner ear is remarkably efficient.

The semicircular canals are three fluid-filled pipes that are oriented in different directions from each other and are used (by means of the vestibular nerve) by the body for balance.

The part of the inner ear that is most pertinent to our discussion on hearing is the *cochlea*, a spiral-shaped, fluid-filled organ that converts waves of air pressure into electrical impulses that are sent to the brain for deciphering and processing. The cochlea is a snail-shaped bony structure that turns $2^5/_8$ rotations and terminates at a point called the "helicotrema". The overall length of the cochlea is about 3.5 centimeters when uncoiled. The entire cochlea is divided into what is termed the "top half" and the "bottom half", or the *scala vestibuli* and the *scala tympani*, respectively. Through the top half, a *cochlear sac* runs through the cochlea, nearly to the end. As the stapes pushes and pulls on the oval window, the fluid in the inner ear vibrates through the cochlea. The vibrations travel the length of the cochlea through the scala vestibuli, around the helicotrema and back down the scala tympani. As the vibrations get to the end of the bottom of their 7cm journey down and back the cochlea they hit a membrane called the "round window membrane," which dissipates the vibrations back into the tympanum (middle ear cavity).

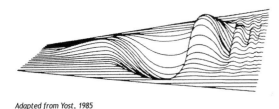

Adapted from Yost, 1985

FIGURE 6.3: The Motion of the Basilar Membrane

The "shelf" that divides the cochlea is created by a piece of bone and a thin membrane called the "basilar membrane." At the beginning of the cochlea, the cochlea is wider and the majority of the width of it is spanned by the above referenced bone (or *osseous spiral lamina*). Only .15mm of the beginning of the cochlea is spanned by the basilar membrane. Even though the cochlea decreases in diameter as it coils, the basilar membrane becomes wider, such that by the end of the cochlear sac, the basilar membrane is three and a half times wider than it was at the entrance to the cochlea. The basilar membrane is essentially "stretched" across the gap, firmly affixed at either side and not able to move. In the center, however, it is freely floating in the fluids and able to vibrate as the fluids around it vibrate. Because the basilar membrane changes in width, but is still affixed at both sides, different frequencies will be able to cause the membrane to resonate more efficiently at certain locations. At the start of the cochlea, where the membrane is taut and narrow, lower frequencies are less able to cause the membrane to vibrate than at the end of the cochlea where the membrane is wider and has more play. Higher frequencies are only able to vibrate the beginning of the basilar membrane, as the *apical end* of the basilar membrane is too loose to allow high frequency waves to take effect. This means that any particular point on the basilar membrane is most efficient at resonating at a specific frequency. The converse is also true: that any frequency will most efficiently resonate a single location on the basilar membrane. A 300Hz sine wave, for example, has optimum effect in resonating the basilar membrane at a distance of 26mm from the stapes, whereas a 200Hz sine wave has its optimum effect at 27mm, and a 100Hz sine wave has its optimum effect at around 30mm. The movement and behavior of the basilar membrane is indicated in Figure 6.3.

Sitting atop the basilar membrane is the *organ of corti*, a complex arrangement of different types of cells that form a layer above the membrane no thicker than that of one or two cells. On the side of the basilar membrane are a series of "hair cells." The cells are aligned in a single-file line from the beginning of the cochlea to the end of the cochlear sac (the hair cells are within the cochlear sac). Closest to the inside is a single-file line of the *inner hair cells*, which are only one cell abreast and around 3500 cells long. A series of *inner pillar cells* separates the inner hair cells from the outer hair cells, which are three abreast. There are about 12,000 outer hair cells in a human cochlea. The hair cells are elongated cells, sitting vertically atop the basilar membrane, supported by other cells on the outside. Atop the hair cells are a series of very small *cilia*, or hair-like fibers that are essentially free floating in "the breeze" of waves of fluid passing by. These specific cilia are called "stereocilia," and they are arranged in rows of varying heights in a U or V shaped pattern atop the cell. Inner hair cells have approximately 40 stereocilia and outer hair cells have about 150. Hovering slightly above the stereocilia is a piece of material called the "tectorial membrane," which is firmly affixed on the inside above the osseous spiral lamina and is free floating above the stereocilia, reaching out over the outermost hair cells and running the length of the cochlea parallel to the basilar membrane. As the basilar membrane moves, the tectorial membrane moves in parallel to it because it is affixed to the organ of Corti, which is atop the basilar membrane itself. As the basilar membrane and the tectorial membrane move up and down with the vibrations of the fluid, the stereocilia get "blown over" by the sheering force of the tectorial membrane, as demonstrated in the diagram in Figure 6.4.

Attached to the base of the inner hair cells is a network of nerve fibers. Nerve fibers are chains of nerve cells called "neurons." The *synapse*, or the cell at the nerve ending where it connects to the hair cell, discharges electrical pulses which are sent from neuron to neuron all the way to the brain for processing. The signal travels through the nerve fibers, which are spread throughout the body in a manner similar to that of the blood system: all nerve fibers start at a single location and branch out with various stems branching off as the network expands. A difference between the circulatory system and the nervous system is that the circulatory system is composed of a series of "pipes", and the blood flows freely through the pipes. The blood in the circulatory system can find its way to any location in the circulatory system. Particular red blood cells are not destined for a particular capillary. The nervous system, on the other hand, is composed of individual strands, or nerve fibers, that travel through the body in "bundles" of anywhere from as few as two to as many as hundreds of thousands of nerve fibers. Each fiber that connects to a hair cell in the cochlea is a complete strand that extends from a given neuron in the ear to a given place in the brain. A neuron connected to an inner hair cell discharges an electronic pulse that is sent to the brain. Because that nerve fiber terminates at a particular location, a message sent through that nerve fiber indicates to the brain exactly which neuron discharged.

Each inner hair cell has approximately twenty nerve fibers attached to it. Even though the inner hair cells account for only 25% of the total number of hair cells in the ear, the nerve fibers attached to the inner hair cells account for 95% of the nerve fibers in the cochlea. The other 5% of the nerve fibers are connected to the outer hair cells with one fiber connecting to perhaps ten different outer hair cells. The fibers are bundled together and travel through the cochlea where they are joined together with the vestibular nerves (for balance) and create the VIIIth (auditory) nerve.

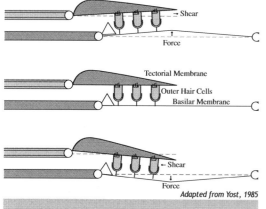

Adapted from Yost, 1985

FIGURE 6.4: The Shearing Force of the Tectorial Membrane Against the Stereocilia

As the basilar membrane moves up and down, the stereocilia atop the hair cells on top of the basilar membrane shear against the tectorial membrane, which hovers above them.

NEURAL DISCHARGES

A neuron discharges in an "all or nothing" capacity. An analogy is often made to the firing of a gun: the gun at a state of rest does not fire until the trigger is pulled far enough to discharge. When a discharge occurs it fires a complete blast and then has to "relax," recharge, and reload. A gun cannot fire at only half capacity, and any discharge is not stronger than any other.

Each neuron has what is known as a "spontaneous discharge rate." Each neuron "fires" at a nominal rate without stimulation (neurons in the ear fire without any "sound" being present). The shearing force of the stereocilia, however, causes that rate to change. A single neuron may have a spontaneous discharge rate of as low as a few discharges per minute or as high as over

100 discharges per second. An individual neuron cannot discharge faster than it can "recharge." The fastest "recharge" rate of any given neuron is 1000 times per second, so a neuron cannot fire repeatedly at a rate greater than 1kHz. The movements of the stereocilia cause the attached neurons to discharge at a faster rate than their individual spontaneous discharge rates. The effect that differing frequencies can have on indi-

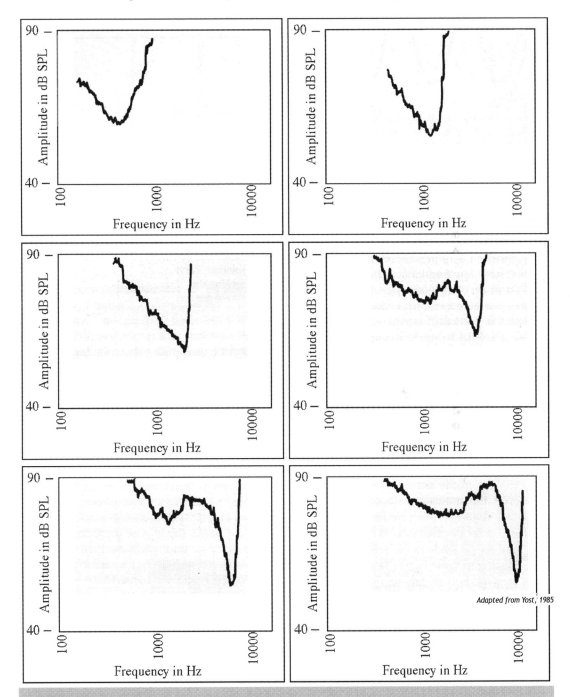

Adapted from Yost, 1985

FIGURE 6.5: Signal Required to Cause Neurons to Fire at Greater than their Spontaneous Discharge Rate

Each neuron in the ear has sensitivity to different frequencies at differing intensities. Some require very little signal to discharge at a given frequency whereas the same amount of signal at the same frequency may be inadequate to cause a reaction in another neuron.

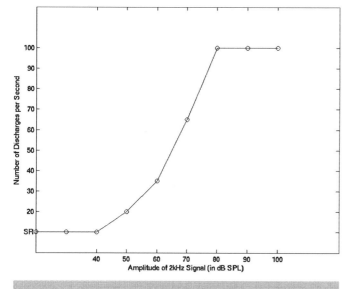

FIGURE 6.6: Response at 2kHz for a Single Neuron

vidual neurons is able to be plotted, and the resulting curve is called a "tuning curve." A tuning curve of a particular neuron may show that it takes a signal of very low amplitude at, say, 500Hz for it to discharge faster than its spontaneous discharge rate, but it may take a very high amplitude of a signal at, say, 100Hz for it to discharge faster than its spontaneous discharge rate.

The tuning curve tells us at what amplitudes and at what frequencies a particular neuron will suddenly become "active" by telling us what is required to cause it to discharge at a rate that is faster than it normally discharges under unstimulated conditions. Other analysis, however, tells us specifically how many times the neuron discharges per second for the various amplitudes of a given frequency. At 2.0kHz, for example, a neuron may discharge at its spontaneous rate (say, 10 times per second) until after the incoming amplitude is greater than 40dB SPL. At 50dB SPL it may discharge 20 times per second, at 60dB SPL it may discharge 35 times per second, and so on. Figure 6.6 shows a tuning curve for a particular neuron at 2.0kHz.

The same neuron, however, may have a different chart of its discharge rate in relation to amplitude of a 4.0kHz tone (Figure 6.7).

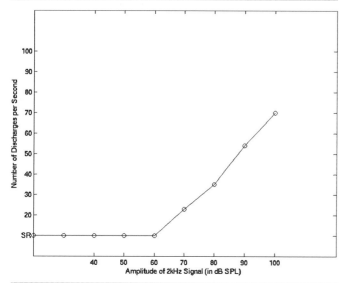

FIGURE 6.7: Response at 4kHz for the Neuron Shown in Figure 6.6

A thorough analysis of a series of frequencies at varying amplitudes would give us a relatively complete picture of the discharge rate of a particular neuron.

A more complete analysis for a neuron is shown in Figure 6.8.

This type of analysis tells us the "best frequency" for that particular neuron, or the frequency that the neuron is most sensitive to. It is not surprising that the neurons with higher "best frequencies" are generally located toward the beginning, or stapes end of the basilar membrane, as that is where the basilar membrane is capable of vibrating at higher frequencies. The neurons with lower "best frequencies" are generally located toward the apical end of the basilar membrane, where lower frequencies have more of an effect on the basilar membrane. Thus, not only are certain neurons situated in places where they are more prone to receiving certain frequencies, but also individual neurons are "tuned" to respond to particular frequencies more than others.

The neurons fire in what is called a "phase locked response," meaning that the timing of the neurons' discharges is in tempo with the cycles of the waveform. An example of this is shown in Figure 6.9.

The discharge does not necessarily happen at every cycle of a waveform, but discharges occur increasingly more often as the amplitude increases, within the tuning curve of that particular neuron. We have already discussed that the fastest discharge rate of a single neuron is 1000 times per second, or 1kHz. For waveforms above 1kHz the neuron will discharge, still in a phase locked response, but will not discharge with every cycle. Two neurons connected to the same inner hair cell may both have a 4kHz best frequency, and when a 4kHz sine wave is presented, they will fire at phase locked, but *asynchronous* discharge rates. The net result of this is still a phase locked waveform but created by two neurons. No single neuron in the ear can present a 4kHz waveform to the brain. A 4kHz waveform can only

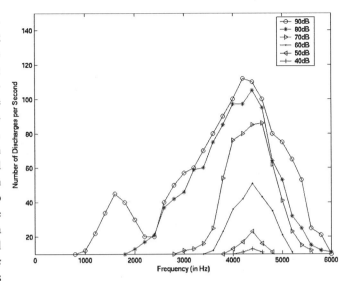

FIGURE 6.8: **Response for a Single Neuron at Different Frequencies and Intensities**

be created indirectly by means of multiple neurons firing in conjunction with each other. An example of asynchronous neural discharges is shown in Figure 6.10.

For single tones above 4kHz or so, neurons are incapable of firing at completely phase locked rates. This does not mean, however, that we cannot hear above 4kHz, or that the neurons do not still fire in a phase locked manner. When two sine waves of differing frequencies are added together a unique situation occurs providing what are called "beat frequencies." Any two sine waves that are added together in the ear produce these tones, providing that both tones cause sufficient vibrations on the basilar membrane. The addition of two tones will create what "appears" to be two additional tones, one at the frequency that is the sum of the original two, and the other at the frequency that is the difference of the two. Thus, two sine waves present at 5kHz and 6kHz will produce a *beat tone* at 1kHz and a *combination tone* at 11kHz. The reason for this is easily understood with a simple graphic. Figure 6.11 shows the results of a 5kHz and 6kHz sine wave summed together.

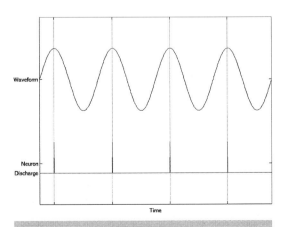

FIGURE 6.9: **Phase Locked Response of Neuron Discharges**

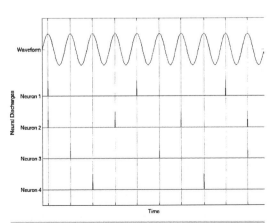

FIGURE 6.10: **Asynchronous Neural Discharges**

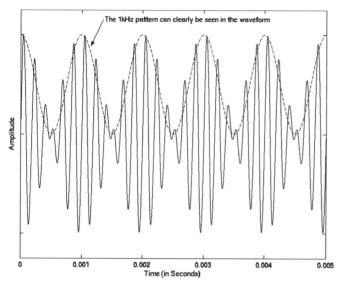

FIGURE 6.11: 5kHz and 6kHz Sine Waves Summed and the Resultant Waveform

The 5kHz and 6kHz waveforms, when added together, create the illusion (and audible "illusion") of an 11kHz and a 1kHz waveform.

The 1kHz result of this sine wave does not truly "exist." In other words, a Fourier Transform of the resulting waveform would not yield the presence of the two additional tones, but would rather show only the presence of 5kHz and a 6kHz tones. A spectrograph plot of this waveform, indicating that the tones at 1kHz and 11kHz do not truly exist as a part of the waveform, is given in Figure 6.12.

The brain uses the presence of the sum and difference tones to determine the actual frequencies present. The fact that the waveform in Figure 6.11 contains 5kHz and 6kHz tones can be concluded because no other combination of tones would create the resulting waveform. A 3kHz and a 4kHz tone would produce the 1kHz discharges but not the 11kHz response. Neurons do fire in a phase locked response to beat tones even though they are not a "valid" part of the signal. In the situation with 5kHz and 6kHz sine waves present, the 1kHz result would cause the neurons with a 1kHz best frequency to discharge at their normal rate based on the amplitude of the 1kHz resultant waveform. The 11kHz tone would be too high in frequency for any neuron to discharge in a phase locked response. The 11kHz tone would only register through the "location method," in that it would only get detected by the neurons that happened to sit on the basilar membrane where 11kHz was capable of resonating. Further, the original 5kHz and 6kHz tones still resonate certain areas on the basilar membrane causing the neurons associated with hair fibers on those areas of the basilar membrane to discharge as well. The result of this is that the overall waveform is still communicated to the brain through neural impulses but in an indirect fashion.

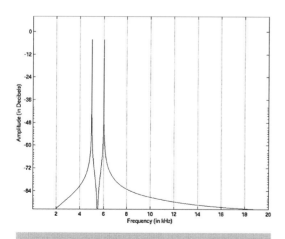

FIGURE 6.12: The Spectrograph Plot of the Waveform in Figure 6.11

The 11kHz and 1kHz waveforms are not, however, present in the resultant waveform, as a Fourier Analysis shows.

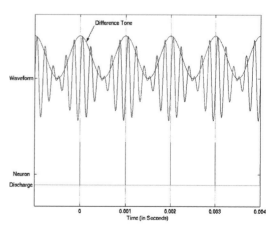

FIGURE 6.13: Neural Discharges Phase Locked to the Difference Tone of Two Waveforms

Neurons can discharge in a phase locked response to beat frequencies created when two waveforms of different frequencies are summed together.

As two sine waves create beat frequencies, neurons can discharge in a phase locked response to the beat frequencies that are created even if they cannot discharge in a phase locked response to the original tones (Figure 6.13).

It is only when single tones (sine waves) are generated above about 4kHz that the ear is incapable of using the phase lock responses of neurons to cue the frequencies available. Above about 4kHz the only way that the ear can decipher waveforms is from one of two methods: beat frequencies and the phase locked response of neurons to those beat frequencies, or through the location method – that being the neurons discharging respective to the area on the basilar membrane that resonates best with those frequencies.

If the beat tones created are lower than the lowest frequency at which the basilar membrane can resonate then the beats begin to sound like fast swells of amplitude. The closer the two tones are to each other the lower the beat frequency becomes. Thus, a 100Hz and a 101Hz tone played at equal amplitude will yield a 1Hz beat frequency. This 1Hz tone is well below the lowest frequency that the ear can hear, so it instead causes what we hear as an amplitude change, causing the ear to hear the 100Hz and 101Hz tones getting louder and softer. The change in the amplitude happens in a sinusoidal manner (Figure 6.14).

This effect is frequently used to tune guitars and other instruments. Two notes are played that are supposed to be at the same frequency. If the sound of beating occurs, however, then one of the notes is

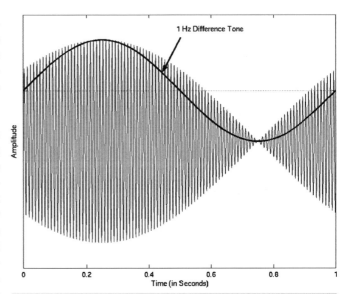

FIGURE 6.14: 100Hz and 101Hz Sine Waves Summed Together.

When 100Hz and 101Hz sine waves are added together the "beat frequency" that results is 1Hz, or one pulse per second. One can see in the graph above the 1Hz waveform present in the result of the summing of the two sine waves.

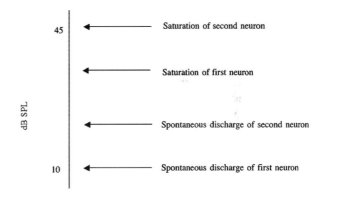

With 1kHz sine wave presented to the ear

FIGURE 6.15: Two Neurons Cover Overlapping Dynamic Ranges

Though each neuron can only cover approximately 20dB of dynamic range between the signal required to get it to exceed its spontaneous discharge rate and its saturation point, multiple neurons work cooperatively to represent the entire dynamic range the ear is capable of hearing

re-tuned until the beats get slow enough and become inaudible. At this point the difference between the two frequencies becomes so small as to be inaudible, indicating that the notes played are of the same frequency.

If the difference between the two frequencies becomes too great then the beat tones again become inaudible.

While other devices can generate beat frequencies, they would cause the beat frequency to become a "real" tone that the ear would hear. If a 2.5kHz tone and a 3.5kHz tone were played through an amplifier that created the 1kHz as a byproduct of its distortions then the 1kHz tone becomes a "real" part of the waveform, and the waveform that enters the ear would include this tone. Any beat tones that are created by the cochlea are not "real" tones, as the additional beat tone does not represent a real air pressure waveform. The consequence of this is that if one or both of the tones is inaudible to the ear then the beat frequencies will not be heard. For example, if a 14kHz tone and a 21kHz tone were played into the ear and the 21kHz tone was not directly audible by the ear then the 7kHz beat frequency would also not be audibly present.

COCHLEAR DYNAMICS

We discussed earlier that each neuron has a tuning curve. That tuning curve represents the minimum amount of stimulation required to cause the neuron to fire at a rate faster than its spontaneous discharge rate. The tuning curve also tells us at what decibel level the neuron stops firing any faster with additional amplitude. This means that a single neuron can only provide amplitude information for a given frequency within a specific and limited range. If the amplitude presented to the neuron at a given frequency is less than the neuron's lower threshold then it will not provide any discharges faster than its spontaneous discharge rate. If the same frequency is presented at an amplitude that exceeds the decibel level required to cause the neuron to discharge at its fastest rate then any further increase in amplitude is not "heard" as any louder by that neuron. An individual neuron connected to a hair cell therefore has a minimum signal level required to cause it to discharge faster than its spontaneous discharge rate, and a maximum signal level before it is saturated and cannot discharge any faster. The difference between the minimum and maximum amplitudes recognized by an individual neuron is essentially the *dynamic range* of that neuron. An individual neuron has a maximum dynamic range at any given frequency of about 20dB.

Attached to any one hair cell are approximately twenty nerve fibers. Each nerve fiber has a maximum dynamic range of 20dB, but not all neurons respond to the *same* dynamic range. For example, one neuron may exceed its spontaneous discharge rate when a 1kHz sine wave is presented to it at 10dB SPL. This neuron may reach its maximum discharge rate when that 1kHz sine wave is presented to it at 30dB SPL. Another neuron attached to the same inner hair cell, on the other hand, may not exceed its spontaneous discharge rate with the same 1kHz sine wave until it is presented at greater than 25dB SPL. That second neuron may not reach its maximum discharge rate until the sine wave is played at 45dB SPL. The result is that between the two, the total dynamic range available reaches from 10dB SPL to 45dB SPL with a 1kHz tone. If a tone is played at 20dB SPL, for example, the first neuron fires at a certain rate and the second neuron fires at its spontaneous discharge rate. If the tone is presented at 26dB SPL, for example, the first neuron fires at near its maximum rate and the second neuron fires at just over its spontaneous discharge rate. If the tone is presented at 40dB SPL the first neuron fires at its maximum discharge rate and the second neuron fires near its maximum discharge rate. If an 80dB SPL 1kHz tone is played then both neurons fire at their maximum discharge rates. An example of how multiple neurons work to cover an extended dynamic range is shown in Figure 6.15.

The synapses of the twenty nerve fibers attached to the inner hair cells are of different sizes. The size of the synapse is directly related to the sound pressure level range, or dynamic range that the synapse operates in. Any given inner hair cell, on the other hand, can yield absolutely no more than a 60dB dynamic range, and most experts say that this number is more realistically in the range of 40dB. Each cell, however, also does not cover the same range of sound pressure levels. The combination of multiple cells is what gives us the total dynamic range that the human auditory system is capable of hearing: around 120dB. This covers the approximate range of (depending on the person) 0dB SPL to 120dB SPL.

If two neurons have tuning curves that represent the same frequencies but one of them covers a higher sound pressure level than the other, then when the sound pressure level is high enough the first neuron discharges at its maximum discharge rate. The second neuron, however, has not reached the point of saturation and continues to discharge appropriately. At this amplitude the first neuron is at the point of saturation and the level and frequency of the signal is being described for the brain by the second neuron (Figure 6.16).

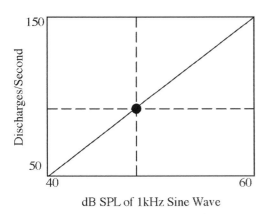

FIGURE 6.16A: **Neuron 1 Discharge Rate Vs. Intensity at 1kHz**

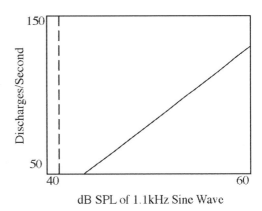

FIGURE 6.17A: **Neuron 1 Discharge Rate Vs. Intensity at 1.1kHz**

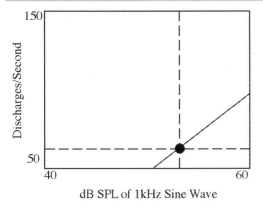

FIGURE 6.16B: **Neuron 2 Discharge Rate Vs. Intensity at 1kHz**

If a 1kHz sine wave is presented to the ear at an amplitude of 50dB SPL, Neuron 1 will discharge 90 times per second and Neuron 2 will discharge 60 times per second.

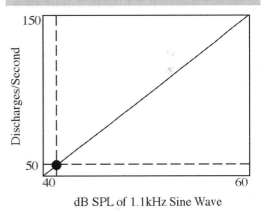

FIGURE 6.17B: **Neuron 2 Discharge Rate Vs. Intensity at 1.1kHz**

The same neurons shown in Figure 6.16 will respond to 1.1kHz sine waves. Figures 6.17A and 6.17B show the discharge rate versus intensity for the same neurons when presented with 1.1kHz sine waves. Therefore, if a 1.1kHz sine wave is presented to the ear with an amplitude of 40dB SPL, Neuron 1 will discharge at its spontaneous discharge rate and Neuron 2 will discharge 50 times per second.

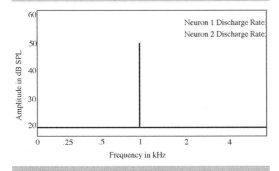

FIGURE 6.16C: **Response of Neurons to 1kHz Sine Wave**

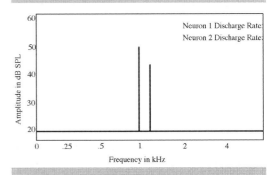

FIGURE 6.17C: **Response of Neurons to 1kHz and 1.1kHz Waveform**

If we then introduce a second tone a few frequencies away from the first tone, played at the same time but at a much lower amplitude, the two neurons would fire as given in Figure 6.17.

We notice that the second tone is not conveyed to the brain by these neurons because the neuron that would be responsible for conveying this tone to the brain is already at a point of saturation, firing at its maximum discharge rate. If we look at a more complex situation, such as four neurons that have different tuning curves and also represent different dynamic ranges, we will notice that the second tone still does not get conveyed to the brain by the neurons (Figure 6.18).

We can see that even with more complex arrangements of neurons, each representing their own frequencies and covering differing dynamic ranges, that the lower amplitude tone does not get represented. The second tone will not get represented by the ear until either the amplitude of the second tone increases to the point

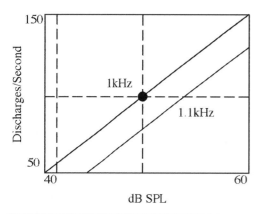

FIGURE 6.18A: Neuron 1 Discharge Rate Vs. Intensity at 1kHz and 1.1kHz

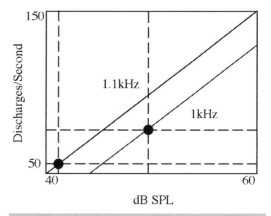

FIGURE 6.18B: Neuron 2 Discharge Rate Vs. Intensity at 1kHz and 1.1kHz

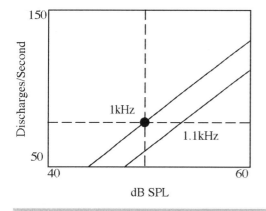

FIGURE 6.18C: Neuron 3 Discharge Rate Vs. Intensity at 1kHz and 1.1kHz

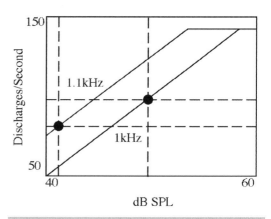

FIGURE 6.18D: Neuron 4 Discharge Rate Vs. Intensity at 1kHz and 1.1kHz

If the waveform in Figure 6.17 is presented to each of these four neurons each neuron will respond the same as if a 1kHz sine wave was presented by itself. In other words, the 1.1kHz tone added to the 1kHz does not get recognized at all by these four neurons and thus the signal is heard as only a 1kHz tone. The 1.1kHz tone is inaudible when played with a 1kHz at the amplitude shown.

that it causes some neurons to fire faster than they were for the first presented frequency alone, or until the second tone becomes far enough removed (in frequency) from the first tone that it causes different neurons to discharge. One could therefore create a curve that represents the amplitude range in which a second tone could be introduced to the ear in the presence of a louder tone and not be recognized. This curve would reflect our observations above: that as a second tone is played at a close frequency to a first tone it will not be recognized if it falls within a certain frequency range and amplitude. An example of a "masking curve" such as this is shown in Figure 6.19.

This curve would not be the same at all frequencies, as our ability to discern between differing tones is much more acute in certain frequency ranges. In these situations, the threshold of hearing of certain frequencies is raised above 0dB SPL. The threshold of hearing a tone in the presence of another tone is also shifted because other material is "masking" it. The effect of this is indeed known as "masking" and is a very demonstrable phenomenon, in fact a characteristic of hearing upon which we humans are very dependent. Masking is the name given for the effect of a tone not being audible because it is in the presence of another, louder tone at a close frequency. It occurs because neural activity that would be used to represent the lower amplitude tone is already busy representing the higher amplitude tone.

Earlier in the book we discussed that white noise is the combination of all frequencies at equal amplitudes. This means that if white noise is present, even though relevant and identifiable sound may be below the noise floor, it will be masked by all of the frequencies that are present. Because the sound below the noise floor is not masked by steady tones but is rather masked by a random combination of all frequencies, the masking is not as effective and we can still hear and recognize material below the noise floor. In 1953 Harvey Fletcher published in <u>Speech and Hearing in Communication</u> the results of a study of his that yielded that the threshold of hearing below a white noise floor was 14dB. More recent studies have shown this number to be as low as 25dB below a white noise floor. This means that if a white noise floor is present at 40dB SPL that the ear is capable of hearing and discerning signals within the noise floor that are present at no less than 15dB SPL. Any signal that is present below that amplitude would not be recognized by the neurons of the ear because the

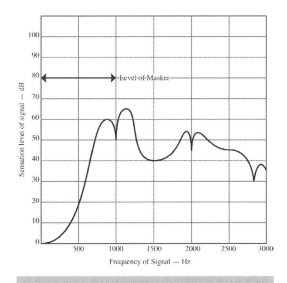

FIGURE 6.19: Masking Curve for 1kHz at 60dB SPL

The curve above shows what the masking curve might look like for 1kHz. This shows the amplitude of signal that would be required to be detectable at different frequencies when a 1kHz signal is present at 60dB SPL.

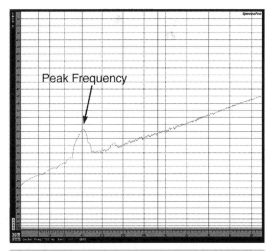

FIGURE 6.20: Signals Present Lower Than the Peak Noise Floor

The noise floor shown above contains some 60-cycle hum from electrical issues. The peak noise floor, as established by the peak of the hum, is much higher than the white noise floor of the signal. The signal present at 1kHz is valid signal that is not masked by the noise floor of the hum because it is far removed from the frequency of the hum.

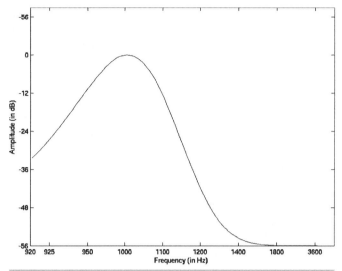

FIGURE 6.21: **Frequency Response Curve of a Portion of the Basilar Membrane**

The frequency response curve above is for a particular portion of the basilar membrane. Every point on the basilar membrane has a frequency response curve akin to the one above in that the membrane vibrates at different frequencies at different points along its surface.

neurons responsible for recognizing that signal and discharging at that rate would already have been firing faster than that rate because of their response to other tones present in the noise.

The inability for the human hearing system to identify signals further below the noise floor is due to what is called "noise masking." Noise masking is not consistent at all amplitudes. At lower amplitudes we cannot hear as far below the noise floor as we can at higher amplitudes, presumably because not as many neurons cover the dynamic range representing the lowest amplitudes we can hear.

We can now see why it is important to quantify the dynamic range present in a signal as it relates to the *white* noise floor as opposed to the *peak frequency* in the noise floor as was discussed in Chapter Five. If only the white noise floor is used then we can determine how far below that and at what rate the audibility of the signal decreases. If the peak noise floor is used then some amount of masking will occur, but much more signal may be present below the noise floor that is still discernable than would be if the noise floor is white. A characteristic example of this is noise present in a signal due to electrical problems that create a "hum" at 60Hz. Perhaps the peak level of this noise is 25dB louder than the white noise floor of that signal. While, due to masking, we will not be able to perceive any signal present in the vicinity of 60Hz and at lower amplitudes than the "hum", material at 1kHz (for example) will be perfectly audible all the way down to the white noise floor and below. An example is given in Figure 6.20.

The effect of masking underscores the importance of identifying the noise floor in a signal as established in Chapter Five.

COCHLEAR FILTERS

It should be noted that there are two, distinct types of filters present in the ear. First, any point on the basilar membrane functions as a filter, attenuating frequencies that are both higher and lower than its optimal frequency. If a single place on the basilar membrane were the only part of the ear that worked, any waveform that came into the ear would be filtered by the frequency response curve of that area of the basilar membrane. The frequency response curve of a particular portion of the basilar membrane is shown in Figure 6.21.

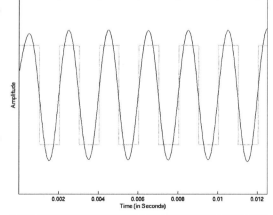

FIGURE 6.22: **The Response of the Portion of the Basilar Membrane to a Square Wave**

The waveform above is how a 1kHz square wave will vibrate the basilar membrane at the point referred to in Figure 6.21.

Based on our studies in Chapter Four, band-limited waveforms have certain properties, so any waveform that hits any part of the basilar membrane is subjected to those properties. For example, that specific point on the basilar membrane cannot resonate in the shape of a high frequency square wave because it is not capable of resonating at the frequency of its third harmonic at all, not to mention its fifth, seventh, ninth, and subsequent harmonics. A square wave fed into that part of the basilar membrane would not yield anything resembling a square wave, as shown in Figure 6.22.

The overall movement of the basilar membrane represents the range of frequencies that the human can hear, but the movement at any particular point on the membrane represents is much less complex.

Second, any individual neuron is essentially a filter as well. A neuron that discharges more with certain frequencies and less with surrounding frequencies functions as a filter. Its action can be said to be fully recreating the amplitude of particular frequencies and recreating other surrounding frequencies with less amplitude. At a certain point it no longer precipitates (more than its spontaneous amount of) discharges at all. If we fed a waveform into this one neuron the result would also represent a band-limited waveform. A square wave fed into a single neuron with a particular discharge curve would be communicated to the brain as a waveform that had much less information than the original waveform. We already know that the neuron cannot discharge any faster than 1000 times per second. We would therefore not be able to observe the discharges that a neuron releases after looking at one cycle of a 1000Hz square wave because no more than one discharge would be present (Figure 6.23)

This information is very incomplete and tells us very little about the ability for the neuron to respond to a square wave. If, however, we plotted the discharges over time we would be able to observe the tendencies of that neuron and its long-term effects. For example, a square wave has a leading edge and a tailing edge. If we played a square wave for many complete cycles and then laid the graph of the discharge during each cycle over each other we would be able to see what the long term discharging of that neuron was for that frequency.

This type of chart (called a "histogram") tells us that that neuron acts as a filter over many cycles, indicating to us that each particular neuron is a unique filter. Once again, the waveform represented by the neuron represents a band-limited waveform. An example of a histogram such as this is given in Figure 6.24.

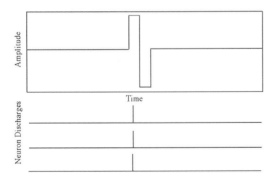

FIGURE 6.23: Neural Discharges to a Single Cycle Waveform

The neurons fire in a phase-locked capacity to the waveform presented, but they provide no further information about the frequencies present because they each only fire one time, and they discharge in phase with each other. The result is that the neurons have acted as filters, filtering out information and only providing minimal content to the nervous system.

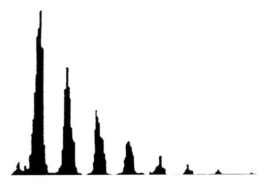

FIGURE 6.24: Discharge of a Neuron to a Repeating Square Wave

A given neuron discharges synchronously to a square wave, though not necessarily at the same time in relation to the square wave's pulse every time.

There are essentially two, discrete types of filters at play in the cochlea: the filter due to position along the basilar membrane and the filter due to each, individual neuron. These filters are called "cochlear filters." We will soon see that the cumulative effect of all of these filters is that the ear, itself, behaves as one large filter, a composite of the individual filters within the ear.

SUMMARY OF THE ANATOMY OF THE EAR

The anatomy of the ear is quite complex, making it one of the most complicated and intricate organs in the body. An understanding of the ear's anatomy is important for the understanding of how and what the ear hears. The ear has several components and different mediums and environments that a waveform must pass through.

First, the waveforms pass by the pinna and into the external auditory canal where certain frequencies are amplified and other frequencies are attenuated. The waveforms then hit the eardrum (tympanic membrane), which resonates between the outer ear and the middle ear, which are kept at equal air pressure by the Eustachian tubes. The eardrum is connected to a series of small bones called "ossicles" that transfer the vibrations of the eardrum to another membrane called the oval window membrane, essentially transferring the waveforms from the eardrum through the middle ear to the inner ear. At the oval window, the waveforms are propelled through a liquid into a long, spiral tunnel called the cochlea. Stretched across the middle of the cochlea is a taut membrane that vibrates as the waves of liquid pass over it. Hovering above that membrane is another membrane that effectively moves in parallel with it. A series of cells on the basilar membrane are topped with micro-fibers called "cilia." As the cilia get sheered against the tectorial membrane above them, momentary electronic pulses are sent through nerve fibers to the brain..

Essentially, changes in air pressure going into the ear get turned into a series of momentary electronic pulses that, somehow, represent the original waveforms. These pulses are then sent to the brain, which has the complex task of deciphering the millions of electronic pulses coming in on the tens of thousands of nerve fibers and determining what waveforms were present. This process is what is called "hearing." Somehow, from this series of momentary pulses the brain is able to reconstruct the original waveforms of air pressure change. We identified in Chapter Two that there are four identifying characteristics of any waveform: frequency, amplitude, phase, and dynamic range. The human auditory system can discern between changes in frequency, changes in amplitude, and some changes in phase. This means that those momentary electronic pulses include enough useful information to decipher what actually, acoustically happens. Understanding how it does this helps us to establish what the sensitivity of the ear is to each of these characteristics. By understanding the sensitivity of the ear we are given an idea of what the tolerances of any communication or recording means would need to be in order to be audibly indistinguishable from the source.

The observant reader will curiously notice at this point that a series of electronic pulses is apparently all that is necessary to communicate very complex waveforms. Actually, momentary electronic pulses are all that is necessary to communicate everything to the brain that the ear can hear.

WHAT THE BRAIN HEARS

We now have a reasonable understanding of the anatomy and physiology of the ear. We understand how the sound gets converted from air pressure waves to neuron pulses that get sent to the complex systems in the human brain. A lot has been determined about the functionality of various parts of the human auditory system that lie between the nerve fibers of the ear and the auditory cortex in the brain, where it is believed that the sensation of "hearing" takes place.

Our purpose of understanding the human auditory system is to determine what it is capable of hearing and what its limitations are. The ear is a device that converts air pressure changes into electrical voltages, and a lot of the signal is lost in the conversion process in terms of amplitude, phase, frequency, and dynamic range. Because the ear itself is the cause of these losses and thus determines the limiting factors of human hearing, and because our purpose of studying the ear is to determine precisely what those limitations are, it is not necessary to continue our study of the human auditory system into the auditory cortex. We really need to understand the anatomy and physiology, as that is where the capabilities of the auditory system are defined. In other words, the limiting factors of human hearing exist at the ear itself, and understanding what the limits of human hearing are defines the needs of any audio recording system. Now that we understand the anatomy and physiology of the ear we can review the four characteristics of waveforms and determine more about what the ear is capable of hearing with regard to each.

FREQUENCY

We have already identified two ways in which the ear transmits unique frequencies to the brain. The first method is based on the location of the neurons that discharge faster than their spontaneous discharge rate. Individual frequencies are more effectively reproduced by different areas on the basilar membrane making *which specific neurons* fire an identifying characteristic of the frequencies that are present. The other method that the auditory system uses is the speed at which the neurons discharge, based on individual tuning curves of each neuron. Every neuron is most sensitive to particular frequencies and discharges more frequently when those frequencies are present. The discharges are (in most situations) phase locked, so the frequency is also represented by the timing of the discharges. Thus, specific neural discharges are the other way in which the auditory system identifies specific frequencies in waveforms.

Enough information is available about the specific physiological capabilities of the ear to give a complete picture of the sensitivity that the human being has to frequencies. Since the second method of identifying frequencies is limited to frequencies under approximately 4kHz, limitations of the vibrations of the basilar membrane become the limiting factor of our ears' frequency range. Due to the anatomical characteristics of the basilar membrane, including its makeup, tension, elasticity, and size, the basilar membrane is a band-limited device. While the basilar membrane can theoretically resonate at any frequency, the amplitude at which it can resonate for frequencies above 20kHz is so low that it does not generate neural discharges. For this reason, the high frequency limitation of the basilar membrane is said to be 20kHz. On the low frequency end of the spectrum, the ear is limited by the same issues regarding the basilar membrane and has a minimum frequency of approximately 20Hz. The ear is therefore said to cover a frequency range of approximately 20Hz to 20kHz, though with each of these frequency extremes a significant amount of signal must be present for human audibility. Human hearing is much more sensitive in some frequency ranges than it is in other ranges. At very high frequencies the ear has a difficult time discerning between different frequencies, and most extremely high frequency content is used by the ear for *localization* of sounds, or the location from which a sound emanates.

Since the ear is a band-limited device it follows all of the rules established in Chapter Four. The ear has a filter that rolls off almost entirely at a frequency that generally falls between 11kHz and 20kHz depending on the person and their age. Very young children are believed to be able to hear well above 20kHz but lose this ability quickly. Most people, when doing a regimented listening test, will notice that their hearing decreases steadily over a range of a few kilohertz. Further, people notice that as material is presented to the ear at higher and higher frequencies, the sound of the waveforms becomes less identifiable and distinguishable because the ear is incapable of hearing anything but sine waves at its highest frequencies of audibility. A square wave played to the ear with proper test equipment within the top octave of a human's hearing capabilities will sound identical to a sine wave. If a human can hear up to 15kHz then a 10kHz square wave (which has no harmonic content from 10kHz to 30kHz) will consist of only the 10kHz component and will thus sound like a sine wave after being filtered by the various filters at work in the ear. Just as with any filter, frequency content above the filter's cutoff frequency has no effect on the audibility of the signals within the ear's audible range. As of the time of this writing there has been no study that indicates that material above the highest audible frequency of any given person has any audible effect at all. This supports the notion that the ear has a filter similar to that of any analog filter and, that while its attenuation curves are not as simple, the ear's sensitivity and limitations to frequencies are easily identifiable per person, and that for the vast majority of the population the upper limit of frequency response is *no higher than* 20kHz. The low frequency range is less significant for this particular text, but the 20Hz limit suggested earlier is a safe working value. For the sake of this text, the generally accepted values are understood to be extremely conservative, but we must also recognize that these values are not completely immune to exceptions, such as that of young children.

AMPLITUDE

The method by which the ear discerns different amplitudes is similar to the way in which it discerns frequencies. The individual tuning curves of the different neurons indicate to the brain not only that certain frequencies are present but also at what amplitude they are present. We know from Chapter Two that the lower limit of amplitude audibility has been established by means of a rigorous study done in the 1900s. This amplitude level of $.0002^{dynes}/_{cm}^{2}$ has been established as the reference level for comparing all amplitude levels. Most frequencies that are present in a signal that are below 0dB SPL are inaudible, and for most people the threshold is likely higher.

The maximum level we can hear is slightly less defined, but is not particularly relevant because of the sheer physical pain experienced at extremely loud volumes. Based on our understanding of the physiology of the ear, we know that the neurons in the ear will reach a maximum discharge rate and once exceeded nothing will cause them to indicate to the brain that the signal has suddenly gotten even louder. If a neuron has a dynamic range from 30dB SPL to 50dB SPL then whether the sound pressure coming in is at 70dB SPL or 90dB SPL that neuron gives no further information other than that the signal is coming in with *at least* 50dB SPL. There-

220dB SPL - Inside a Diesel Engine

200dB SPL - Jet Engine at Takeoff

170dB SPL - Ear Drum Disintegrates

120dB SPL - Threshold of Pain
105dB SPL - Rock Concert
90dB SPL - Downtown Urban Traffic from Curbside
85dB SPL - Typical Music Listening Level
80dB SPL - Noisy Office Environment
70dB SPL - Small Orchestra
60dB SPL - Typical Conversation Between Two People
50dB SPL - Background Office Noise
40dB SPL - Quiet House at Night
30dB SPL - Typical Recording Studio

0dB SPL - Threshold of Hearing

FIGURE 6.25: Sound Pressure Levels of Some Common Sounds

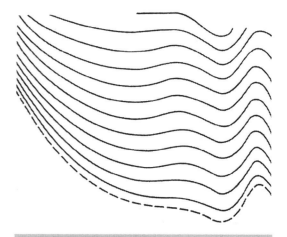

FIGURE 6.26: Equal Loudness Contours

The "Equal Loudness Contours" chart, also called the "Fletcher-Munson Curves" shows the amplitude required at any frequency to sound as loud to the ear as a signal present at another frequency. A signal presented to the ear at 4kHz and 20dB SPL will sound as loud to the ear as a signal presented to the ear at 100Hz and 40dB SPL.

fore, as signals get louder there is nothing that indicates that the ear has reached its upper limit of discerning amplitude other than the occurrence of physical damage to the ear.

Because there is not an upper limit of amplitude audibility we generally refer to the levels at which people would no longer want to be in the presence of audio. This level would be that at which physical pain is experienced. The "threshold of pain" is widely understood to be around 120dB SPL. General "loud" listening levels for music are certainly not standardized, but in an attempt to mix at the levels that most people listen to music, the mixing and mastering communities work with their levels at around 85dB SPL. Most listeners would describe this level as definitely "loud," especially in contrast to the quiet control room environment. Since an increase of 6dB causes the perception of doubling the "loudness," 120dB SPL is around 32 times louder than "loud" listening levels used to mix and master albums. Figure 6.25 again shows us typical sound pressure levels of some common sounds.

While we accept the 0dB SPL to 120dB SPL range as the audible range of amplitude for the ear, and while we understand the physiological constraints in the ear that limit the range, we should recognize that the amplitude range of the ear is not completely linear. This means that as the amplitude of the signal entering the ear changes by a certain amount, the perception of this change is not necessarily the same amount. The combination of the structure of the outside ear, the cochlear filters and cochlear dynamics cause some frequencies to be more pronounced than others. As the amplitudes of some frequencies change, the audibility of the increase changes differently than with other frequencies. This was studied and charted in 1935 by Harvey Fletcher and W.A. Munson and the chart that identifies the relative amplitudes of audibility at various frequencies is often referred to as the "Fletcher-Munson Curves." More formally this material is known as the "Equal Loudness Contours." The chart shows the amplitude levels at which various frequencies would need to be played if they were to sound to the ear like they were presented at the same amplitude. More recent analysis of this has also been done further refining the original analysis. The original data as presented by Fletcher and Munson is shown in Figure 6.26.

We also know that amplitude audibility varies depending on what other frequencies are present and how loud they are. The 0dB SPL threshold of audibility is based on studies done at 1kHz. The ear is more sensitive to low amplitude information at 4kHz than at 1kHz, with some studies recently saying that the most sensitive demographic of the population is capable of hearing as low as –6 or –8dB SPL at 4kHz. Further, the threshold of hearing of particular frequencies increases if frequencies around it are present at louder amplitudes, per the earlier discussion on "masking."

Due to all of the complexities of the ear's physiology, defining the amplitude range of the ear is not simple. Suffice it to say, however, that approximately 120dB of dynamic range is a usable figure for the sake of audio recording and playback.

PHASE

For the most part, the ear is not capable of discerning a change in phase of a signal by itself. An example of phase variations of a signal is shown in Figure 6.27.

A lot of debate has transpired about phase changes of sinusoids of specific frequencies within a waveform. For example, if all frequencies above 1kHz are slightly delayed and frequencies below 1kHz within the same signal are not, then the higher frequencies will be out

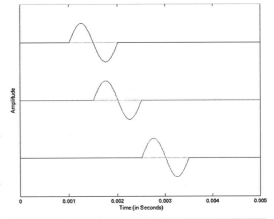

FIGURE 6.27: Phase Variations of a Signal

of phase with how they originally occurred in the waveform in comparison with the lower frequencies. This type of phase change is called "group delay" because particular "groups" of frequencies are delayed. This is the reason that the waveform shown in Figure 3.8 in Chapter Three is often thought to be indiscernible from a square wave: it is a square wave that has undergone a particular group delay. A further example of group delay on a waveform is shown in Figure 6.28.

Phase does, however, become very consequential when the fact that the human has two ears is taken into regard. If a sound source is directly in front of the ear then the time that the sound takes to get to the ears is the same. If the sound source is on the right side of the head, for example, the amount of time needed for the sound to get to the right ear is different than the time it takes for the sound to get to the left ear. The distance between the two ears is approximately 17cm, so the sound will get to the right ear approximately six milliseconds before it hits the left ear. As the sound source moves, so does the difference in arrival times at each ear (Figure 6.29).

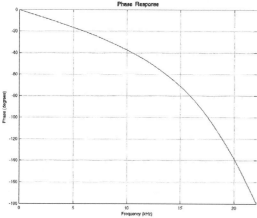

FIGURE 6.28A: Group Delay Chart

The chart above shows the amount of group delay that a particular device imparts on a signal. Higher frequencies are shifted more degrees out of phase than lower frequencies. A waveform that experiences this group delay may sound the same to the ear but will not look the same.

The human ear is remarkably acute to changes in arrival times of waveforms between the two ears. Though the ear can only discern the sound source's location based on phase differences for signals within specific frequency ranges, the ear is capable of hearing shifts in space of a sound source by as little as one degree. Studies have shown that the human auditory system is sensitive to timing variations between the two ears of as little as 2 microseconds (2 millionths of a second). We discussed earlier that the phase of a signal is always a comparison of the signal (or part of a signal) with another. A single signal cannot be "out of phase." It can only be out of phase with something else. We now understand that the phase of two signals is important for the sake of localization, or the ear's ability to hear the location of a source in an open sound field. Examples of transient arrival times are shown in Figure 6.30.

The ear is far more adept at hearing localization cues from very high frequencies than from any other fre-

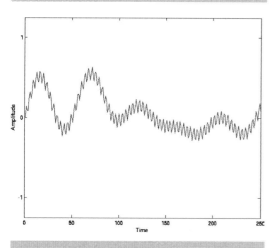

FIGURE 6.28B: A Waveform

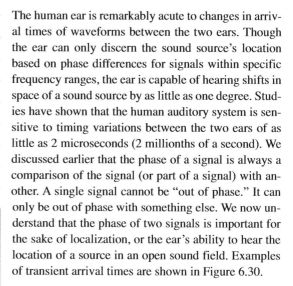

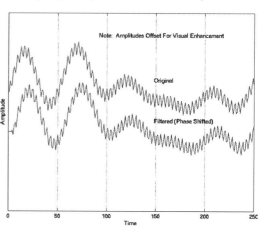

FIGURE 6.28C: A Waveform After Experiencing the Group Delay Seen in Figure 6.28A

quency range. Content in the top octave of our hearing range tells us the most about a sound space and our location and a sound source's location within it. In this capacity, relative phase between two signals is crucial. In many other cases the ear is incapable of discerning the phase relationships between two signals.

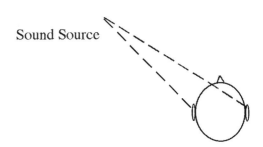

Sound Source

DYNAMIC RANGE

We have already discussed at length the dynamic range of the ear. The ear is capable of a dynamic range of around 120dB, though the dynamic range at particular frequencies is not as good (as the Equal Loudness Contours chart in Figure 6.26 above has shown us).

FIGURE 6.29: Binaural Audibility

The human head is approximately 17cm wide, so sound that occurs on either side of the head takes longer to get to one ear or the other depending on how far on the side the sound occurs. The ear that is on the side near to the source of the sound will receive and process the sound first.

We have also shown that the human can hear approximately 25dB below a white noise floor before the noise completely masks the sound source. The actual dynamic range of the ear extends from a high amplitude of approximately 120dB SPL to a low amplitude of either 25dB below the white noise floor of a signal or around 0dB SPL, whichever is lower (Figure 6.31).

If a signal is played for the ear that has a white noise floor 80dB below the peak, and the signal is recreated in an anechoic chamber (no acoustic noise present above the atmospheric noise level) at 60dB SPL then the audible dynamic range of this signal is approximately 60dB, as we can only hear the range of the signal between 0dB SPL and 60dB SPL. 20dB of the signal gets "lost" below the threshold of hearing. If the same signal is reproduced at 90dB SPL then the audible dynamic range of the signal is 90dB, as we could hear the full 80dB range of the signal down to the white noise floor, and possibly an additional 10dB below that before we once again hit the threshold of hearing (0dB SPL). If the same signal is reproduced at 110dB SPL then the audible dynamic range of the signal is 105dB, as we will be able to hear from the peak at 110dB SPL down to the

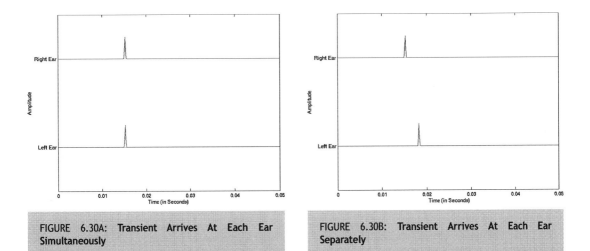

FIGURE 6.30A: Transient Arrives At Each Ear Simultaneously

FIGURE 6.30B: Transient Arrives At Each Ear Separately

In Figure 6.30A sound comes from straight in front and the transient arrives at each ear at the same time. In Figure 6.30B the sound comes from the right side as can be seen and heard because the transient arrives at the right ear first.

signal's noise floor at 30dB SPL (80dB below the peak) and an additional 25dB below that (down to 5dB SPL, or 105dB below the peak). See Figure 6.32.

SUMMARY

Developing a model of the ear is difficult because of the many variations that can occur based on various aspects of the signal presented. Further complicating the development of an ear model, however, is that humans do not all have the same ears. As the researchers at Bell Labs noticed, black women between the ages of 18 and 22 have the lowest threshold of hearing. Makers of hearing aids and ear plugs tell us that people of Asian decent have narrower external auditory canals, making the frequencies they are most sensitive to different than people of Western descent. Children have a more extended high frequency response. Specific people are more sensitive to frequency changes. Still others find it painful to listen to music played at amplitudes well below the supposed "threshold of pain." The variations from person to person are complex and wide.

Beside the variations from person to person, the ear is complex enough that to identify any thresholds is potentially oversimplifying the situation, and those very oversimplifications are the most significant contributors of the confusion that abounds and that this book attempts to alleviate.

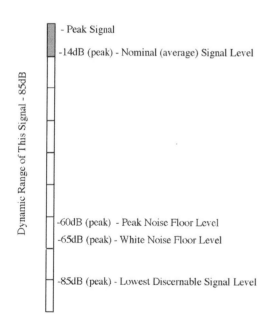

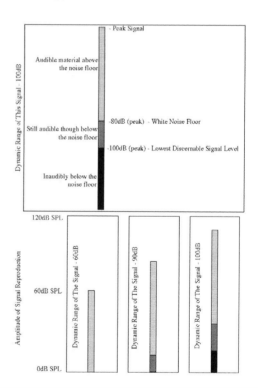

FIGURE 6.31: **Dynamic Range and Signal Levels**

The dynamic range of this signal is 85dB. Often the dynamic range is thought to be the difference between the peak signal and the peak of the noise floor, but since the ear can hear below that level it is important to consider the entire dynamic range that the ear is capable of hearing. In this example that is 85dB.

FIGURE 6.32: **Dynamic Range and Signal Levels**

Since audio recording is for the masses, however, we should probably identify the extreme and most rare boundaries of the ear for the sake of creating an auditory model for which we are communicating audio to the majority of people. A *vast* oversimplification shows us that the ear is sensitive to the four identifying characteristics of a waveform in the following ways:

Frequency: *20Hz to 20kHz*

Amplitude: *-8dB SPL (at 4kHz, or 0dB SPL at 1kHz) to 120dB SPL*

Phase: *Degrees of phase depends on the frequency, but time variations from ear to ear of as little as 2μs*

Dynamic Range: *From the peak amplitude to as low as 25dB below the white noise floor, but no greater than 120dB overall*

Part Two

Digital Recording and Transmission

Chapter Seven

The Basics of Recording

THE PURPOSE OF RECORDING

This book is entitled *Digital Audio Explained For The Audio Engineer*. We are therefore primarily concerned with recording audio for the sake of listening. It was with this in mind that we studied the restrictions of the human auditory system. The eventual goal of nearly any audio recording is the reproduction of the material. This reproduction can either come after recording the audio and playing it back at a later time or it can come after transmitting the audio and playing it back in *real time* in the context of radio, television, internet, telephone lines, or any other means of transmission. In order to attempt to reproduce audio accurately it is necessary to understand what needs to be reproduced. In order to duplicate the original audio, it is not practical to attempt to recreate the audio perfectly, reproducing the entire waveform without flaw. This is senseless for two reasons.

First, it is impossible. The simple fact that measurement equipment needs to be involved negates the idea of recording anything absolutely perfectly anyway. Much of what we are talking about in terms of waveforms happens at the atomic level, with individual molecules having consequential importance in quiet waveforms. At levels around 0dB SPL, the presence of a single, individual hydrogen molecule can tip the scales between a pressure wave being audible and not being loud enough. On a daily level we may be fooled into thinking that accurate duplication is possible, but on an atomic level this is most definitely not the case, especially because the introduction of any piece of equipment to take the measurements cannot avoid having an effect on the results. Since audio delves into the atomic world it becomes apparent that audio cannot be flawlessly duplicated.

Second, the majority of air pressure waves have no effect on our auditory systems. Attempting to record or transmit these waves for the sake of reproduction is senseless if they have no bearing on human auditory systems. Logically, the needs for recording and reproduction change if the human auditory system is not the eventual receiver. If the air pressure waves are recorded for scientific purposes, finding fish with SONAR, or studying the age of the universe by studying low pressure waves, then the needs for transmission or recording change. Since, however, this book is specifically for the audio engineer we only need to keep in mind the subject of that particular engineer's work: the human auditory system. That audio system is limited in its capabilities as we learned in Chapter Six. This makes the reproduction needs (and in turn the transmission and recording needs) much easier with which to work.

Because we can accept that the waveform will not be reproduced with 100% accuracy, we now need to determine what level of accuracy is necessary.

HOW WE RECORD

Since we are interested in recording changes in air pressure we somehow need to capture these changes in air pressure. Currently this is done using a device called a "transducer" that is allowed to freely vibrate in the air, responding to the changes in the air pressure as they occur. The transducer is a part of an electrical circuit such that the movement of the transducer results in a change in electrical current. This occurs in different ways. One method involves the transducer (or "diaphragm") being mounted to a wire coil that surrounds a piece of iron, such that the movement of the diaphragm causes a change in the electromagnetic field within the device. The changes in air pressure then get turned into changes in electrical voltage, such that a 1000Hz sine wave of air pressure changes becomes a 1000Hz sine wave of voltage changes. Another method uses a very thin piece of a synthetic material that has gold "sputtered" ("atomically evaporated," say) onto it and an electrical signal sent to it. This diaphragm hovers parallel to another piece of metal called a "backplate." As the diaphragm moves back and forth the electrical capacitance between the diaphragm and the backplate changes. This change in capacitance then gets converted into a change in voltage. Still another method uses a thin ribbon of a conductive metal suspended between two magnets. As the metal diaphragm moves, the magnetic field changes

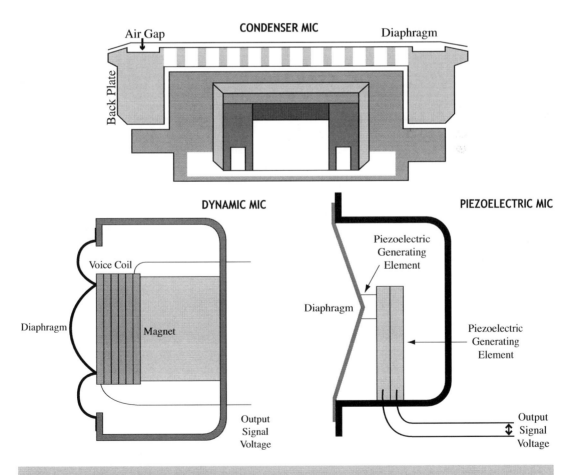

FIGURE 7.1: Various Microphone Designs

respectively, resulting in a change of voltage. Other methods have been also been used to convert air pressure changes into electrical changes since the first "microphone" was used in 1861.[1] See Figure 7.1.

Similar to our discussion on recording, microphones are incapable of perfectly transferring air pressure waves into electrical voltage waves. Not only is it physically impossible, it is also unnecessary for all of the reasons discussed previously. In the case of microphone transducers, the physical restrictions are difficult to overcome and nearly all microphones make sacrifices in their amplitude, frequency, relative phase, and dynamic range capabilities. Designing a microphone with better frequency response provides a nearly direct trade-off in the inherent self-noise of the microphone, compromising its dynamic range capabilities. A microphone with lower self-noise characteristics trades off its ability to handle high amplitudes. Microphone manufacturers try to find an appropriate balance of tradeoffs between the various microphone specifications. Certain microphones may appear to be underwhelming for the majority of applications but may have a unique application for which they are optimized by means of a set of tradeoffs that are more conducive to a specified use.

While other methods of capturing air pressure changes have been theorized, to date a microphone for the audio industry has yet to be successfully manufactured using lasers or any other method that does not use an electromechanical transducer.

The other method for recording air pressure waves is to record the *movements of the instrument* that creates the air pressure changes rather than record the subsequent air pressure changes. An electric guitar (or any instrument with a "pick up") is an example of this. The metal guitar strings not only create changes in air pressure, but as they vibrate they are made to pass through an electromagnetic field, causing a subsequent change in electrical voltage. This method does not convert air pressure waves to electrical voltage waves directly, but is effective at simulating the same.

WHAT WE NEED TO RECORD

Respecting the four characteristics of audio waveforms, we should identify the specific criteria that we need to meet for each in order to provide a recording that is "perfect" for the sake of the human ear. We know that it is not possible to make a "perfect" recording, but the recording could be perfect when the limitations of the ear are taken into regard. It is the goal of the audio recording and transmission media to not have any effect upon the audio integrity in any way, though we would concede that any lack of "perfect" accuracy (with regard to the ear) that microphones and speakers yield restricts the ability for audio to be perfectly recorded and transmitted. Nonetheless, it is our business to discuss the recording itself and we will leave microphone and speaker perfection to those respective industries.

AMPLITUDE

It is not necessary for us to record the overall amplitude of the signal. Since the signal changes media (i.e. from air pressure changes to electrical voltage changes) the absolute amplitude of the signal is almost irrelevant. In the end, a waveform amplitude of 100dB SPL does not get converted into an electrical voltage amplitude of 100V. It instead gets converted to some relative amplitude that can then get converted back to air pressure. So long as the *relative amplitudes* of each of the individual frequencies, respective to each other, are accurately captured the overall signal strength need not be. In other words, a waveform with a fundamental at 76dB SPL and a third harmonic at 70dB SPL need only be recorded such that the fundamental is 6dB greater in amplitude than the third harmonic. The *actual* sound pressure levels of each are irrelevant. Respecting the capabilities of the human ear, however, any recording medium needs to have 120dB of amplitude variability in order to cover the entire range of audibility. The only way in which a signal with 120dB of dynamic range can be completely recreated would be if the playback system (amplifiers and speakers) were turned up to recreate the signal at 120dB SPL. If the playback system only recreates the audio at an amplitude of 90dB SPL then only 90dB SPL need be captured, as any harmonics that contribute to the waveform that are lower than 90dB below the peak amplitude will be recreated below 0dB SPL and will be inaudible (ignoring, for the sake of explanation, the fact that the ear is sometimes capable of hearing as low as –8dB SPL, as was discussed in Chapter Six). Therefore, the eventual playback system is an important part of determining the actual amplitude range necessary to record. Covering a range of 120dB, however, ensures that the most extreme playback system can accurately play the audio back for the benefit of the human ear in a "perfect" capacity.

FREQUENCY

We have already discussed the frequency range that needs to be covered in depth throughout Chapter Six. We specifically identified the limiting factors of the human ear's frequency response and determined that recording any material above the 20kHz range is unnecessary as human *auditory* sensing is concerned. There are exceptions, however, to the principle that there is not a reason to record a wider frequency range than the human ear can hear. As these exceptions do not relate to the human ear they were not covered in Chapter Six, though as they relate to the holistic "sensing" of our environment they are worth briefly discussing.

First, the human's low frequency threshold for hearing is given at around 20Hz, but air pressure waves below 20Hz are still capable of being sensed by humans through other parts of the nervous system. Low frequency rumble can easily be felt even when it cannot be heard. Though we would not call this material "audible" because the nerves in the cochlea are not responsible for transmitting this sensation to the brain, such waves can still be a viable part of a listening experience when the nerves from these low frequency waves are combined with the audible overtones. Oftentimes subwoofers in hi-fi reproduction systems are capable of reproducing waveforms as low as 5Hz in order to provide the listener with low frequency effects akin to those experienced in real life. Explosions, trains passing by, machinery operating and other events involving massive amounts of energy are capable of generating these low frequency waves, so for the sake of the human experience it is plausibly beneficial to recreate these in a listening environment.

Second, there are some theories about the potential ability for humans to *perceive* higher frequency air pressure changes through means other than the auditory system. The ear's limitations are well understood and documented, but there are other senses that could contribute to the ability for higher frequency waveforms to somehow be conveyed to the brain, perhaps through very sensitive skin cells or otherwise. A study done in Japan by a research group spearheaded by Tsutomu Oohashi and presented in 1991 at the 91st Audio Engineering Society convention tested levels of brainwave activity when higher frequency audio signals were present. The study tested a number of subjects with an audio reproduction system that reproduced audio from 20Hz to 20kHz followed by the same system with an additional high frequency tweeter that reproduced "missing content" in the music at frequencies above the human hearing range. Subjects were asked to discern between the same waveforms played on the system that was band-limited to 20kHz reproduction and the system with the extended high frequency response. According to the study, not a single subject was capable of identifying the signal with the extended response with any sort of statistical accuracy. Most subjects, however, showed through an alpha electroencephalogram (Alpha EEG) an increase in the brain's electrical activity when the additional high frequency waveforms were present. This study was presented both to the Audio Engineering Society and to the American Physiological Society but has undergone criticism for its testing methods and has apparently not been reproduced since.

Other studies have indicated that people with hearing disorders have benefited from having high frequency audio (above 20kHz) transmitted through bone conduction to the skull. This has apparently improved speech understanding in test subjects. The amount of air pressure required to equal the vibrations yielded through bone conduction, however, is significantly higher than the threshold of pain.

Regardless of the validity or applicability of these tests, they pose an interesting philosophical question: if high frequency material is not audible and not discernable by humans is there any benefit to recording it? This question will have to be dealt with by each audio engineer on his or her own.

PHASE

We need to record audio with minimal phase variation. Phase variations in the form of group delay can cause changes in the arrival time of very high frequencies, which are crucial to our ability to localize sources within the sound field.

DYNAMIC RANGE

The dynamic range requirements for a recording are directly related to the dynamic range of the material being recorded. There is no reason to record a range greater than the audible range of the original waveform. This means that for a particular waveform we only need to capture, record and describe it with a precision reflective of the dynamic range of the signal. Any movement within the waveform that is so small as to be below the threshold of detectability, whether because it is lower than the threshold of hearing (approximately 0dB SPL) or because it is too far below the noise floor to be audible is considered irrelevant because the ear cannot discern it. It is critical that we understand this and is worthy of repeating. Any part of the waveform that is quieter than the quietest signal that we can hear below the noise floor is irrelevant and can be ignored. "Ignoring" is not necessarily simple, however, as simply redrawing that waveform without that part of the signal there yields a different waveform.

So far we have discussed easing the needs of our recording because of the limits of the human ear. We have talked about not needing to record large amplitude variations, and not needing to record very high frequencies. Now, in discussing the maximum dynamic range that we need to record we discuss that we can remove some of the signal at very low levels.

If we can record the accuracy of the waveform within the bounds specified above, which are derived from the maximum capabilities of the human auditory system, then we would be able to record the waveforms *perfectly* with regard to the human's ability to discern the recording from the original source. What we are really concerned with is how much of a waveform is both *necessary* and *sufficient* to record in order to completely accurately reproduce the waveform for the benefit of the human ear. Based on our understanding of the ear from the preceding chapter we now know what aspects of any waveform the ear is able to hear and can thereby determine how much of any audible waveform is both necessary and sufficient to record in order to yield accuracy. It is the goal of audio recording to meet this objective and thus to perfectly accurately record audio waveforms, at least insomuch as the ear can discern.

ANALOG RECORDING

The first audio recording system used a crude, mechanical technology involving wax cylinders. Essentially a large horn, perhaps eighteen inches across, had a small diaphragm about 1/4" across at its base. Attached to the diaphragm was a small piece of sharp metal called a "stylus." A cylinder made of soft wax was put in motion spinning under the stylus. As a person yelled (and it did require actually yelling to get enough sound pressure level to record using this method) into the large horn the air pressure moved the diaphragm, which in turn caused the stylus to dig into and "carve" the wax in a way that paralleled the changes in the air pressure waves.

The higher the air pressure the deeper the stylus cut into the wax. If one were to look at the grooves cut in the wax cylinder with a magnifying glass they would find that the grooves looked like audio waveforms. See Figure 7.2.

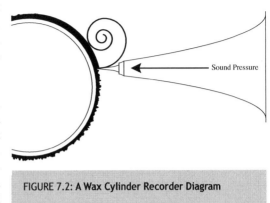

Once the wax cylinder had been recorded upon, a mold was made and copies of it were manufactured using a type of hard resin (instead of soft wax) that would not allow any further recording to happen to it by accident. This recording was then played back by consumers using the same type of device. As the stylus was applied to the cylinder and the cylinder spun, the stylus tracked along with the waveforms, causing the diaphragm attached to it to vibrate. The diaphragm, vibrating at the base of the horn, was amplified by the horn and could then be heard.

FIGURE 7.2: A Wax Cylinder Recorder Diagram

Numerous problems existed with this primitive recording system that make it hardly worth discussing seriously. For one, the transducer at the base of the horn suffered from the same types of problems that microphones do, but being a primitive design and utilizing a heavy diaphragm, the frequency response was poor. Natural inconsistencies in the wax caused variations in the signal being recorded. The friction between the stylus and the wax provided resistance that affected the accuracy of the recording. Further, the amplification system of the simple horn was inadequate for many of the needs of audio recording. The science of sound reproduction and amplification has undergone great developments since a simple horn was used to amplify sound. Regardless, being the basis of recording technology it is important for us to be aware of the wax cylinder recording system. Further, it is interesting to note the parallels between a wax cylinder recorder and the human ear: The horn functions like the pinna, the diaphragm functions like the eardrum, and the stylus functions the same as the ossicles, impressing the wax instead of pushing fluid waves through the cochlea.

The primitive "wax cylinder" recording method is very closely related to the more modern phonograph in that a flexible piece of material is carved to represent audio waveforms. A stylus then tracks in the groove of the medium as the device turns, allowing the conversion of the waveforms represented in the carved medium into air pressure waves.

The more common types of recorders use the properties of magnetism to record audio signals. Primitive versions of this, called "wire recorders," recorded the magnetism onto a small gauge of wire that passed along a recording head. More practical and modern, however, is the use of "tape" to record analog audio waveforms.

In a tape recording system, the recording medium is a piece of a substrate (such as mylar) that is cut like a roll of tape. Very small particles of oxidized iron (rust) are adhered to the tape using a process called "calendering." The elongated particles are generally adhered to the tape oriented in parallel with the length of the tape. The tape then passes over a special type of electromagnet (a recording head) that "orients" the magnetism of the particles. The recording head is actually an electromagnet that, depending on the amount of voltage

FIGURE 7.3: Magnetism on Tape
Dark regions represent areas of high magnetic polarization; light areas represent areas of low magnetic polarization.

provided to it, can supply varying amounts of magnetism with which to orient the particles. The tape passes across the head at a constant velocity so that a roughly consistent number of magnetic particles pass across the head in a given amount of time.

While this happens, the audio signal enters the machine represented by changes in electrical voltage. The voltage changes are fed into the tape's recording head, which subsequently changes the amount of magnetism applied to the particles on the tape. The changing of the magnetism of the particles on the tape represents changes in the waveform. In other words, the changes in voltage over time are converted to changes in magnetism of the linear tape over time (Figure 7.3).

There are several inherent problems with this recording method, though many of them can be drastically improved through modifications to the recording equipment. First, particles do not respond linearly to magnetism. This means that if one were to provide a steadily increasing amount of magnetism to a tape as it passed over a magnetic head and then one were to measure the amount of magnetism "assumed" by the particles on the tape, one would find that the tape does not respond linearly to this change in magnetism. In other words, if we were to plot the input voltage supplied to the recording head against the amount of magnetism assumed by the tape we would find that an increase in voltage of a given amount does not necessarily yield a change on the tape of that same amount of magnetism. There are two reasons for this.

First, the particles have a characteristic called "reluctance." This refers to the resistance that a particle has to assuming a magnetic charge, affecting the particles primarily at low levels of magnetic response. In other words, it takes a certain amount of magnetic charge to overcome the particle's "reluctance" to assuming a

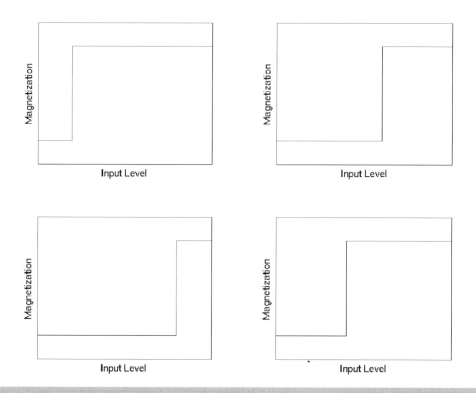

FIGURE 7.4A: **The Non-Linear Response of Several Tape Particles**

Particles on tape have different, unique magnetization characteristics. Above is a chart showing the magnetic response versus the input signal for several different particles.

magnetic charge. Therefore, with low amplitude signals the response of the magnetic tape is inconsistent and uneven with respect to the voltage applied to the magnetic head.

Second, particles experience magnetic "saturation" wherein the particles are fully magnetically polarized and cannot assume any additional magnetic charge. When saturation occurs any additional voltage supplied to the magnetic head will have no further effect on the particle and thus the response of the magnetic tape is again inconsistent and uneven with respect to the voltage applied to the head.

Each individual particle is unique with regards to its reluctance and it's the magnetism corresponding to its saturation. Each particle, individually, has a unique non-linear response with respect to amplitude such that a given signal amplitude entering the system will not necessarily correspond to an equivalent amount of magnetism. The combined effect of this is that the tape itself has a non-linear response that is the cumulative result of the individual responses of each of the particles. The non-linear response of individual tape particles and of the cumulative effect of them is shown in Figure 7.4.

It is in the interest of accurate recording, however, to have a "linear response" in our recording media. A non-linear response yields distortion to the signal as will be discussed in later chapters. Because magnetic tape has a remarkably poor linear response both at high amplitudes and at low amplitudes it is desirable to use the middle of the tape's magnetic range, where it is the most linear, for recording. In order to do this, any audio waveform put on tape is "biased," bringing the signal into the middle of the tape's magnetic range. An example of the range to which a signal is biased is shown in Figure 7.5.

It is important to note, however, that the middle of the tape's range is not completely linear either. Further, as the signal increases in amplitude it gets toward the outside of the tape's optimal magnetic range and becomes *increasingly* non-linear. This means that tape, as a recording medium, is inherently non-linear and thus creates distorted recordings, but becomes even more so as the signal being recorded increases to high amplitudes.

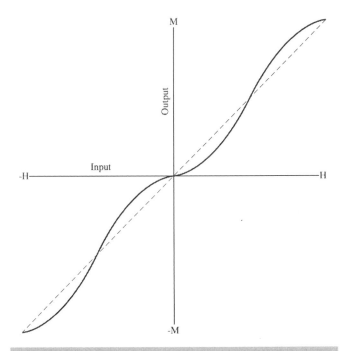

Beside the fact that tape is inherently non-linear, it is also fairly noisy. The magnetic particles on the tape are composed of many "magnetic domains," each of which is polarized either positively or negatively. Each of the domains requires a unique but inconsistent amount of magnetic charge to flip its polarity. This inconsistency causes seemingly random variations in the magnetic response of the domains on a particle, and thus causes inconsistency in the magnetic response of the particle itself. Since the particle is inconsistent and has a seeming random variation to it, the tape itself yields the net result of all of this inconsistency. Because of this, tape itself has random error to it that yields, as discussed in Chapter Five, noise added to the signal when a waveform is recorded onto it. This noise can be decreased in amplitude in several ways but the fact that properties of magnetism result in random error cannot be avoided.

FIGURE 7.4B: **The Non-Linear Response of Tape**

The combined non-linearity of each of the particles on a tape provides for an overall non-linearity of the tape.

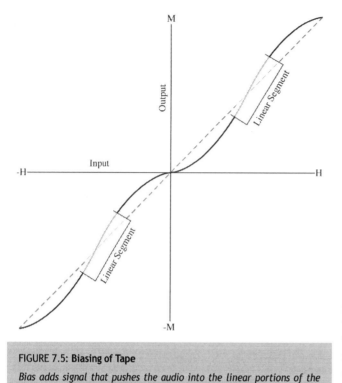

FIGURE 7.5: Biasing of Tape

Bias adds signal that pushes the audio into the linear portions of the tape.

The most effective way to reduce the amplitude of the noise is to double the number of particles. One particle has a tremendous amount of random error but two particles averaged together only have half the error. Four, averaged together, have half the error of two, and so on. By doubling the number of particles the error in any given particle averages out to have a lower effect on the total. In other words, the average performance of the tape increases with twice the number of particles. With a given tape there are three ways to increase the number of particles used. First, we can double the width of the tape used. Oftentimes a piece of tape is used to record several, separate audio tracks. By halving the number of tracks recorded, the portion of the tape used to record each subsequent track doubles, doubling the number of magnetic particles used to represent the analog signal. Another means of increasing the number of particles is to pass the tape across the head faster. By doubling the speed of the tape across the head the number of particles per given increment of time doubles. A third solution is to use a type of tape that has a higher density of particles on it. Such tapes do exist and are known to have a lower noise floor.

Practical limitations of these methods exist, however. For example, doubling the width of each track has mechanical limitations based on imperfections in the manufacturing of the recording head. If the recording head has any variations of its own then the accuracy of the recording decreases. As heads are designed wider, the ability to keep those variations at a low enough level to avoid other errors becomes tenuous.

The net result is that random variations (errors) simply do exist with magnetic media (such as tape) due to the simple nature of the medium itself. As a result, magnetic tape has an inherently high noise floor and thus relatively low dynamic range. The dynamic range of tape is inherently lower than the dynamic range of the human ear, with the most highly tuned and calibrated analog tape machines yielding dynamic range of barely over 80dB. This means that analog tape recorders are inadequate for capturing all of the audio waveforms that the ear can hear. Analog tape recorders are thereby not *sufficient* for audio recording for the human ear based on the criteria we have already defined. Having said this, many audio tape recorders are capable of recording music within the bounds that are necessary on a given audio recording. For example in a noisy playback environment or with limited dynamic range audio material, a given tape recorder may be perfectly capable of recording the audio material in a capacity that is indiscernible from the source to the human ear.

Analog tape has a few other unique characteristics as a recording method. Analog machines, for example, are composed of analog devices such as resistors, capacitors, transformers, wire, and more. Each electronic device has certain characteristics of its own, including random error due to characteristics of the device itself and its own non-linearity. Better-quality components can reduce these characteristics. Any such device also suffers from band limitation. No device made of natural material can pass all frequencies. For the most part this problem is inconsequential because the frequency limitations of devices such as resistors far exceeds those needed by audio systems. Having stated this, it does mean that all analog electronic devices essentially function as filters. One characteristic of filters that is covered in a later chapter is that all filters pass some frequencies through the system faster than they pass other frequencies through the system. In other words, a resistor allows some frequencies of waveforms through at a faster rate than others. This means that some parts of the waveform will be shifted in phase by a slight amount with respect to other frequencies. If a square wave is put through a resistor, for example, what comes out the other side will not be square because the frequencies that are higher pass through faster and the various harmonics that create the waveform no longer align at the zero crossing properly (Figure 7.6).

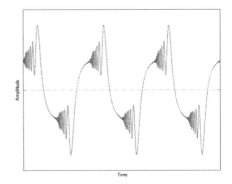

FIGURE 7.6: A Group Delayed "Square Wave"

While within one resistor or capacitor the effect is minimal, the effect of all of the components in the tape recording machine or the tape medium can act as band limiting filters that limit the speed at which some frequencies pass through the system. Because this happens, the phase of the waveforms recorded are subsequently altered. One specification of analog tape machines is their "square wave response," which indicates the amount of phase shift that a tape machine imparts on a signal, thus affecting how much a square wave that enters the system resembles a square wave on tape. This specification, amongst other things, gives an idea of the amount of phase shifting of signals a tape machine causes.

Many of the other problems with analog tape systems can be minimized, though they do still exist. One example is the well-known problem of "wow and flutter," caused by the tape passing through the various capstans and rollers at an inconsistent and oscillating rate. One perpetual problem with analog tape, however, is the fact that magnetizing the tape and then "reading" the magnetization off of the tape requires that the tape pass atop the magnetic heads of the machines. The friction involved in this causes particles to shed from the substrate to which they are attached, thus changing the amount of magnetization of the particles on the tape by reducing the number of particles available to be magnetized. As this occurs the amplitude of the signal is changed and the noise floor increases (because fewer particles are available to average out the random error). Recording engineers are known to report a change to the sound of the tape as a particular piece of tape gets used.

Analog tape, therefore, has several inherent flaws when used for recording. First, its noise floor does not meet the requirements specified in order to transparently record sound for audio purposes. Second, its non-linear properties cause the manifestation of distortion when the signal is played back off of the tape. Third, the mechanical characteristics of the systems create problems, such as the shedding of particles due to friction. Fourth, because the system is analog it inherently has phase errors created due to the inherent filtering done by the system. In total, analog tape is capable of recording recognizable audio as none of these problems is so great that it completely negates the effectiveness of the medium, but it is incapable of meeting the requirements of accurate audio reproduction for the sake of the boundaries of the ear's capabilities.

Other methods of recording audio waveforms have also been used besides wax cylinders and analog magnetic tape recorders. The most popular alternate form of recording audio signals is carving the waveform onto a flat, circular, vinyl disc. This method, very similar to the wax cylinder, involves a stylus that fits into a groove in the disc that "tracks" with the rises and falls in the vinyl that correspond to the compression and rarefaction portions of the waveform they represent. The stylus, however, functions as a transducer connected to an electro magnetic device. As the stylus moves up and down the magnetic field changes, much as occurs in a microphone.

The specifics of this type of technology are not worth comprehensively analyzing, as the results are in many ways similar to magnetic tape. The method is capable of reproducing audio to a large degree, but incapable of accurately reproducing audio to a degree that matches the ears' capabilities. For example, being a physical device made of a manmade material, imperfections in the vinyl cause random errors upon playback of the system, creating noise and decreasing dynamic range. The fact that the system is composed of several mechanical and electrical components means that it is inherently band-limited and thus has phase issues in the audible range, even if the band it covers exceeds the human audible range. The friction of the needle on the disk causes permanent damage to the disk every time the material is played back, causing a change to the recording medium when used. Finally, other limiting factors of the size of the disc and the properties of the medium have negative effects on other characteristics that affect its performance as relates to its ability to accurately record audio for human ears. One example is the inability to record high amplitude, low frequency waveforms without the needle potentially "bouncing" out of the groove. This necessitates the application of an EQ curve to the material before and after it is put on the vinyl disk. Many of these issues have comprehensively engineered solutions that make these recording systems viable for audio recordings, and due to these solutions these mediums have become tremendously more effective at recording audio for humans over time.

A more mathematical way to look at the various issues that plague analog recording techniques utilizes what is called a "transfer function." In essence this refers to the relationship between what goes into a system and what leaves the system. The "function" refers to the fact that a mathematical formula can be used to describe the differences such that any signal going in and put through the formula would yield the signal that leaves a given system. For example, if we had a box that turned the signal up approximately 6dB and did nothing else then we could say that the transfer function of that box is as follows:

$$y = 2x$$

Where x is the inbound signal and y is the outbound signal. The outbound signal is simply equal to twice the inbound signal. The transfer function of a box can also be plotted on a graph, as is given in Figure 7.7.

Oftentimes several transfer functions are discussed for a given device, one for each of the characteristics of the signal. For example, one can look at the input vs. output of a resistor in several different ways. One can look at the *frequency* transfer function of the resistor, or what happens to frequencies that enter the resistor. Most resistors have an excellent transfer function of frequencies up to a very high point. One can also look, for example, at the *phase* transfer function of a given device, noting how the phases of the signals that enter change upon leaving the device.

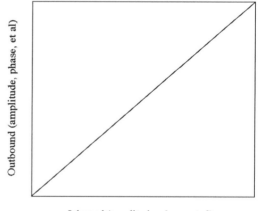

FIGURE 7.7: A y=x Transfer Function

If the outbound signal is precisely the same as the inbound signal then the "transfer function" is as shown above.

All analog devices (including electrical components, transducers, magnetic devices, wire, and even air) have transfer functions that are not perfect. Sending signal into any of those devices produces a different output (to some degree) than what went in, especially in extreme circumstances. Several of these devices are notably worse than others. For example, the frequency and phase transfer functions of transducers such as microphones, styli on recording apparatuses and speakers is generally far worse than the transfer function of wire. Regardless, all analog components have transfer functions that are imperfect. When a series of devices, such as: transducer, circuit board trace, resistor, circuit board trace, resistor, circuit board trace, capacitor, transformer, electrical connector, wire, etc. are chained together (as occurs in a microphone, for example), the transfer function of the first component creates a different signal than went in, which is compounded by the second component, and so on.

Since all analog recorders are dependent upon the actual signal being transferred to a storage medium, the transfer function of several components, the actual mechanical device that transfers the signal to the recording medium, and the rest of the entire system enter into play. As of yet a method has not been developed for transferring the analog sound pressure waves, converted into electrical signals by a microphone, onto a recording system, that causes only an inaudible amount of variation. The likelihood that an audibly perfect analog recording system could be devised is minimal simply because of the vast range of sensitivity to amplitude, frequency, and phase that the human species has, in combination with the inability for the materials used and the manufacturing of them to represent (without error) such great ranges as the ear can discern.

CONCLUSION

Respecting the accuracy with which audio needs to be recorded for human use, and further respecting the inability for this to happen using analog, or continuously variable methods, another method of transmitting and recording audio is clearly necessary if audible perfection is to occur.

This is not to say that analog recording methods are entirely unviable. Analog tape and phonographs, for example, are highly respected for their sonic capabilities and can be, as stated above, perfect audio recording devices for certain audio signals, many of which might be of the most common variety recorded. They are incapable, however, of recording *audible perfection*. Further, at a time when a replacement for this type of recording was under development, the analog recording methods had simply not been improved upon to the degree in which they are in modern times. Still, the analog recording methods have some inherent issues that have simply not been overcome, which leads to the need for a different type of recording system that is not prone to these types of problems.

FOOTNOTES

[1] The first "microphone" would have been part of the transmitter portion of the first "telephone," as was presented on October 26, 1861 by Phillip Reis in Frankfurt, Germany.

Chapter Eight

Introducing Digital Audio

The word "digital" comes from the Latin word "digitalis," which refers to the human fingers (digits). The word refers to things that can be counted, as in the fingers and toes. Digital audio refers analog voltage changes that have been turned into simple numerical values. The advantage to this is that numbers somehow representing a waveform can be effectively communicated and recorded with much greater precision than continuously changing analog voltages. We learned in Chapter Seven that analog voltages are difficult to record or transmit without inducing variance. By simply dealing with numbers, any signal can be accurately transmitted so long as the numerical values that represent the audio are not accidentally altered by the transmission or storage system. An extremely crude example of this gives an indication of why this is the case.

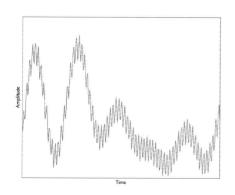

FIGURE 8.1 : A Complex Waveform

Attempting to communicate a waveform verbally on the telephone is nearly impossible. Communicating the waveform in Figure 8.1 as an analog signal verbally would be akin to saying "up a little, then down not quite as much, then a little up, down, up, wiggle, etc.". If we communicated this to a friend via telephone and then compared his drawing of the waveform with the original, the difference would yield a very distorted image of the waveform. To some degree this is what occurs whenever analog signals are transmitted or re-corded. If we were somehow able to turn this wave-form into some sort of numerical code that accurately represented the waveform, however, and if the friend on the other end of the phone line understood that code, we could very accurately communicate the waveform to him. His rendition would be remarkably accurate, pending the accuracy in which we could turn the waveform into a numerical code. Such accuracy is indeed a concern, but the communication of it would be nearly foolproof:

"439261028947294845823874747487404894763487346103459468574389098"

It was this precise reason that scientists and mathematicians in the communications industry (telegraph, primarily) in the early 1900s were looking for a way to "encode" audio waveforms as numerical data.

In reality, even the numbers need to get recorded or communicated in an analog form in one sense or another. The storage media used for digital recordings is still a blank template to which changes are made, and the transmission media for digital communication are still electrical voltages on analog wires. The method for using these analog means for digital work typically uses pulses of electricity to represent numbers.

ENCODING NUMBERS AS PULSES

There are several ways in which pulses can represent numbers. One method, similar to Morse Code, simply uses one pulse to represent the number one, seven pulses to represent the number seven, and so on. The number 13 would be represented by one pulse followed by three pulses. The number zero might be represented by a pause of a fixed length. This type of digital coding is called PNM, or Pulse Number Modulation, and is shown in Figure 8.2.

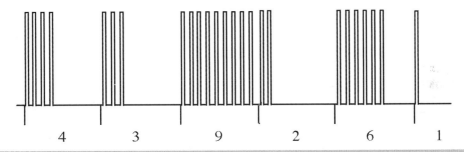

FIGURE 8.2: A PNM Encoded Signal

The PNM system uses pulses to transmit numbers by using several sequential pulses to transmit particular values. For example, one pulse above represents the number "1." Nine pulses represent the number "9." Long numbers can be transmitted simply by varying the number of pulses between brief pauses of no values.

Another method of using analog pulses to communicate digital information might involve a series of consistent pulses within fixed intervals of time. A "number" would be represented by varying the *timing* of the pulses. If, for instance, pulses were sent out ten times a second, the number "one" might be represented by changing the timing between two of the pulses by one millisecond. The number "seven" would be represented by changing said timing by seven milliseconds. The number "13" would be represented by changing the timing between two pulses by one millisecond, and the next interval by three milliseconds. This method of digital coding would be called PPM, or Pulse Position Modulation, as the position of the pulse changes in time. This is shown in Figure 8.3.

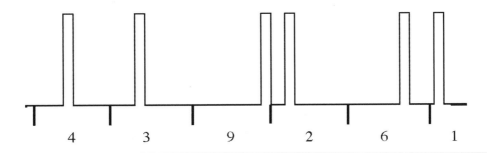

FIGURE 8.3: A PPM Encoded Signal

The PPM system uses pulses to transmit numbers by varying the position of the pulses against unique measures of time. For example, a pulse displaced from its time reference by, perhaps, 1 microsecond would represent the number "1." Nine microseconds of displacement represents the number "9."

Yet another method of digital coding would involve sending out a steady stream of pulses but changing the width of the pulses. A wide pulse would represent a high number and a narrow pulse would represent a low number. Each pulse would theoretically be a fixed length when combined with its subsequent "valley," so wider pulses would be followed by a narrower "valley." A complete pulse and valley might be $11\mu m$ long so that a pulse that is $1\mu m$ (micrometer) long would represent the number zero and the number nine would be a pulse $11\mu m$ long. This way, whether the number represented was any number from zero to nine there would still be a pulse and a valley for each number. The number seven might be represented by a pulse wavelength of $8\mu m$ and a valley wavelength of $3\mu m$. The number thirteen would be represented by a wavelength of $2\mu m$ followed by a valley of $9\mu m$, then a pulse $4\mu m$ long followed by a valley $7\mu m$ long. This method of digital coding is called PWM, or Pulse Width Modulation, and is given in Figure 8.4.

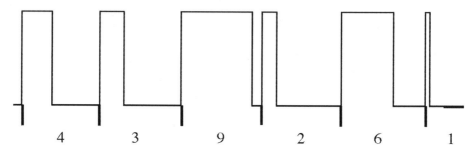

FIGURE 8.4: A PWM Encoded Signal

The PWM system uses pulses to transmit numbers by using differing widths of pulses to transmit particular values. For example, a narrow pulse above represents the number "1." A pulse nine times as wide represents the number "9." This method is very similar to PPM as referenced above.

The most efficient means of transmitting numbers using pulses for the purposes needed is through a means devised at International Telephone and Telegraph Company in France in 1937. Sir Alec Reeves developed a way of transmitting telegraph information down telephone lines. The method involves determining a code that is associated with each number. This code is determined using both the pulses and valleys, or the "ups" and "downs" of the signal in organized arrangements that convey specific numbers. All of the ups and downs are of the same length. A certain number of either up or down positions are used to transmit every number whether the number is zero or much higher. The number of positions is dependant on the range of numbers that need to be communicated, but is no more than the number of up/down variations that are possible with a specific number of positions. For instance, if only four numbers need to be represented they can be represented with only two positions: down-down, down-up, up-down, and up-up. Each of these represents a distinctly different number and can be used to represent the numbers one through four.

The most efficient use of up and down positions, Reeves determined, is that which takes advantage of the *binary* counting method. We humans have ten fingers, so when we started using numbers and counting we got into the habit of counting in units of ten. This numbering system is called "base 10," or "decimal." In the decimal system we count up to nine numbers, and when we reach the next number we start a second "column" that represents "ten". This counting method is so ingrained in our behavior and thinking that it may seem odd to think about it in this analytical sense. We start counting in the "ones" place, and when we reach the number nine and add one more we use the "tens" column (much like an abacus) to keep tally of how many complete sets of "ones" have passed by. As soon as more than nine of the "tens" have passed we start keeping track of the "hundreds," and so on. The number 13 in base ten is used by denoting 1 group of "ten" plus 3 individual "ones." The number 4,329 is 4 thousands plus 3 hundreds plus 2 tens plus 9 ones. See Figure 8.5.

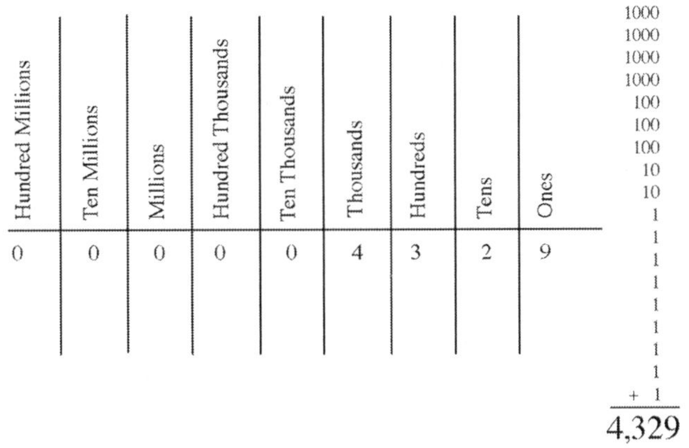

The Base 10 Numbering Scale is the conventional method of describing numerical values in western cultures, but is not the only means for describing numbers. Base 10 most likely comes from the fact that ten digits exist on our two hands combined, making the number a logical choice for the basis of our counting system.

The decimal system is not, however, the only way of counting. In the Mesopotamian culture counting was done in a combination of base 10 and base 6, and the fact that there are 60 seconds in a minute and 60 minutes in an hour, as well as the 360° in a circle stems from their original counting system.

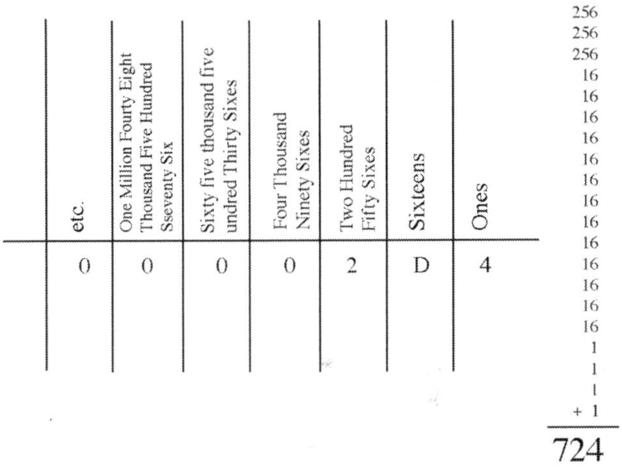

A lot of computer programmers use the "hexidecimal" system (base 16) to make programming language easier to decipher. In the hexidecimal system the second column does not start until the sixteenth number is tallied, and the third column is not used until sixteen of those have been tallied, or the value of two hundred and fifty six is reached. This means that the number "10" in hexidecimal is actually the number sixteen. The number "100" is two hundred and fifty six. Because only ten digits are identified in our Base 10 numbering scale, the letters A, B, C, D, E, and F substitute for ten, eleven, twelve, thirteen, fourteen, and fifteen respectively in the Base 16 system. In hexidecimal the number 2D4 is equivalent to 2 two-fifty-sixes plus D (thirteen) sixteens plus 4 ones for a total of seven hundred twenty four. See Figure 8.6.

Hundred Millions	Ten Millions	Millions	Hundred Thousands	Ten Thousands	Thousands	Hundreds	Tens	Ones	
0	0	0	0	0	4	3	2	9	1000 1000 1000 1000 100 100 100 10 10 1 1 1 1 1 1 1 1 + 1

4,329

FIGURE 8.5: **The Base 10 Numbering Scale**

etc.	One Million Fourty Eight Thousand Five Hundred Seventy Six	Sixty five thousand five undred Thirty Sixes	Four Thousand Ninety Sixes	Two Hundred Fifty Sixes	Sixteens	Ones	
0	0	0	0	2	D	4	256 256 256 16 16 16 16 16 16 16 16 16 16 16 1 1 1 + 1

724

FIGURE 8.6: **The Base 16 Numbering Scale**

Back to discussing the coding of numbers in pulses, if there were ten possible positions of a pulse then the base 10 system could be used to code numbers very effectively. The different amplitudes of the pulses could be used to transmit numbers. The number 7 would be represented by a pulse 7 units high. The number 13 could be represented two different ways. One way would be to send a single pulse 13 units high. This would require that there would be enough amplitude levels available for pulses to cover the entire scale of numbers necessary. If it is known that the largest number that will be sent through this system is the number 25 then only 26 different amplitude levels are necessary (one for each of the values including and between 0 and 25). We will soon determine that the number of amplitude levels necessary to communicate digital audio effectively in this manner would be in the millions. This would mean that a single pulse would need to have millions of steps that it could represent, which puts this type of system as capable of having flaws as the analog systems that were refuted in Chapter Seven. This because of inaccuracies and variances in the recording system and the transmission method that could slightly vary the amplitude of a given pulse, changing it to a different value, defeating the desired goal of this digital communication and recording system. This type of communication of numbers, however, is called PAM, or Pulse Amplitude Modulation.

The other way to represent the number 13 with amplitude modulation would be with one pulse one unit high followed by another that was three units high. If this system were used then the system would have to be aware that this was not a 1 and then a 3 as two separate numbers, but rather a 13 as a single number. In other words, if we sent a stream of numbers like 7 – 13 – 42 – 2 – 31 – 1 then they could be misread as 7 – 1 – 3 – 4 – 2 – 2 – 3 – 1 – 1. We would really have to set the system up so that all numbers were two digits, such as 07 – 13 – 42 – 02 – 31 – 01. If the deciphering system knows that every two pulses represent one number then the numbers could be adequately communicated without confusion, and the number 0 would have to be represented by a pulse of some form, such as a pulse of the lowest amplitude. The problem with this system is again that if the range of numbers that need to be transmitted are in the millions then not only must there be ten different amplitude variations per pulse that are distinct and able to be transmitted without accidental change, but seven such pulses would have to be transmitted to yield a single answer (to cover the range from 0,000,000 to 9,999,999). Each series of pulses representing a single number is called a "word," and is the number of pulses necessary to represent a complete number. The number 3,427,005 would be represented as given in Figure 8.7.

The PAM system uses pulses of differing amplitudes to express numbers. In the Base 10 numerical system, ten different amplitude levels must be able to be used and recognized.

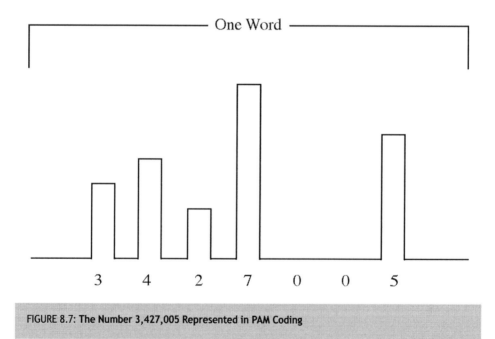

FIGURE 8.7: The Number 3,427,005 Represented in PAM Coding

The more efficient method of transmitting these numbers was to use the base 2 counting system, or "binary." In binary code the highest value that can be counted in any numerical "column" is 1.

As soon as more than "1" is needed in any column the next column is used. The rightmost column counts the "ones," the next column counts the "twos," the next the "fours," the next the "eights," and so on (Figure 8.8).

The binary numbering scale only uses zeros and ones to represent all numbers, but takes many more digits to represent numbers than Base 10.

The entire binary counting system utilizes a series of 1s and 0s. Because of this many more columns are required to describe a number but there are fewer variations in the values in each column. The number 4,572,349 in decimal is the same as 45C4BD in hexidecimal, and the same as 10010110001001011111101 in binary. The higher the base of the counting system the fewer digits necessary to represent it, but the more variations of the individual values are necessary. The number above took only six digits to represent in hexidecimal, but each digit had sixteen possible variations; in decimal it took seven digits, but each digit had ten possible variations; and in binary 22 digits are needed, but each digit only had two possible states.

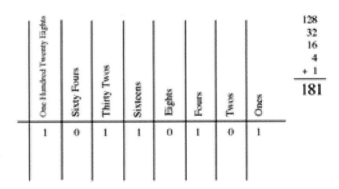

FIGURE 8.8: The Base 2 (Binary) Numbering Scale

To determine how many digits are necessary to communicate a number in various numbering systems we need to take the number of values that can be counted in one digit and raise it to the number of digits available. For example, in base 10 we can count ten values with one digit (zero through nine). If we want to find out how many numbers we can represent with three digits we raise ten to the third, or 10^3. The mathematical formula we use to calculate this is:

If

v = number of values that can be represented with one digit (what the base counting system is)

n = number of digits to be used, and

R = range of numbers that can be represented in total, then

$R = v^n$

If we know the range of values we are representing and we know the base counting system then we can determine how many digits are necessary by using the formula:

$n = log_v R$

Using these simple formulas we can determine that in hexidecimal, three digits gives us the ability to represent 65,536 numbers; in the decimal system three digits gives us the ability to represent 1,000 numbers; and in binary three digits gives us the ability to represent 8 numbers.

If binary code is used to transmit and record numbers then pulses could be used very effectively. First, the range of numbers needs to be established. A range of a million values can be represented, for example, with nineteen digits. This means that if our range of values is one million that each *word* will require nineteen pulses (either on or off pulses). The number zero would be represented as 0000000000000000000, the number one by 0000000000000000001, the number two by 0000000000000000010, and so on. Whenever the number 1 comes up a pulse "on" message will be sent, and whenever a 0 comes up a pulse "off" message will be sent. After nineteen pulse positions are transmitted the word is over and the value that it represents can be determined. The next nineteen values represent the next complete number, or word. This type of digital coding is called PCM, or Pulse Code Modulation, and is the primary form of digital communication used today.

PCM is much easier to use, as digital storage devices do not have to be able to record a variety of amplitudes; they only need to be able to record on or off positions. These values can be stored by means of holes punched or not-punched in cards, such as was used in the computers from the 1950s. They can be stored as "pits" or "lands," as compact discs use nowadays. Any method of storing simply two variations of values can be used to store PCM digital information. Transmitting PCM information in binary is much less complicated than other methods as well. Light can be used to transmit digital signals simply by turning the light on or off. Electronic pulses can be used in the same way.

In the computer world, each digit is called a "bit." Eight bits is called a "byte." The number of bits/bytes needed to transmit a stream of digital numbers is dependant on the range of numbers. If the range of numbers needed is from zero through two hundred fifty five then each "word" can be as little as eight bits, or one byte. If the range of numbers to be transmitted is larger then each word will need to have more bits. If the range of numbers is smaller than two hundred fifty six then fewer bits may be used to transmit digital information. Both the sending device and the receiving device must know how many bits are associated with each numerical word so that the codes that are sent are properly received.

We now have a way to transmit numerical information through a series of off-on pulses. Numbers are turned into binary numbers, which are associated with pulses. All pulses are the same amplitude so that variances in amplitude cannot be mistaken for incorrect numbers. A number of pulses are used together in a binary code to most effectively transmit or store a range of numbers. The numerical word is an established length, all words are the same length, and every word that gets transmitted represents a single value.

VARIATIONS OF BINARY PCM

There are three variations of binary PCM that are worth discussing. The first is the "floating-point" counting system. In order to understand floating-point systems we should revisit our decimal system again.

The field of mathematics has determined an easier way to refer to numbers that are very large or very small. Rather than write out the number in its entirety, a numerical system called "scientific notation" is used in which we write some of the number and then imply how many decimal places to the left or the right it needs to get "shifted." The "mantissa" represents the number and the "exponent" represents how many decimal places need to be added. This is essentially represented by two numbers that are multiplied times each other: the first indicates the accuracy of the number and the second is the number 10 raised to a power, shifting the decimal places. 10^1 is equal to 10. 10^2 is equal to 100. 10^3 is equal to 1000, and so on. If a number is multiplied times 10 raised to a power, then the power that it is raised to tells how many zeros to add to the number. As an example, 6.55×10^4 is the same as 65,500, as the decimal point shifts four places to the right. If the exponent is a negative number, such as 10^{-3} (.001) then the decimal place gets moved to the left the number of places in the exponent. The number 6.55×10^{-3} is equal to .00655. By using this form of scientific notation, very large numbers and very small numbers can be used with less confusion as fewer zeros need be written.

There is another advantage, however, of scientific notation that has to do with accuracy. The number 6.55×10^4 is inherently different than the number 65,500. In the latter we have defined that the last two digits are definitely "00" but the former version does not actually specify that 6.55×10^4 ends in "00" at all. For all we know, 6.55 x 10^4 was rounded, and there is not any way of knowing whether or not it was indeed rounded to this value. It does not tell us if the last two numbers really *are* two zeros or not. When the number is written 65,500 the last two numbers are clearly defined as two zeros when they may not actually be. A more accurate way to write this number would be 65,5xx if the last two numbers are not really known, though this is not a convention in typical numerical notation. An example of this is as follows: the speed of sound is approximately 406,080 feet per hour. This could be written as ~4.06 x 10^5 $^{ft}/_{hr}$. If this is then turned into *fixed-point* notation it would have to be written as 406,000 $^{ft}/_{hr}$, which is not actually accurate. If we were to figure out how far sound would travel in a day or in a month our math would be very inaccurate if we were to use this latter number. For this reason, adding the zeros makes the number actually *less accurate* than using scientific notation. When scientists and mathematicians use numbers with scientific notation they have certain rules that prevent the result from yielding an answer that seems to imply more accuracy than the numbers really represent. It is important to recognize that when numbers are written in scientific notation that the numbers are really only as accurate as they are presented. There is not an accurate way of representing numbers without scientific notation in our current numbering system without putting additional numbers (zeros) at the end. By putting additional numbers in we are *committing* those values to zeros when they may not actually be zeros.

Relating this to binary notation the same thing can be done. The number 1011 in binary notation is equivalent to the number eleven (1 eight, 0 fours, 1 two, and 1 one equals eleven). Applying scientific notation to this we could write 1011 x 2^{100} (1011 x 2^4), which shifts the decimal place four spaces to the right, adding four decimal places to this number. This will give us the number 1011xxxx. This number is not the same as 10110000, which we are implied to write, which is actually one hundred seventy six. If this were the number that were meant then the original number would have been written 1011.0000 x 2^4. Since the four zeros were not originally present, the actual answer can really be any number between 10101000 and 10110111, because any numbers in this range would be rounded to 10110000, or 1011 x 2^4. Therefore this number can actually represent any number from one hundred sixty eight to one hundred eight five, and the number is not specific enough to be one hundred seventy six. The same rules that apply to decimal scientific notation apply to such notation in binary: positive exponents after the "x 2" shift the decimal point to the right while negative exponents shift the decimal point to the left. Also, adding zeros is not actually as accurate as leaving the number in scientific notation because adding zeros *implies* a level of accuracy not given, and further math with those zeros in place gives answers that also imply that they have more accuracy than they actually do.

If we use scientific notation in binary, the decimal *point* is not in a *fixed* location, such as at the end of the numbers. Instead the decimal *point floats* around depending on the quantity represented by the exponent. This type of notation is descriptively called "floating-point" notation, and is the same as scientific notation in the decimal system.

Floating-point notation is written in binary by using the first few bits to represent the exponent and the remaining bits to represent the mantissa. 1011 x 2^{0100} would be written simply as 0100 1011, removing the "x 2" from the code. This floating-point notation would have a four-digit exponent and a four-digit mantissa (noting that, counter to how it is written in scientific-type notation, the exponent comes first). Just as with fixed-point notation described earlier, both the sending and receiving devices have to be prepared to accept floating-point binary PCM code. In addition to this, the "formatting" of the floating-point notation must be the same between both devices, meaning that each device must know not only the length of the numerical word, but also how much of the word represents the exponent and how much of the word represents the mantissa. The most common formatting of floating-point binary PCM code in the professional audio industry is 32-bit floating-point as defined by the I.E.E.E. in which the first eight bits are the exponent and the remaining 24 bits are the mantissa.

In decimal based scientific notation the convention is that all of the zeros on the left of the first "valid" numerical value are removed and the first valid number is put in front of the decimal point and the rest are placed behind the decimal point.

Ex: 000000000063556 is represented by removing all of the zeros on the left, putting the first "6" in front of the decimal point and then determining the appropriate scientific notion to describe the rest: 6.3556 x 10[5]

In binary-based floating-point notation the convention is that all of the zeros on the left of the first "valid" numerical value (the first "1") are removed and the floating-point notation is then determined.

Ex: 00000000110101000100100100110000.01001111101 is represented by removing all of the zeros on the left, putting the first "1" as the first number represented. Then the number of digits in front of the decimal point determines the value of the exponent.

In 32-bit floating-point notation the first eight bits establish the exponent (how many places in front or behind the decimal point the number exists) and the next twenty-four bits represent the number. Since, however, every floating-point number inherently then starts with a "1," there is not a reason to indicate this first digit. Therefore, in floating-point notation the first "1" is implied and the next twenty-four bits are noted. For this reason, 32-bit floating-point notation actually represents 25 bits instead of 24.

*Ex: 00000000**110101000100100100110000**.0**1001111101 is represented by removing all of the zeros on the left and then representing the next twenty five bits:*

1101010001001001001100000

Since all numbers start with a "1" however, the first one is removed so that all 25 bits are "represented," but only 24 are used. The result, removing the first "1," is:

101010001001001001100000

We need to be clear that 32-bit floating-point notation only has 25 valid bits of precision and that the 8-bit exponent only "scales" the numbers. While floating-point notation is capable of representing very large and very small numbers, the precision of those numbers is not maintained. For example, we can look at a set of potential numbers:

0000000000000000100101010010101010111010101001010100101010110101

0000101000010010101110101010101101010101011010110101011010100101011

0000000000000000000111101011010110101010101001011010100101010010

00000000000000000000000000111101010010100101010010010101001001

000000000000000000000000000101010100010101010100100010010100101001

If we want to represent these numbers in a 24-bit *fixed-point* numerical system we would only be able to represent 24 digits within these numbers, and they would have to be the same 24 bits in each number. We have to pay attention to the largest value and base our "scaling" on that. The results are that all of the **bold** values are kept:

*00000000000000000**100101010010**10101011101010100101010010101010110101*

*0000**1010000100101011101010101**101010101010110101101010110101001010 11*

*000000000000000000001**1101011**0101101010101010100101101010010101 0010*

*00000000000000000000000000000**011101010010100101010010010101001001*

00000000000000000000000000000101010100010101010010001001010010100 1

Notice that the last two values did not get represented at all because their values were too small in comparison to the second value in the series. 24 Bits only give us the ability to represent a certain range of numbers, and the five numbers in the series above far exceed the range that 24 bits can give us.

If, however, we used 32-bit floating-point to represent these numbers then the values that would be represented are as follows, again in **bold**,

*00000000000000000**10010101001010101011101010**100101010010101010110101*

*0000**10100001001010111010101011**01010101011010110101011010100101011*

*0000000000000000000001**11010110101101010101010100**10110101001010100 10*

*0000000000000000000000000000000**11101010010100101010010010**101001001*

*0000000000000000000000000000000**10101010001010101001000100**10100101001*

Notice that with 32-bit floating-point a much wider range of numbers can be represented, but each number is still limited to only having 25 bits of precision. Very large and very small numbers can both be represented, but neither with more accuracy than their equivalent fixed-bit counterparts.

SIGN BIT

Typically, the bit on the far left is referred to as the "Most Significant Bit," or MSB, as this bit has the largest effect on the number. Just as in the decimal system where the value of the digit on the left is the largest and most significant number, the same is true in binary. The bit on the far right is subsequently called the "Least Significant Bit," or LSB. In actuality, in most binary systems, the bit on the far left is used to indicate whether the number is a positive or a negative number as it indicates whether a + sign or a – sign is present in front of the number. For this reason the bit the furthest to the left is actually called the "sign bit," and the bit to the right of it is actually the MSB. If the sign bit is a 0 the number is positive and if it is 1 the number is negative. This is true in both the case of the exponent and the mantissa. Using eight bit words wherein the first four are the exponent and the remaining four are the mantissa, the number ***0***100 ***1***011 would actually be a negative number as the sign bit of the mantissa (the fifth bit from the left) is a 1, and therefore implies that the mantissa is a negative number. This number could just as accurately be written –011 x 2^{+100} ("100" being binary for the number four), where the positive and negative signs represent bits, so there are only actually three numerical bits in the exponent and the mantissa. This number is the same as:

Magnitude Bits
Sign Bit
Fours
Twos
Ones
MSB
0 000 0000 0000 0000 0000 0000.
LSB
Decimal Point Goes Here

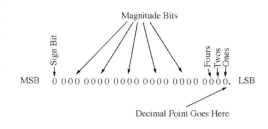

FIGURE 8.9: 24-Bit Fixed Point Notation

-011 x 2^4

-3 x 2^4 *(decimal)*

-011xxxx

~-48 (decimal)

Any in the range of numbers from 0101000 to 0110111

Any in the range of numbers from 40 to 55 (decimal)

We now know that a 24-bit fixed-point number is generally laid out as given in Figure 8.9.

A typical 32-bit floating-point number is laid out as given in Figure 8.10.

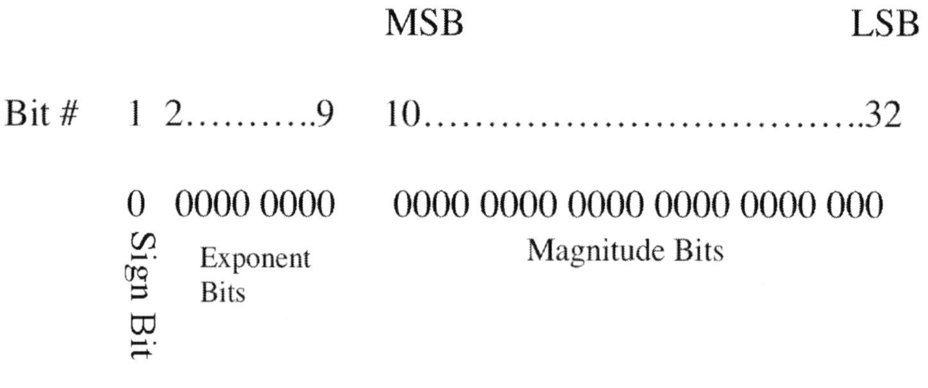

MSB
LSB
Bit # 1 2..........9 10...................................32
0 0000 0000 0000 0000 0000 0000 0000 000
Sign Bit
Exponent Bits
Magnitude Bits

FIGURE 8.10: 32-Bit Floating Point Notation

TWO'S COMPLEMENT

The final variation to typical binary coding is called "two's complement" and makes doing math to the binary numbers easier for computer processors. The two's complement of a positive number is the negative version of that number and is determined by taking the opposite of all of the digits in that number and adding a "1" to the result. The number 01001 represents a positive number nine. The two's complement of this would be the negative number nine. We could determine the number "negative nine" by taking the number "positive nine" and "flipping" all of the bits and adding a "1" to the result. Therefore, if the number "nine" is 01001, then "negative nine" is 10110 + 1, or 10111. The leftmost bit again tells us the sign, but if the number is a negative then it cannot be read as a traditional binary number. Instead it has to be determined by converting it back to a positive number. The advantage of this is that the addition of positive and negative numbers can be handled by a computer by simply adding numbers together, ignoring the sign.

In fixed-point,

> *0011 1001 (57)*
>
> + *0001 1100 (28)*
>
> *0101 0101 (85)*

> *0011 1001 (57)*
>
> + *1001 1100 (-0110 0100 represented in two's complement, or –100)*
>
> *1101 0101 (-0010 1011 represented in two's complement, or –43)*

Subtraction of two numbers in computers is done by making the second number a negative number by determining its two's complement. If we wanted to subtract 9 from 16 we would take the two numbers: 010000 (16) and 001001 (9) and determine the two's complement of the second number: 110111. Then the two numbers are added together rather than subtracted:

> *010000 (16)*
>
> + *110111 (-9 in two's complement)*
>
> *000111 (7)*

Two's complement notation is dependent upon the use of the sign bit. Digital audio coding typically uses two's complement (and therefore the sign bit) though floating-point notation is not always used. We will discuss more about floating-point math and its practical and impractical uses in Chapter Fourteen.

Chapter Nine

Digital Sampling

Because of the problems with analog transmission and because of the recognition of the benefits of digital transmission, the engineers at the major telegraph companies in the early 1900s worked to find a way to convert analog signals into digital signals. The research into ways to do this happened on both sides of the ocean and a few people determined the most efficient way of doing this on their own. In Russia an engineer by the name of Kotelnikov worked on the problem, in Europe a pair of engineers by the names of Whittaker and Cauchy arrived at the same conclusion, and in the United States a Swedish born engineer by the name of Harold Nyquist did the same. The challenge was to record all of the characteristics of a waveform as a series of numerical codes such that the entire waveform could be re-created at the other end of a telephone or telegraph line.

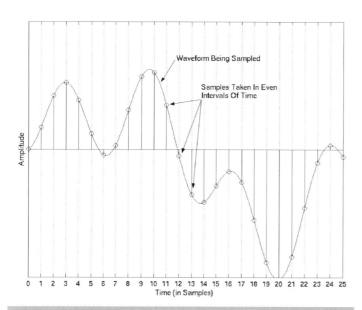

FIGURE 9.1: Digital Sampling

The amplitude of the waveform is recorded at even intervals of time, per Nyquist's Theorem.

Nyquist, an engineer with AT&T research, had spent the years from 1918 to 1924 studying the field of telephotography which culminated in a device that could create *facsimiles* of photographs through telephone lines and resulted in a successful transmission between "fax machines" in 1924. Starting in the late 1920s he began working on a way to transmit audio through telephone lines more accurately and with less distortion. In January of 1928 he published a groundbreaking paper in Transactions of the A.I.E.E. His paper, "Certain Topics In Telegraph Transmission Theory" presented a theory about the most efficient and accurate method of converting analog waveforms into digital numbers. He theorized, over 28 pages full of mathematical analysis, that an analog waveform could be completely captured and reconstructed if the signal could be band-limited. The amplitude of the waveform would need to be captured at equal increments in time, at a speed more than twice the frequency of the highest frequency present. This means that if the waveform is limited so that no frequency content is available above a certain frequency, say, 1000Hz that the entire waveform could be recorded and re-constructed if the amplitude of the waveform is recorded more than 2000 times per second, or at a rate of more than 2kS/s (2 kilo Samples per second). It is very important to understand (and it will be explained here) that by recording only the amplitude this often that *the entire waveform can be accurately reconstructed, including its amplitude, frequency, phase, and dynamic range.* An example is provided in Figure 9.1.

N. Erd described the recording of the waveform at regular intervals of time as "sampling" and the term has been used ever since. In 1948 Claude E Shannon, a mathematician, derived the mathematical proof of Nyquist's theory, nearly twenty years after Nyquist first published his paper. Shannon's proof was offered in the Proceedings of the Institution of Radio Engineers vol. 37, no. 1, 1949, pp. 10-21 and is entitled "Communication in the Presence of Noise." As mathematical proof had thus been offered for the *theory* it would hence become a "*theorem,*" and Shannon's original text from his paper is as follows:

> *Theorem 1: If a function f(t) contains no frequencies higher than W cps [ed: cycles per second, or "Hz"], it is completely determined by giving its ordinates at a series of points spaced 1/2W seconds apart.*

A paraphrasing of this yields, "If a waveform contains no frequencies higher than some number of Hz it can be completely defined by determining its amplitude at a series of points spaced no more than twice the frequency of the highest frequency contained within the waveform." By the time Shannon provided his proof, mathematicians in no less than three different languages had already provided other proofs, but Shannon's proof is regarded by U.S. scholars as being the basis of digital theory. In Russian textbooks the theorem used as the basis of digital audio is called the Kotelnikov Theorem. In other countries it is known as the Nyquist Theorem, the Shannon Theorem, and the Sampling Theorem, all of which refer to the same concept.

Shannon alludes to the fact that his theorem had already been well accepted in the field of communications but had not yet been proven. Nyquist was actually frustrated by the result of his work because his interest was in transmitting audio for telephone lines, which had been shown to have valid frequency content up to 15kHz, meaning that he would have to sample the waveforms 30,000 times per second, a rate that was not sustainable on equipment of that time.

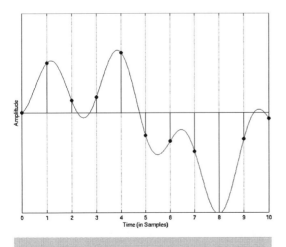

FIGURE 9.2A: A Sampled Waveform

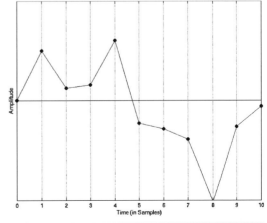

FIGURE 9.2B: A Misrepresentation of How Digitally Sampled Material is Reconstructed

Oftentimes the sampling theorem is misunderstood to infer the obvious about waveforms, that since a waveform has a compression wave and a rarefaction wave that the general frequency content of the wave could be noted by digital sampling but without appropriate amplitude or phase accuracy. An example of this misinterpretation is shown in Figure 9.2.

The waveform in Figure 9.2A is shown digitally sampled according to the Nyquist Theorem. Figure 9.2B shows a misinterpretation of how the waveform is often thought to be reconstructed. Clearly the two waveforms are not the same. Nyquist's Theorem, as substantiated by Shannon's proof, however, tells us that the waveform can and will be reconstructed to exactly the same waveform that was originally sampled. In other words, the waveform in Figure 9.2A, after being properly sampled and reconstructed, will look exactly like the waveform in Figure 9.2A.

The simplified understanding that yields the waveform in Figure 9.2B is specifically *not* what Shannon mathematically proved. He writes, "The intuitive justification is that, if f(t) contains no frequencies higher than W, it cannot change to a substantially new value in a time less than one-half cycle of the highest frequency, that is, 1/2W. A mathematical proof showing that this is not only approximately, but *exactly*, true can be given as follows." What Shannon is referring to is something that we have already determined in Chapter Four: that band-limited waveforms exhibit very predictable behavior in that they cannot have any content in them that is indicative of higher frequency content. Since higher frequency content is needed in order to create sharp edges or straight lines in a waveform, any waveform without those frequencies will behave in a specific and mathematically determinable fashion. The behavior of the waveform is such that sampling it twice for the highest frequency that is contained within it *completely* determines the entire waveform. The mathematical proof of this is substantial, complex and beyond the scope of this book.

In essence the proof tells us that if we take a waveform that is restricted to a certain set of frequencies, sampling it twice will give us enough information to reconstruct the original waveform. The reconstruction of that waveform, however, involves somehow recreating the waveform through the sample points in a manner that resembles the original waveform. At first glance it may seem that this would not be possible because the sampling points do not give a comprehensive enough description of exactly what happens with the waveform between the sample points. Nyquist and Shannon say, however, that what happens between the sample points can be completely determined based on the requirements given – that the waveform contain only specific frequencies, and that the samples be taken at a specific and related frequency. The only way that a waveform, band-limited to the same frequencies as the original, can be recreated through the original sampling points is in the same manner that the original signal passed through those points.

Figure 9.3 shows a waveform that has been sampled, indicating certain sampling points. Several different methods of recreating the waveforms are also shown, each of which shows that it contains the same frequency content within the "legal" band. All of the alternatives, however, also show frequency content *above* the legal band. A Fourier Transform analysis of each of the alternate recreations is shown along with the waveforms (Figures 9.3A-9.3J).

All of the potential alternate reconstructions of the waveform utilizing the sampling points in Figure 9.3A produce artifacts that are above the Nyquist frequency and therefore do not conform to the Nyquist Theorem. The only method of reconstructing a waveform using the sampling points in Figure 9.3A and not exceeding the determined limiting frequency is using the waveform in Figure 9.3A, per the Shannon proof of the Nyquist Theorem.

The only way that a waveform can be reconstructed within the legal range is in the fashion with which it originally occurred. Shannon's Theorem essentially unveils the mathematical law that a waveform can only be drawn through a series of points along an axis one possible way if it is band-limited to half of the sample rate. Said another way, limiting the bandwidth and sampling at the appropriate rate limits the number of valid

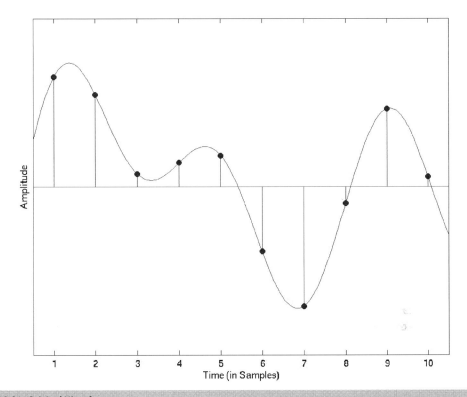

FIGURE 9.3A: Original Waveform

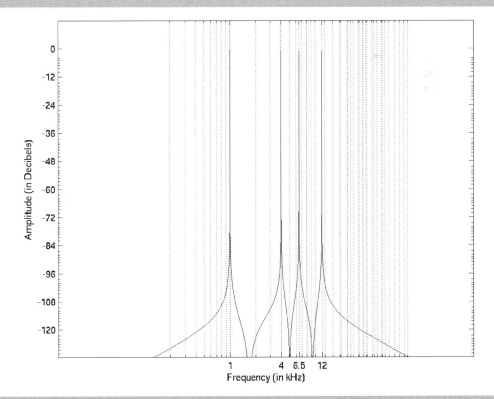

FIGURE 9.3B: Spectrograph of the Waveform in Figure 9.3A

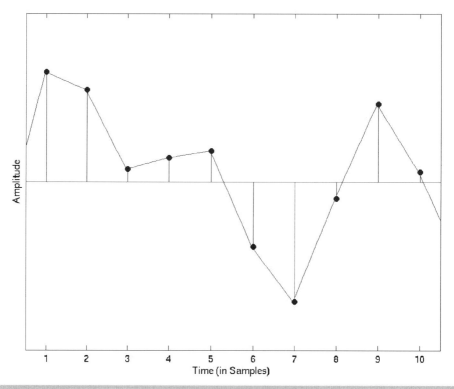

FIGURE 9.3C: A Potential Reconstruction of the Sampling Points in Figure 9.3A

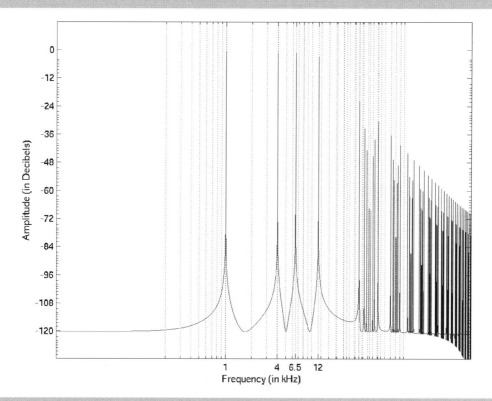

FIGURE 9.3D: Spectrograph of the Waveform in Figure 9.3C

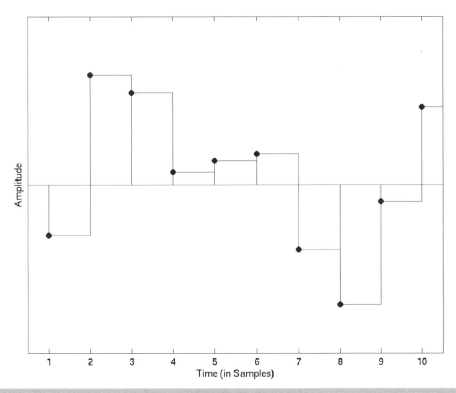

FIGURE 9.3E: A Potential Reconstruction of the Sampling Points in Figure 9.3A

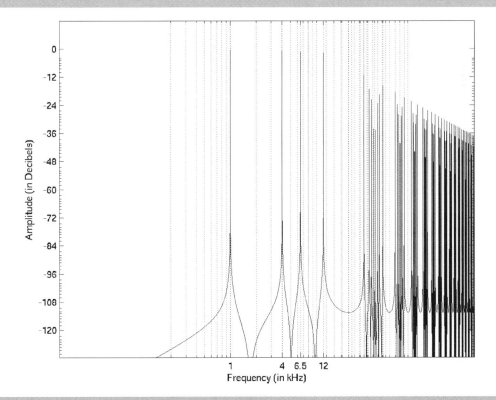

FIGURE 9.3F: Spectrograph of the Waveform in Figure 9.3E

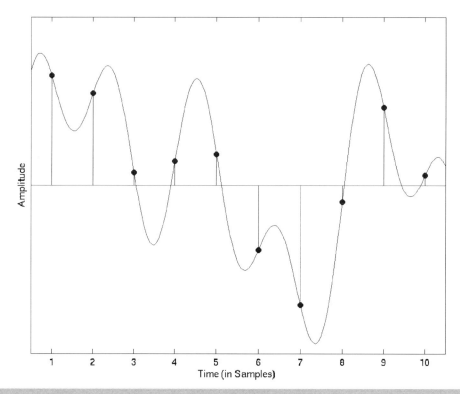

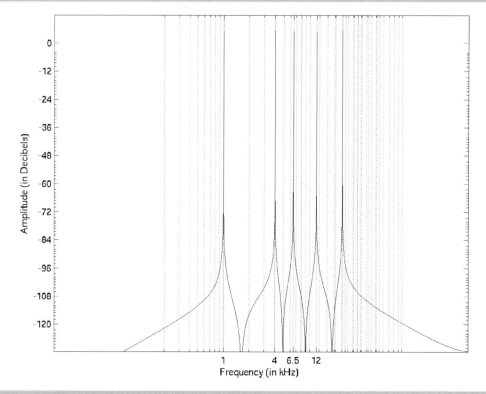

FIGURE 9.3H: Spectrograph of the Waveform in Figure 9.3G

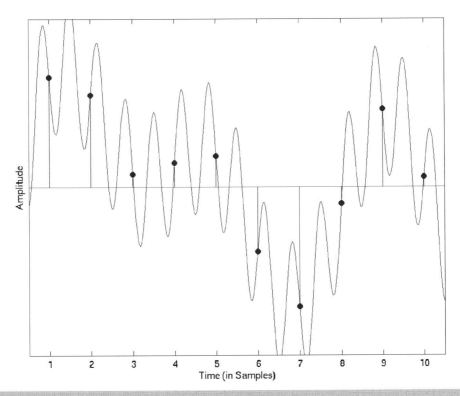

FIGURE 9.3I: A Potential Reconstruction of the Sampling Points in Figure 9.3A

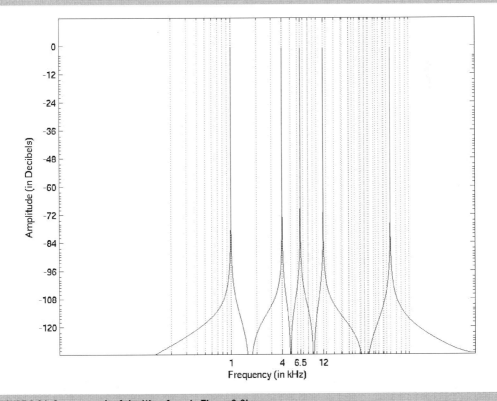

FIGURE 9.3J: Spectrograph of the Waveform in Figure 9.3I

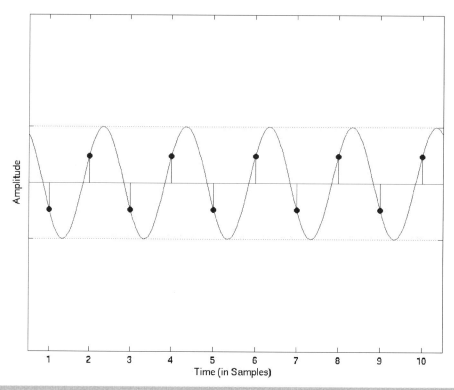

FIGURE 9.4A: Original Waveform

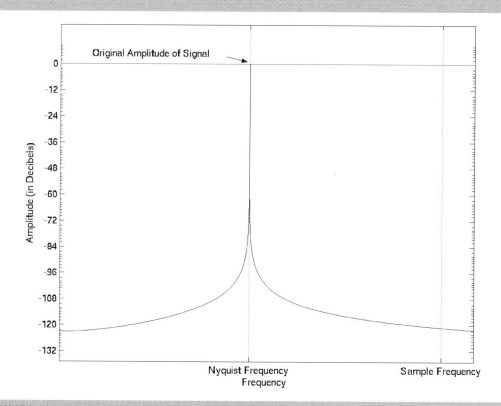

FIGURE 9.4B: Spectrograph of the Waveform in Figure 9.4A

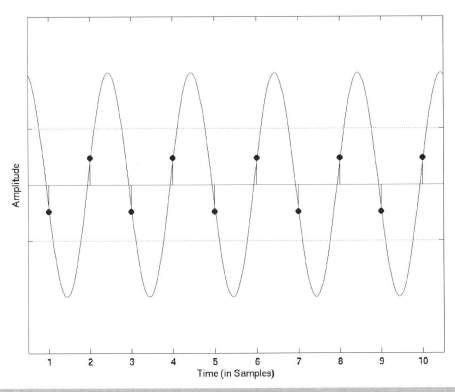

FIGURE 9.4C: A Potential Reconstruction of the Sampling Points in Figure 9.4A

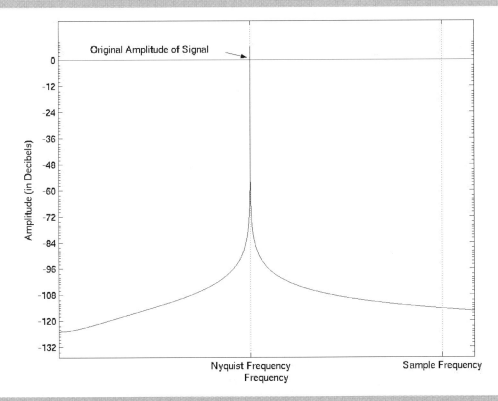

FIGURE 9.4D: Spectrograph of the Waveform in Figure 9.4C

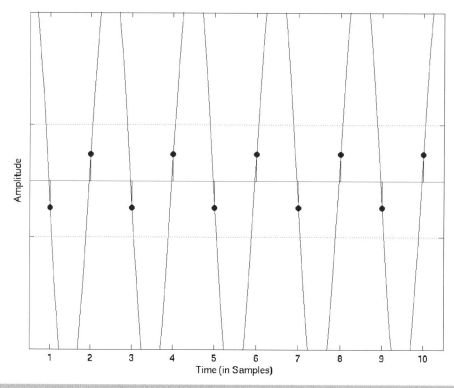

FIGURE 9.4E: A Potential Reconstruction of the Sampling Points in Figure 9.4A

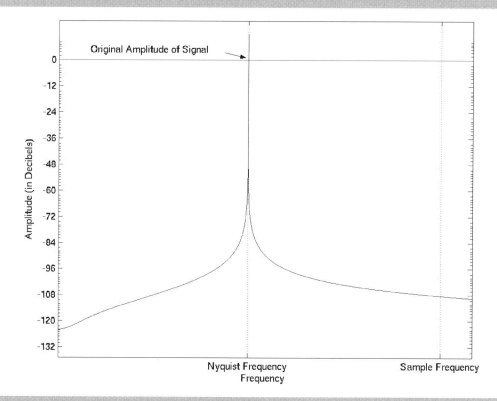

FIGURE 9.4F: Spectrograph of the Waveform in Figure 9.4E

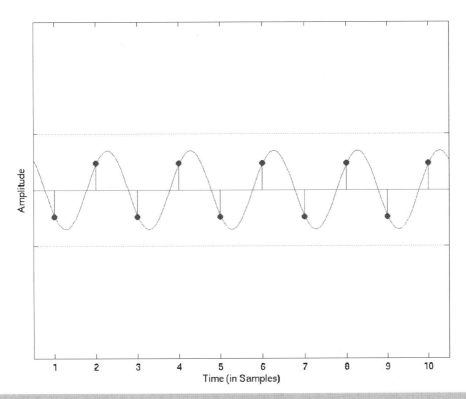

FIGURE 9.4G: A Potential Reconstruction of the Sampling Points in Figure 9.4A

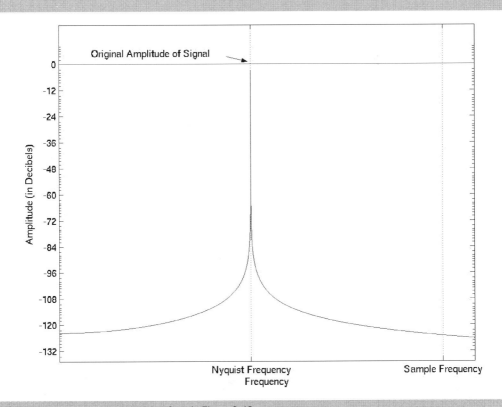

FIGURE 9.4H: Spectrograph of the Waveform in Figure 9.4G

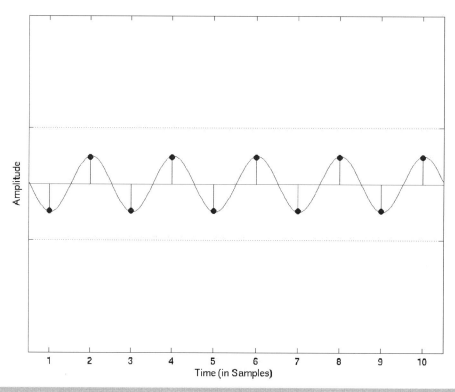

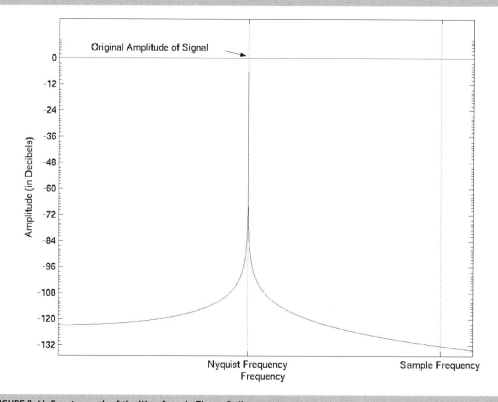

lines to connect the dots to exactly one. The actual methodology for *recreating* the original waveform will be discussed later.

HALF THE SAMPLING RATE

The frequency at half of the sampling frequency is called the "Nyquist Frequency." The Nyquist Theorem holds true with waveforms that are at exactly the Nyquist Frequency (for a 30kS/s sampling rate, frequencies at exactly 15kHz) but only if the sampling continues forever. A waveform at exactly half the sampling rate will be sampled exactly once per half cycle (compression or rarefaction cycle) and there are many possible ways to recreate a "legal" waveform through those two sampling points as seen in Figure 9.4.

When sampling frequencies that are precisely at the Nyquist Frequency, the Nyquist Theorem no longer works as multiple methods of reconstructing the original waveform can be used, all of which create only frequencies that are within the bounds of the Nyquist Theorem.

The Fourier Transform analysis of each waveform provided in Figure 9.4 shows that each waveform presented is indeed "legal" as each contains exactly the same frequencies and none of them contain frequencies above half the sampling rate. Each, however, contains frequencies of differing amplitudes and phases. If this waveform continues on indefinitely and we continue to sample it for an infinitely long period of time then exactly half the sampling frequency would still be capable of being captured accurately. In reality we treat the Shannon Theorem to say that the waveforms to be sampled must be *less than* half the sample frequencies. This way we do not have to deal with infinite numbers of samples over an infinite duration of time. Even if the frequency is just slightly less than half the sampling frequency, and the samples are taken at the "zero crossing," enough information is still captured to accurately redraw the waveform. Even if the samples are taken when the waveform's amplitude is a minutely small increment above the zero crossing there would still be only one legal way of recreating the waveform through said sample points.

This bears repeating. So long as a waveform contains only frequency content at less than half the sampling frequency there is only one possible way of recreating the waveform that fits within the required frequency boundaries. Even if the samples are taken at very low amplitudes, the waveform represented by them can only yield one result when properly reconstructed, and will be reconstructed at the same amplitude as the original waveform.

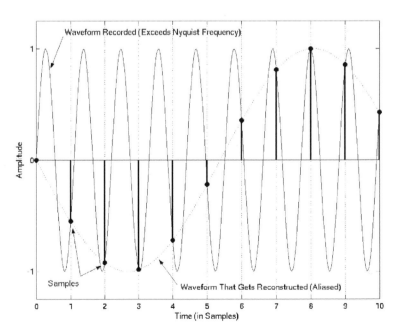

FIGURE 9.5: Aliasing

Aliasing occurs when frequencies above the Nyquist Frequency are sampled. The waveform that gets reconstructed is different than the waveform that is sampled, as can be seen above.

ALIASING

If the material to be sampled contains frequency content above the Nyquist Frequency then a type of distortion to the signal called "aliasing" occurs (Figure 9.5). If frequencies above the Nyquist Frequency are present then the samples will not be taken twice per highest frequency, but will be *assumed* to have been taken twice per highest frequency and the signal will be reconstructed differently than it original existed.

Since there is only one possible way to reconstruct a "legal" signal through the sampling points, and since we assume that the waveform is indeed a legal waveform and will be reconstructed as a legal waveform, any frequencies *above* the Nyquist Frequency will be re-created as frequencies *below* the Nyquist Frequency. The frequencies created are actually very predictable and mathematically determinable. The Nyquist Frequency acts as a sort of mirror in that any frequency content above it gets mirrored around it and creates frequency content below it. See Figure 9.6.

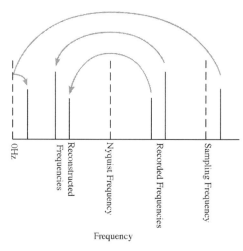

Frequency

FIGURE 9.6: The Mirroring Effect of Aliasing

When aliasing occurs the frequency of the signal that is recorded "mirrors" around the Nyquist Frequency when reconstructed. If the frequency of the recorded signal is above the sampling frequency then the reconstructed result "mirrors" around the Nyquist Frequency and "bounces" off of 0Hz.

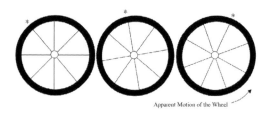

Apparent Motion of the Wheel

FIGURE 9.7: Aliasing on Film

In films a car's wheels are sometimes seen moving backwards when the car is moving forwards because the "sampling" done by the picture frames in the film occurs slower than the movement of the wheels. In the progression above from left to right, as the identified spoke moves clockwise, the apparent effect is that the wheel moves counterclockwise.

If the frequency content sampled is higher than the Nyquist frequency and is also higher than the *sampling* frequency then the aliasing mirrors again around 0Hz such that if the sampling frequency is 30kS/s and a waveform of 31kHz is sampled then it will create a sampled waveform of 1kHz. As the frequency content in the waveform being sampled continues to rise, the mirroring continues to bounce around between 0Hz and the Nyquist Frequency so that any frequency, clear up into the megahertz or gigahertz range or beyond will create aliasing content within the legal range of frequencies.

A visual example of aliasing can be seen in the movies when a car is shown accelerating. Since the movie is a series of visual "samples" occurring 24 times per second, the position of the spokes on a car's wheels are shown speeding up until the speed of the wheels is faster than the "legal" speed for the sampling rate. As the wheels pass this point the wheels appear to come to a stop because the samples are taken at a rate such that the wheels' spokes appear to be at the same position when the pictures are taken. As the car speeds up beyond this speed the wheels appear to move backward because the position of the wheels moves faster than the pictures allow demonstration of, as is shown in Figure 9.7. This is aliasing, and the wheels' apparent speed mirrors around a certain speed, dependant upon how many spokes are on the wheel and how many samples are taken per second.

Aliasing can actually be used in a beneficial capacity. Since aliasing is predictable, mathematically determinable, and organized as simple mirroring around the two outside boundaries of the legal range, much higher frequencies can be sampled using these principles, so long as they use a narrow frequency band. For example, if the sampling frequency is 30kS/s then as the frequencies to be sampled increase between 0Hz and 15kHz they are accurately sampled. As they increase from 15kHz to 30kHz they are mirrored backwards and decrease from 15kHz to 0kHz. As the frequencies to be sampled increase from 30kHz to 45kHz the resultant frequencies are represented as increasing between 0kHz and 15kHz again. This means that if the waveforms to be sampled are band-limited to a specific range such as 30kHz to 45kHz then they can be represented by sampling at only 30kS/s, though the results of this are going to be represented between 0kHz and 30kHz. Additional processes can return this material again to the range of 30kHz to 45kHz. The practical implications of this in the audio industry are few, but scientific research can use much lower sampling rates to sample material that has a limited bandwidth that may be up in the megahertz range. Material between, say, 1MHz and 1.05MHz (a 50kHz bandwidth) can be accurately sampled using only a 100kS/s sampling frequency, so long as the results are interpreted properly. If any material below 1MHz or above 1.05MHz were to be introduced then unwanted aliasing would occur causing a distortion in the interpreted information.

For the sake of audio we will be discussing aliasing as a type of distortion and not as a beneficial occurrence. Even though aliasing occurs at mathematically predictable frequencies, the frequencies that are generated are most likely not harmonically related to the original frequencies or to the other frequencies present in the original waveform and therefore create *in*harmonic content. Let us, for a moment, consider how a square wave would be sampled. If a square wave existed at 5kHz then we know that it contains harmonic content of 5kHz, 15kHz, 25kHz, 35kHz, 45kHz, 55kHz, and so on, each with decreasing amplitudes. If we tried to sample this square wave with a sampling frequency of 48kS/s then all of the harmonics in the square wave below 24kHz would be accurately captured but all of the harmonics above 24kHz would alias back into the range from 0Hz to 24kHz. This is shown in Figures 9.8 and 9.9.

Note that the original square wave content is harmonic in nature, as the frequencies that exist are at odd multiples of the fundamental. In the sampled version, the additional frequencies added are not related to the fundamental and are therefore inharmonic and the audible results from this are a harsh, brittle sounding type of distortion. The only situation where aliasing would be considered acceptable would be when it is created well enough below the noise floor that it is masked by the noise floor and is therefore inaudible. If the square wave we intended to record was at, say 100Hz and 40dB SPL then the mathematical formula for a square wave tells us that the harmonic content of the square wave that exists at 24.1kHz would be no greater in amplitude than $^1/_{120}$th the amplitude of the 100Hz fundamental, or -1dB SPL. As this is well below the threshold of human

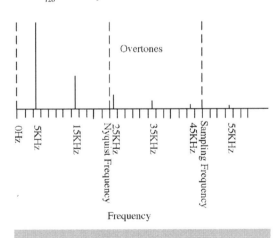

FIGURE 9.8: Sampling a 5kHz Square Wave

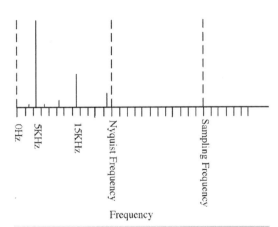

FIGURE 9.9: Reconstruction of a 5kHz Sampled Square Wave

The 5kHz square wave's overtones almost all end up above the Nyquist Frequency, thus "mirror" or "fold back" into the tolerable range upon reconstruction, creating an undesirable, distorted result.

hearing at that frequency, the aliasing created from sampling this square wave is inconsequential and is not audible. Aliasing (as with any other type of audio signal) is only important for us if it is audible. Aliasing that occurs below the noise floor is inconsequential to us (Figure 9.10).

Again, for the sake of accurate audio sampling and reproduction, aliasing is only a negative characteristic if it is above the threshold of hearing within whatever noise is present.

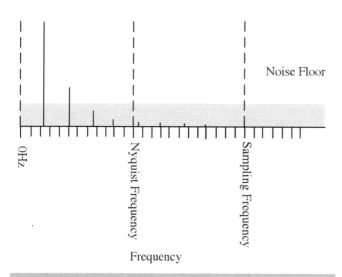

FIGURE 9.10: Aliasing Resulting in Artifacts Below the Noise Floor

If the waveform represented in the diagram above were to be sampled some aliasing would occur due to the fact that frequency information exists above the Nyquist Frequency. The aliased artifacts would be so far below the noise floor, however, that the distortion resulting would be inaudible and is therefore not of concern.

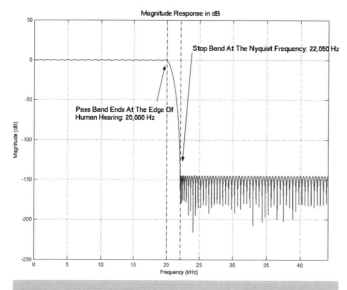

FIGURE 9.11: An Anti-Aliasing Filter

The anti-aliasing filter removes all content above the Nyquist Frequency in order to prevent aliasing

In order to prevent aliasing from occurring, a filter is put in place to prevent any frequency content above the Nyquist Frequency from getting into the recording process. This "anti-aliasing filter" needs to allow all of the frequency content within the human hearing range to pass but attenuate all of the information between the top of the hearing range and the Nyquist Frequency. We will discuss filters later, but building what is called a "brick wall" filter that has an infinitely steep slope is impossible. The filters therefore "roll off" all of the high frequencies over a frequency range so that at one frequency the filter has no effect but with a smooth slope it tapers off to fully "attenuating" frequencies at and above the Nyquist Frequency. A typical anti-aliasing filter's response is shown in Figure 9.11.

QUANTIZING

The purpose of digital sampling is to take the analog waveform and turn it into a series of numbers that represent the waveform. This is done by measuring the amplitude of the waveform at uniform increments of time and assigning numerical values to those amplitude levels. Being that the amplitude levels are analog voltage levels, the values that are then measured can vary by infinitely small increments. Somehow the value that is sampled has to be "rounded" to a certain, close voltage level. We will therefore need to determine how many voltage options are required between the bottom and the top of the scale to which the amplitudes are to be rounded. We also need to determine at what specific values those voltage levels are to be placed. A demonstration of this rounding is shown in Figure 9.12. The number of quantization steps required is directly tied to the amplitude at which the signal is sent into the system. Figure 9.13 hints to us that we need to be aware of the amplitude of the quantization steps in relation to the amplitude of the signal we feed into the system and adjust accordingly.

An arbitrary voltage level is used as the maximum level and 0V is used as the lowest level, and all of the various voltage levels are in the middle at equal increments apart. These amplitude levels are called "quanta" or "quantization steps." To determine how many quantization steps are necessary we need to determine what the effect on the audio is of having to round ("quantize") the waveform to the closest quantization step.

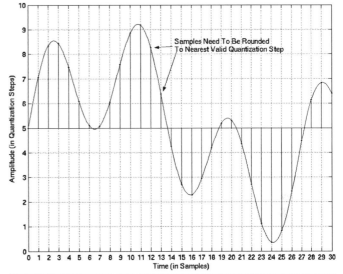

When a waveform's values are quantized, the shape of the waveform inherently changes. We learned in Chapter Three that all waveforms are created by adding different frequencies together. In order to take one waveform and turn it into another waveform additional frequencies must be added to it. Therefore the original waveform is actually still present, but some additional harmonic content will have been added by the process of quantizing (Figure 9.14).

FIGURE 9.12: Rounding to the Nearest Level

The two waveforms above are identical other than their amplitude. In order to sample effectively the signal amplitude has to be appropriate for the amplitude of the levels in the sampling system.

The actual voltage level recorded is irrelevant, as the equipment prior to this stage can turn the amplitude up as high or down as low as is necessary so that the amplitude of the waveform is fulfilling the entire range of levels (Figure 9.13).

We already know that we add two waveforms together by summing them together "point for point", or at each successive increment of time. We can also, then, determine that the waveform that is added to the original waveform to create the quantized waveform is simply the subtraction of the quantized waveform and the original waveform. In other words, if we subtract the original waveform from the quantized waveform we get a result that is the waveform that was added by the action of quantizing. Since quantizing a waveform inherently changes its shape, this can be said to introduce "error" into the signal. The error that gets added to any particular sample value by the process of quantizing is called "quantization error." Therefore if the original waveform is subtracted from the sampled waveform the difference signal is the quantized error signal.

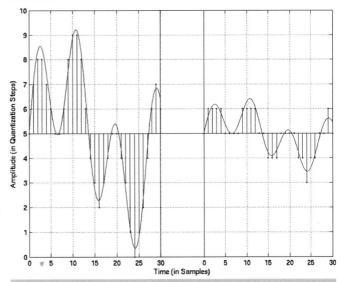

FIGURE 9.13: The Levels For Recording Need to be Appropriate

The quantization error from a signal is related to the signal itself. While on a complex waveform the values of the quantization error from sample to sample may seem to be nearly random, they are in fact determined by the original waveform. A 10.25kHz waveform, sampled at 44.1kS/s will repeat its sample values ad infinitum. Because of this the quantization error that is added to the signal is also repeated. If a signal is added to the waveform that is random we know that this creates the addition of noise to the signal, thereby lowering the dynamic range of the waveform. If, however, a signal is added to a waveform that is *not* random but is in fact *correlated* to the waveform itself then it creates distortion instead of noise. Quantization error is in fact distortion and all quantization errors on every sample are in fact related to the characteristics of the waveform itself. If the waveform is repeated then the quantization error is repeated, making it decidedly *not* random. The name for the distortion yielded to a waveform through quantization is called "quantization distortion."

If, however, a random noise waveform is sampled then the quantization error induced will be as random as the noise waveform itself. While it is still related to the noisy waveform in the same manner described above, and is therefore "distortion" of the noise, such distortion is as random as the noise itself and can therefore be considered simply additional random noise. If a noise waveform is sampled there is no statistical probability that any sample is any closer to one quantization step than it is to another. There is as little of a chance of the waveform hitting the quantization step dead-on as there is to it being halfway between two steps. The statistical probability of the waveform being at any amplitude in relation to the nearest quantization step is completely random. An example is shown in Figure 9.15.

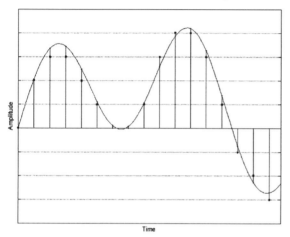

FIGURE 9.14: **The Waveform in Figure 9.12 After Quantizing**

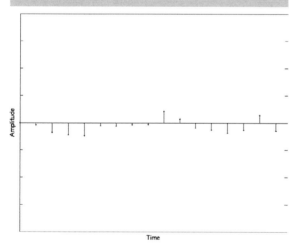

FIGURE 9.15: **The Random Probability of Quantization Error**

When properly sampled, the statistical probability of a waveform being any closer to any given quantization step is random. Therefore, the quantization error signal yields noise.

The waveform that is created by quantizing noise is simply a stream of random values. In Chapter Five we learned that this (a stream of random amplitudes, or sample values) is specifically the definition of noise. Therefore, the difference between the original waveform and the quantized waveform is actually just pure, random noise, or, said the other way, the waveform added to a noise waveform that creates a quantized waveform is pure, random noise. In this case the noise is white noise and its makeup is not Gaussian in probability, but is rather completely random in probability and has the title "Rectangular Probability Density Function," or "RPDF" noise. This noise (that is created by the process of quantizing a random signal) can be called "quantization noise" as opposed to "quantization distortion." See Figure 9.16.

The amplitude of the noise is also easy to determine. We know that the noise is not going to have a greater amplitude at any one sample than half of the size of a quantization step. We know this because if the amplitude of the waveform is more than one half an amplitude step away from a quantization step then it will not be rounded to that step but will rather be rounded to its next closest step. The maximum quantization error (rounding error) is shown in Figure 9.17).

Because quantization really happens as a result of rounding to the next closest step, the amplitude of the quantization noise or quantization distortion is never greater than half of the amplitude of the quantization steps. If the quantization steps are .1V apart then the quantization error will not ever be greater than .05V, or half of the amplitude difference of the quantization steps. We learned in Chapter Two that doubling the amplitude of a waveform raises its amplitude 6dB. We can also infer from this that half of the amplitude is a loss of 6dB. If the

quantization error is (at most) half of the amplitude of the difference in quantization steps then the quantization noise or distortion is 6dB less then the amplitude difference of those steps. We could also say that the quantization noise is half of the amplitude of the *first* quantization step, as the amplitude of the first step is the same as the difference between each successive step.

We therefore know exactly what happens when we quantize a waveform: *quantizing a waveform adds distortion to the waveform at an amplitude of 6dB less than the amplitude of the first quantization step.*

If, however, the sampled waveform is random noise, then when we quantize a waveform we add *white noise to the waveform at an amplitude of 6dB less than the amplitude of the first quantization step.*

We would much rather have white noise added to our waveforms than distortion. One way to accomplish this is to add some noise to the waveform prior to the sampling process. If we add white noise that is of a mathematically required amplitude then we can randomize the quantization error with respect to the noise that is present rather than simply quantizing the signal itself. This way the error that gets added to the waveform is randomized and not predictable and we add white noise to the waveform instead of distortion during sampling. In actuality, we do not need to actually *add* noise to a waveform because all waveforms inherently have noise in them anyway. We must simply ensure that the amplitude of the noise is high enough with

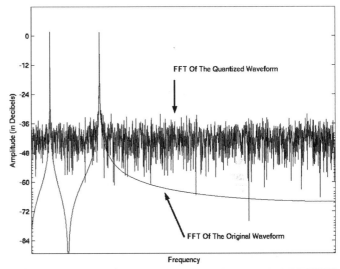

FIGURE 9.16A: FFT of a Waveform Before Quantization

This FFT analysis shows the difference between the FFT of a simple waveform prior to being sampled and an FFT of it after it is quantized.

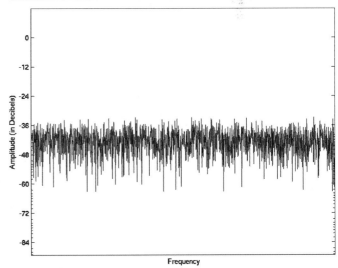

FIGURE 9.16B: The Difference of the Signals in Figure 9.16A

The difference signal between the two signals in Figure 9.16A showing that the error added to the signal because of quantization manifests itself as noise.

respect to the amplitude of the quantization steps to ensure that the quantization error yielded is randomized. This way the quantization error yielded from sampling any given waveform is white noise instead of distortion. Therefore, proper quantizing of a waveform requires that the amplitude of the noise within the waveform be high enough to ensure that the quantization error is white noise. Since the amplitude of the quantization error will be lower than the amplitude of the noise that was already within the waveform, the addition of this quantization noise is of low amplitude and is often inconsequential. We will learn in Chapter Fifteen exactly how much higher the amplitude of the noise within the signal must be than the amplitude of the quantization steps in order to ensure that the quantization noise that is produced is truly random.

We need to remember that properly quantizing a waveform does not take anything *away* from the waveform; it only adds noise. All of the original waveform is still present and nothing was removed, but noise was simply added to it.

Now that we know what happens when we quantize the waveform, the next thing we need to determine is how many quantization steps are actually needed to describe the waveform without changing the four identifying characteristics of that waveform. We already know that quantizing a signal is not going to change its amplitude (because the amplitude of the signal is determined by how much we turn it up, and therefore all we are concerned with in regards to amplitude is the amplitude of certain frequencies relative to each other). Quantizing a waveform does not remove or add frequency content other than the addition of the noise, nor does it affect the phase of the waveform. All that quantizing does is add noise, which affects only the dynamic range of the waveform. What we need to do is make sure that the quantization noise is more than 25dB lower than the white noise floor of our material. This will ensure that the quantization noise that is added is lower than the quietest content in the waveform that we can hear.

We established in Chapter Two that the dynamic range of different waveforms varies depending on the noise level in the room being recorded, the equipment being used and the overall amplitude of the signal. The "audible" dynamic range is up to 25dB greater than the dynamic range from the peak amplitude to the amplitude of the white noise floor. If the quantization noise is more than 25dB below the noise level of the signal then the quantization noise will have no audible effect on the signal and will thus not affect our dynamic range. We simply need to determine how to ensure that the quantization noise stays that low.

If we record a pure sine wave with only two quantization steps (which is the minimum) then the quantization error we add will be 6dB less than sine wave's amplitude because the error added is half of the overall amplitude of the waveform. An example is shown in Figure 9.18.

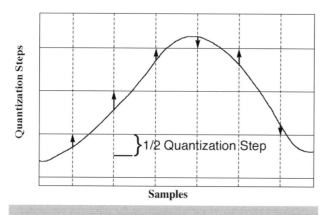

FIGURE 9.17: Rounding Error

The maximum amount of quantization error is +/- 1/2 quantization step. Any more than that and it would round to the next step.

Therefore, two quantization steps of recording give us a maximum of 6dB of dynamic range (though in reality two quantization steps cannot accurately represent 6dB of dynamic range because the noise would not be able to be of a high enough amplitude to ensure that the quantization error was random). If we double the number of quantization steps then the amplitude of the noise halves and the dynamic range doubles to 12dB. If we double the quantization steps again we again reduce the amplitude of each quantization step by half. This subsequently lowers the quantization noise level by half. Lowering the noise level by half lowers it an additional 6dB, thereby increasing the dynamic range of the system by 6dB. We can therefore determine that each doubling of the number of quantization steps (starting with two) gives us 6dB of additional dynamic range. To determine the number of quantization steps necessary to capture a signal in an audibly perfect capacity all we need to do is determine the audible dynamic range of a signal and use enough quantization steps to ensure that the digital system's dynamic range capability exceeds that. We can do this by taking the dynamic range of the signal and figure out how many times 6dB divides into it. That is how many times we need to double the number of quantization steps we need (starting with two). The mathematical formula that yields this number is as follows:

If Q is the number of quantization steps and D is the dynamic range then

$$Q = 2^{(D/6)}, \text{ or } D = 6 \, Log_2 \, Q$$

It may seem counterintuitive that only two quantization steps can describe a complete waveform with all of its complexity and detail, but it very effectively does. Any portion of that waveform that is present with an amplitude quieter than 6dB below the peak will be present but below the level of all of the induced quantization error created by the sampling process. The fact that two quantization steps are actually able to completely describe a waveform (albeit with added distortion) will become a crucial concept as we talk about current recording techniques. Most of the digital recording world today is actually dependant on the ability for two quanta to record audio accurately, as we will see in Chapter Eleven.

Using the formulas above we can discern that 48dB of dynamic range can be obtained by using 256 quanta and that 96dB of dynamic range will require 65,536 quanta. To obtain 144dB of dynamic range (better than the human ear can handle) 16,777,216 quantization steps are necessary

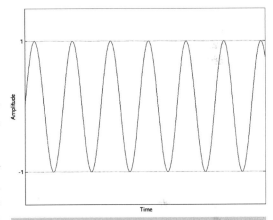

FIGURE 9.18A: A Sine Wave

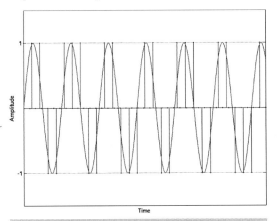

FIGURE 9.18B: The Waveform in Figure 9.18A Quantized to 1 Bit

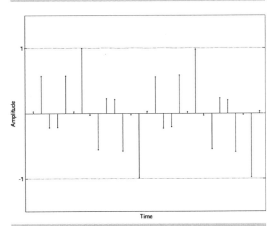

FIGURE 9.18C: The Difference Between Figure 9.18A and Figure 9.18B

The difference signal between the original signal and the quantized signal in Figure 9.18B shows the quantization error from quantizing the signal to only 1 bit.

Figure 9.19 shows a waveform prior to sampling and its Fourier Transform. It also shows the waveform after being sampled and conformed to very few quantization steps. The Fourier Transform plots show us that indeed all frequency content in the original waveform was maintained, but the dynamic range was affected by the sampling process. The increased noise floor in Figure 9.119D is evidence of this.

We now know how to turn analog voltages of waveforms representing air pressure waves into streams of numbers. First we sample the amplitude of the voltage a certain number of times per second dependent on the frequency limits of the audio band. Then we round each of those voltage levels to the nearest quantization step; the more the quantization steps the larger the dynamic range that this methodology is capable of representing. All we need to do at this point is turn the quantization steps into binary PCM code so that the digital numbers can be transmitted or recorded. We learned in Chapter Eight how to determine how many binary digits are necessary to represent a value with the formula $n = \log_v R$. This tells us how many "bits" or digital numbers in a word will be necessary to transmit an accurate dynamic range for the audibility of the human ear.

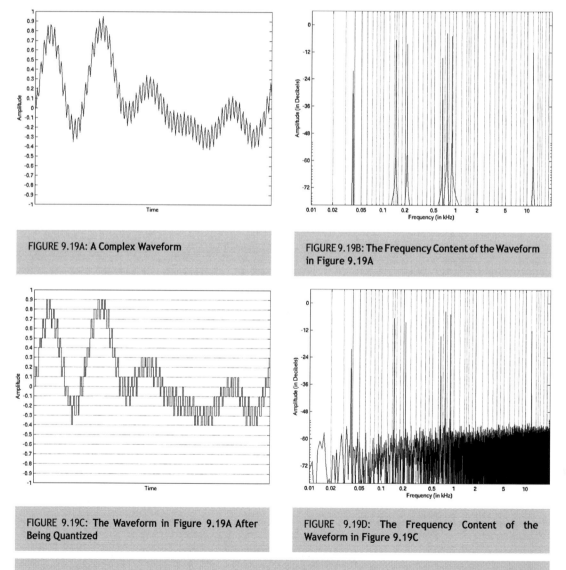

FIGURE 9.19A: A Complex Waveform

FIGURE 9.19B: The Frequency Content of the Waveform in Figure 9.19A

FIGURE 9.19C: The Waveform in Figure 9.19A After Being Quantized

FIGURE 9.19D: The Frequency Content of the Waveform in Figure 9.19C

Figure 9.19D shows that all of the frequency content of the waveform in Figure 9.19A was recorded during the sampling process, though much additional content is added in the form of quantization error because of the sampling process.

We can further simplify the formulas to tell us that when using binary coding, the number of bits (digits) necessary to transmit a number is equal to the dynamic range divided by (approximately) six.

Therefore, if we wish to transmit a dynamic range of 72dB, for example, we need to use 12 bits (72/6).

When we use enough bits to transmit a waveform we are able to transmit the entire dynamic range of the waveform completely transparently for the benefit of the human auditory system. If we use more bits than are necessary then we do not gain any benefits as far as the human auditory is concerned. The waveform will sound completely accurate with the fewest number of required bits, and more bits only lowers the quantization noise further below the noise inherent in the waveform. If this noise is already below the lowest level we can hear then the waveform does not sound any different if we lower the level of the quantization noise even further.

GAIN STAGING

When we convert analog audio into digital numbers we need to have the entire range of analog audio fit into the established range of quantization steps. The waveform has to be set at an appropriate amplitude so that the

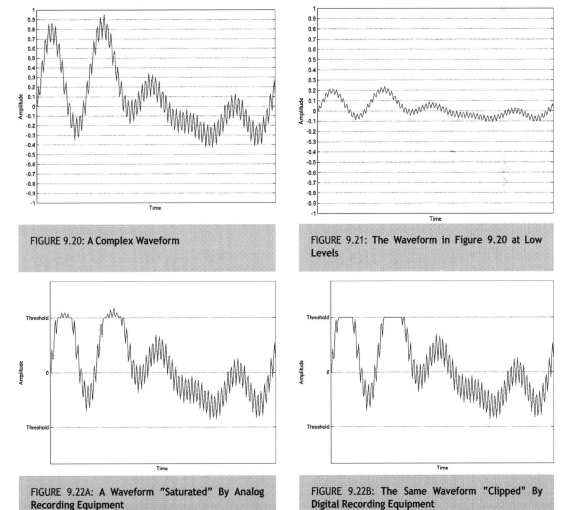

FIGURE 9.20: A Complex Waveform

FIGURE 9.21: The Waveform in Figure 9.20 at Low Levels

FIGURE 9.22A: A Waveform "Saturated" By Analog Recording Equipment

FIGURE 9.22B: The Same Waveform "Clipped" By Digital Recording Equipment waveform can be captured without losing any of its dynamic range, but not so high that it exceeds the range of quantization steps (Figure 9.20).

If the amplitude of this waveform is too quiet then fewer quanta are essentially used to sample it and the dynamic range may be affected. This acts the same as simply using fewer quantization steps to start with (Figure 9.21).

If the amplitude is too high then it will exceed the highest value allowed and will *clip*. This highest quantization step is called "full scale," and a signal whose amplitude reaches that amplitude at a particular sample is said to "exceed full scale." If a signal is recorded with its amplitude too high overall, the amplitude over several of the samples will exceed full scale and the full scale level will be recorded for each of those samples. The same principle occurs when recording using analog equipment such as analog tape. When the amount of magnetism in the tape is exceeded then the tape is "saturated" and clips the waveform. Clipping a waveform essentially turns a waveform into a square wave, or at least a waveform with "square-ish" properties. If a sine wave of very high amplitude clips it gets very close to being a square wave, increasingly so the more over full scale the amplitude gets. An example of a clipped waveform and a saturated waveform are shown in Figure 9.22.

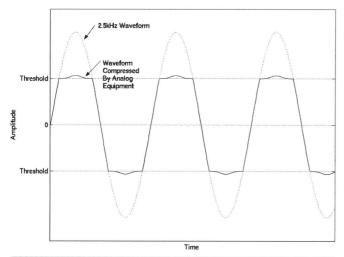

From our study of square waves in Chapter Three we know that they are comprised of odd order harmonics. When clipping a waveform, the more "square" the waveform becomes the more odd order harmonics are added to it. This means that a sine wave at 2.5kHz that has too much amplitude for its recording mechanism and clips produces the odd order harmonic series based on the fundamental. This 2.5kHz waveform yields some 7.5kHz, 12.5kHz, 17.5kHz, 22.5kHz, 27.5kHz, 32.5kHz and on and on, ad infinitum.

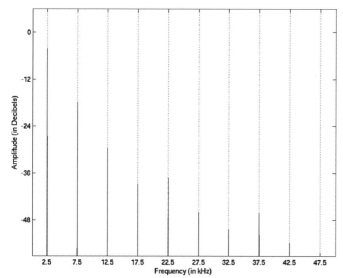

When analog equipment records this waveform that is precisely what is recorded, and when this "saturated," or clipped waveform is reproduced what is heard is 2.5kHz, 7.5kHz, 12.5kHz and 17.5kHz, but all of the other harmonics exceed human hearing abilities and are not heard. Because the overtones that are created by saturating a sine wave (such as our 2.5kHz sine wave) are all harmonic overtones, the result of this is often said to sound "musical" and is a desired effect for certain types of music recording, though this effect is inaccurate with respect to the original audio. As a general rule, slightly saturating analog recording mechanisms creates harmonic overtones that are not considered audibly displeasing. The harmonic effect of saturating a waveform is shown in Figure 9.23.

We remember that an anti-aliasing filter is put in place to prevent the results of the sampling from aliasing. It is after this filter that the sampling actually occurs. If the signal clips in a *digital* recording mechanism then a square-ish wave will be recorded there as well and the same harmonic content will be created. Since, however, the digital system is limited with respect to how high of frequencies can be recorded and reproduced, any frequency content above the Nyquist frequency will alias back into the "legal" range of frequencies. For example, in a 48kS/s sampling system the Nyquist frequency is 24kHz. The 2.5kHz sine wave that heavily clips will create odd order harmonic overtones of 7.5kHz, 12.5kHz, 17.5kHz, 22.5kHz, 27.5kHz, 32.5kHz, 37.5kHz, 42.5kHz, and on and on, ad infinitum. All of the overtones below 24kHz will be accurately reproduced just as they are in analog recording. The overtones from 27.5kHz, to 47.5kHz, however, will

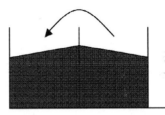

alias, "mirroring" around the Nyquist frequency. The 27.5kHz overtone will mirror around 24kHz and will reproduce as a 21.5kHz overtone. The 33.5kHz overtone will alias and reproduce as a 14.5kHz overtone (Figure 9.24). Each of the overtones up to the 47.5kHz waveform will alias and create overtones that mirror around 24kHz. Again, none of these alias tones are filtered out because this process occurs *after* the application of the anti-aliasing filter.

0Hz   Nyquist   Sampling
                    Frequency

FIGURE 9.24: Aliasing of Harmonics Due To Clipping That Exist Between The Nyquist Frequency And The Sampling Frequency

When clipping occurs, the frequency content created due to the distortion between Nyquist and the sampling frequency fold back, mirroring over the Nyquist frequency, and are reproduced in the "legal" range of 0Hz to the Nyquist Frequency.

All of the overtones above 48kHz and below 72kHz will alias and mirror around 0Hz and the overtones that they create can be ascertained by subtracting 48kHz from the frequency (Figure 9.25). The 52.5kHz overtone will be reproduced at 4.5kHz, etc.

The result when this clipped 2.5kHz waveform is reproduced is that all of the overtones that would have existed above 24kHz and would have been inaudible are now reproduced *in the audible range*. Because these overtones are not whole number multiples of the original waveform they are *in*harmonic overtones and are *not* audibly appealing to the ear. This type of distortion in the digital world is known to sound very harsh for specifically this reason. Because of this, clipping (saturation) in the analog realm sounds very different than clipping in the digital realm.

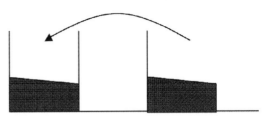

0Hz   Nyquist   Sampling
                    Frequency

DATA CAPACITY

Digital audio is comprised of samples of amplitudes taken at regular intervals of time that are noted in binary codes. Each sample yields a number that is represented by a series of on and off pulses called "bits," eight of which are called a "byte." The larger the range of quantization values the more bits and bytes are

FIGURE 9.25: Aliasing of Harmonics Due To Clipping That Exist Above The Sampling Frequency

When clipping occurs, the frequency content created due to the distortion that exists above sampling frequency folds back similarly to harmonic content below the sampling frequency.

needed for each sample. The number of samples taken per second is dependent upon the range of frequencies that need to be reproduced.

If we establish that 8-bit sampling is adequate then each sample will require one byte of storage capacity to record it, or one byte of transmission capability to communicate it. If we establish that 12-bit sampling or 16-bit sampling or more is required then more storage capacity is needed to record it.

The number of samples per second yields the total speed with which the bits pass. If, as Harry Nyquist determined, 30,000 samples are taken per second and each sample yields, say, 2 bytes (16 bits) then 60,000 bytes (480,000 bits, or pulses) will pass through the digital audio system per second. Because technology that was capable of handling such a high bandwidth of information had not yet been invented, Nyquist was not able to create a digital sampling system for several decades after the publishing of his initial theory. The number of bytes used for each sample, multiplied times the number of samples per second, tells us the bandwidth, or speed with which the digital information needs to pass. This is typically measured in bits (or bytes) per second.

The amount of storage space required for recording the digital audio information can be determined by multiplying the data bandwidth yielded by the sampling by the amount of time that needs to be recorded. If a digital sampling system yields 60,000 bytes per second and the audio lasts for five minutes then we need to multiply 60,000 bytes per second by 300 seconds. This particular piece of audio requires storage capacity of 18,000,000 bytes, or 18MB (18 megabytes). The sheer magnitude of these requirements prevented digital audio from becoming practical for mass use until around 1980.

APPLICATION

We now understand that digital technology is perfectly capable of recording, transmitting, storing, and recreating waveforms, respecting the requirements of the human auditory system. This can happen perfectly, as far as the human auditory system is concerned. Nyquist, Shannon, and others have shown us that amplitude, phase, and frequency information can be accurately recorded if the sample rate is high enough. We know from our understanding of quantization steps that dynamic range can be accurately captured as well. From our understanding of the ear, we can start to determine exactly how the conversion of the analog waveforms into digital numbers needs to be done if it is to be audibly transparent.

Because the ear can hear up to 20kHz, the sampling frequency needs to be at least 40kS/s. If the sampling frequency were 40kS/s then everything below 20kHz would be accurately captured. The only problem with this is that we need to prevent any frequencies above 20kHz from getting into this system. This requires the aforementioned anti-aliasing filter. As we discussed, however, designing filters that are akin to brick walls is impossible. We need some frequency range with which to implement the filter. If the sampling frequency is only 40kS/s then the Nyquist Frequency will be 20kHz, and the filter will roll off over some range of frequencies below 20kHz into our hearing range. Since the goal is to prevent this digital sampling process from having any audible consequences, the sampling frequency needs to be above 40kS/s so that there is room for the anti-aliasing filter to operate without affecting the audible range of frequencies.

44.1kS/s was chosen as the sample rate because it provided adequate enough room for the filter to operate above 20kHz. The Nyquist Frequency would now be 22.05kHz and anti aliasing filters would need to fully attenuate the frequencies at 22.05kHz while allowing 20kHz frequencies to pass unaffected. The 44.1kS/s sample rate stems from clock circuits used in television equipment at the time. Even though compact disks (CDs) have no video component, video equipment was used in the first CD players and was a backbone of CD technology.

After trying 14 bits for consumer media in order to conserve bandwidth, an eventual bit depth of 16 bits was codified for the compact disk. 16 bits is capable of providing 65,536 quantization steps, which provide 96dB of dynamic range capabilities. 96dB of dynamic range was determined to be plenty for most types of recordings as any reproduction of less than 96dB SPL would be more limited by the listening environment than the recording. Further, the only material that could have more than 96dB of valid dynamic range was material that was louder than approximately 96dB SPL at the time of recording (because of the amplitude of atmospheric noise at just below 0dB SPL). The opportunities for audio to have more than 96dB of dynamic range are not common, so 16 bits was determined to be appropriate. Further, most information in the computer industry is handled more efficiently in bytes, so 16 bits gives the opportunity for the data to neatly fall into words of two bytes each.

The CD was originally designed to hold about one hour of music on a smaller disk (11.5cm in diameter). As legend has it, a wife of a Sony executive protested that the disk would not be large enough to hold conductor (and Sony supporter) Herbert von Karajan's version of Beethoven's Ninth Symphony. The current disk, which is 12cm in diameter, was a compromise between size, bandwidth (bit depth and sample frequency), and length of the material it could hold. The finalized implementation was 16 bits and 44.1kS/s in stereo on a 12cm disk, which conveniently allows 74 minutes recording time – presumably enough to hold the entire Ninth Symphony, even at slow tempos.

For these reasons, the CD standard is 16-bit 44.1kS/s, and this standard is now called "CD Quality" and has been written into the governing texts that define how a CD is created.

BEYOND CD QUALITY

Humans have been pushing to improve the quality of recordings since recording first became a possibility. It is without surprise that common people, record companies, audiophiles and audio engineers have been pushing to record with "better than CD quality" sound. The first major, sustained movement was to increase the bit depth of recordings and the delivery media to more than 16 bits. More recently the push has been to raise the sample rates. Now that equipment is readily available to sample at greater than 44.1kS/s and music and other audio can easily be recorded at sample rates up to 192kS/s, murmurings are surfacing that the next improvement will be to again increase the bit depth of the recordings to 32-bit or 32-bit floating-point or more. On top of all of that, the buzzwords "DSD" and "SACD" are emerging and drawing interest. (We will be discussing DSD and SACD comprehensively in later chapters.)

With the understanding that we have now of how digital audio works, can there be any benefit to recording at higher rates for the benefit of the human auditory system? The explanations given above are not incorrect nor are they overly simplistic. The breakdown with CD quality does not have to do with the inability for it to provide audibly perfect sound. The breakdown has to do with the implementation of the digital audio foundations in practice. If the digital audio basis is implemented properly, and if we accept the boundaries of the human auditory system that we defined in Chapter Three, then there can be no benefit to higher sampling rates and there can only be benefit to higher bit depths in extreme (and extremely loud) conditions. Now that we understand what the limitations and requirements of digital audio are, the next task will be to understand how it is implemented, for this is a crucial aspect of the potential success of digital audio to deliver perfect audio reproduction.

With analog recording we discussed that the recording methods themselves were inherently flawed due to the inherent inconsistencies of the media, the "transfer function" of the devices that were used to record the material, and the fact that changes in the media result in changes to the material represented on it. With digital audio the values are absolute. The theory is firm and has been proven. The ability for digital audio to provide perfect audio reproduction is evident on paper. The breakdown only comes with the how the systems are implemented. If perfect implementation is accomplished there will be no potential benefit to using higher sampling rates or higher bit depths. If, however, the errors accumulated throughout the devices involved yield changes to the audio that can be improved with higher sampling rates or bit depths then a plausible notion exists that such advancements are warranted. It is important to recognize at this point, however, that, provided the implementation is accurate enough for human discernability, increasing the bit depth or the sample rate is unnecessary for the sake of recording or playing back audio.

In the ensuing chapters we will discuss the actual hardware and how it converts analog signals into digital signals and back again. We will also discuss how processing these digital numbers occurs so that we will be able to piece together the potential advantages of extending the sampling conventions.

NOTES:

Chapter Ten

Conversion between Analog and Digital

Until now we have been discussing how digital audio works from a conceptual perspective. We now need to discuss how the concepts are actually implemented so that we may understand where potential breakdowns exist and how different types of implementations can yield differing results. From the intuitive approach, since digital audio is merely a series of numbers, the opportunities for problems seem far fewer. Perhaps the largest area for disparity arises in the devices that actually turn analog waveforms into digital numbers and then back again. These devices are called "analog to digital converters" (ADC or A/D converter) and "digital to analog converters" (DAC, or D/A converter), respectively.

Any device that converts analog signals into digital signals, by definition alone, has an analog to digital converter in it, including CD burners with analog inputs, keyboard samplers, computer sound cards with analog inputs, some children's toys, DAT machines, interfaces to digital equipment, digital mixers with analog inputs, digital effects processors and more. Any device that turn turns digital signals into analog signals, by definition alone, has a digital to analog converter in it, including CD players, computer sound cards, musical greeting cards, many children's toys, digital effects processors, digital mixers, digital keyboards and synthesizers, computer interfaces and more. Since most current audio recording and playback is done digitally, nearly anything that plays audio requires a digital to analog converter. The price range of A/D and D/A converters range from a few cents to around $10,000, so something must account for the disparity. In the following chapter we will discuss how the two types of converters are actually made so as to understand any deficiencies in this crucial area of implementation.

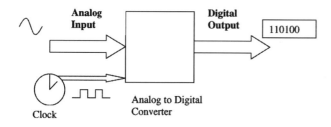

FIGURE 10.1: An Analog to Digital Converter

An analog to digital converter has an input for the analog signal as well as an input for the clock signal that controls the timing of the taking of samples.

PRIMITIVE A/D CONVERTERS

The most primitive type of A/D converter is called a Flash A/D and utilizes a series of resistors in series as a way of converting the signals. The analog signal enters this converter as a series of waves of voltage change that represent the air pressure changes.

A clock of some form sends a stream of pulses to the converter circuit at the speed of the sample rate, indicating when the converter is to take its samples. We will cover the implementation of these clocks much more comprehensively in Chapter Twelve. By default, the voltages fed into a converter bypass all of the conversion circuitry. When the converter components get a clock pulse indicating that they need to take a sample, a device in the converter is triggered to siphon the voltage off and route it through the electrical circuit that does the actual conversion (Figure 10.1).

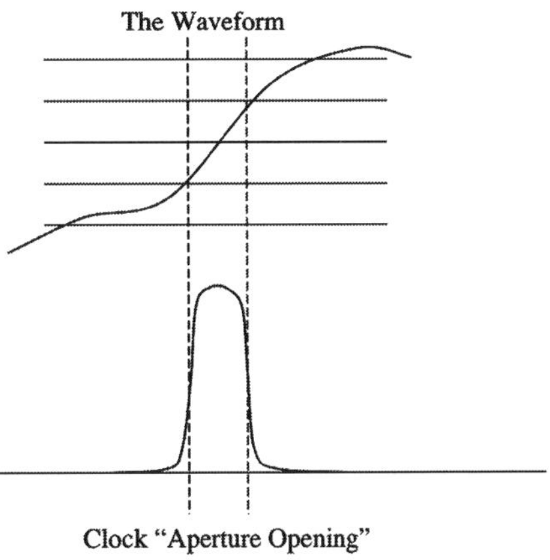

The voltage amount that is siphoned off to the rest of the circuitry is theoretically the amplitude of the voltage of the waveform at an infinitely small amount of time. An example of this "aperture" of the sample taking process is shown in Figure 10.2.

The Waveform

Clock "Aperture Opening"

FIGURE 10.2: **The Timing of the Taking of Samples**

If a clock's aperture opening is wider than an infinitely short amount of time then the waveform can be sampled over wide a time-span, creating a sampling error.

This spike of voltage is then sent into a series of resistors that are scaled to represent all of the quantization steps. The value of the smallest quantization step is represented by a very small-valued resistor while the largest quantization step is represented by a much larger-valued resistor. If, for example, we were to create a converter that covered an amplitude change between 0V and 1V with 64 quantization steps then 64 resistors would be needed. The range between 0V and 1V is equally divided into 64 equal portions.

Ohm's law says that voltage is equal to the product of current and resistance (V=IR) where voltage is measured in volts, current is measured in amperes, and resistance is measured in ohms. If we keep a constant current of, say, 1 amp, then the amount of voltage is equal to the amount of resistance. 1V = 1Ohm (1Ω). 2V = 2Ω. If we need 64 equal steps between 0V and 1V then we need to simply divide 1/64 and determine the value of each resistor. The value of the resistors would be as follows:

0.015625	0.265625	0.515625	0.765625
0.03125	0.28125	0.53125	0.78125
0.046875	0.296875	0.546875	0.796875
0.0625	0.3125	0.5625	0.8125
0.078125	0.328125	0.578125	0.828125
0.09375	0.34375	0.59375	0.84375
0.109375	0.359375	0.609375	0.859375
0.125	0.375	0.625	0.875
0.140625	0.390625	0.640625	0.890625
0.15625	0.40625	0.65625	0.90625
0.171875	0.421875	0.671875	0.921875
0.1875	0.4375	0.6875	0.9375
0.203125	0.453125	0.703125	0.953125
0.21875	0.46875	0.71875	0.96875
0.234375	0.484375	0.734375	0.984375
0.25	0.5	0.75	1

These 64 resistors provide resistances that, when fed the equivalent voltage, keep the current at a value of 1 amp. This type of setup is called a "resistor ladder" and is shown in Figure 10.3.

Since the same voltage is sent through all of the resistors, the current coming out of the other side of the resistors changes accordingly. If a voltage of 718.75mV were sent through the resistors defined above then the highest valued resistor would yield current on the other side of 1.391304amps whereas the smallest valued resistor would yield a current of .02173913amps. On the other side of each of the resistors is a "comparator," a device that compares two different voltage levels and, if they are the same, puts out an electronic pulse. The

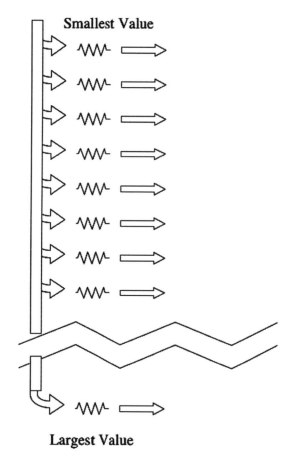

Smallest Value

Largest Value

FIGURE 10.3: **A Resistor Ladder Converter**

The signal is sent to multiple resistors, organized so that with a given signal level the smallest value resistor represents the highest amplitude. The largest value resistor represents the lowest amplitude. One resistor is used for each quantization step.

comparators are each fed two signals. The first signal comes from a fixed power source inside the converter component and has current of 1amp. The second signal comes from its own resistor. If the comparator gets the same value of current from the fixed signal and the resistor-fed signal then it sends out a pulse. If the current of the fixed source is 1amp then only one resistor will feed back an current level that is the same as this for any inbound signal. For example, if a .5V signal comes through, only the 32nd resistor will put out current of 1amp. That circuit then sends an electronic pulse. If a .234375V signal comes through, only the 15th resistor will put out current of 1amp and *that* circuit instead will put out an electronic pulse. A basic resistor ladder converter is visually described in Figure 10.4.

The net result from this contraption is that the sample of the voltage is sent through a series of differently weighted resistors, each of which feeds a comparator. Because all of the resistors are weighted differently, only one resistor can yield the same current as the fixed reference value sent to all of the comparators, so only one comparator sends on a pulse. The pulse gets sent to a digital signal processor that analyzes which comparator yielded the pulse, and sends an appropriate binary code associated with that particular resistor/comparator pairing.

In summary, a flash A/D converter works in the following steps. A clock pulse indicates to divert the voltage through the converter circuitry. That voltage spike is sent in parallel through a series of differently weighted resistors corresponding to the amplitude variations. The voltage spike yields differing results from every resistor, only one of which matches the current of a fixed reference signal. Comparators compare the currents coming from each resistor and one of them yields a match and releases an electrical pulse. A digital signal processing chip then generates the binary code relating to that comparator.

PROBLEMS WITH PRIMITIVE A/D CONVERTERS

There are many potential problems with a primitive converter design such as a flash A/D. The first problem is the sheer number of components that are required to make one. Each quantization step requires a unique resistor and an identical comparator. In our example above, only 64 quantization steps were used, making it equivalent to a 6-bit converter. A 6-bit converter is only capable of providing 36 dB of dynamic range, well below the requirements of the human auditory system's capabilities and well below the requirements for CD quality. To make a flash A/D with CD quality we would need 16 bits, 65,536 quantization steps, and thus 65,536 resistors and comparators. The sheer quantity of components provides a tremendous difficulty in manufacturing this type of converter. The larger problem, however, is the precision of the components that need to be involved.

The range of precision for the resistors is tremendously large. On a 4V, 16-bit flash A/D converter the difference between each resistor would be calibrated to correspond with a difference of .0000610V. The first problem is simply obtaining the specific values of resistors required. The resistors have to be custom manufactured to get the range of very specific values needed for a device like this. Finding a .0000061Ω value resistor or a .9999490Ω value resistor is implausible. Therefore, beside the sheer magnitude of components required, the specific components needed provide a substantial problem. Because of these problems the typical flash converter is most often used as a low bit-depth converter in crude applications not fit for an audio recording engineer.

Beyond just the difficulty and cost of the design, the quality of such a design would be very suspect because of precision issues. Each resistor has a certain, specified tolerance, or "slop factor." The average consumer looking to purchase resistors will find a variety of resistors for each value, which represent varying degrees of accuracy. A 5% 1Ω resistor is actually 1Ω plus or minus a 5% tolerance. This means that it is actually a resistor of somewhere between .95Ω and 1.05Ω. If the same valued resistor were a 1% resistor it would actually resist somewhere between .99Ω and 1.01Ω. The more accurate the resistor the more expensive it is, and resistors can easily be purchased with .1% tolerance.

The practical application of this problem with our A/D converter has to do with the very wide range of values that need to be represented. The smallest value resistor

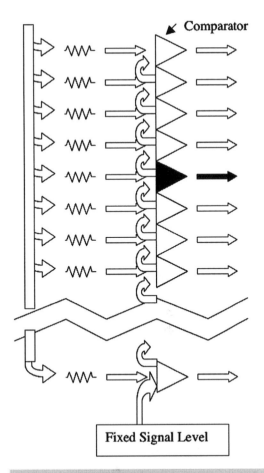

FIGURE 10.4: A Resistor Ladder Converter

The signal is simultaneously sent to a series of resistors that all represent different values of resistance. The signal coming off of each resistor is compared to a fixed reference signal. Only one such resistor puts out the appropriate signal level for any given waveform amplitude. The sample level is determined by which comparator indicates it has a match.

in our simple example above is .015625Ω and the largest resistor is 1.000000Ω. Even if resistors are used that are .01% resistors the highest value resistor can actually be any value between 1.010000Ω and .990000Ω. Since each resistor is only supposed to represent a very narrow range of .015625Ω it is not only possible, but rather very likely that some of the highest valued resistors are going to overlap each other, especially in converters with a higher bit depth than our 6-bit example above. Even if they manage to not overlap each other it can almost be guaranteed that the difference between each of the resistors is not going to be the same. "Perfect" and "imperfect" resistors and their effects are shown in Figure 10.5.

The inconsistent size of the quantization steps causes a type of irregularity called "non-linearity." If an A/D converter were completely "linear" then any voltage going in would yield the proper binary PCM values for its amplitude. In a perfectly linear A/D converter, any change in voltage of the amount commensurate to the size of the quantization steps would yield an increase in the binary code output by 1 number (Figure 10.6). In a non-linear converter, some increases in voltage of that amount does not yield a change in binary code (such as when the resistor values are too far apart) or yields a change in binary code of more than just one value (such as when the resistor values are too close together). The amount of non-linearity that a converter exhibits

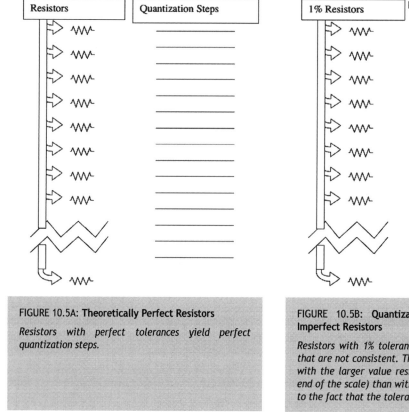
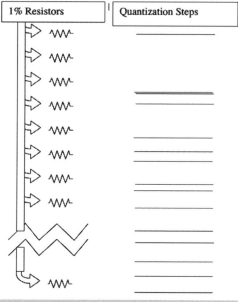

FIGURE 10.5A: **Theoretically Perfect Resistors**

Resistors with perfect tolerances yield perfect quantization steps.

FIGURE 10.5B: **Quantization Steps Yielded From Imperfect Resistors**

Resistors with 1% tolerances yield quantization steps that are not consistent. The effect would be far worse with the larger value resistors (which are at the top end of the scale) than with smaller value resistors due to the fact that the tolerances are in percentages.

reflects the amount of variation that the converter has from perfection. Four different non-linearity measurements are often evaluated for converters.

The first type of non-linearity is called differential non-linearity and has to do with the maximum amount of deviation of the amplitude difference between adjacent quantization steps. If the amplitude difference between two specific quantization steps is supposed to be 250nV apart and instead, because of the tolerances of the resistors, they are 450nV apart then non-linearity is present. In a flash A/D converter design, this type of non-linearity manifests itself in the form of distortion on the signal and has the largest effect on the highest bit values because of the tolerances in resistors discussed above. The differential non-linearity of a converter is typically measured in terms of the greatest variation from the ideal quantization step size that is present in the converter. If the ideal step size is 250nV and the greatest variation from that between a given pair of quantization steps is 187nV then this determines the differential non-linearity for that converter circuit. Differential non-linearity is shown in Figure 10.7.

Integral non-linearity has to do with the combined effect of the differential non-linearity at each quantization step. If the ideal linearity of a converter is plotted from the lowest step to the highest step against the re-

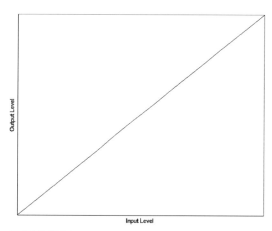

FIGURE 10.6: **Perfect Linearity**

"Perfect Linearity" is represented by each like-increase in inbound level yielding a commensurate increase in quantization values.

spective inbound voltage amplitudes that trigger them then we would see a diagonal line from the lower left corner of the plot to the right. This is where the term "linearity" comes from – what comes in to the converter goes out of the converter, reflecting a linear relationship between all of the amplitudes and binary codes. Differential non-linearity has to do with the individual steps and the amount of variance that they have. Integral non-linearity refers to the *total variation* from ideal demonstrated by the converter. If the amplitudes coming in result in very different binary codes than are ideal then the box is said to have high "integral non-linearity." Integral non-linearity is measured as the greatest amount of deviation exhibited by a converter between its relationship of amplitudes to binary codes and the linear relationship of amplitudes to binary codes. Integral non-linearity is shown in Figure 10.8.

Integral non-linearity and differential non-linearity both cause distortion, but each is a unique problem. A particular converter can exhibit excellent statistics in either type of distortion while being far less than ideal in the other. Integral non-linearity is measured as the greatest amount of overall variation from all the steps

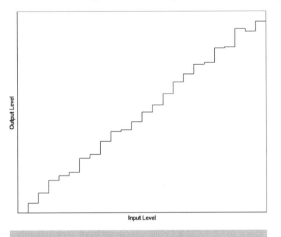

FIGURE 10.7: Differential Non-Linearity

"Differential Non-Linearity" is represented by each like-increase in inbound level yielding differing increases in quantization values. The differential non-linearity specification is given as the greatest variation from the ideal amplitude change that would characterize a quantization step.

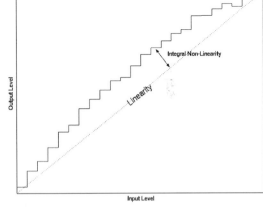

Figure 10.8: Integral Non-Linearity

"Integral Non-Linearity" is represented by wide variances from perfect linearity over the entire allowable amplitude range. The integral non-linearity specification is highlighted above as the greatest deviance from the ideal linearity plot over the complete amplitude range of the converter.

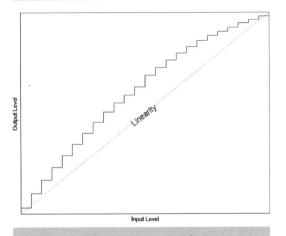

FIGURE 10.9: Adequate Differential Linearity Coupled With Poor Integral Linearity

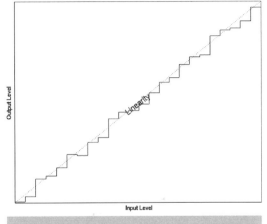

FIGURE 10.10: Adequate Integral Linearity Coupled With Poor Differential Linearity

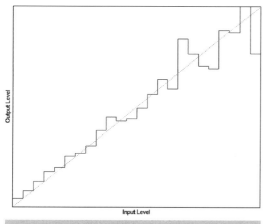

FIGURE 10.11: Linearity of a Typical Flash A/D Converter

The typical flash A/D converter has increasingly poor linearity at lower levels

to perfect and differential non-linearity is measured as the greatest amount of variation from step to step. A particular converter can have very good step-to-step specifications, only deviating just slightly from perfect, but if each step is off by the same amount in the same direction then the integral non-linearity suffers (Figure 10.9).

On the other hand, a box can have very poor step-to-step consistency but follow the ideal slope very closely overall (Figure 10.10).

Our flash A/D converter would likely fit into the latter category. The non-linearity of this converter is caused because of the significant variations due to the tolerance percentages of the individual resistors. This type of A/D converter would likely exhibit a linearity plot similar to that shown in Figure 10.11.

Our flash A/D converter will also likely exhibit *non-monotonicity* errors. Non-monotonicity refers to situations wherein the converter's differential non-linearity is so extreme that a particular quantization step overlaps the value previous to it (Figure 10.12). In this situation, as the amplitude of the voltage increases, the binary code move *down* a value instead of up. Flash A/D converters often have non-monotonicity errors (especially in the higher amplitudes) because of the percentage tolerances from resistor to resistor.

Linearity problems cause distortion that is not random like noise. Quantization noise is random when the probability of the amplitude of the voltage being closer or further from a quantization step is random. Distortion, on the other hand, is caused by the fact that the error only occurs when the voltage is at a very specific amplitude. This means that the distortion is related to, or "correlated" to the signal in some way as opposed to being random. For example, if a particular converter had poor linearity in its highest amplitudes then the converter would only exhibit these problems when the amplitude was high. If the problems only manifest with high-amplitude signals then by definition the errors are not *random* but are rather *correlated*. When errors are correlated they cause distortion, which yields additional overtones that are likely non-harmonic overtones. These additional frequencies are potentially

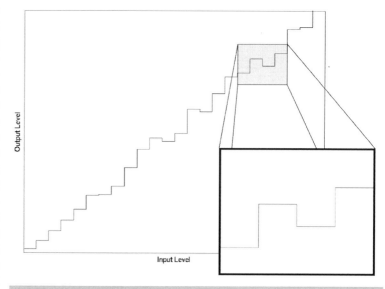

FIGURE 10.12: Non-Monotonicity Error

Non-monotonicity error occurs when one quantization step is so far out of linearity as to exceed the level of one of the neighboring quantization steps

very audible to human beings and can be above the quantization noise floor of the converters. See Figure 10.13.

The linearity of a converter is an essential component of a converter's quality and its ability to record audio transparently and accurately. For all of the reasons discussed above, the flash A/D converter has very poor linearity specifications on top of other design difficulties and is therefore considered primitive and unfit for audio recording.

PRIMITIVE D/A CONVERTERS

The equivalent to a flash A/D converter is a flash D/A converter which works under the same principles but in reverse. A reference voltage is sent to a long series of gates, each followed by a resistor - one for each quantization step. Each resistor has the same values as the equivalent A/D converter but is set up exactly the opposite so that the resistors with the most resistance are on the lowest values and the resistors with the lowest resistance are on the highest values. For a 4V chip, a 4V electrical signal is sent to all of the resistors in parallel

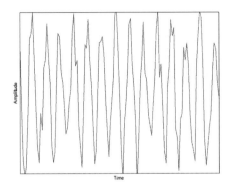
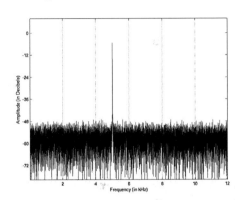

FIGURE 10.13A: A Sine Wave Converted With Noise and its Spectrograph Plot

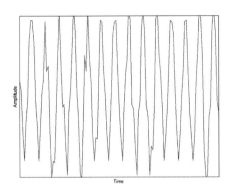
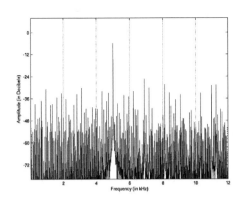

FIGURE 10.13B: A Sine Wave Converted With Poor Differential Linearity And Its Spectrograph Plot

The sine wave converted with noise, or random errors has a noise floor that is random and consistent. A sine wave converted with differential non-linearity has recurring errors and therefore distortion, which is noted in the spectrograph analysis as peaks in the frequency response of the result.

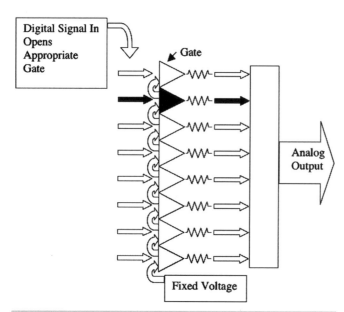

Digital Signal In
Opens
Appropriate
Gate

Gate

Analog
Output

Fixed Voltage

FIGURE 10.14: A Flash D/A Converter

An inbound digital signal opens an appropriate gate. The gate is fed by a fixed voltage signal, and the output of the gate feeds a resistor that turns the fixed voltage signal into the proper amplitude for the digital value represented. The highest amplitude utilizes the smallest value resistor. The smallest amplitude represented utilizes the highest amplitude resistor and puts out the lowest (most resisted) amplitude based on the fixed voltage it is fed.

but the gate prior to the resistor prevents the electricity from passing through it. A flash D/A converter design is shown in Figure 10.14.

When any of the gates opens, the voltage is allowed to pass through that resistor and put out a unique voltage amplitude for that resistor. The voltage continues to pass through that gate until that gate is closed, triggered by a clock circuit.

At the beginning of this converter, a digital signal processing chip takes the inbound binary values and sends specific code to only one gate allowing that gate to open. As the inbound binary values change, the related gates open and close allowing different voltages to emanate from this converter, which can then be amplified and reproduced. The mechanism itself is almost identical to the equivalent A/D converter except that it happens in reverse. On the A/D the signal goes into a resistor, out to a comparator, and out to a digital signal processing chip to establish the binary code. On the D/A the code goes into a digital signal processing chip, which opens the proper gate, then voltage passes through the appropriate resistor and exits. In an A/D converter, the largest resistor is used for the largest value. In a D/A converter the largest value is used for the smallest value.

The similarity between the A/D and the D/A converters means that all of the problems that exist in the A/D converter are manifested in the D/A converter but in reverse: the differential non-linearity is heavily manifested at low levels as that is where the highest value resistors are. This means that the greatest variations due to tolerance percentages happen at the other end of the amplitude spectrum. Integral non-linearity is the same. Non-monotonicity errors are more present at low amplitudes instead of high amplitudes.

One type of error that our flash A/D converter does not reflect but our D/A converter does is "missing codes," another type of non-linearity. If a converter has missing codes it has particular amplitudes that will never be represented by the converter. This can happen in a D/A converter if, because of the loose tolerances of two adjacent resistors, they end up representing the same value. Then, when the appropriate digital code for one of the values is sent through, the proper voltage value is not produced. Instead it produces the same value as if the next quantization step's binary code were sent instead. See Figure 10.15.

In this situation a particular, legitimate voltage level will never be produced by this converter. It is as if that binary code value does not exist. It is for this reason that this type of error is called a "missing code," because that binary code no longer puts out a unique voltage amplitude. Any situation in a D/A converter where two adjacent values produce the same result yields a missing code.

For all of the reasons that a flash A/D converter is not appropriate, a flash D/A converter yields the same conclusion. The concept of this design, however, yields what would become the foundation of converter design for decades of digital audio recording and playback.

R-2R LADDER

A revision that can be done to the flash D/A converter (but *not* to the A/D converter) involves using far fewer resistors and taking advantage of the numerical coincidences of binary numbers.

Rather than use as many resistors as there are quantization steps in our system we instead only use as many resistors as the number of *bits* in our system. Therefore, instead of having 65,536 resistors and gates, we can get by with only using 16. The system involves using (in this example) 16 separate voltages that each represent the value of their respective bits. The lowest voltage in our 4V, 16-bit converter equals .000061V and the highest voltage equals 2V. Each voltage equals twice the voltage of the previous value, just as each bit represents twice the value of the previous bit, as in the diagram to the right.

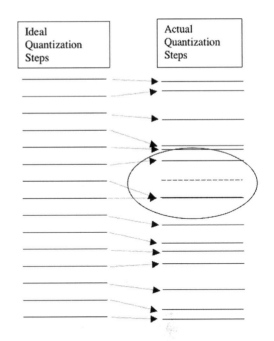

FIGURE 10.15: **Missing Codes**

The highlighted area shows a missing code in the D/A converter. The linearity in this particular implementation is poor enough that a particular voltage level of output cannot possibly be generated because no resistor in the circuit represents that particular value.

Each voltage level is created by a fixed voltage (4V) with a resistor connected to it as identified above, so the resistors als represent binary values with the highest value resistor creating the lowest voltage. Preceding each resistor is again a gate that allows the voltage to pass through the resistor. In the flash D/A converter discussed above, the binary code entered and went to a digital signal processor that sent a message out to turn on particu-

Resistor 1 yields	2V
Resistor 2 yields	1V
Resistor 3 yields	.5V
Resistor 4 yields	.25V
Resistor 5 yields	.125V
Resistor 6 yields	.0625V
Resistor 7 yields	.03125V
Resistor 8 yields	.015625V
Resistor 9 yields	.0078125V
Resistor 10 yields	.00390625V
Resistor 11 yields	.00195313V
Resistor 12 yields	.00097656V
Resistor 13 yields	.00048828V
Resistor 14 yields	.00024414V
Resistor 15 yields	.00012207V
Resistor 16 yields	.0000610V

lar bits. In this new circuit, the binary code enters the circuit and is sent straight to the gates as a binary code. The first bit on the left (the MSB) is sent to the resistor that yields the highest voltage. The second bit on the left is sent to the resistor that yields half of that voltage, and on and on until the bit on the right (the LSB) is send to the resistor that yields the smallest voltage. If the particular numerical value to be converted contains a "0" at any given bit then the respective gate does not open and the voltage is not passed on through the resistor. If a bit contains a "1" then the respective gate opens, allowing the voltage to pass through the resistor and on to the output. As the respective voltage levels are released to the output they are summed together, creating the analog voltage reflective of the binary code that entered. An R-2R digital to analog converter is shown in Figure 10.16.

In this paradigm, the binary code of 0000 0000 0000 0001 is equal to a single quantization step, or the value of an LSB (by definition). When this binary code is sent to this circuit all of the most significant valued resistors stay off and the electrical current flows only through the least significant resistor yielding an output voltage of .0000610V. If the binary code to be converted is equal to 1111 1111 1111 1111 then all of the gates are opened, the voltage passes through all of the resistors and the sum of all of those signals equals the highest voltage allowed to pass from the converter (4V, or full scale). See Figure 10.17.

One caveat to this is that binary codes in digital audio use the two's complement numbering system, so 1111 1111 1111 1111 is not at all the highest amplitude but is rather the first value below the half way point. Since the half way value is called the "zero crossing" the first value below that is considered the first negative value. Along with that, 0000 0000 0000 0001 is not the lowest value but is rather the first positive value above the zero crossing. With the zero crossing at the quantization step half way between the largest and the smallest voltages, the values around the zero crossing in a 16-bit converter are as follows:

Highest = *0111 1111 1111 1111*

         3 = *0000 0000 0000 0011*

         2 = *0000 0000 0000 0010*

         1 = *0000 0000 0000 0001*

         0 = *0000 0000 0000 0000*

        -1 = *1111 1111 1111 1111*

        -2 = *1111 1111 1111 1110*

        -3 = *1111 1111 1111 1100*

Lowest = *1000 0000 0000 0000*

Because of this, a change is made to one of the resistors in the resistor circuit described above. Rather than have the highest voltage (least resistance) bit turned off until a "1" causes the gate to open, instead this resistor is always on unless a "1" value comes through on that bit, at which point the gate closes. This way, whenever the value on that bit is a "0" it indicates that the value is in the top half of the voltages (at or above the zero crossing). Whenever that bit is a "1" it indicates that the value is in the bottom half of the voltages, below the zero crossing, and is therefore considered a negative number (Figure 10.18).

This type of circuit is also called a "resistor ladder," but because of its binary layout it is called an "R-2R ladder." R-2R ladders are very simple in many respects. They have the advantage of having very few components and are therefore still used today in many parts of the audio industry. Of the four major manufacturers of A/D and D/A converter

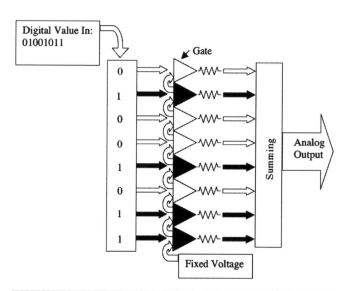

FIGURE 10.16: **An R-2R Ladder D/A Converter**

A digital signal is sent in and the binary values cause various gates to open. A fixed voltage passes through the gates and on to tuned resistors that represent binary values. The now-reduced voltage passes through to a summing amp that combines the signal coming off of each of the resistors that are active and sends the resultant analog voltage value through to the output.

circuits currently on the market, at least one still makes an R-2R ladder D/A converter that is sought after by some audiophiles for its audio quality.

PROBLEMS WITH R-2R LADDER CONVERTERS

While the R-2R ladder solves several of the tremendously large linearity problems found in flash converters by greatly reducing the number of resistors and thus the variances of the resistors in use, it is not immune to linearity problems. The very small resistor values used in the MSB are still not readily available. The smallest resistor size used in the MSB is still only the size relative to the LSB. The resistor used for the LSB still has the greatest value of resistance (the resistor that creates the .0000610V output). Because of this, the tolerance of the resistor used for the LSB is still very crucial, as a tolerance of .1% on that very large valued resistor can still yield very high variations, and the respective differential non-linearity would be great. If the LSB is .0000610V and the current is 1 then the value of the LSB resistor would be .9999490Ω. A .1% tolerance would throw the value of the LSB off from .0000610V to .00106V, an error of 17 times the value! Clearly the accuracy of the components must be very high even with R-2R Ladder converters, but with fewer resistors the errors are more consistent.

A large difference between the flash D/A and the R-2R ladder, however, is that in a flash D/A converter a single resistor is only used for a specific binary code. In an R-2R ladder converter, a single resistor is used in conjunction with other resistors a lot more often. Actually, a single resistor is used in fully half of the voltage levels produced. This means that a single resistor has a much more consequential effect on the linearity of the converter. The resistor used for the MSB contributes whenever the voltage amplitude is not negative. The resistor used for the 2nd bit from the right is used half the time that the amplitude is positive and half the time that the amplitude is negative. The resistor used for the 3rd

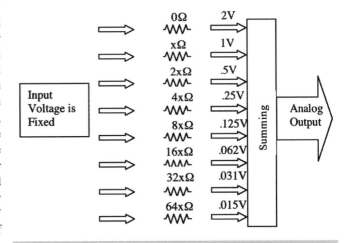

FIGURE 10.17: The Resistors in an R-2R Ladder D/A Converter

The resistors are stacked in a binary pattern, releasing output voltages that are appropriately binary weighted.

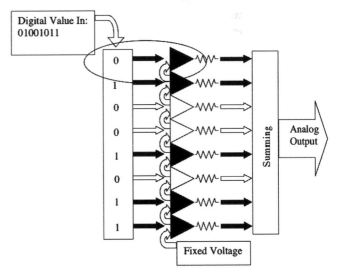

FIGURE 10.18: A "Two's Complement" R-2R Ladder D/A Converter

Note that the first circuit, that representing the highest voltage change, is reversed from the rest to accommodate two's complement digital signals. The gate is opened when the value is a "0" as opposed to versa visa.

bit from the right is used half the time that the 2nd bit is on and half the time the 2nd bit is off, and so on and so on.

This means that if the resistance of the resistor used for the MSB is off by .1% it will affect the entire positive range of voltage amplitudes released. If the value of the resistor used for the 2nd bit is off by .1% then linearity will be poor whenever that resistor is on, affecting half of the positive values and half of the negative values. The result of this is that the extremely drastic swings that can be experienced in the flash converter as far as differential linearity (step-to-step linearity) are much less affected. On the other hand, changes to a single resistor can have an impact over a large range of values, yielding potentially poor integral linearity.

Because of the layout of the R-2R converter, the fluctuations in the resistance of the LSB resistor affect the variation from one step to the next, as that resistor is in use for every other quantization step. If the resistor is errant by .00001Ω then each increase in amplitude equivalent to a step will no longer be .0000610V, but will rather be .0000710V, yielding high differential non-linearity (thought not as poor as the flash converter). The variations in the accuracy of the MSB, on the other hand, have very little effect on the individual steps but have more impact on the entire positive amplitude range in comparison to the negative range. Therefore the MSB resistor has the most impact on integral non-linearity. Because of this, some R-2R ladder converters used a type of *variable* resistor circuit on the MSB, or even the first few most significant bit resistors. By doing so the manufacturers allowed the converter to be calibrated so that the integral non-linearity could be improved by fine-tuning the accuracy of the MSBs.

Another problem experienced by R-2R ladder converters is caused when the voltage amplitude passes from the positive numbers to the negative numbers. When this happens the binary values change from 0000 0000 0000 0000 to 1111 1111 1111 1111. At the zero crossing, no pulses are sent to any of the gates. At the first negative value pulses are sent to all of the gates. The amount of electrical power required to do this is not inconsequential, momentarily lowering the amount of voltage available. Because the voltage is lowered, the voltage sent through each of the resistors is subsequently lowered (although only slightly) and the total voltage reproduced is not accurately represented. Since at that point the total voltage at the output of the converter is being created by the sum of fully half of the resistor circuits, and since none of them put out the proper voltage, the voltage drop causes a substantial error.

The distortion yielded by this phenomenon theoretically occurs when binary values in a waveform use fewer "on" bits to represent it than the previous value required, but the consequence from a change of only one bit, or one pulse, is not particularly significant. The problem really manifests itself most notably around the zero

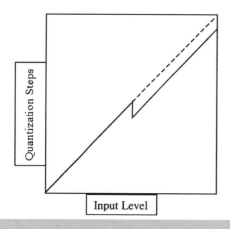

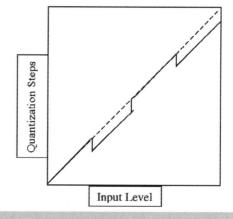

FIGURE 10.19A: **Example of Non-Linearity Caused by a Poorly Calibrated MSB Resistor**

FIGURE 10.19B: **Example of Non-Linearity Caused by a Poorly Calibrated 2nd MSB Resistor**

crossing because of the tremendous number of bits that change simultaneously. The distortion that this yields is therefore called "zero crossing distortion" and is especially noticeable on R-2R converter designs.

Regardless of the zero crossing distortion or the integral non-linearity that R-2R converters yield, their performance is markedly better than their flash D/A converter counterparts.

R–2R A/D CONVERTERS

An R-2R ladder A/D converter cannot actually exist in the same sense that it does in a D/A converter. There is not a direct but opposite parallel because there is no way of knowing what the binary code will be in order to send the signal to the proper resistors. We could not simply reverse the circuit like we could with flash converters and hope that the signal goes to the proper resistors. See Figure 10.20.

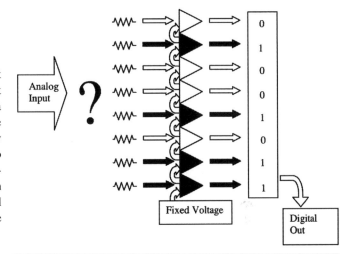

FIGURE 10.20: An R-2R A/D Converter Cannot Exist

An R-2R A/D converter cannot exist in the way that an R-2R D/A converter exists because of the missing link of determining which of the binary circuits should be allowed to pass signal.

Somehow, though, we want to improve A/D converters in the same way that the R-2R ladder was able to improve D/A converters. The scheme that was created is called a "Successive Approximation Register" or "SAR."

In order to take advantage of the improvements with R-2R ladder D/A converters, an entire one is put into every SAR A/D converter. The way it works is as follows: A counter counts through all of the binary values, starting with the lowest value and going to the highest value, from 1000 0000 0000 0000 to 0111 1111 1111 1111 (in two's complement binary notation). These binary values are fed into an R-2R ladder D/A converter, which converts these values into their respective analog voltages. Those voltages, which essentially represent a voltage sweep from bottom to top, are fed into a comparator. The other side of the comparator is fed by the incoming analog signal. When the voltage of the incoming analog signal matches the voltage coming from the internal R-2R ladder converter, the comparator recognizes the match and sends a pulse back to the counter, indicating that it has

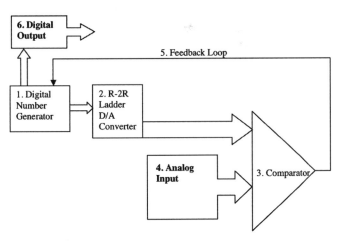

FIGURE 10.21: An SAR A/D Converter

An SAR A/D converter uses an R-2R D/A converter within it. A digital number generator (1) generates binary numbers and sends the values to a D/A converter (2) which turns those into an analog signal. This analog signal is then sent to a comparator (3), which compares the results of the D/A converter with the analog input (4) that is to be converted. When the comparator finds a match between the D/A converter's signal and the analog input it sends a message back (5) to the number generator telling it got a match. The appropriate code then becomes the digital output (6).

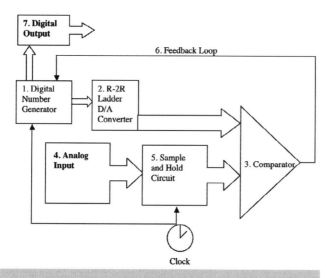

Clock

FIGURE 10.22: A More Realistic SAR A/D Converter

An actual SAR converter uses a clock and a sample and hold circuit. The analog signal is held by the sample and hold circuit at the specific moment when the sample is to be taken. The comparator then compares the held, momentary sample of the analog signal with the signal generated by the number generator until it finds its matching voltage. The clock controls the speed of the number generator as well as the sample and hold circuit, essentially telling everything to "start over again" when the next sample period arrives.

found the proper value and to send that value out. The counter circuit, triggered by the pulse from the comparator, sends the representative binary code (to which it had counted) out its digital output. This process determines the appropriate binary code to represent an analog voltage. This circuit is visually demonstrated in Figure 10.21.

The "counter" as described above does not actually count through all of the numbers as indicated. Instead, it uses a logical deduction path with which to find the appropriate value. It might first send out a zero value, representing the zero-crossing voltage value. The comparator on the other side of the R-2R ladder DAC compares the zero-crossing voltage with the incoming voltage and determines if the incoming voltage was too high or too low and sends a signal back to the counter indicating its conclusion. The counter then picks another value half way between the peak amplitude and the zero crossing and sends this binary code out to the R-2R ladder DAC, yielding another comparison. The comparator then indicates again whether this value is too high or too low. This system continues to hone in on the specific quantization value that compares to the inbound voltage. The number of "honing in" steps is the same as the number of bits in the DAC, and the two have a logical relationship. The first comparison essentially defines the value of the first bit (positive or negative). The second comparison defines the value of the second bit (top half or bottom half within the positive or negative range). The third comparison defines the third bit, and so on. The continued "guessing" and refining of the value of the voltage is called "successive approximation," thus the name of this type of converter.

The problem with this particular design as we understand it so far is that there is nothing to control the timing with which the samples are taken. The analog voltage is fed into the comparator and it takes a certain amount of time for the counter and D/A converter to work through the successive approximations to produce the correct voltage. In the meantime the analog voltage coming in from the inbound source changes.

To prevent this problem from occurring, a clock is used to determine exactly when a sample is to be taken. The clock sends a pulse to a circuit that samples the value of the analog voltage coming in and holds it for some time. This way the amplitude of the voltage coming in is maintained at the value when the sample should have been taken. Therefore, as the counter counts the voltage being compared at the comparator does not change. This circuit is called a "sample and hold" circuit and typically uses a capacitor to store the voltage until the next clock pulse comes through and indicates that the next sample needs to be taken. A revised SAR analog to digital converter is shown in Figure 10.22.

PROBLEMS WITH AN SAR A/D CONVERTER

The biggest shortcoming of an SAR A/D converter is that its reliability is completely based on the accuracy of the D/A converter inside of it. The same problems that are produced by an R-2R ladder D/A converter are inherently present in the A/D converter in which it resides. Therefore, the SAR A/D converters available on the market can never be better than their corresponding D/A converters. They also cost more because the D/A converter is just a portion of the total amount of circuitry needed for the A/D converter. The improvements, however, over the flash A/D converters are beyond compare. The SAR A/D converter has been the staple in the audio market for decades. Its use is still respected and some companies still make them, though newer designs for converter circuits are less prone to the errors found in SAR converters.

ANTI–ALIASING AND RECONSTRUCTION FILTERS

Until now we have not discussed the fact that every A/D converter needs to have an anti-aliasing filter in front of it to prevent frequencies above the Nyquist frequency from getting into the conversion process and causing aliasing. It is assumed that the converter types discussed above have some sort of filter in front of them. These filters are made using a series of analog components and implemented to filter out frequency content above the Nyquist frequency. We will discuss filters more comprehensively in later chapters.

In Chapter Nine we hinted at the fact that the waveform that comes out of any D/A converter should be a complete reconstruction of the original waveform, even though the sample values only *indicate* what the waveform originally was; the simple recreating of the sample points does not yield the original waveform. We also learned that any method of recreating the waveform that passes through the sample points and does not represent the original waveform contains high frequencies that are above the Nyquist frequency.

As of yet we have shown that the signal that comes out of the D/A converter is really just the sample points and not the complete reconstruction. The complete reconstruction is done using another filter called a "reconstruction filter." The function of the reconstruction filter is to fully attenuate all of the overtones that are present in the signal coming out of the D/A converter that are above the Nyquist frequency. If all of that content is removed then the only waveform that can possibly remain is the waveform that the sample points *indicate* should exist (Figure 10.23). If a reconstruction filter is used then the waveform that results from it will be

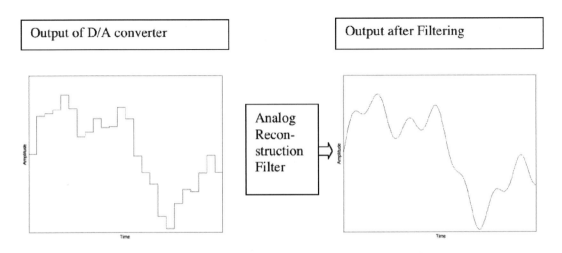

FIGURE 10.23: **The Reconstruction Process**

completely and properly reconstructed. (Of course, errors due to non-linearity in the converters yield the fact that what the sample points *indicate* should exist is not what originally existed, but is rather a distorted version of such.)

The circuit for the reconstruction filter can be exactly the same as the anti-aliasing filter as it serves the same function: to remove all of the frequency content above the Nyquist frequency. Therefore, every A/D converter is *prec*eded by an anti-aliasing filter and every D/A converter is *succ*eeded by a reconstruction filter. While one prevents aliasing and the other prevents artificial high frequency content from being generated, one is required in every converter.

As mentioned above, the filters are generally created using a series of capacitors. A capacitor is a device that stores electricity and releases it over time. A simple spark fed into a capacitor indicates the rate at which this dissipation occurs. As the analog voltage streams into the capacitor it is summed together with previous voltage values that have not yet dissipated. The summing of delayed signals to themselves causes higher frequencies to decrease in amplitude and lower frequencies to pass less affected. A much more comprehensive look at filters fills Chapter Seventeen.

In the meantime, what we need to know is that the rate of the dissipation of the capacitor is consistent, but the time it takes for specific voltages to dissipate changes because the amplitude is different. The dissipation of the waveform over time causes a delay of some frequencies with respect to others of getting through the filter. This delay of specific "groups" of frequencies is called "group delay." This specific example of group delay is similar to the group delay caused by the cochlear filters that we covered in Chapter Six.

The group delay causes a phase shift of frequencies that becomes increasingly larger as the frequencies roll off. At high enough frequencies, the waveform undergoes enough phase shift that frequencies are not passed through the system, thus causing the filter to attenuate high frequencies. The steeper the filter the more phase shift there is of the frequencies that pass. The problem with this is that we have discussed the human ear's sensitivity to phase shifts, especially in high frequencies. As the filter gets too steep, the shift in phase causes inconsistencies in the timing of transients that are used to facilitate the ear's ability to localize events in space.

The anti aliasing filters that are used need to roll off the entire dynamic range of the converter over the frequency range of 20kHz to the Nyquist frequency. Since the Nyquist frequency for CD quality audio is 22.05kHz, the total frequency range is only about a 15th of an octave, and for CD quality digital audio the material above the Nyquist frequency needs to be attenuated 96dB. This calls for a very steep filter, which results in a high amount of inevitable phase shift of frequencies that are in the audible range.

The reconstruction filters have the same problem. Reconstruction filters need to attenuate all frequencies above the Nyquist frequency while allowing all frequency content below 20kHz to pass without attenuation. This again has a high amount of phase shift, further distorting the timing of the frequency content within the human hearing range.

Because this type of distortion is inherent in all of the examples of converter design discussed above, a technique was established to help eliminate the phase shift caused by these filters.

OVERSAMPLING

What would really be ideal is to just raise the sample rate high enough that the filters could be much higher than the audible range of human hearing and could also roll off much more gently. If the sample rate were at 88.2kS/s, for example, the Nyquist frequency would be twice as high, up at 44.1kHz. This would provide over an octave for the filter to operate, reducing the group delay and phase shift in the audible range dramatically.

Raising the sample rate, however, would double the storage and transmission requirements of the digital audio, and this may not even be a high enough sample rate to eliminate the audibility of the group delay. Preferably, we would like to keep the sample rate at 44.1kS/s and find another way to make the filters inaudible. The solution is called "oversampling."

We have briefly discussed the problems inherent in analog converters with respect to time and phase. While the same problems occur when filtering digital signals using digital signal processing there are ways to avoid these problems. As we will learn in Chapter Seventeen, it is very possible to design "linear phase" filters, or filters that have no group delay at all. By taking advantage of digital technology we can use digital signal processing to perform our anti-aliasing and reconstruction filters. The problem with this is quite obvious: we have to get the analog signals into and out of the digital systems somehow, and that process is precisely what we are trying to improve. The solution is to do the initial digital sampling (conversion) at a much higher rate than the eventual sample rate. If the eventual sample rate is 44.1kS/s then the initial conversion is done at 2x, 4x, or more times this sample rate. In many situations in which R-2R ladder converters or SAR converters are used, the oversampling rate is eight times higher (8x) than the eventual sample rate. When sampling at 44.1kS/s this means that the initial conversion is done at 352.8kS/s instead. This means that the Nyquist frequency of this sampling is 176.4kHz and the analog anti-aliasing filter does not have to actually roll off completely until that frequency. The analog anti-aliasing filter would now have from 20kHz to 176.4kHz to fully operate, more than three full octaves with which to attenuate material without causing audible phase shift below 20kHz. This avoids any chance that the analog filter will have any audible phase distortion effect on the material to be sampled.

Once the material is sampled at the oversampled rate it represents audio waveforms that are band-limited to 176.4kHz. Each sample point represents the amplitude of the waveform at a specific moment in time. We can think of this as representing a complete analog waveform that now needs to get sampled at the rate of 44.1kS/s. In order to *resample* this waveform at the

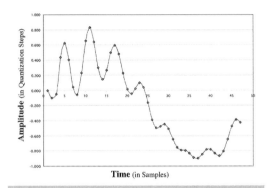

FIGURE 10.24A

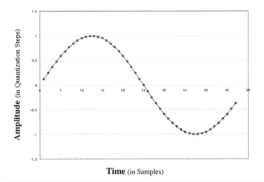

FIGURE 10.24B: Sample Data from Figure 10.26A Filtered to (1/2)*fs*

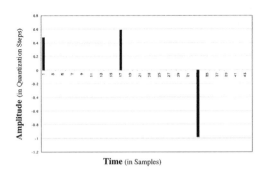

FIGURE 10.24C: Sample Data from Figure 10.24A Fully Decimated

A waveform is sampled at 16 times the eventual sampler rate or 16fs in Figure 10.24A. As a part of downsampling it, all frequency content above half of the eventual sampling frequency (1x) is removed as is shown in Figure 10.24B. Finally, excess samples are removed leaving only the necessary data per the Nyquist Theorem, as is shown above in Figure 10.24C.

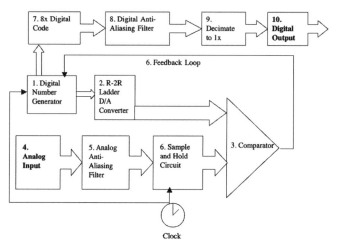

FIGURE 10.25: An 8x Oversampling SAR A/D Converter

An 8x Oversampling SAR has an analog anti-aliasing filter at the input (5) that filters the incoming analog signal at 1/2 of the sampling frequency (of 8x). After the digital code is released (7) a digital anti-aliasing filter removes all frequency content above 1/2 of the eventual sampling frequency (8) before excess samples are removed (9) and the final 1x digital output is released (10).

new, lower rate we need to once again use an anti-aliasing filter, but this time to prevent aliasing with a Nyquist frequency of 22.05kHz. Since the signal is now a digital signal, the "linear phase" filter can be implemented by digital signal processing in a way that can effectively operate within the very narrow range of 20kHz to 22.05kHz and with no phase distortion.

Once this *digital* filter is implemented we end up with new digital information that represents the following: a sample rate of 352.8kS/s but with no frequency content represented at all that is above 22.05kHz. At this point we have a tremendous amount of wasted information as we already know that we do not need the sample rate to be any higher than 44.1kS/s, yet we have eight times that amount of information. Nyquist tells us that we only need one eighth that number of samples in order to accurately reconstruct the waveform, so there is effectively eight times the necessary amount of data representing it at this point. We can now reduce this amount of information to the eventual sample rate of 44.1kS/s. If we look at this sample data as *representing* an analog waveform, but with every sample point representing the amplitude at a specific point in time, we can simply reapply the Nyquist Theorem and sample the waveform as though it were an actual analog waveform. The easiest and most accurate way to do this is simply to keep every eighth sample and discard the rest. By doing so we have essentially sampled the already sampled information. We now have a 44.1kS/s sample rate with no "illegal" frequencies in it that cause aliasing. On top of this, we have eliminated the opportunity for audible phase distortion. The process is shown in Figure 10.24.

The process of converting the sample rate from a higher rate using digital filters and removing excess samples is called "downsampling." When the process is done from a sample rate that is an even multiple of the eventual sample rate (such as 2x or 4x) then the process is called "decimating," which means "to reduce markedly in amount."

An 8x oversampling SAR converter therefore has the following layout: audio enters the converter and goes through an analog anti-aliasing filter that rolls off at 176.4kHz. The band-limited signal then enters an SAR converter where it gets converted at the rate of 352.8kS/s. The digital information then leaves the converter

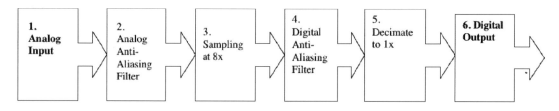

FIGURE 10.26: An 8x Oversampling SAR A/D Converter

mechanism and goes to a digital processing mechanism where the *digital* anti-aliasing filter is implemented. Seven of every eight samples are then removed and the sampling process is complete with a 44.1kS/s sample rate. The schematic for the revised, oversampling SAR analog to digital converter is shown in Figure 10.25.

A waveform, converted in an 8x oversampling SAR converter would goes through the stages shown in Figure 10.26.

The same principles can be applied to a D/A converter. We have already established that there is only one possible way to properly reconstruct a waveform coming out of a D/A converter that includes only "legal" frequencies. What we want to do is "upsample" the material to a higher frequency so that we can convert from digital to analog at a higher sample rate so that the analog reconstruction filter can be less steep and cause less phase distortion in the conversion back to analog.

Upsampling is the same as downsampling except that we need to *add* sample values rather than take them away. Somehow we need to determine what the additional sample values should be. In the end we want to add seven additional samples that represent the original waveform and no harmonic content over 22.05kHz (for an 8x oversampling 44.1kS/s D/A converter). We do this by multiplying each sample value times eight and then inserting seven successive samples, all with the value of the zero crossing. The process is shown in Figure 10.27.

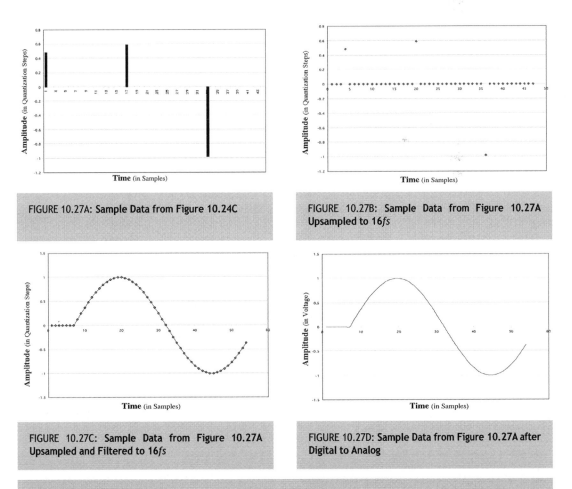

FIGURE 10.27A: Sample Data from Figure 10.24C

FIGURE 10.27B: Sample Data from Figure 10.27A Upsampled to 16*fs*

FIGURE 10.27C: Sample Data from Figure 10.27A Upsampled and Filtered to 16*fs*

FIGURE 10.27D: Sample Data from Figure 10.27A after Digital to Analog

Conversion and Further Analog Filtering

We then use a digital reconstruction filter to remove all of the high frequency content represented by the samples, which now contain a lot of high frequency information because the additional samples clearly do not represent the original waveform. By definition the additional samples must represent additional frequency content above 22.05kHz. When those frequencies are removed we are left with the original waveform represented by the sampling points. The fact that the additional values we added were zeros lowered the amplitude of the remaining sample points a respective amount. This is why we initially multiplied all values by eight. This ensured that when the amplitude was lowered it resumed its original amplitude.

The waveform now has a Nyquist frequency of 176.4kHz, but without frequency content above 22.05kHz. We now have the same issues of the D/A converters discussed prior: that there is only one way of reconstructing the waveform through those sample values without the inclusion of frequency content above 176.4kHz. What the samples really represent is a waveform with no frequency content between 22.05kHz and 176.4kHz, but the D/A conversion process will itself create harmonic content above that. An analog reconstruction filter still needs to be added after the signal is turned to analog to remove the frequency content created by the D/A above the new Nyquist frequency. Fortunately this new reconstruction filter only has to filter the information above 176.4kHz, so the same filter used for anti-aliasing in the A/D converter will work.

The complete 8x oversampling digital to analog converter circuit now works as follows: Digital information enters and goes through a digital signal processing stage where seven additional zero values are added and then all of the values are multiplied times eight to maintain the proper amplitude. The digital data, which is now representative of a sample rate of 352.8kS/s, is then filtered with a digital reconstruction filter to remove all content between 22.05kHz and 176.4kHz. The material then passes through the D/A circuit and is turned into analog waveforms. The analog waveforms then pass through an analog reconstruction filter to complete the reconstruction process. The waveform is then the same as the waveform that the samples implied, but with a slight amount of inaudible phase distortion from the final, gentle, analog reconstruction filter. A flow-chart is shown in Figure 10.28.

Most SAR A/D converters and R-2R ladder D/A converters made since the mid 1980s are oversampling converters because of the benefits that the oversampling process provides. The first such converters on the market were 2x. 4x and 8x oversampling converters soon followed.

The terms 2x, 4x, 8x and more refer to the sample rate, given a particular "base rate," such as 44.1kS/s. 2x means simply two times that rate. Another nomenclature often used is fs, which stands for "frequency of sampling." $2fs$ means two times the frequency of sampling – essentially the same thing as "2x." The nomenclatures of "x" and "fs" are used interchangeably throughout this book and through the industry as a whole. "fs" should not be confused with "FS" with stands for Full Scale, or the maximum sample value in a digital system. The usage alone should distinguish the terms. "-6 dBFS" refers, obviously, to six decibels below Full Scale, whereas $2fs$ refers to two times the base sample rate.

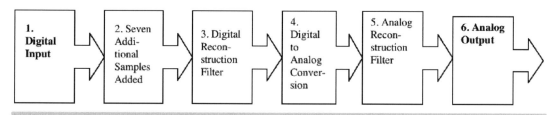

FIGURE 10.28: An 8x Oversampling R-2R D/A Converter

THE USE OF MORE THAN ONE CONVERTER

We have just finished talking about the problems with implementing transparent anti-aliasing and reconstruction filters in the conversion process. Another problem we have discussed with converters is linearity. The linearity problems that we have discussed so far stem from the inaccuracies of the resistors. Conceptually, the R-2R ladder DAC and the SAR ADC are great solutions, but implementation-wise we have to deal with the deficiencies in the components. The precision required is more than can be met even by modern manufacturing techniques. If the linearity problems in a converter could be fixed then the converter would have less distortion. There are ways of doing this that simply utilize multiple converters for each signal. Each converter works under the premise that the resistors all have tolerances and that the tolerance of the resistor within a known range is random. This means that if the resistor is supposed to be a 1Ω resistor, +/- 1%, that its resistance is somewhere between .99Ω and 1.01Ω, but its specific resistance within that range is random.

One solution to solving linearity problems is to use two R-2R ladder digital to analog converters for each channel of output and average the two output levels together. If a converter has a resistor with a 1% tolerance that is actually off by .5% in the positive direction then the odds are that a second converter would have the same resistor, off by less than that amount. Odds are that the

Ideal Values	Resistor 1	% Error	Resistor 2	% Error	Average	% Error
10	9.79	2.11	10.35	-3.46	10.07	-0.67
20	19.76	1.22	19.34	3.31	19.55	2.27
30	30.48	-1.61	29.07	3.09	29.78	0.74
40	39.83	0.43	40.58	-1.46	40.21	-0.52
50	49.97	0.06	48.92	2.16	49.44	1.11
60	62.99	-4.99	61.65	-2.76	62.32	-3.87
70	68.17	2.62	66.88	4.46	67.52	3.54
80	76.72	4.10	76.84	3.95	76.78	4.03
90	86.16	4.26	90.26	-0.28	88.21	1.99
100	100.07	-0.07	102.23	-2.23	101.15	-1.15
Total Error		**21.48**		**27.16**		**19.88**

FIGURE 10.29: Improving Linearity by Combining Converters

second converter's same resistor would be off by somewhere between –1% and .5%, and not .5% and 1%. If the two resistor values are averaged together then the odds are that the total amount of variance yielded will be less than .5%. If the second converter's resistor is off by -.5% then the two, averaged together, yield a perfect average value. If the second converter's resistor is off by an extreme –1% then the average between the two would still only yield a variance of -.25%, which is better than either one converter on its own (Figure 10.29).

The only way that adding a second converter would cause the overall performance to decrease would be if the average of any two resistors were worse than one resistor by itself. This would happen if, for instance, one

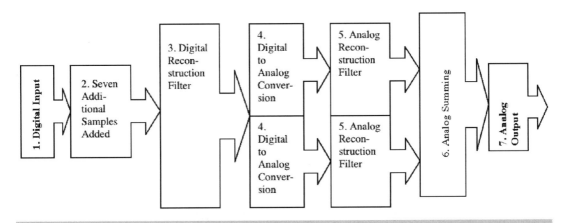

FIGURE 10.30: An 8x Oversampling Averaging R-2R D/A Converter

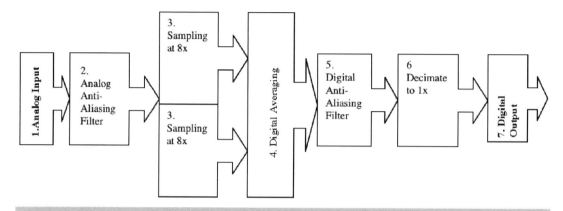

FIGURE 10.31: An 8x Oversampling Averaging SAR A/D Converter

resistor had a variance of .1% but the second one had a variance of .9%. The resulting .5% variance average would be worse than using only the first resistor by itself. Over the entire range of the converter, however, a statistical analysis would show that the odds would be that the performance improves overall by the addition of a second converter. The downside to this type of converter design is only the additional expense involved of doubling the circuitry. See the flowchart in Figure 10.30.

Since this can be done with an R-2R ladder DAC, the same idea can be applied to an SAR ADC as shown in Figure 10.31.

The problem with using the "averaging" method by using two converters is that the effect is really no different than simply utilizing slightly different (and hopefully better) resistors in the first place. The distortion characteristics are slightly improved, but are still consistent; in other words, every time a waveform lands on a particular quantization step the same error occurs.

Other methods also exist for using multiple converters, including having the converters cover different amplitude ranges of the conversion process. Converter manufacturers worked for many years at improving the specifications of SAR and R-2R ladder designs because of some of the inherent weaknesses of using components with such specific tolerance requirements.

CONCLUSION

So far we have discussed the implementation of the analog to digital and digital to analog converters and discovered that, while ideally the digital systems should stand up to (and exceed) their analog counterparts, the actual implementation of these systems is difficult because of the wide range of human audibility. Manufacturing techniques simply are not advanced enough to refine the electrical components in these converters at this time. The type of converters we have talked about in this chapter can be called "ladder" converters as they all work on the principle of a resistor ladder, whether the ladder is a completely parallel ladder as in the flash converters or it is an R-2R binary ladder as in the R-2R ladder DAC or the SAR ADC.

The ladder type converters all use the principles put forth by Nyquist, Shannon, and others in a traditional sense: remove all harmonic content above the Nyquist frequency, sample at the sample rate, use as many quantization steps as the dynamic range of the material requires, and then convert to those quantization steps. Oversampling is a simple variation on this involving sampling twice in the process. First we start with an infinite sample rate (analog signals) and add an anti-aliasing filter and sample. Then we add another filter and sample the results again from the already sampled material but at a lower sample rate. Conceptually this still follows the traditional approach to conversion as explained above. It was not until the late 1980s that a major departure from traditional conversion was introduced that fosters a much larger conversation about digital sampling and digital technology altogether. In Chapter Eleven we discuss a new, potentially counterintuitive approach to the conversion process.

Chapter Eleven

Low Bit Converters

We know that each bit gives us approximately 6dB of dynamic range. This means that any part of a waveform that is contained within the top 6dB of its overall amplitude can be accurately captured but that a noise floor is added to the signal a certain number of decibels below the peak that is determined by the number of quantization steps used. We also know that said noise floor represents random, white noise when proper conversion is done. Any part of the waveform that was below the noise floor is still represented in the converted signal but is swamped by the noise and will at some level be audibly masked by that noise.

We also know about noise, however, that white noise has a lot more high frequency content than low frequency content. White noise has 1000 times the energy between 20,000Hz and 40,000Hz as it does between 20Hz and 40Hz, though each range represents one musical octave. With white noise, the amplitude of the noise decreases at a rate of 3dB per decreasing octave, so that the octave from 5kHz to 10kHz has 3dB less amplitude of noise than the octave from 10kHz to 20kHz. The octave from 20Hz to 40Hz has 54dB less noise content than does the top octave. See Figure 11.1.

This means that if we digitally sample low frequency material we will actually get more than 6dB of dynamic range per bit in the low frequency range because the noise induced by quantization error has less amplitude in this range. It is not that less noise is present, but rather that amongst that noise, very little of its energy is in the low frequency range. Using 16 bits, for example, we can actually record very low frequency instruments with far greater than 96dB of dynamic range! A double bass, for example, can be recorded with much better than 96dB of dynamic range, still using only 16 bits. For that matter, if we determine that we only need a certain amount of dynamic range and we were only interested in low frequency instruments we

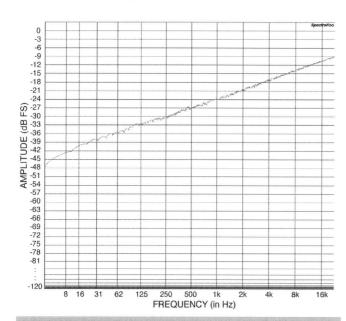

FIGURE 11.1: White Noise Spectrum

White noise decreases in amplitude by 3 decibels per octave as octaves get lower in amplitude.

could choose to keep the sampling rate at 44.1kS/s and lower the bit depth accordingly. We would still have the same amount of noise present overall, most of which is in the high frequency ranges (such as the top audible octave). If, however, we choose to filter out all of the signal above the frequencies produced by the double bass we would inherently, then, end up filtering out much of the noise caused by sampling. This would leave us much greater dynamic range than only 6dB per bit in the frequency band that remains.

In fact, we could actually record the bass with only 1-bit (two quantization steps) and get much more than 6dB of dynamic range out of it, so long as the material was filtered afterwards to remove all of the content above the double bass' frequencies, as is shown in Figure 11.2.

The quantization error level is actually going to be very loud, but the error level *in the range of the frequency content we are trying to record* is going to be very low. After filtering we would get a far better than 6dB dynamic range throughout the remaining frequencies and would experience a fairly decent recording for only having used a single bit (two quantization steps) to record the material. This is shown in Figure 11.3.

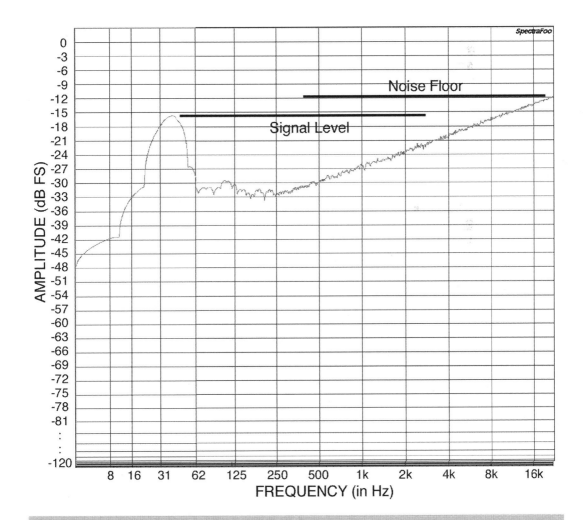

FIGURE 11.2: A Bass Guitar Playing With a High White Noise Floor

The bass guitar note and its harmonics are seen peaking above the amplitude of the white noise floor on the low frequency range of this spectrograph plot.

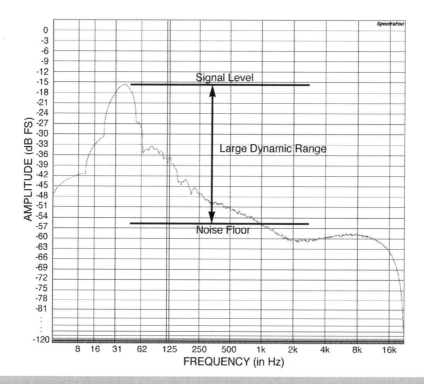

FIGURE 11.3: A Bass Guitar Playing With a High Filtered White Noise Floor

When the high frequencies of the noise floor are removed by a filter the remaining noise floor is much lower in amplitude than its original level, leaving a larger dynamic range.

The application of this is a further implementation of the work of Nyquist, Shannon and the others. We can use a lower bit depth (fewer quantization steps) if we sample at a higher rate and then filter out all of the unneeded high frequency material. In fact, we can actually record the entire audio range with only one bit if the sample rate is high enough. Yes, there will be a lot of noise in the results, but if the noise *within the audible range* is low enough (because the noise is white) then two quantization steps are theoretically plenty to accurately capture the material. This concept is extremely important to understand as this entire chapter is based on this premise, making a review of the content leading up to this concept worthwhile if there is confusion.

We can now calculate the sample rate necessary for recording the entire audio range with only 1-bit. First we need to establish what overall dynamic range we want within the human hearing range. We have already settled on 120dB as the maximum dynamic range of human audibility, so it is reasonable to say that we would like 120dB of audible dynamic range from this 1-bit system. Therefore, from 20Hz to 20kHz we would like the noise to be 120dB below the maximum level. The maximum level in digital audio occurs when the bits are "full on" or at "full scale." For this reason, signals are often measured in reference to the highest allowable signal level, or 0dB FS (exactly at Full Scale). What we want to achieve is therefore a noise level at −120dB FS (120dB below Full Scale). We know that the quantization noise decreases within a given frequency band by 3dB for every octave added and that the noise across the entire band from 0Hz to the Nyquist frequency is −6dB FS. Therefore, with a 40kS/s sample rate, the amplitude of the noise in the audible range is −6dB FS, but if we double the sample rate then the quantization noise *in the audible range* decreases by 3dB because much of the noise then ends up in the frequency range *above* the audible range. The quantization noise is still −6dB FS, but most of that noise is above the hearing range, and the amount of that noise that is in the audible range is less – by 3dB. If we double the sample rate again then the level of the quantization noise in the audible range drops another 3dB relative to the full scale level. The overall noise is still −6dB FS (across the entire frequency band from 0Hz to the Nyquist frequency) but most of the noise is above the audible range, which makes the noise in the audible range lower by another 3dB. If we keep raising the sampling rate for this 1-bit

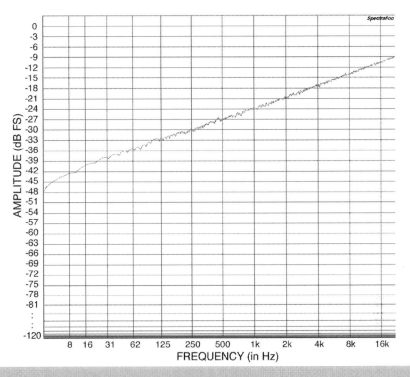

FIGURE 11.4A: Noise Floor from 44.1kS/s, 1-Bit Recording

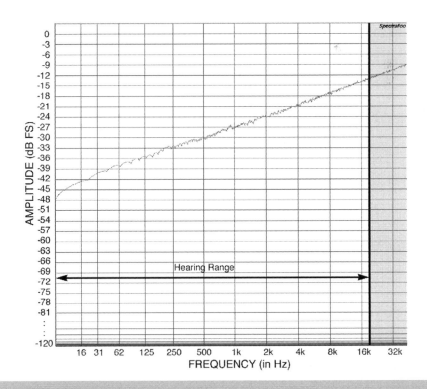

FIGURE 11.4B: Noise Floor from 88.2kS/s, 1-Bit Recording

DIGITAL AUDIO EXPLAINED

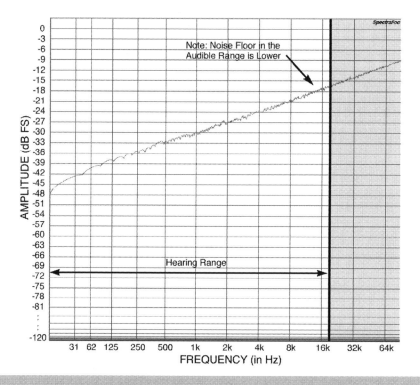

FIGURE 11.4C: Noise Floor from 176.4kS/s, 1-Bit Recording

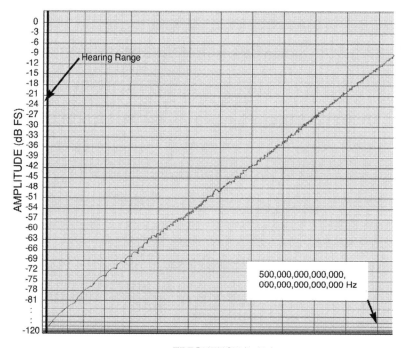

FIGURE 11.5: Noise Floor from 1.1 x 10¹³kS/s, 1-Bit Recording

recording then we can continue to lower the noise floor in the audible range (Figure 11.4).

Recognizing this we can figure out what sample rate we would have to use if we wanted to capture the entire audible spectrum with 120dB of dynamic range with only 1-bit. If we want to push the audible range noise floor from –6dB FS to –120dB FS and we get to subtract 3dB for every doubling of the sample rate then we can calculate the sample rate we would need to use. It would take 38 doublings of the sample rate (above 40kS/s) to give us the recording that we want, or about 1.1 x 10^{13}kS/s, or 11,000,000,000,000kS/s. This is represented in the graph in Figure 11.5.

If we sample at this extremely high rate then, even though there are only two quantization steps and the resultant samples would simply be a series of on-off pulses, the entire audible range would be captured accurately. If this system were to be played back there would be a tremendous amount of noise present, but the vast majority of that noise would be above our audible range and the material within our audible range would be recreated with perfect audible fidelity.

Again, the premise that the entire audible range can be captured with only two quantization steps may seem counterintuitive, but it is a very real phenomenon and is easily demonstrable. This is much easier to understand when we remember that the quantization noise is *the result of having to add energy to the waveform to get it to be represented by the quantization steps*. The fewer the quantization steps the higher the amplitude of that noise, but even two steps fully represents the waveform – just with a lot of noise present. Again, there is only one possible way that a sinusoidal waveform can be drawn through a series of sampling points legally, and even with two quantization steps the only way to draw a waveform through those points still has the original complex waveform present, underneath all of the noise created by the quantization. See Figure 11.6.

The notion of sampling at rates like 11,000,000,000,000kS/s is unreasonable, but it represents the very valid point that a 1-bit recording can theoretically give us our required audio fidelity. Regardless of the impracticality of such a converter, however, there is a significant advantage to using a system like this. A 1-bit system would be immune to having the non-linearity we discussed in the conversion process. With only two quantization steps there is only one "step size." As such, all "step sizes" are inherently the

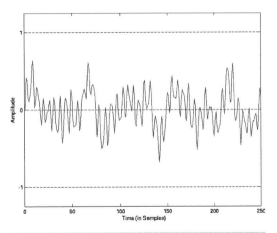

FIGURE 11.6A: A Complex Waveform

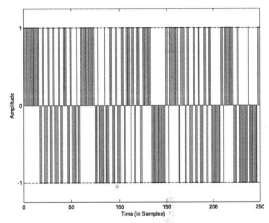

FIGURE 11.6B: 1-Bit Quantized Version of the Waveform in Figure 11.6A

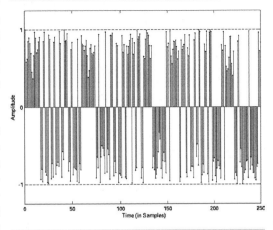

FIGURE 11.6C: The Quantization Error Between Figure 11.6A and 11.6B

same. Differing step sizes are the culprit of both integral and differential non-linearity as discussed in Chapter Ten. By definition, a 1-bit converter would have perfect differential and integral linearity! For an example, see Figure 11.7.

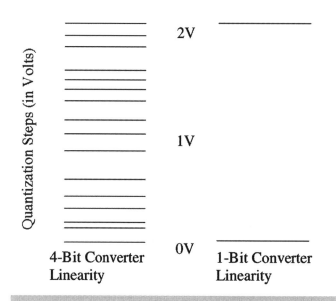

FIGURE 11.7: Quantization Steps For 4-Bit and 1-Bit Converters

The quantization steps on a multi-bit converter such as a 4-bit converter above are likely to be inconsistent and this creates high differential non-linearity. On the 1-bit converter all steps are the same size (since it has only one step) so it has essentially perfect differential linearity.

Because of the improved linearity, the concept of the high frequency 1-bit converter should be considered, but the implementation will have to be modified for practical usage. The result is the method of converter design that has dominated the audio industry since the 1990s.

The problem with 1-bit conversion is really that the slope of the noise floor, octave upon octave, is not steep enough. If the noise amplitude changed at a rate of, say, 6dB per octave then the sampling frequency necessary to transparently record audio with 1-bit would no longer be an exorbitant 11 e*xa*S/s, but would drop to a measly 2.06×10^7kS/s, or 20,600,000kS/s, or 20.6GS/s (20 giga samples per second). While this sample rate is still too high for current technology it gets us closer to being able to use this concept. The question to explore is how we can get the quantization noise to drop off at a rate of more than 3dB per octave. We remember that the reason the quantization noise decreases at a rate of 3dB per octave is because it is white, and white noise has equal energy at all frequencies. Some quick math would prove to us that for noise to have equal energy at all frequencies each octave must have 3dB less noise amplitude in it than the octave above it. The only way to get the quantization noise to drop off at a faster rate than 3dB per octave is to get it to somehow be something other than white noise. The reason that quantization noise is white noise is because the amount of variation between the actual amplitude at a specific moment in time and the amplitude of the quantization step is random. This random variation added to the signal to get the waveform to adhere to quantization steps is therefore random. We covered this extensively in Chapter Nine.

The only way to change the quantization noise is to somehow change the probability with which the signal passes near the quantization steps so that it is no longer completely random but instead tends toward creating a type of quantization noise that has much more high frequency content than low frequency content – more so than pure white noise.

One way we can change the shape of the noise floor is to add some filtering to the noise. Remember that the noise is, in effect, the result of the quantization error from the quantizing process. If the quantization error could be filtered to remove the low frequencies in the quantization error then the noise floor would no longer be white. One way we could do this is to utilize "feedback."

A feedback loop inherently functions as a filter. The classic example of this is given with a guitar and an amplifier. As a guitar feeds back into an amplifier the circuit filters out low frequency content and increases the amplification of the high frequency content, which causes the guitar to "squeal." One can change the filter specifications of the guitar/amplifier circuit by pulling the guitar away or pushing it closer to the amp. By doing so the cutoff frequency of the filter is changed. The type of filter created through this type of feedback loop is a high pass filter, or one that takes away low frequency information.

We can do the same with our sampling system. We can take the quantization error and "feed it back" in a loop so that it filters out its own low frequency content. If we do this – filter the noise present in the system by means of a feedback loop so that it has less low frequency noise - then we can use a single bit at a much lower sample rate. The way in which this is done is we take a sample, quantizing it to either the upper quantization step or the lower quantization step. We then take the quantization error from that sample – the amount we had to round the sample up or down – and we add that error to the next sample. By doing so we are feeding the error from one sample into the next sample and this creates the effect of filtering. The signal itself is still completely maintained and sampled accurately, but this process feeds the error signal from sample to sample, allowing a change in the shape of the quantization error noise floor.

This type of quantization noise is no longer white in nature as the noise generated by the quantization error is no longer equal at all frequencies. There is much more noise now in the higher frequencies than there is in the lower frequencies. The total amount of noise, or the total power of the noise is the same, but most of it is now high frequency energy. The noise is still random but is no longer white in nature, and it now gives us a steeper roll-off of the noise so that we can reduce the sample rate. The energy of the noise merely shifted from the low frequencies to the high frequencies to make the noise in the lower frequencies have a much lower amplitude than it would with white noise. This altering of the noise to generate a different "shape" to the plot of the noise is called "noise shaping."

By implementing noise shaping we can create a 1-bit converter that can operate at a lower frequency than we would need otherwise. The amount of noise that can be shifted from the low frequencies to the high frequencies dictates how low the sample frequency can be that will still give 120dB dynamic range in the audible range of 20Hz to 20kHz. Different amounts of noise shaping can be accomplished by how much of the error is fed into the next sample. One can, for example, not only feed a sample with the previous sample's error, but could also feed it with error from the sample before that. One can change the ratio of how much error from previous samples is fed, etc. One could take all of the error from the previous sample plus 50% of the error from the sample before that. The control of the amount and type of feeding changes the shape of the noise floor in a similar way to how changing the relationship between a guitar and its amp changes the frequencies affected by that particular feedback loop.

The device used in this type of converter is called a delta sigma modulator (or sigma delta modulator). The name of this comes from the premise that it takes the difference, or "delta" between the signal and the quantization step (the quantization error) and adds it (adding is referred to as "sigma") to the next sample. The type of converter that uses a delta sigma modulator is often identified as $\Delta\Sigma$.

DELTA SIGMA MODULATORS

The delta sigma modulator essentially has three components that cause the error from the sample prior to get added to the next sample before the sampling takes place. The basic delta sigma modulator schematic is shown in Figure 11.8.

The first event is the subtraction of the inbound voltage value from the value of the last sample. This results in the dif-

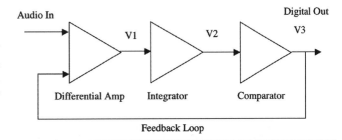

FIGURE 11.8: A Delta Sigma Modulator Schematic

ference between the voltage of the signal and the voltage of the quantization step, or the quantization error. The voltage for the quantization error is then added to the previous quantization error. Finally, the resulting voltage (the subtraction of the quantization error of both samples) is quantized to either plus 1 or –1 (the two quantization steps). If the total error is greater than zero then the value 1 is sent out and if it is less than zero then a 0 is sent out.

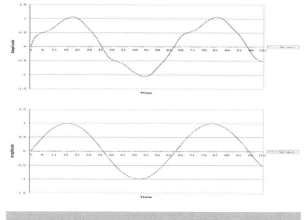

FIGURE 11.9A: Two Complex Waveforms

In Figure 11.8 the incoming voltage is sent to a differential amplifier where it is subtracted from the previous quantization value. The resulting voltage (the quantization error) is referred to as V_1. This is sent to an "integrator," whose output is referred to as V_2. The integrator stores the value for V_2 until the next sample. The V_2 value is determined by summing together the previous V_2 value with the current V_1 value. The V_2 value is then sent to a "comparator" which determines if the voltage is greater than 0V or less. If V_2 is greater than 0V then a "1" value is sent out, and if it is less than 0V then a "-1" is sent out. The voltage coming out of the comparator is V_3.

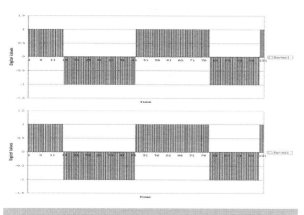

FIGURE 11.9B: Delta Modulator Codes For The Waveforms In Figure 11.9A

The voltage coming out of the comparator represents a (1-bit) binary code. The voltage V_3 is sent out the device as a digital signal but is also sent back into the front of the device where the cycle starts over again. This is the "feedback" part of the system. The net result of this circuit is that when a sample is taken the quantization error is stored and added to the next sample prior to sampling.

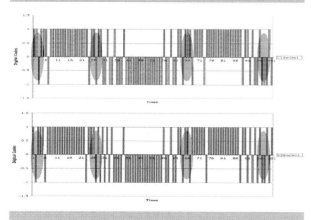

FIGURE 11.9C: Delta *Sigma* Modulator Codes For The Waveforms In Figure 11.9A

A delta sigma modulator is often confused with a device called a "delta modulator" that simply measures the difference between the amplitude of the waveform at subsequent moments in time. A delta modulator would measure the amplitude of the voltage at one moment in time, and at the next sample would measure the difference between the current sample and the previous sample. A 1-bit delta modulator would only be able to tell this difference with two quantization steps, essentially whether the difference in amplitudes was positive or negative. If the current sample is greater than the last sample value then the delta modulator would send out a "1" and if the current sample is less than the last sample value then the delta modulator would send out a "0." A delta modulator sends out an indication of the relative *movement* or *direction* of a waveform, but would not give an indication of the *amplitude* of the waveform. For example, the two waveforms in Figure 11.9A yield the same 1-bit delta modulator codes, but yield differing 1-bit delta *sigma* modulator codes, as indicated in Figures 11.9B and 11.9C.

A delta modulator only gives an indication of whether or not the amplitude is moving positively or negatively (north or south). The delta sigma modulator also gives an indication of how much it is moving positive vs. negative by feeding back the error to the next sample and incorporating that. Further, a delta modulator does not respond to direct current (DC, or unchanging voltage). If the voltage between two samples does not change then the delta modulator randomly fluctuates back and forth between its two quantization steps. A delta *sigma* modulator, on the other hand, fluctuates back and forth in a pattern that indicates the voltage being sampled.

Input Voltage	V1	V2	Digital Output (V3)	Input Voltage	V1	V2	Digital Output (V3)
0.2	0.2	0.2	1	0.6	0.6	0.2	1
0.2	-0.8	-0.6	-1	0.6	-0.4	-0.2	-1
0.2	1.2	0.6	-1	0.6	1.6	1.4	1
0.2	1.2	1.8	1	0.6	-0.4	1	1
0.2	-0.8	1	1	0.6	-0.4	0.6	-1
0.2	-0.8	0.2	-1	0.6	1.6	2.2	1
0.2	1.2	1.4	1	0.6	-0.4	1.8	1
0.2	-0.8	0.6	-1	0.6	-0.4	1.4	1
0.2	1.2	1.8	1	0.6	-0.4	1	1
0.2	-0.8	1	1	0.6	-0.4	0.6	-1
0.2	-0.8	0.2	-1	0.6	1.6	2.2	1
0.2	1.2	1.4	1	0.6	-0.4	1.8	1
0.2	-0.8	0.6	-1	0.6	-0.4	1.4	1
0.2	1.2	1.8	1	0.6	-0.4	1	1
0.2	-0.8	1	1	0.6	-0.4	0.6	-1

The Average Over Any (5) Codes is 0.2   The Average Over Any (5) Codes is 0.6

FIGURE 11.10: Delta Sigma Modulator Ouputs For Differing DC Voltages

In the chart on the left, an inbound voltage of .2V is fed into the delta sigma modulator and we can see that the average output over a fixed period of time is .2V. In the chart on the right an inbound voltage of .6V is fed into the delta sigma modulator and it the average output over a fixed period of time is .6V

We can clearly see this in the examples in Figure 11.10.

We can see in the examples above that the binary values given by the delta sigma modulator give an indication of the voltage that created them. We also notice that the results are giving an ongoing averaging of the voltage – if all of the values are averaged together it yields the amplitude of the voltage that generated the signal. We can look at a delta sigma modulator as doing precisely this: providing a rolling average of the voltage that was fed into it. In this context, a straight slope will show a constant changing average of the binary values as the slope increases (Figure 11.11).

A delta modulator would simply put out a stream of 1s for a slope like this because the difference between the amplitudes is always positive. The delta *sigma* modulator, on the other hand, puts out a signal that shows the constant changing average, and looks remarkably similar to a pulse width modulation (PWM) binary code such as we studied in Chapter Eight. It is important that we think of this code in terms of what it really is: a traditional PCM code that only has 6dB of dynamic range, but that does not have a white noise floor but rather has a noise shaped noise floor so that the dynamic range in the lower frequencies is much greater than the dynamic range in the higher frequencies.

A 1-bit delta sigma analog to digital converter utilizes a 1-bit delta sigma modulator operating at a very high sample rate. Most of the time the preliminary sample rate for these converters is 64x or 128x, meaning either 64 or 128 times the sample rate that the data will end up at after decimation. For 44.1kS/s audio systems the modulator's sample rate would therefore be either 2.8224MS/s or 5.6448MS/s. An analog anti-aliasing filter still needs to be inserted to avoid aliasing of any content above the Nyquist frequency (half of the modulator's sample rate). The analog signal is then sent into the delta sigma modulator, which results in a 1-bit data stream. This sample stream is then sent into a digital filter, which removes all of the content above the "base rate."

Obviously it would be impossible to remove all of the high frequency con-

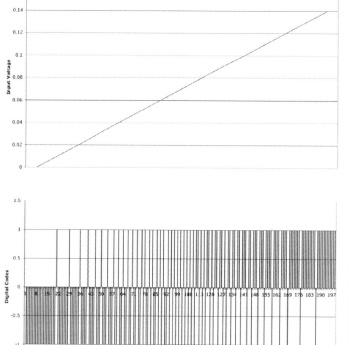

Input Voltage	V1	V2	Digital Output (V3)
0	0	0	0
0.01	0.01	0.01	-1
0.02	1.02	1.03	1
0.03	-0.97	0.06	-1
0.04	1.04	1.1	1
0.05	-0.95	0.15	-1
0.06	1.06	1.21	1
0.07	-0.93	0.28	-1
0.08	1.08	1.36	1
0.09	-0.91	0.45	-1
0.1	1.1	1.55	1
0.11	-0.89	0.66	-1
0.12	1.12	1.78	1
0.13	-0.87	0.91	-1
0.14	1.14	0.1	-1

FIGURE 11.11: Delta Sigma Modulator Conversion of a Slope

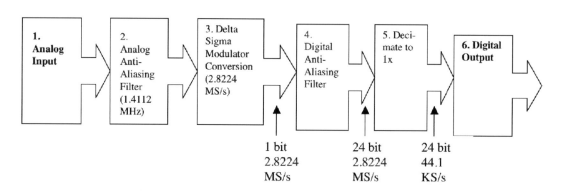

FIGURE 11.12: A Digital Delta Sigma Modulator Schematic

tent and still only have a 1-bit signal. We know that filtering out all of the high frequency information (noise) created in this sampling process will yield much more than 6dB of dynamic range across the range from 0Hz to the Nyquist frequency, requiring more than one bit to be present. As long as the high frequency noise is in the system, the *broadband* dynamic range is still 6dB and one bit is still adequate to describe it. As soon as the high frequency noise is removed (through filtering) then the *broadband* dynamic range increases dramatically, requiring more quantization steps. Our understanding of the number of bits that are needed to represent this 120dB of dynamic range without the additional noise above the audio range tells us that at least several hundred thousand quantization steps are needed.

A digital filter is implemented to do specifically that – to remove the high frequency noise leaving only the desired frequency range. A digital filter may be designed to only yield 16-bit words, indicating that some of the 120dB dynamic range provided by the 1-bit delta sigma converter is sacrificed. Most digital filters used for this application put out 24-bit words, exceeding the dynamic range provided by the delta sigma modulator. After the material has been filtered, the

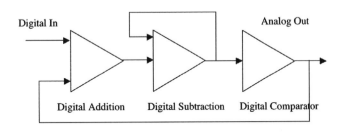

FIGURE 11.13: A Delta Sigma Modulator Schematic

remaining data is then re-digitally sampled, resulting in the reduction of the number of samples to the base rate number of samples. In the case of a 64x delta sigma modulator putting out 24-bit, 44.1kS/s data, 63 of every 64 samples are removed after the digital filters are implemented. The result is a 24-bit, 44.1kS/s data path (Figure 11.12).

A 1-bit delta sigma digital to analog converter utilizes the same concept but works in reverse order. Rather than having an analog delta sigma modulator, a digital to analog converter utilizes a *digital* delta sigma modulator. Instead of comparing analog voltages as described above, a digital modulator compares the numerical, binary, digital values and does the entire process numerically. The schematic for this is given in Figure 11.13.

After the digital to analog conversion, a final analog reconstruction filter removes all of the harmonic content above the modulator's Nyquist frequency, leaving only the waveform implied by the original, multi-bit data. A delta sigma modulator digital to analog converter is shown in Figure 11.14.

The most significant advantage of using 1-bit conversion is that the differential and integral linearity can be improved by reducing the amount of quantization steps from the conversion process, as the resistors used in previously mentioned conversion processes are inherently of questionable tolerances.

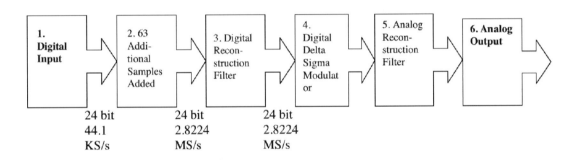

FIGURE 11.14: A Delta Sigma Modulator D/A Converter

There are, however, disadvantages to delta sigma modulator based A/D and D/A conversion circuits.

One disadvantage to this type of circuit is that the noise floor is difficult to keep low in the audible range. Although the concept of using noise shaping to reduce the noise floor sounds plausible, the amount of noise floor filtering that needs to be done to reduce the sample frequency requirements from 11,000,000,000,000kS/s to 2,822kS/s is quite drastic. This filtering is done using analog components, which, as we have been saying for several chapters now, have degrees of random tolerances and weaknesses of their own. Noise shaping is therefore implemented that uses several "orders," each order representing an additional feedback circuit, but also increasing the steepness of the filter in use by 6dB per octave. A 7th ordered noise shaping circuit would feedback some of the last sample's quantization error, plus a commensurate amount of the quantization error from the sample before that, plus a commensurate amount of the quantization error from the sample before that, plus commensurate amounts of the quantization errors from a total of 7 samples. This can create a very steep filter, allowing for a very low noise floor, helping us get close to our 120dB of dynamic range with only one bit.

A problem is in creating such devices. The most finely tuned delta sigma modulators used in audio applications only provide up to around 106dB of dynamic range in the human's audible frequency spectrum.

The larger problem, however, is an issue we raised in the "Quantizing" portion of Chapter Nine. We discussed that quantization error is not actually noise but is actually distortion. This is because the error of a signal is related to the signal in some capacity. We discussed that, in order to turn the quantization error into noise we had to add some sort of random noise to the signal at a *great enough amplitude* that we could randomize the quantization error, turning the quantization error into distortion of noise (which is still just noise). We also discussed that in order to do this, noise did not actually have to be *added* to a waveform (as all waveforms have plenty of noise in them) but rather that we had to turn the waveform up high enough in amplitude that the noise was greater than the amplitude of two quantization steps. This number – that of two quantization steps – is mathematically determined and substantiated as the amount of noise that must be in a signal in order to statistically randomize the quantization error.

The problem that we have is that, using only one total quantization step (from 0 to 1) the noise can never be present at the amplitude of two quantization steps - a high enough amplitude to fully decorrelate the quantization error from the signal.

Even though we take the error from each sample and feed it backward to the next sample, thereby changing that sample value to some degree, the error at each quantization step is still in some way related to the signal itself. Even using a 7th order noise-shaping delta sigma modulator, where some of the previous 7 samples' errors are fed backward and added to a signal before it is quantized, the resulting quantization error is still correlated to the signal in some capacity. For this reason, a 1-bit converter does not actually have a "noise" floor but actually has a "distortion" floor. All of the talking we have been doing about shaping the "noise" floor is actually incorrect. We have been talking about shaping the underlying amount of "distortion" present in the signal. The problem, here, is that the resulting distortion can manifest itself audibly in various situations.

Several attempts have been made to improve upon 1-bit delta sigma modulator based converters by adding some amount of noise or random variations in some capacity that could hopefully decorrelate the quantization error from the signal itself. Various ideas have included adding some random variations to the feedback circuit so that what gets fed backward is not necessarily the quantization error exclusively, but is the quantization error plus a bit of noise added to it. Unfortunately, not enough noise can get added in this manner to properly decorrelate the error. Another method involved intentionally varying the timing of the sampling circuit in a random capacity so as to add enough random error to *when* the samples were taken that this could decorrelate the quantization error from the signal. This method, called "jither" was introduced at an AES convention in 1999. Still other methods have been tried.

To this day, however, the inherent problem persists that if only one bit is used to sample a signal it is mathematically impossible to decorrelate the quantization error signal from the signal itself. Because of this, high distortion is *ipso facto* a characteristic of such converter designs. In fact because of this, a 1-bit design is inherently *not* linear, contrary to the objective of its design. It is, however, significantly more linear with regards to the measurements of differential and integral linearity studied in the previous chapter. As we look at newer technologies this fact will become a significant issue.

In the meantime, the problem with such converters was improved upon by once again going to multiple bit designs as opposed to staying with a 1-bit design.

MULTI-BIT MODULATORS

The delta sigma modulator improved digital converters by providing better differential and integral linearity, but the dynamic range available in the audible frequencies is a less than desirable 106dB and the distortion yielded by the inherent problems in the circuits is problematic. An additional 3dB of dynamic range can be obtained for each doubling of the sampling frequency, but 120dB of dynamic range still put the modulator's sampling rate too high for practical designs.

In 1999, AKM Semiconductor, Inc. derived a way to improve upon delta sigma modulator technology by releasing a converter that provides a full 120dB of dynamic range in the audible range while at the same time improving the distortion specification. The converter still uses delta sigma modulators, but puts out a several-bit output, which represent more quantization steps. By doubling the number of quantization steps (going from 1 to 2 bits, for example) the dynamic range is improved by 6dB. More so, by going from 1 bit to 2 bits enough room now exists to add the proper amount of noise to decorrelate the quantization error, removing the distortion talked about prior. Therefore, a delta sigma modulator that puts out a few bits instead of one bit can indeed reach 120dB of clean dynamic range.

The logical approach would involve using a delta sigma modulator where the comparator at the end of the chain is able to recognize more than whether the signal is higher or lower than 0V. If the comparator, for example, was able to decipher whether or not it was one of four levels (greater than 3V, between 3V and 2V, between 2V and 1V, or less than 1V, for example) then we could have a 2-bit delta sigma modulator. The problem with this approach is that the feedback part of the converter would have to turn the 2-bit number back into four different voltages. By definition this involves a D/A converter, similar to the R-2R ladder DAC that we have been trying to get away from because of linearity problems (Figure 11.15).

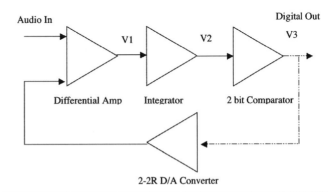

FIGURE 11.15: A 2-bit Delta Sigma Modulator Schematic

This multi-bit modulator uses a 2-bit comparator that sends out codes from 00 to 11 instead of just 0 and 1, but these must be converted into analog voltages in the feedback loop. Therefore, this converter utilizes an R-2R D/A converter in the feedback loop, presenting differential non-linearity problems. Dashed signals represent 2-bit digital values. Solid lines represent analog voltages.

An improvement would be to use several 1-bit delta sigma modulators in parallel and then sum the results together. To do this, each modulator represents a specific amplitude range. One modulator may be calibrated to represent the range from 0V to 1V. Another may be calibrated to represent the range from 1V to 2V, and so on. Each of these modulators puts out appropriate values and the results get summed together in digital signal processing, turning the four modulators into a 2-bit result. This would essentially work like the neurons in the ear: each covers a specific dynamic range, the combination of many covering the entire dynamic range of the ear. A multi-level variation on the delta sigma modulator is shown in Figure 11.16.

The problem with this solution is that we introduce the same linearity problems that we did with R-2R digital to analog converters and SAR analog to digital converters: each component (in this case, modulator) represents a specific range, and any slight electrical variations in the components causes differential or integral non-linearity because the size of the quantization steps is different. This is the same problem we experienced with the variations in the resistor values in the R-2R ladder and SAR converters. The way this is avoided is that the range that each modulator represents changes randomly. Rather than having one of these modulators cover just the 0V to 1V range, its range randomly changes so that any variances in the tolerances of each modulator are no longer correlated to the waveform. If, by chance, the modulator that covers the range from 0V to 1V and the modulator that covers the range from 1V to 2V do not meet up well in the middle then non-linearity will occur whenever the signal passes through these ranges. By randomizing which converter covers which range, the variations are made random and what was a predictable and repeatable error (distortion) is turned into a

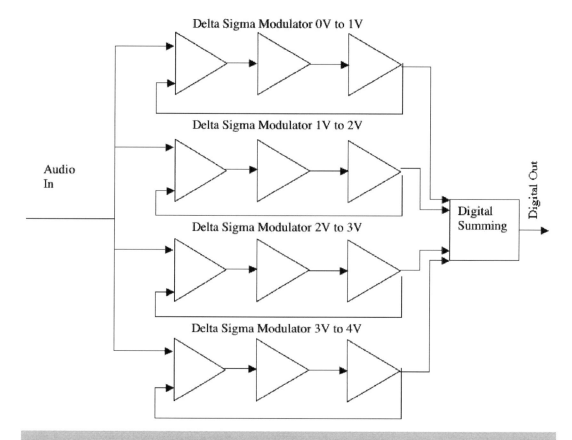

FIGURE 11.16: A Multi Level Delta Sigma Modulator Schematic

This multi-level modulator has four different delta-sigma modulators within it, each representing a different part of the audio amplitude range. The outputs of each are sent to a digital summing calculator that adds the results appropriately. A 2-bit code is then released from the converter.

random error (noise). Therefore, four modulators could be used, each covers a range that is randomly derived and changes over time so that the point where two modulators' ranges meet up does not cause *predictable* non-linearity, but rather *randomly changing* non-linearity. The concept of randomizing which component does what and when is a successful means of reducing non-linearity and turning distortion instead into a noise floor. In order to use this converter we need four different delta sigma modulators running simultaneously, each covering a different range, but the more modulators we have available to pick from the more random our results become and the more linear we can make the results. A converter manufacturer typically uses one less than an even binary multiple's (1, 2, 4, 8, 16, etc.) worth of modulators, such as 7 or 15. If 15 modulators are used then there are 32,760 available combinations of four modulators in four different ranges. This provides for a large amount of randomness, almost completely linearizing the results. Any non-linearity remaining would produce distortion well below the noise floor and would therefore be inaudible and would not affect the conversion quality for audio recording purposes. If more randomness is needed, more than 15 modulators can be used.

This converter type therefore works as follows: 15 delta sigma modulators are used, each putting out a 1-bit result. A random number generator selects which four of the modulators are to be used and determines the range that each chip represents. All of these 1-bit values are then sent to a digital signal processor that adds them together. The problem is that since each modulator covers a different amplitude range, and since that

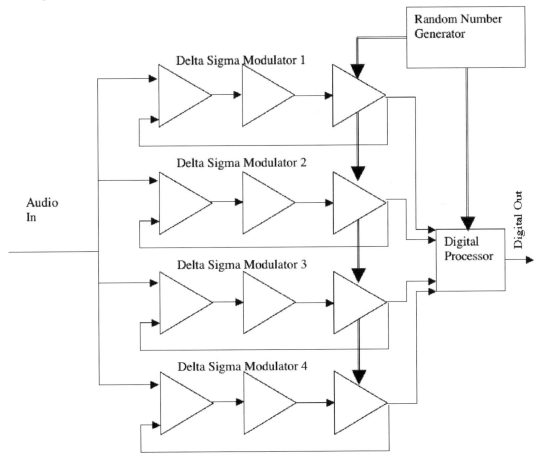

FIGURE 11.17: A Multi-Level Delta Sigma Modulator Schematic

In this multi-level modulator design, each modulator carries a different "weight" as is determined by a random number generator. The random number generator then conveys that code to the digital processor, which adds the results together with the appropriate weights given to the different modulators. This randomizes the error between the modulators, turning the error into noise instead of predictable and repeatable non-linear behavior (distortion).

is all randomly determined, the digital signal processor that sums the results has to know which modulator is putting out the most significant bit's worth of information as opposed to which one is putting out the least significant bit's worth of information. The digital signal processor must know the random code used to control the modulators so that it can decode the results and give the value from each modulator the proper weighting. Therefore, the random number generator also must send its random code to the digital signal processor at the end of the chain so that it can decipher the random weightings that the modulators provide to it. In this way we have a converter that puts out multiple bits but utilizes the advantages that delta sigma modulators provide. This type of converter is called a "multi-level modulator" or a "multi-bit modulator." Nearly all converters built currently are multi-bit modulator converters (Figure 11.17).

A multi-bit modulator D/A converter works much in the same way as its equivalent A/D converter. In the D/A converter, however, the entire process of modulating the signal is done digitally, prior to the conversion to analog. The digital signal is upsampled and filtered to a high sample frequency to reconstruct the analog waveform, removing high frequency content up to the range of the oversampling.

The resultant data then passes through a digital multi-bit modulator. This modulator does not have any of the non-linearity problems that an analog one does because it compares numerical values as opposed to analog voltage levels and can be made to be perfectly precise because there is not any ambiguity with the relative values of numerical values. The entire multi-bit modulation process can be done with one digital processor, producing a four-bit digital output. This process is not as simple as other forms of bit reduction. It requires going through the same process as the analog signal did including comparing the value of the inbound signal with the quantization steps but adding back in the quantization error from the previous sample(s). The result is a 4-bit version of the waveform with the same shape of noise on it that the analog versions of the signal had. This 4-bit signal can then be turned into an analog waveform.

Converting the 16-bit or 24-bit digital signal at "base rate" (44.1kS/s, for example) into a 4-bit modulated signal provides all of the benefits that oversampling provides while removing the non-linearity present in R-2R ladder converters and providing lower noise distortion than 1-bit delta sigma modulator converters. The problem is that we now have to convert the 4-bit signal into an analog signal. One way to do this would be to use a small R-2R ladder, but we just reviewed that part of the benefit of this converter was to remove the linearity problems present in such converters. Fortunately, there is an alternate way to convert this signal to analog because it has so few quantization steps.

Rather than having four different resistors, each of which represents a different binary value, and turning on or off the signal passing through the resistors, sixteen identical voltage "elements" can be used, each of which puts out the same voltage. The digital processor that puts out the 4-bit signal can, instead of putting out a 4 bit signal in binary code, put out what is called "unary" code. In unary code a series of pulses represents a number, but each bit has equal weighting. For example, 00000111 and 01101000 both represent the number three because three bits are "on" with each number. Each bit only equals one, and all ones simply get added together. To represent the number sixteen at least sixteen bits need to be used. This type of code is very inefficient for most applications but provides a benefit for this specific application. The digital processor needs to put out, not specifically a 4-bit binary code, but rather a way to convey up to sixteen quantization steps. This is done using 16-bit unary code. The unary code is sent to gates that open and close the sixteen voltage elements causing them to turn on and off. The output voltages are then summed together creating the appropriate analog voltage for the digital signal that represents it. A digital code of 0000000000000001 turns on the first element. A digital code of 0000000000000011 turns on the first and second elements, etc. Since all of the elements put out the same voltage, the voltage is recreated when the appropriate number of elements are turned on and added together. See Figure 11.18.

The problem with this is that we once again are relying on analog components that have varying degrees of accuracy and are difficult to manufacture with the precision needed for transparent audio. The alternative is to randomize which of the elements are used. This way the same element is not used every time the converter puts out the lowest value. Rather than having the lowest value always be represented by 0000000000000001, and turning on the first element, a random element can be turned on, such as 0001000000000000, or 0000000010000000. This way the inaccuracy of the element is removed from causing non-linearity and instead simply generates a small increase in noise because the error is decorrelated from the waveform and is random. Therefore, the digital processor does not put out straight unary code, but rather randomizes the code so that random elements are turned on instead of the same elements every time.

There still lies, however, a statistical problem. When only one element is to be turned on there are sixteen different random possibilities of which element is to be turned on. When two elements are turned on there are 120 different possibilities of which elements can be turned on. When three elements are turned on there are 560 different possibilities. When all sixteen elements are turned on there is only one possible combination of elements to be turned on. This "randomness" is not completely random, as the number of elements that need to be used dictates the randomness available for their use. This creates error that is clearly correlated to the waveform as the amplitude of the waveform affects the randomness with which the noise is created. In order to avoid this, extra elements are brought into the possible range of elements so that even a full scale value of 16 can be randomly constructed. By using, say, 31 elements, even a full-on 16-bit unary number has a high amount of random potential for which elements are used to create its analog output.

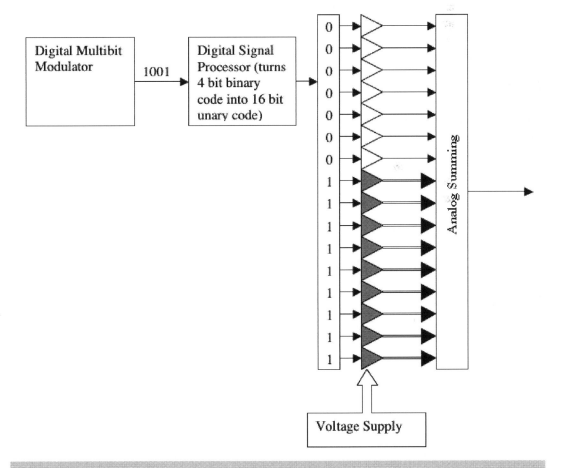

FIGURE 11.18: A Multi-Bit Modulator DAC

In this digital multi-bit modulator design several "elements" all release the same voltage. The multi-bit output from the modulator is turned into unary code and this triggers the turning on of the various elements. Their outputs are summed, creating the appropriate voltage level output.

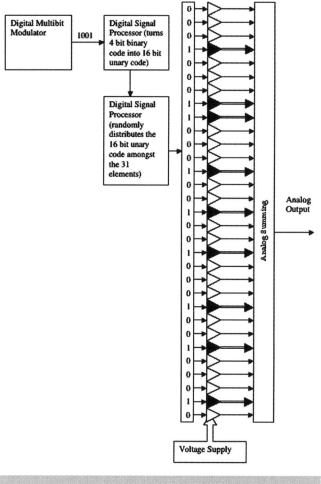

FIGURE 11.19: A Complete Multi-Bit Modulator DAC

Therefore, a 4-bit multi-bit modulator digital to analog converter is actually created as follows: The base rate, multi-bit data is upsampled to a higher sample frequency and filtered to remove the non-harmonic overtones generated by the sampling process. Once the material is oversampled to a high enough rate the digital signals are modulated using a digital multi-bit modulator that releases, not 4-bit *binary* codes, but rather 16-bit *unary* codes where the bit structures are randomized amongst a possible, say, 31-bits. These 31 values are then sent to a series of 31 voltage elements that turn on appropriately and all pass the same voltage when on. The sum of those voltages yields the appropriate analog value. This system is shown in Figure 11.19

While significantly more complicated than their lower frequency predecessors, modulator based converters provide many advantages, including lower noise floors and better linearity. The specific implementations can vary to some degree between specific designs. Converter manufacturers use anywhere from 2-bit to 5-bit modulators, and the methods they use to randomize the various components is a highly guarded industry secret. The premise, however, is consistent. While multi-bit modulators were only introduced to the audio industry in 1999, nearly all of the digital audio equipment made since the year 2000 utilizes them. They can be made to provide in excess of 120dB of dynamic range, extremely low integral and differential non-linearity, and can operate at various frequencies above the intended base rate. Most converter chips use 64x sample frequencies, though 128x and 256x sample frequencies are in use as well.

NOTES:

Chapter Twelve

Clocks

The concept of digital sampling is based on the measurements of the amplitude of an analog waveform getting at equal intervals of time. So far we have discussed the parts of a converter that measure the waveform and have discussed to some degree the speed at which that happens. We have not, however, discussed what controls the timing of the samples.

The timing of the samples is controlled by some form of a "clock" contained within each piece of digital equipment. The clock is not a conventional clock that reads the time of day. It does not tell "what time it is," but rather indicates only the passing of time, much like a metronome. It does this simply through the sending of electronic pulses much like a metronome conveys the passing of time by means of a series of audible "tick tocks."

The accuracy of the clock is absolutely critical because timing variations negate the accuracy of digital audio systems. Because a digital audio system is designed around the principles of digital sampling, any digital audio system inherently assumes that the conversion process was implemented perfectly. Errors in the timing of the samples do not get corrected, accounted for or accommodated for in digital audio systems. The system simply assumes that the samples were taken correctly. Therefore, if the analog to digital converter samples

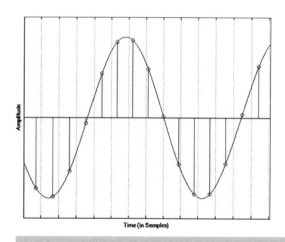
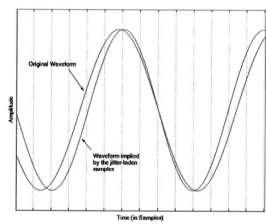

FIGURE 12.1: Jitter During the Analog to Digital Conversion Stage

At the analog to digital conversion stage, samples taken at the wrong moments in time yield the capturing of a waveform that is different than the original waveform.

the amplitude of the waveform but at the wrong time the waveform does not get properly represented. When the waveform gets reconstructed by the digital to analog converter at the other end of the signal chain the reconstruction will not yield the waveform that went into the system originally but will rather yield some sort of variation upon it. The effect of this timing error at the analog to digital converter is shown in Figure 12.1.

Conversely, if the analog to digital converter took its samples at the correct times but the digital to analog converter turns them back into analog waveforms at the wrong times then the same type of error will occur. This situation is shown in Figure 12.2.

Either way, any device that converts between analog and digital signals needs to have meticulous timing to ensure that the samples occur at and represent equal lengths of time. Timing variations that manifest in inaccurate conversion are called "jitter."

Another type of error regarding clocks can occur when two digital devices each have their own digital clocks but the clocks are slightly different. If one clock runs slightly faster than the other then the digital communication between the two devices breaks because the digital words are not properly reconciled between them. If the analog to digital converter takes its samples at 44.1kS/s and the digital to analog converter reconverts at 48kS/s, each slaving the process to their own individual clocks, then the system will not work properly. A more common

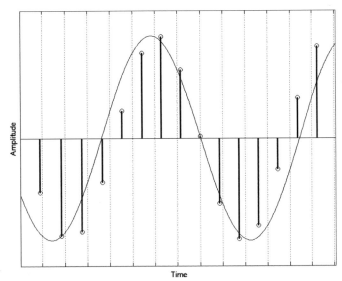

FIGURE 12.2A: Jitter During the Digital to Analog Conversion Stage

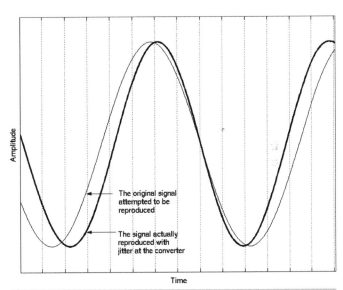

The original signal attempted to be reproduced

The signal actually reproduced with jitter at the converter

FIGURE 12.2B: Jitter Manifestation after Reconstruction in the Digital to Analog Converter

situation occurs when both converters are running at 44.1kS/s but each is running off of its own clock. If one clock is even just slightly faster than the other (perhaps an extra clock pulse or two a minute) then the digital information will flow freely between them until the slight variances in the clocking cause the wrong bits to be registered by the digital to analog converter. When this happens the system truly "breaks" for a moment until the clocks reconcile once again. In most cases this manifests as a "click" or a "pop" in the result as some number of samples go by with no associated digital words.

This type of error does not only happen when sending digital information from an A/D converter to a D/A converter. It can happen anytime that any information is sent to a D/A converter when the clocks are not resolved.

It can also happen any time the A/D converter sends the information to any other device, such as a recorder, if the clocks are not synchronized.

Every piece of digital audio circuitry contains some sort of clock. In an A/D or D/A converter, that clock controls the timing of the digital conversion, but this is an over simplification. In our SAR converter from Chapter Nine there were actually several separate steps that occurred for each sample. First, the analog voltage was sampled and held for comparison. Then, the processor that controlled the successive approximation started "guessing" voltages to be converted, which got converted by the D/A converter. When a match was made, the digital code was sent on its way. One manufacturer of such converters indicated that for every sample taken by the A/D converter six different events need to be "triggered" by the clock. In a digital signal processor a clock is used to control the speed of the processing. Every piece of digital equipment inherently has a clock in it, but when any digital audio device is used in conjunction with other digital audio devices all of them must be resolved to each other in order for the audio data to pass between them properly.

The problem of unresolved clocks (two devices running off of two different clocks) is completely separate and unrelated to jitter (erratic timing in a clock) - each problem is a unique issue. See Figure 12.3. The clock signals in this graphic are represented as square wave "pulses," as that is how they are transmitted between electronic devices.

Accurate

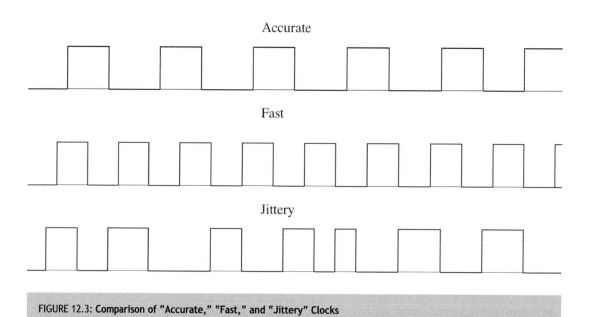

Fast

Jittery

FIGURE 12.3: Comparison of "Accurate," "Fast," and "Jittery" Clocks

Both because of the potential for jitter and because of clocking errors, the clocking circuits in digital audio systems are of great concern.

JITTER

Jitter only manifests itself as problematic at a conversion stage. Digital audio processors are immune to variations in clock timing, as are digital recording devices. A digital recorder that records the information erratically with respect to time does not, unto itself, create an audible problem. A digital processor that processes the audio and releases the results with erratic timing also does not, unto itself, create an audible problem. The problem only manifests if the digital to analog converter converts the information back to analog using that erratic timing. Theoretically, if both devices utilize the same master clock then any timing variations in the digital signal processor would also yield timing variations in the digital to analog converters. Much of the problem with jitter, however, does not come from an erratic master clock but rather comes from the communication of those clock pulses to the other devices slaved to it. It is therefore very possible, in fact likely, to have different amounts of jitter in every digital audio device in a digital audio system.

Since any jitter manifested at the digital signal processors or the digital recorders has no audible effect, only the jitter at the converters need cause concern.

The actual effect of a jittery clock on a waveform is mathematically determinable. The problem with jitter is that samples get taken (or reproduced) at the wrong times and the wrong values get recorded (or played back). Jitter would obviously be worse in a situation where a slight change in sample time can yield a dramatic difference in the sample value. This effect is therefore greatest when the voltage has the largest changes in amplitude in the shortest amounts of time. Low frequency waveforms do not change amplitude particularly quickly but high frequency waveforms do. Further, a waveform changes amplitude the fastest when it is near the zero crossing and it changes amplitude the slowest when it is near the peak. Erratic timing

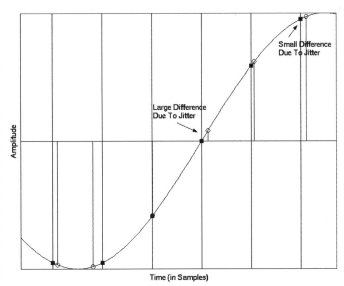

FIGURE 12.4A: **The Effect of Jitter on Low Frequency Waveforms**

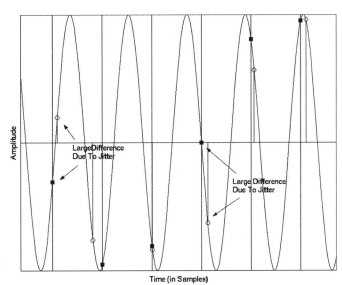

FIGURE 12.4B: **The Effect of Jitter on High Frequency Waveforms**

Note that the largest amplitude change due to jitter on either waveform occurred near the zero crossing, but the higher frequency waveform in Figure 12.4B showed much more drastic errors.

of the sampling mechanism has much less effect on a low frequency waveform than it has on a high frequency waveform (Figure 12.4). Further, jitter has less effect near the peak amplitude of a waveform and has increasingly greater effect toward the zero crossing. With these realizations about the areas of the greatest effect of clocking variations, it becomes easier to understand that clocking variations give very determinable results.

If the variations in the timing are plotted on a chart where the amount of the variation is plotted as amplitude then the result would yield some type of waveform. This waveform represents what we call the "frequency content" of the jitter. If the frequency content of the jitter in a clock is 1kHz, for example, then the clock variations oscillate back and forth between being ahead of true time and being behind true time 1000 times per second and in a sinusoidal fashion (Figure 12.5).

A Fourier Transform of the waveform of the *jitter* yields which frequencies of jitter are present. The frequency of the jitter manifests itself as audible "sidebands" around the actual waveform recorded. For example, if a 5kHz sine wave is recorded and the clock controlling the sampling has 1kHz jitter then the result is a 5kHz sine wave with some 4kHz and 6kHz harmonics present. The effect of 1kHz jitter on a 5kHz waveform is shown in Figure 12.6.

The amplitude of the sidebands is dependent upon three things: the amplitude of the jitter (the maximum timing variations), the amplitude of the waveform being recorded, and the frequency of the material being sampled. A 10kHz sine wave recording yields sidebands of greater amplitude than an equivalent 1kHz sine wave recording for the reason we specified above: higher frequency waveforms are more susceptible to distortion due to timing variations than lower frequency waveforms because the waveform amplitude changes much faster. A low amplitude waveform produces lower amplitude sidebands than a higher amplitude waveform because low amplitude waveforms do not change amplitude very fast (they do not change amplitude much at all!)

If the *jitter waveform* has two frequencies present then two sidebands appear around the sampled material. A 5kHz sine wave recorded with a jittery clock containing both 1kHz and 2kHz content produces a digital recording of the 5kHz waveform with sidebands around the recorded frequency of both 1kHz and 2kHz. Thus the resultant recording contains the 5kHz sine wave with additional frequency content at 3kHz and 4kHz on the low side and 6kHz and 7kHz on the high side (Figure 12.7).

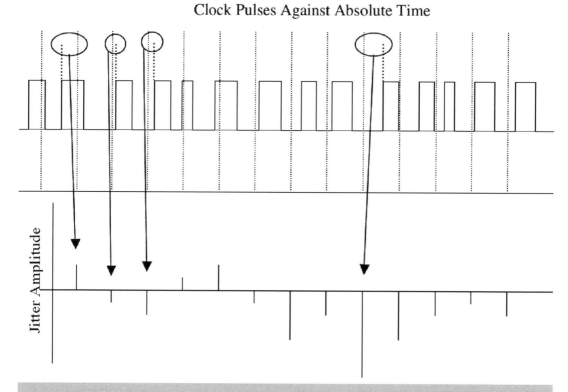

FIGURE 12.5: **Plotting Jitter**
The amount of timing error at each sample is determined and the results are plotted on a graph.

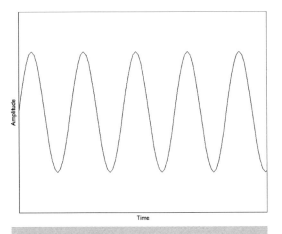

FIGURE 12.6A: A 5kHz Sine Wave

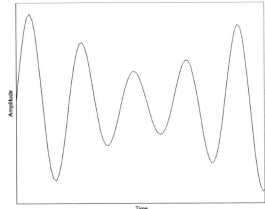

FIGURE 12.6B: A 5kHz Sine Wave Sampled With 1kHz Jitter

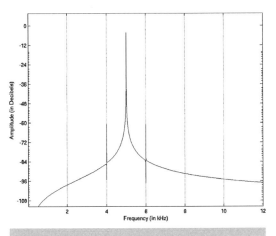

FIGURE 12.6C: A Spectrograph Plot of the Waveform in Figure 12.6B

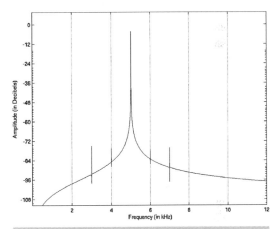

FIGURE 12.7: The Spectrograph Plot of a 5kHz Sine Wave Sampled With 1kHz and 2kHz Jitter

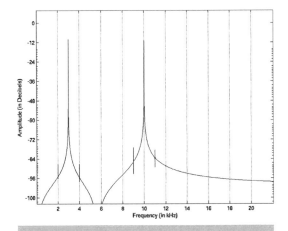

FIGURE 12.8: The Spectrograph Plot of 3kHz and 10kHz Sine Wave Sampled With 1kHz Jitter

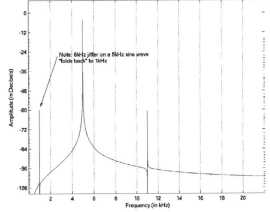

FIGURE 12.9: The Spectrograph Plot of a 5kHz Sine Wave Sampled With 6kHz Jitter

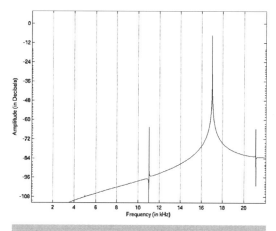

FIGURE 12.10: **The Spectrograph Plot of a 17kHz Sine Wave Sampled With 6kHz Jitter**

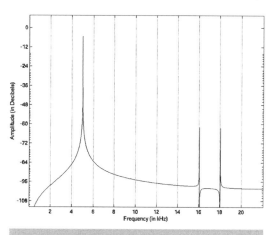

FIGURE 12.11: **The Spectrograph Plot of a 5kHz Sine Wave Sampled With 23.05kHz Jitter**

The sidebands end up around every frequency recorded, so if the recording contains two frequencies of, say, 3kHz and 10kHz and 1kHz jitter is present then sidebands will be present around the 3kHz and the 10kHz tones. The sidebands around the 10kHz band, however, have greater amplitude because the frequency being recorded is higher, making it more susceptible to jitter (Figure 12.8).

If a sampling system is designed to cover the range of 0Hz to 22.05kHz (such as a 44.1kS/s system) then the reconstruction filter does not allow any frequency content outside of that range to be reproduced. This means that if the jitter sidebands occur outside of that range they are reconstructed by the filters as having an effect *within* the audible range. If the sampling system allows the range of 0Hz to 22.05kHz then the sidebands always end up within that range. When the frequency of the timing variations is greater than the frequency recorded then the lower sideband "aliases" around 0Hz and ends up back in the "legal" range. If a sampling system, for example, has 6kHz jitter but a 5kHz tone is recorded then the two tones sidebands will appear at 11kHz and 1kHz. The 11kHz is the 5kHz tone plus the 6kHz jitter as explained above. The 1kHz tone is the 5kHz tone minus the 6kHz, mirrored around 0kHz and back to 1kHz. The 1kHz tone is the absolute value of the 5kHz minus 6kHz result. This is shown in Figure 12.9.

The same is true as we reach the top end of the "legal" frequency range. A 17kHz tone with 6kHz jitter yields sidebands at 11kHz and 21.05kHz, the 11kHz tone being the lower sideband of the 17kHz tone as would be expected. The 21.05kHz tone is the upper sideband, mirrored around the Nyquist frequency of 22.05kHz and aliased back to 21.05kHz (Figure 12.10).

If the frequency of the jitter is above the Nyquist frequency but below the sample frequency then the same rules apply. In this situation, however, we can be guaranteed that *both* of the sidebands are going to have to alias around their respective boundaries. If, for instance, a 5kHz tone were recorded and the jitter was present at 23.05kHz (1kHz above the Nyquist frequency) then the "lower" sideband would alias around 0kHz and end up at 18.05kHz. The "upper" sideband would alias around 22.05kHz and end up back at 16.05kHz. The "upper" sideband ends up lower in frequency than the "lower" sideband. This can be seen in Figure 12.11.

A simple observation can be made of the effect from any jitter that is between the Nyquist frequency and the sample frequency. The sidebands end up removed from a "center frequency" by the difference between the jitter frequency and the Nyquist frequency. In the case above, the sidebands ended up only 2kHz apart, so they are 1kHz removed from a center frequency, just as the jitter frequency of 23.05kHz is 1kHz removed from the Nyquist frequency. The center frequency is the difference between the Nyquist frequency and the frequency of the tone being recorded. In this case the center frequency is 17.05kHz (halfway between the sidebands of 16.05kHz and 18.05kHz), which is the difference between the Nyquist frequency and the original tone frequency of 5kHz.

If the timing variations occur at the same frequency as the clock frequency itself then no effect from jitter will occur. If, for example, the clock is supposed to be sending a pulse 10 times per second but it varies with jitter of 2.5 cycles per second at an amplitude of 1/4 second then the first clock pulse would be on time and every fifth clock pulse would also be on time, but the intermediate samples would be early and late.

If, however, the clocking variations happen at the same frequency as the clock itself then the clock may be "off" the entire time, but its pulses will always be off the same amount and no jitter will therefore be manifested, as in Figure 12.12.

Once the clock variations exceed the sample frequency, the aliasing of the clock variations causes the sideband distortion to be the same as the jitter frequency minus the sampling frequency. In our 10Hz clock rate example, jitter of 11Hz will have the same effect on the sampling process as 1Hz jitter (Figure 12.14).

One other observation to be made about jitter is that the sidebands are a lot more offensive to the human ear

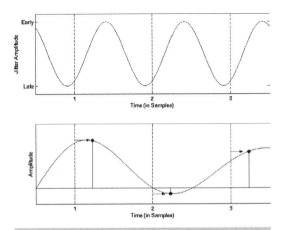

than they may "look." The reason for this is that the frequency content created by jitter is linear with respect to frequency in that the upper sideband is constructed the same number of Hertz up from the recorded tone as the lower sideband is constructed down from the recorded tone. A 5kHz tone recorded with 1kHz jitter yields sidebands evenly removed in frequency, at 4kHz and 6kHz. The human perception of pitch and the musical scale, on the other hand, are not linear in frequency. At one place in the musical scale 1kHz equals an octave whereas at another place it represents a very small interval. 5kHz is approximately equivalent to the musical note E. 6kHz is approximately equivalent to the musical note F#, a whole step away. 4kHz, on the other hand, is approximately equivalent to the note B, a musical fourth away.

As the content of the jitter becomes more complex the effect on the recorded material becomes greater. So far we have been discussing very "pretty" jitter that is

FIGURE 12.12: **Jitter Frequency At The Sampling Frequency**

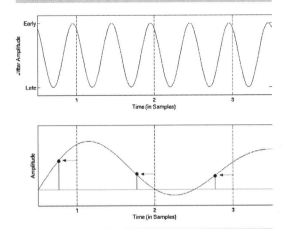

FIGURE 12.13: **Jitter Frequency at a Multiple of the Sampling Frequency**

If jitter occurs at a multiple of the sample frequency then all samples get taken early or late the same amount, such that the samples are all taken consistently, without the effect of jitter.

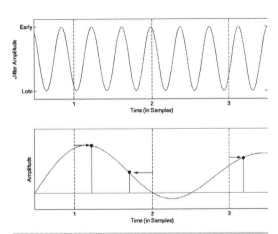

FIGURE 12.14: **Jitter Frequency At Higher Than The Sampling Frequency**

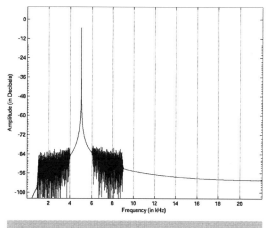

FIGURE 12.15: The Spectrograph Plot of a 5kHz Sine Wave Sampled With Random Jitter Between 1kHz and 4kHz

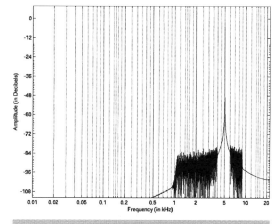

FIGURE 12.16: The Spectrograph Plot of a 5kHz Sine Wave Sampled With Random Jitter Between 1kHz and 4kHz - Linear Octave Representation

neatly organized for analysis. Most often a plot of the jitter content yields far more complex variations in timing than simple, cyclical variations, such as our 1kHz example. Jitter that is completely random, for example, causes random sideband distortion across the whole frequency spectrum. If the content of the jitter is random noise between the frequencies of 1kHz and 4kHz then the result is random sidebands removed from the original tone by a range of 1kHz to 4kHz. If a 5kHz tone were to be sampled using this jittery clock then sidebands would be present between 1kHz and 4kHz and between 6kHz and 9kHz. This can be seen in Figure 12.15.

Because the sidebands are closely related to linear frequencies and are not closely related to musical content, the lower sidebands cover a range of two complete octaves whereas the upper sidebands only cover a range of a musical fifth. A scaled representation of the sidebands to human hearing can be seen in Figure 12.16.

The upper sideband will always be a different musical interval removed from the initial tone than the lower sideband, and the frequency of the sidebands will almost never be related to the frequency content of the material recorded. For this reason, jitter is never considered "musical" or acceptable. Its results are not harmonically related to the material.

If the frequency content of the jitter is completely random then the effect of this on a signal is sidebands of completely random content covering the entire audible range. Because the random variations in the sidebands are directly related to the signal (without any signal there are no sidebands, with signal there are sidebands, with higher amplitude signals there are higher amplitude sidebands) the frequency content caused by jitter is not "noise," but is rather a type of distortion. Jitter causes a "distortion" of the audio signal being recorded. Semantically we should be clear that jitter itself is not distortion. Jitter, itself, is only the timing variations with which samples are taken or reproduced. Jitter *causes* a type of distortion – "sideband distortion" to be precise.

JITTER AND THE SAMPLE RATE CONVERTER

A Sample Rate Converter (SRC) is a device that can convert digital material recorded at one sample rate to another sample rate. Sample rate converters can function to increase or decrease the sample rate of a piece of digital audio, such as converting from 44.1kS/s to 48kS/s for film purposes or from 96kS/s to 44.1kS/s to put a high frequency recording on a compact disc. The type of sample rate converter that analyzes and converts the sample rate offline is called a "synchronous" sample rate converter. The "synchronous" part refers to the

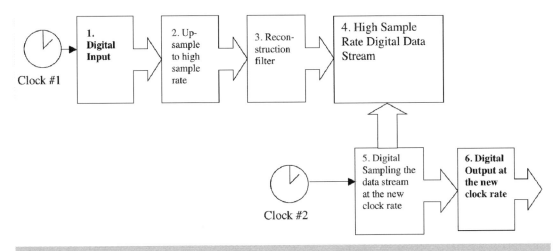

FIGURE 12.17: An Asynchronous Sample Rate Converter

fact that the starting sample rate and the final sample rate are synchronized, even if they are at odd multiples of each other.

Sample rate converters can also, however, be used to convert material in real time from two different clocks that are completely independent of each other and not assumed to be synchronized at all. This type of sample rate converter is called an "asynchronous" sample rate converter. Asynchronous sample rate converters can convert digital audio synchronized with one clock at, perhaps, ~44.1kHz to another clock at ~44.1kHz that are not the same, each of which have their own crystals and their own jitter. The first clock may actually generate 44.1000002kHz and the other may generate 44.099996kHz, both of which are considered ~44.1kHz.

Sample rate converters are covered more in depth in a later chapter, but the basic function of a sample rate converter is to upsample the incoming material to a very high frequency while using the inbound clock. Using the second clock the samples closest to the clock pulses are "pulled" from the pool of very high frequency sampling data as it goes by. In effect a *near* analog signal is created, slaved to the inbound clock rate and a digital converter then "samples" the near analog signal according to its own clock rate. An asynchronous sample rate converter flowchart is shown in Figure 12.17.

Because this process involves digitally sampling a waveform using an independent clock, jitter manifests itself in asynchronous sample rate converters as well. An asynchronous sample rate converter can be thought of as converting a signal to analog using a digital to analog converter, then resampling it at a different rate using an analog to digital converter, though this process is shortchanged just short of the final conversion from a very high rate digital waveform to an analog waveform. Nonetheless, even though an asynchronous SRC is a digital-to-digital converter, jitter affects this process in the same way that it affects analog to digital and digital to analog converters.

THE AUDIBLE EFFECT OF JITTER

Consistent amongst all jitter effects is the fact that higher frequency and higher amplitude material produce higher amplitude sidebands than lower frequency and lower amplitude material. Since, as we learned in Chapter Six, high frequency material is what humans use for localization cues and stereo placement, jitter has the most detrimental audible effect on recorded material through clouding the sense of space or stereo image in the recorded content. Often the ability to localize events in the stereo field and the ability to accurately discern the physical space that the recording was done in is hampered by excessive jitter at the analog to digital and digital to analog conversion stages.

We also know from Chapter Six that frequencies that have high amplitudes mask the presence of nearby frequencies of lower amplitudes so that they are inaudible. The audible effect of jitter can vary as the frequency content of the jitter varies. If the frequency content of the jitter is 20Hz then its effect on low frequency material, such as material in the 20Hz to 40Hz octave or the few octaves above that, may be consequential. In the octave between 10kHz and 20kHz, however, sidebands removed from the source material by only 20Hz will easily get masked. The difference between, say, 11,500Hz and its sidebands at 11,480Hz and 11,520Hz is so small that the jitter would have no audible effect at all even though the sidebands would be relatively high in amplitude because the source material is high in frequency.

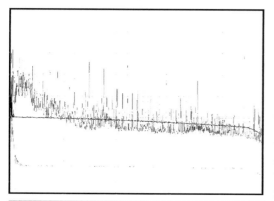

FIGURE 12.18: A Typical Jitter Frequency Specification Chart

The amount of jitter that is audible is dependent upon the frequency content of the jitter and the frequency content of the material recorded. Jitter in the nanosecond range (timing variations on the order of billionths of a second) is considered clearly audible and unacceptable for many professionals. Jitter in the picosecond range, especially under 100ps is considered acceptable (100 trillionths of a second, or .0000000001seconds), though the frequency content of the jitter is still consequential. Many manufacturers only specify the overall "peak" jitter indicating the maximum amount of timing variation produced. This statistic is not particularly useful because very high amplitude timing variations at low frequencies (such as 10Hz) are often inconsequential, though much lower amplitude timing variations at much higher frequencies such as 3kHz are much more easily audible. Many manufacturers also list in their specifications only timing variations up to the sample rate. As we discussed above, however, the jitter above the sample frequency is just as consequential as the jitter at frequencies within the audible range. Some manufacturers provide a chart showing the frequency dispersion of their jitter rather than simply provide a peak jitter specification (Figure 12.18). Even this approach can be difficult to interpret as the method of testing can produce highly varied results.

The fact that jitter on the order of trillionths of a second is audible should not be misinterpreted to deduce that the human ear is sensitive to higher frequency content or that phase shifts on the magnitude of very slight portions of a second are audible. The reason that timing variations on the order of this magnitude are audible is because one sample point provides a lot of information that is used to interpret the audio passing through the converter. If the sampling information is only slightly off due to timing inaccuracies then the effect from that affects the audible material over a long period of time. When we start to discuss digital filters we will realize that bad sampling data can affect the audible material over the next 500 samples or more. The precise measurement of every sample is therefore crucially important for digital audio to work properly. Very small timing inaccuracies are not an indication of the sensitivity of the ear to timing variations, but are rather an indication of the sensitivity of the ear to the audible sidebands that get created in the sampling and reconstruction processes because of the errors. It is rather a testament to the ear's extraordinary sensitivity to frequencies in its audible range.

Most jitter is divided into two categories: random jitter and systematic jitter. Random jitter is exactly what it sounds like: random changes in the clock's timing that create random sidebands, creating distortion that functions like a noise floor (though it is correlated with the signal in a random capacity). Systematic jitter is any type of jitter that is non-random. Inherently, systematic jitter must repeat or be organized in some capacity. The 1kHz jitter we discussed above is an example of systematic jitter, though we will soon learn that systematic jitter can be introduced from many means and that it does not necessarily produce simple results like constant jitter at specific frequencies.

The clock is, as we addressed above, more like a metronome in nature than an actual clock. The clock signals are transmitted as simple pulses of electricity down a wire. The pulses are often sent as square waves so that the same part of the square wave can be used as the "trigger point." Many devices use the leading edge of the square wave as the trigger point so that as soon as the square wave flips from zero volts to its maximum voltage the receiving device acts accordingly. (For our purposes, this action is likely the taking of a digital sample.) We discussed in Chapter Three that true square waves are composed of the entire, infinite frequency range of a fundamental. We also discussed that perfect transmission of analog signals cannot be realized.

We therefore know that the square wave pulses are not truly square waves but are only very close to square waves. The trigger point used for most electronic circuits is not actually when the square wave switches, because the switch from 0V to maximum voltage does not happen immediately. The trigger point is often taken from whenever the voltage of the square wave passes through a particular amplitude level. See Figure 12.19.

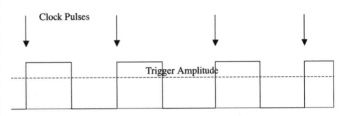

FIGURE 12.19: **Clock Pulse Trigger Amplitude**

Jitter can occur because of one of two changes to the perfect square wave clock transmission. One change would be the erratic spacing of the clock pulses. This type of clock distortion would likely occur because of the variables of the clock circuitry itself. In other words, the source of the type of clock distortion where the square waves are unevenly spaced stems from erraticism in the device that generates the original clock signal and can be seen in Figure 12.20.

The light lines show accurate clock placement. The solid lines show when the clock pulses are taken, showing jitter due to an erratic clock generator.

The other type of clock distortion that happens is a change in shape of the square wave pulses. If the shape of the square waves change then the voltage level used for triggering may occur at odd spacings from pulse to pulse. With this type of jitter, the pulses coming from the original clock circuit may be evenly spaced but distortion of the square wave causes the receiving device to trigger at incorrect times, as is shown in Figure 12.21.

In order to understand the jitter from the clock circuitry better we need to understand more about how clock signals are generated. We can then learn how jitter is manifested by means of transmission of the clock signal.

TYPES OF CLOCKS

There are several ways of developing a pulsating electronic clock. The easiest and least expensive method is to use what is called an "RC" circuit, or a "resistor-capacitor" circuit. The implication here is that a few electrical components put together on a circuit board can be made to oscillate on their own. There are many ways to create a stand-alone oscillating circuit but we will only cover one as a means of exploring the use of such circuits as a master clock.

A capacitor is a device that stores an electrical charge like a battery. If it is connected to electrical ground it dissipates its charge to ground. If a resistor is placed between the capacitor and the electrical ground then the resistor inhibits the ability for the capacitor to dissipate its charge, to some degree, slowing the rate at which it can do so. The more resistance provided by the resistor the slower the discharge rate of the capacitor. The larger a charge the capacitor has the slower the discharge time of the circuit. This can be thought of like an hourglass timer. The top of the hourglass represents the capacitor and the lower half represents electrical ground. The two are interconnected by a "throat" in the hourglass, and the sand represents the electrical charge. If we widen the throat then the charge drains to ground faster. If the throat is narrow then the charge drains to ground slower. If more sand is put in the top it will take longer for the discharge to occur.

This resistor and capacitor can then be coupled with a device called an "inverter," which functions like a gate. The inverter puts out voltage when it is fed no incoming signal. It puts out no voltage if it is fed any signal at all. The inverter is fed by the capacitor. The capacitor and the inverter are configured in a loop so that the output of the inverter feeds the input of the capacitor. A basic RC clock circuit is shown in Figure 12.22.

As the capacitor drains completely it puts out zero volts to the inverter and the inverter then sends out a higher voltage, which goes back to the capacitor. Almost instantaneously, the capacitor sends out a higher voltage to the inverter so the inverter shuts off and sends out zero volts. This gives time for the capacitor to drain through the resistor to electrical ground. When the capacitor has drained low enough the inverter in turn flips back on and sends out a high voltage and the cycle repeats. This repetition happens consistently so long as voltage is

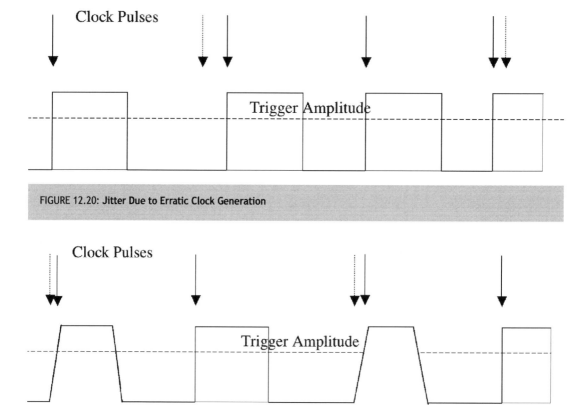

FIGURE 12.20: Jitter Due to Erratic Clock Generation

FIGURE 12.21: Jitter Due to Clock Waveform Distortion

The light lines show accurate clock placement. The solid lines show when the clock pulse will be recognized (when it passes the trigger amplitude) which is jittery due to mis-shaping of clock pulses.

supplied to the inverter from the power source. A clock can be derived simply by tapping off of the inverter so that whenever the inverter flips on and sends out voltage, that voltage is also sent to another device as a clocking pulse. Because of the *nearly* instantaneous speed with which the inverter snaps on and then snaps back off, the clock pulse that it produces is a square wave pulse.

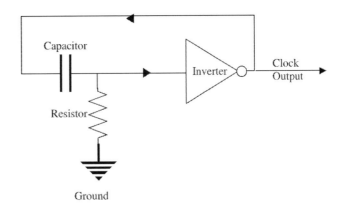

The advantage of using an RC circuit for clock design is that it is very inexpensive. The problem with it is that very small variations in the electrical current supplying the inverter (in this example) can cause a drastic change in the rate of the pulses that it discharges, because small voltage changes to the capacitor from the inverter drastically change the rate at which the capacitor dissipates. This, thus, changes the speed of the clock. This type of RC circuit can also

FIGURE 12.22: Clock Generation Using an RC Circuit

In this example of an RC circuit, the inverter charges the capacitor. The capacitor feeds the inverter. If the capacitor puts out a charge then the inverter feeds it no signal. The longer the capacitor takes to drain its charge the longer before the inverter flips position again and sends the capacitor another charge, in turn, sending a clock pulse to the output. The speed of the circuit can be controlled by the value of the resistor, effectively controlling the speed at which the capacitor drains its charge to ground.

be called a Voltage-Controlled Oscillator, or "VCO," because a change in voltage can increase or decrease the frequency of the clock signal it puts out. Because they are so susceptible to voltage changes, RC circuits are inherently unstable and inadequate for use as a sampling clock, though we will soon find out that simple VCO circuits are still a valuable part of digital audio circuitry, and the fact that they are voltage controllable has its benefits elsewhere in the clocking chain.

For digital audio sampling, a more stable clock source is needed. The most common solution involves the use of something that oscillates at an unchanging, specific frequency. The source of the constantly oscillating, unchanging, stable device can vary. The most accurate clocks in the world use the frequency of the light that is emitted from a specific type of atom (often cesium or radium) as a source of a stable, unchanging pulse. Unfortunately, while cesium and radium make the best clocks, both elements are highly volatile and therefore dangerous to work with. The use of these "atomic" clocks is relegated to scientific and government work, and the price of them can run between $12,000 and $250,000 or more. The advantage of atomic clocks is that, because they work on the atomic level, their accuracy is unapproachable by other means. Atomic clocks are known to not vary by more than a second over a million (or millions) of years. While in extreme situations atomic clocks can be found in recording applications, they are of little concern to us because the advantages of using them are negated by their expense and the fact that other clock sources provide enough stability for audio applications.

A more practical approach for audio applications (as well as many other applications) involves using a small piece of crystal. If we apply an electrical current to a crystal the crystal will physically vibrate back and forth. The frequency at which it resonates is based on the size of the crystal and can therefore be controlled by the way the crystal is cut. The thicker the crystal the lower its inherent frequency. When the electrical current is fed into a crystal it resonates and the current that is emitted comes out as a steady oscillation at a very low level. Quartz is often used as the crystal for a few reasons: it is relatively inexpensive, very reliable, and easy to work with because of its consistency.

The extremely low amplitude pulse that comes off of an "excited" quartz crystal is then amplified to a voltage level that can be transmitted with less susceptibility to noise and other sources of distorting of the pulse stream. This clock pulse is then ready to be used for applications requiring a clock.

CRYSTAL IMPERFECTIONS AND JITTER

Just as we discussed in regards to atmospheric noise, there is a degree of random variation in any device including the crystals and other components in the clock circuit. This random variation is equivalent to noise and it stems from the random behavior of the atoms and molecules that make up the quartz and other components. Random variations in the clock result in jitter of the first type mentioned: random, broadband noise jitter. Generally, this broadband jitter from the clock circuit itself is of less concern to designers than the jitter that gets induced into the clock during transmission. All clocks (as with any devices) inherently have some degree of random activity.

Aside from the random variations, there are two other issues regarding the variations in clocks. First, when the quartz is cut it is cut to meet a specific tolerance requirement, just as with resistors and other electrical components. A quartz crystal is cut and specified by the preparer as being within a specific tolerance, say, 100ppm (parts per million). A clock that is sold as a 10MHz clock +/- 100ppm might actually have a nominal resonating frequency of 10.00002MHz instead of 10MHz. The nominal oscillating frequency of a crystal also fluctuates dependent upon its temperature. Heat causes quartz to expand, changing the size of the crystal, changing its inherent resonant frequency. Every crystal has an accompanying specification indicating the susceptibility it has to temperature changes. The susceptibility of the crystal to temperature changes can be somewhat controlled by the angle at which it is cut off of the rock from which it is taken.

Many clock circuits used in digital audio use a simple crystal oscillator to control the conversion process. The clock's inherent variation from the optimal frequency is considered inconsequential because a timing variation of a fraction of a percent does not have any audible impact on the audio so long as the clock rate stays constant. The temperature variations are often considered inconsequential as the temperature inside a piece of equipment generally heats up to a relatively fixed temperature over the course of its operation shortly after the equipment is turned on.

Having said this, some designers of converters do take these variances in crystal accuracy into regard. Temperature variations can be dealt with in two ways. A Temperature Compensated Crystal Oscillator (TCXO) is designed to compensate for temperature variations by altering the circuitry that encompasses the crystal. Another method used for reducing the effects of temperature variations involves simply heating the crystal until the crystal is hotter than any of the temperature variations in the surrounding environment. An OCXO is an Oven Controlled Crystal Oscillator and is exactly what it sounds like: a crystal oscillator placed in an oven that keeps the crystal at a constant temperature. Often an OCXO is designed to heat a crystal to 10°F above the hottest temperature the crystal is expected to face. The oven is then thermostatically controlled so that large variations in temperature in the environment from cooling fans, tubes, or neighboring equipment and circuits heating up or cooling down do not affect the crystal. By doing so, the crystal's accuracy can be increased to .0001ppm when the environmental changes might have caused the accuracy to only be 10ppm. OCXOs are prohibitively expensive, costing around 100 times the price of a regular crystal oscillator (XO) and five to ten times as much as a TCXO. Very few pieces of audio equipment use OCXOs for clocking. An OCXO circuit, oven and all, is built onto the circuit board of equipment utilizing this type of clock design.

The variations in the clock frequency from the optimal clock frequency can also be improved upon. A type of crystal called a Voltage Controlled Crystal Oscillator, or "VCXO" has the ability to "pull" the frequency of the crystal to a slightly different frequency than the nominal frequency of the crystal. Pulling a crystal by a few hundred parts per million is possible by varying the electrical circuitry that surrounds and effects the crystal making it possible to pull the crystal back to the optimal nominal frequency. A specific type of VCXO called a VCTCXO, or Voltage Controlled Temperature Compensated Crystal Oscillator can not only pull the crystal's oscillating frequency to the optimal frequency, but it can also compensate for the fluctuations in the clock's resonance due to temperature variations.

In audio applications that use delta sigma modulators (nearly every converter design since 1990) the sample frequency is actually 64x or 128x (64 or 128 times the "base" frequency of either 44.1kS/s or 48kS/s). The crystal clock needs to oscillate at no less than that frequency, and because so many different components of the converter that need to get clocked at different times over the course of one sample being taken, the crystals used actually oscillate at 256x. When an audio system runs at a sample frequency that is a multiple of 44.1kS/s (such as 44.1kS/s, 88.2kS/s, or 176.4kS/s) the clock oscillation rate is often 256 times 44,100, or 11.2896MHz. If the audio system runs at a sample frequency that is a multiple of 48kS/s (such as 48kS/s, 96kS/s, or 192kS/s) the clock oscillation rate is often 256 times 48,000, or 12.288MHz.

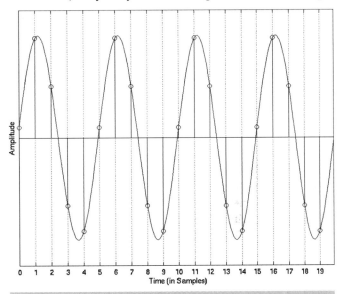

Figure 12.23: A 4kHz Sine Wave Represented with a 10kS/s Sample Rate

NUMERICALLY CONTROLLED OSCILLATORS

Since digital audio uses two different and unrelated base rate frequencies (44.1kHz and 48kHz), two different crystal clocks are needed inside every device. Beside those two rates, however, there are several other rates used in film post-production for dealing with the multitude of frame rates used in video. Often audio needs to be "pulled up" or "pulled down" to slightly differing rates when video is transferred from film to color television or from European television to US television. Rates such as 44.144kHz, 48.048kHz and others are needed in these situations, but attempting to derive these frequencies from a clock that is an even multiple of 44.1kHz does not yield an even conversion. In pieces of equipment that need to produce multiple frequencies, a type of circuit called a "numerically controlled oscillator," or "NCO" can be used.

If we want to derive a 5kHz clock from a 10kHz crystal we would use a simple divider that removes every other clock pulse. If, on the other hand, we want to produce a 4kHz clock from the 10kHz crystal, an even multiple divider cannot be used. One way we can accomplish this is by creating a multi-bit digital waveform at the clock rate that represents the clock signal desired. For example, if a 4kHz clock signal is required then we can simply create a 4kHz digital waveform, treating 10kHz as the sample rate. What we want to do is to math-

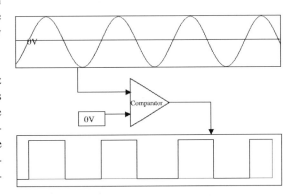

FIGURE 12.24: Turning a Sine Wave Pulse Into Square Wave Pulses

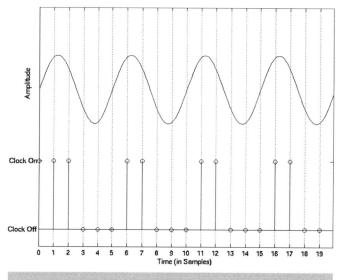

FIGURE 12.25: A 4kHz Sine Wave Represented with a 10kS/s Sample Rate

ematically create what a 4kHz sine wave sampled at 10kHz would yield. If we create this as 16-bit data then we can more effectively "see" the 4kHz sine wave created. See Figure 12.23.

We can then run this digital information through a digital to analog converter to reconstruct it into an actual, analog 4kHz sine wave using any of our known digital to analog conversion methods. The conversion will happen locked to the 10kHz clock rate. The analog 4kHz sine wave can now be emitted as a clock signal. If we want the clock pulses to be square then this can be done with a simple comparator. If the digital to analog converter puts out a 1V 4kHz sine wave then a comparator can determine whenever the signal is greater than .5V (the zero crossing of a 1V sine wave) and "turn on," emitting a pulse when that occurs. The result is that whenever the sine wave is positive a pulse is emitted and whenever it is negative, no pulse is emitted, thus producing a 4kHz square wave (Figure 12.24).

In reality, however, we do not need a 16-bit signal to create a sine wave. We only need a 16-bit sine wave if we want the sine wave to have high dynamic range, which is somewhat unnecessary when the sine wave is only used to trigger the creation of a square wave that is used to create a clock pulse. For this reason, very low-bit sine waves are created, most often using just one bit. The sine wave that is produced is no different than a 1-bit sine wave produced in a simple 1-bit A/D converter (not a delta sigma modulator). If a 4kHz sine wave is sampled using a 10kHz sample rate and only one bit, then statistically, over a period of time, every sine wave will average out to covering 2.5 samples. This means that the sine waves will alternate using two samples then three samples over and over again, as in Figure 12.25.

The 1-bit sampled data can be created simply by turning the first sample in the waveform on, as is shown in Figure 12.26.

When this is filtered, the result becomes a noisy 4kHz sine wave, which can then be turned into a square wave for a clock output.

Another way to look at this circuit is that if 5kHz is needed we use a "divide by 2" divider and simply send out every other clock pulse. If 3.333kHz is needed we use a "divide by 3" divider and send out every third clock pulse. If 4kHz is needed we use a programmable divider that can divide by 2 and then 3 and then 2 and then 3, so that it lets the first clock pulse go by, then skips one and lets the third clock pulse go by, then skips two and lets the fifth clock pulse go by, then skips one

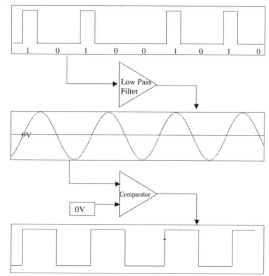

FIGURE 12.26: A Numerically Controlled Oscillator

and lets the seventh clock pulse go by, then skips two, etc. Over 10 pulses it let 4 go, creating a 4kHz pulse. This 4kHz pulse, on the other hand, has a tremendous amount of jitter as its clock varies .5kHz up and down from its overall clock rate. This clock pulse needs significant filtering in order to generate a relatively jitter free clock.

One observation we might make is that the higher the initial clock rate the less jitter will occur. For example, if the 4kHz clock needs to be derived from a 102kHz clock instead of a 10kHz clock then the divider still has to be programmable. Having said this, the divider will let the first pulse go, then skip 24, then let the next pulse go and skip 25, and so on. This can be seen in Figure 12.27.

The timing variations from sample to sample are reduced to less than $1/10^{th}$ of what they would be with a 10kHz clock. If the initial clock frequency is high enough it is possible that the jitter could be reduced to the point of being negligible without the need for analog filtering of the signal.

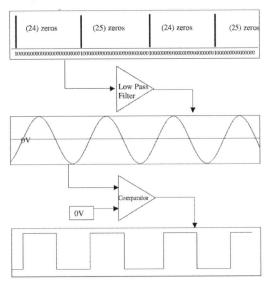

FIGURE 12.27: Generating a 4kHz Clock From a 102kHz Clock Rate In An NCO

This type of circuit, that which uses either multi-bit binary data to generate digital waveforms that then get converted to analog and filtered, or a 1-bit system that is essentially a programmable divider, uses numerical patterns to generate an odd clock rate from a given clock and is the basic implementation of an NCO. Several manufacturers in the audio industry use NCOs as the basis of their clocks, though the technology is significantly more involved than simple crystal clocks at even integer frequencies of the base rate, and the price of such boxes is therefore inherently more expensive. Manufacturers that use NCOs often start with an internal clock of 80MHz to 100MHz and derive from that, through numerically programmed dividers or multi-bit sine wave creation, several different sample rates, each of which, when filtered, can have very low jitter.

One advantage of using NCO circuitry is that a single quartz crystal resonating at 80MHz, for example, can be used to generate clock signals at any sample rate lower than that simply by changing the math done internally. An 80MHz NCO circuit can be used to derive 44.1kHz clocks, 48kHz clocks, 11.2896MHz clocks, 2.8224MHz clocks, and any odd clock rates that need to be generated. Because of the filtering used, NCOs are often more stable and have less jitter than other clock design methodologies.

CLOCK TRANSMISSION

As we discussed above, the clock signal is generated and transmitted as a square wave. If the clock is generated within the same piece of equipment in which the analog to digital or digital to analog conversion happens then the clock is simply transmitted to the converter on circuit board traces and jumper wires. Electrically conductive materials, such as wire, function as low pass filters, however, and the longer the length (and the higher the capacitance) of the wire the more high frequency attenuation occurs. If the square waves are transmitted at 44.1kHz then the frequencies transmitted are all of the odd harmonics of 44.1kHz. In other words, the square waves used for word clock transmission are composed of the following frequencies: 44,100Hz, 132,300Hz, 220,500Hz, 308,700Hz, etc. (all of the odd multiples of 44,100Hz). If the clock signal is transmitted at the rates at which the clock is generated then the frequency content in the clock signal is much higher. A 256x clock of the same 44,100Hz base rate is composed of the following frequencies: 11,289,600Hz, 33,868,800Hz,

56,448,000Hz, etc. These frequencies up in the megahertz range are difficult to accurately transmit because of the low pass filtering that naturally occurs in wire.

In order to avoid the difficulty of accurately transmitting the clock, when the clock signal is sent along any consequential length of cable (such as between two devices) the clock transmission occurs at base rate (44.1kHz or 48kHz). A few manufacturers in the past have developed equipment that transmits or receives clock signals at the original, 256x clock rates at which the conversion happens in most equipment, but because of the deterioration of the clock signal due to the inherent filtering in the cabling, the cable lengths for transmitting the clocks between the devices were limited to eighteen inches (a half meter). Devices that are designed to use this clock rate have their clock inputs labeled as "256x," and the transmission is called "superclock." Most devices transmit or receive clock rates at the base rate, and because this clock rate is used to determine the speed at which digital "words" pass, the clock input is called "wordclock." On most devices accepting either wordclock or superclock, the clock transmission is done on 75ohm cable using BNC connectors.

For boxes that send out base rate wordclock signals, a divider takes the clock from the crystal and divides it down to the base rate. The methodology is very simple: if the clock is to be divided into the base rate of $1/256^{th}$ the clock rate then the divider counts 255 clock pulses and then lets the next one through. While this approach is simplified, and often multiple dividers are used in series to divide the clock, the concept and the electronics involved are relatively simple.

JITTER DUE TO CLOCK TRANSMISSION

Because the clock pulses are square waves, high frequency attenuation causes a change in the shape of the clock pulses. Because the receiving device uses the point at which the amplitude of the square wave reaches a particular voltage, a change in the shape of the square wave causes the clock to be "registered" by the receiving device at a different time. Figure 12.28 demonstrates the difference in clock circuit detection of square wave pulses as opposed to square wave pulses that have been filtered by any of a number of means.

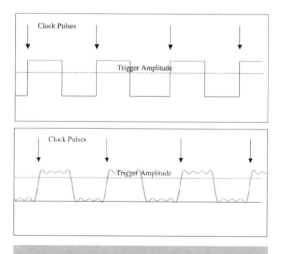

FIGURE 12.28: Square Wave Pulses vs. Filtered Square Wave Pulses

A square wave pulse that gets filtered low enough turns into a sine wave. If the clock pulses become filtered then the trigger points can change.

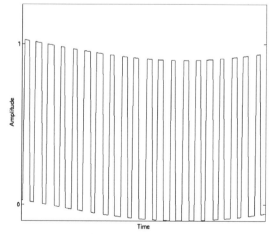

FIGURE 12.29: Square Wave Clock Pulse With A 1kHz Signal Added To The Clock Circuit

If every square wave changes in the same capacity and the same amount, as would typically happen with the high frequency attenuation caused by a cable, then this does not produce jitter, as the trigger point of every square wave is the same distance apart. This modified square wave clock still represents a stable clock. As the square wave becomes less square and more sinusoidal through filtering, the trigger point becomes slightly less defined because the change in voltage is drawn out over a longer period of time. The point in time when the voltage passes a critical frequency is less clearly defined than it is on a true square wave. This causes less square pulses to be more prone to inconsistencies of when, exactly, the trigger amplitude is reached.

Along with erratic changes in the square wave causing the trigger amplitude to change from pulse to pulse, this problem can be exacerbated due to stability problems in the receiving device. The trigger amplitude is established by analog components in the receiving device, but fluctuations in the voltage supply in that device can cause the amplitude that it senses for its trigger to change. If this happens then this can combine with the changes in shape of the square waves so that not only does the square wave change shape, yielding a change in exactly when the trigger amplitude is reached, but exactly what amplitude is used as the trigger amplitude changes as well, compounding the situation.

Another problem with transmission of clock signals via wire is the induction of noise due to radio frequency or electro-magnetic interference. As additional electronic signals infiltrate the wire used for transmission they get added to the clock pulses and create waveforms that are much less consistent. If the signals that get added to the clock pulses are random then the change to the waveform is random and the jitter produced is random. If, however, the signal that gets added to the clock during the transmission process is not random then changes of the timing of the trigger amplitude of the clock pulses fall into the category of *systematic jitter*. A 1kHz signal added to the clock signal causes jitter that is not random. The jitter that gets added due to a 1kHz sine wave being added to the waveform is precisely 1kHz jitter, the amplitude of which is determined by the amplitude of the 1kHz signal that was introduced (Figure 12.29).

The longer the distance that the clock has to travel in its transmission the greater the affect on the integrity of the clock. Transmission of clocks on circuit boards are under little threat to induced jitter because of the short distances they travel, though they are in the middle of a box that can be considered a hotbed of electro-magnetic activity. The clock signals transmited through cables to other pieces of equipment travel much longer lengths but in potentially less hostile environments.

The changing of the shape of the clock pulses is as viable a concern with regards to jitter as the changes in the distance between the clock pulses.

JITTER AND "EMBEDDED CLOCKS"

There are several "languages" used for transmitting digital audio between devices. Examples include S/PDIF, TDIF, ADAT Lightpipe, AES/EBU, S/MUX, SDIF and more. Many of these data transfer methods are designed so that the receiving device can "extract" clocking information from the information coming to it without the need for an extra cable just for communicating wordclock.

AES/EBU and S/PDIF are both digital communication languages that can transmit 24-bit data. The data encoding used for these is called "bi-phase" in that two bits are used to communicate every data bit (48 binary pulses are used to communicate a 24-bit piece of data). Every data bit causes a change in direction of the transmission data. A "0" is indicated with the two transmission bits being the same. A "1" is indicated with the two transmission bits being different. The binary code 0000 would be transmitted as 00-11-00-11, each data bit taking two transmission bits, each "0" causing both transmission bits to be the same, and each data bit causes a change in "direction" or "phase" of the code. 1111 would be transmitted as 01-01-01-01 – the second transmission bit is different than the first, and each data bit changes phase from the previous transmission bit. The binary code for 00101101 would be 00-11-01-00-10-10-11-01. For every new bit, the value changes direction, so that a "0" and a "1" are not indicated by the values of the bits, but by whether they switch once or twice over the course of the two bits used in the bi-phase protocol. By using this method it is impossible for three transmission bits in a row to be the same value.

Since both AES/EBU and S/PDIF transmit two channels of information (left and right) through one cable at one time, the information is put together in blocks of data, including the left and right channel data for a single word (each channel's data within a block is called a "sub-frame"). At the beginning of the block and at the beginning of each sub-frame a "header" is used that is specifically designed to violate the bi-phase protocol established above. Six different header bits are used depending on whether the header is at the beginning of a "block" or at the beginning of the left or right channel sub-frames. The headers are also different depending on what value the previous transmission bit is (the last bit of the last digital code). If the last value transmitted was a "1" then the header starts with a "0" and vice versa. The six header bits are as follows:

Block header, previous value is 0:   *11101000*

Block header, previous value is 1:   *00010111*

Left channel header, previous value is a 0:   *11100010*

Left channel header, previous value is a 1:   *00011101*

Right channel header, previous value is a 0:   *11100100*

Right channel header, previous value is a 1:   *00011011*

Each of these header bits starts with three consecutive bits of the same value, violating the bi-phase code used to transmit the actual data. Because of this, the header data can be used as clock pulse information and clocking information can therefore be derived to clock the rest of the circuitry.

The problem with using clocking information embedded in data signals is that some methods of data transmission formats do not require the same level of integrity that clock signals do. Our clock signals need to be as precise as possible, not causing changes in pulses that result in timing variations of mere picoseconds. The data transmission, on the other hand, only has to maintain whether the pulse is positive or negative and therefore slight timing variations are inconsequential and have no bearing on the integrity of the data.

Optically based S/PDIF and ADAT Lightpipe signals, for example, use fiber optic cable to transmit the data rather than electrical voltages. The fiber optic cable relies on lasers or LEDs (Light Emitting Diodes) at one end to send the pulses of light and an optical receiver at the other end to decode them. In the audio industry lasers are too expensive, so LEDs are used in their stead, and LEDs have limited bandwidth, causing changes in the shapes of the pulses being transmitted which results in resultant data with less accuracy. Fortunately, optical interfaces are adequate for transmitting data, but the more important aspect in regards to jitter – the timing of the data – is sacrificed when optical connections are used.

JITTER AND POWER

Many of the clock designs discussed so far allow voltage changes to "pull" the clock a few parts per million either up or down in frequency. The voltage is supplied by the power supply of the unit in which the master crystal clock is housed. If a voltage drop suddenly occurs then the crystal changes frequency. A voltage drop occurs if some other circuit connected to the power supply suddenly requires a lot of current. This happens frequently in an analog to digital converter. We have already discussed the zero crossing distortion that occurs when the numerical values switch from zero to –1, causing a binary change (in 16-bit communication) from

0000 0000 0000 0000 to

1111 1111 1111 1111

Each "1" bit requires a certain amount of voltage, so the change from no "1s" to sixteen "1s" causes a momentary swing in voltage that is consequential. The effect of this is a drop in voltage at the power supply, potentially causing a drop in voltage at the master crystal, which causes jitter.

The same can occur at the digital to analog converter when the output signal changes amplitude. The analog output of a digital to analog converter represents a change in voltage, and the voltage often comes from the same power supply that produces the voltage that regulates the clock. When the output signal changes amplitude the clock changes its frequency, causing jitter.

SYNCHRONIZING CLOCKS

We discussed earlier that all pieces of equipment in a digital audio system must slave to only one master clock but we have not fully discussed how that is accomplished. With all of the noise that is induced into external wiring we would not want to solely rely on the quality of the clock that is transmitted from the first piece of equipment. Clearly, transmitting a clock is less reliable than simply using an onboard clock (if the clocks are of equal quality). To solve this, the circuit in any piece of equipment synchronizes to an internal clock, but that internal clock is "pulled" into sync with a given external master clock. This relationship between two clocks is called a "master and slave" relationship.

Master and slave clock relationships date back to the 1800s when train stations would all have clocks. Each clock, however, needed to represent precisely the same time as all of the other clocks on that train system. A system was devised for there to be clocks in each train station, but one master clock (perhaps at grand central station) represented the actual time. Each of the clocks would run independently. Once an hour or once a minute, however, an electrical signal was transmitted through telegraph lines from grand central station to all of the satellite stations and the clocks would readjust and synchronize themselves to the master clock.

The same system applies in digital audio equipment: one device functions as the master clock and the remaining devices function as the slaves to that clock, continually re-synchronizing themselves to the master clock. The circuitry in each satellite piece of equipment actually utilizes the clock inside that piece of equip-

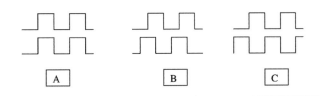

FIGURE 12.30: **Clock Pulses In And Out Of Phase**
Clocks "in" phase (A), 90° out of phase (B) and 180° out of phase (C).

ment, but that clock is in tempo with the master clock. The circuit used to accomplish this slaving is called a "phase lock loop."

The phase lock loop (PLL) is a circuit involving a device called a "phase comparator," which compares the relative phase of two clocks (Figure 12.30). The two clocks are the internal (slave) clock and the master clock coming in from an outside source. Theoretically, if the two clocks are in sync with each other the phase comparator will recognize that both clocks show an "on" pulse at the same time and that both clocks show an "off" pulse at the same time. If one clock shows an "on" pulse while the other shows an "off" pulse then the two clocks are not in phase with each other, but are rather up to 180° out of phase with each other.

The phase comparator, upon establishing how far out of phase with each other the two clocks are, sends an electrical pulse to the internal clock telling it to speed up or slow down to stay in sync with the external clock. This basic PLL circuit design can be seen in Figure 12.31.

Clearly, the internal clock in this situation needs to be "pullable" in some capacity so that it can "correct" itself to the master clock. The degree to which it has to be pulled is related to the stability of the master clock's signal. If the clock pulse coming in from the master clock is not stable then the internal clock needs to be able to adjust quickly and without delay or else it will fall out of sync. If the clock pulse coming in from the master clock only changes slowly then the internal clock does not need to change as fast. The most responsive clock that can be used would be a clock that is highly susceptible to voltage changes. For this reason, a voltage-controlled oscillator, such as the RC circuit discussed at the beginning of the chapter, is often used as the internal clock in slave devices. VCOs are very responsive to voltage changes and react quickly, making them an ideal choice. Since the VCO is directly linked to the PLL circuit, the voltage is somewhat controlled, making it a much more stable clock than it would be on its own. A VCXO could also theoretically be used, but only pending knowledge that its ability to pull up and down is in line with the maximum amount of variance that the master clock's pulse has. If a VCXO can only pull 100ppm, but the master clock's variance is 150ppm then the VCXO would be unable to continue to track along with the master clock in extreme situations.

One problem we have is that the clock signal coming in enters at the base rate of either 44.1kHz or 48kHz. The internal clocks needed for processing or audio conversion need to be up to 256 times the speed of the base rate clock, so we need to somehow increase the clock frequency *and* stay in sync with the master clock. This is done easily with a modification to the PLL. The clock in the PLL runs, not at the same frequency as the master clock, but rather at 256 times that speed. If the master clock comes in at 44.1kHz then the internal clock within the PLL runs at 11.2896Mhz. Before the internal clock's signal is fed back into the front of the PLL, however, it goes through a simple divider that removes 255 of every 256 clock pulses. The result is a PLL wherein the internal clock runs at a higher frequency but gets divided down so that it is only compared with the incoming clock at base rate frequency. See Figure 12.32.

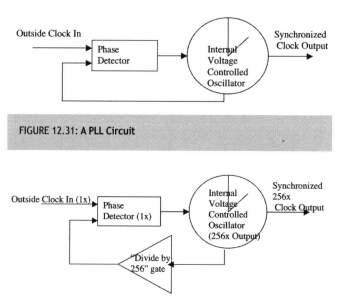

FIGURE 12.31: A PLL Circuit

FIGURE 12.32: A PLL Circuit With 256x Clock Output

Unto itself the PLL circuit does not actually solve any of the problems that we have with jitter. The slave clock does not slave directly to the master clock, per se, but slaves to the clock signal that gets transmitted to it from the master clock, full of noise and transmission induced jitter. If the internal clock simply synchronizes to this noisy, jittery clock pulse then it will have just as much jitter as the pulse that comes into it, solving none of the clocking problems caused by clock transmission. Fortunately, however, the PLL is imperfect and does not have an instant reaction time. The phase detector only tells the voltage-controlled clock internally to "speed up" or "slow down." It does not indicate how much to do so, but if it gets a "speed up" message for long enough it will eventually catch up to the speed of the inbound clock. This reaction time within the PLL causes a form of a clock buffer, so that the speed of the internal, voltage driven clock does not directly track to the speed of the inbound clock. This way, small, erratic movements in the external clock are diffused to some degree by the time that it takes for the internal clock to respond.

The analogy that is best used to describe the actions of a PLL involves two wheels connected by an axis, much like the axis of an automobile. A portion is removed from the center of the axis, however, and the middle is replaced by a spring, as is shown in Figure 12.33.

As the wheel on the left is turned, the spring in the middle begins to contract and tighten. At some point after the left wheel is started, the spring in the middle gets tight enough to cause enough tension to build that the wheel on the right starts turning. After the right wheel "catches up" turning, the tension on the spring comes into balance with the mass of the two wheels. The amount of time that it takes for this to occur is based on the length and the tension of the spring. At this point the two wheels spin at the same speed. If the left wheel speeds up then the spring again tightens and shortly thereafter the right wheel catches up to that tempo. If the left wheel slows down the right wheel eventually slows down. If erratic movement is given to the left wheel – it is turned but at an inconsistent speed - the right wheel also turns at an inconsistent speed, but its own erraticness will be less than that of the left wheel because the spring buffers the fluctuations, providing for the right wheel to move at a more consistent speed. The tighter the spring tension (or the shorter the spring) the less buffering there is, whereas the less taut the spring tension the more buffering there is and the movement of the right wheel is more removed from the movement of the left wheel.

If a mark is put on each wheel once they are moving at the same speed so that the mark on each wheel hits the top at the same time then we can determine when the wheels are in sync or out of sync with each other.

The wheels are in sync with each other so long as the left wheel never passes, or "laps" the right wheel. If the left wheel is suddenly given enough extra energy to spin it faster than the spring and the right wheel cannot catch up, causing the mark on the left wheel to pass the mark on the right wheel, then the left wheel becomes one complete rotation ahead of the right wheel and the two wheels have lost synchronization with each other. The same problem would occur if the left wheel were to slow down fast enough that the right wheel, not "grabbed" by the lessening of tension in the spring yet, would lap the left wheel. Any designer of an axle system like this would need to know the maximum amount of variation in the performance of the left wheel before ascertaining exactly which spring to put between the two wheels that would provide the greatest amount of buffering available while not allowing the wheels to fall out of sync with each other. We would need to know the maximum amount of variance in the speed of the left wheel in order to make sure that the spring was not too long and would not allow the wheels to ever lap each other.

In this analogy, the left wheel represents the inbound clock from an external device. The right wheel represents the internal, voltage-controlled clock. The spring in the middle represents the PLL.

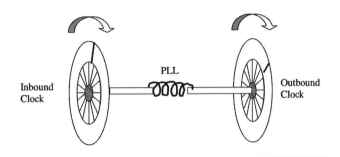

FIGURE 12.33: A PLL Analogy

The PLL can be "tuned" to not allow the voltage-controlled clock to speed up or slow down too fast, similar to having a taut spring in our analogy above. If the PLL is tuned too loosely, though, and the internal clock does not track closely enough to the external clock then the two clocks can fall out of sync with each other. The less closely the internal clock tracks to the external clock the more smoothly and less jittery the internal clock will oscillate. If the PLL is configured too loosely for the circuit, however, the two clocks will fall out of sync with each other. For this reason, the maximum tolerance for a clock is important information, and most clocks used for digital audio systems are tuned to not vary by more than 150ppm.

One other function a PLL can serve is to help "tune" the jitter to specific frequencies. We discussed that low frequency jitter is less audible than high frequency jitter, especially on high frequency content. We also discussed that the "spring" in the above analogy can be adjusted so that the tracking of the internal clock can be tighter or looser. A lot of manufacturers adjust the reaction time of the components in the PLL circuit to "tune" the device to produce mostly low frequency jitter so that the resultant sidebands get masked by the material being recorded. A jittery clock signal entering the system can be "tuned" using a PLL with a slow tracking time to produce mostly low frequency jitter, similar to the way in which noise shaping works to change the shape of the noise floor in delta sigma modulators.

The fact that a PLL is used does not negate that the clock that gets used within the box is still voltage controlled and voltage-controlled clocks are subject to variations due to instability in their power supplies. A PLL is therefore subject to its own jitter. On the other hand, PLLs can help improve jittery sources. A PLL is still always subject to jitter from the incoming clock source, so using a better quality clock source will always help prevent high amounts of jitter, even though the PLL will help buffer the internal clock to some degree. For this reason it is important for an audio engineer to test the various clocks in the various pieces of equipment in the studio and determine which clock source is the best.

INTERFACING DIGITAL AUDIO EQUIPMENT

Due to the incredible sensitivity that we humans have to the very small timing variations in digital audio samples, there are several helpful tips that can be adhered to for improving the sound quality in the studio specifically relating to clocking.

In theory, PLLs will help to buffer clock jitter and reduce its overall effect. Unfortunately, however, two (or more) PLLs in series can actually exaggerate the problems of jitter rather than reduce them. Two PLLs in series function much like a three-wheeled axle as in Figure 12.34, with springs between each pair of wheels.

As the left wheel is turned, the center wheel is pulled into sync with it, and as the center wheel turns, the right wheel is pulled in sync with it. Between each

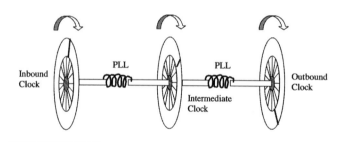

FIGURE 12.34: Two PLLs in Series

When multiple PLL's are put in series the latter wheel is more removed from the first wheel.

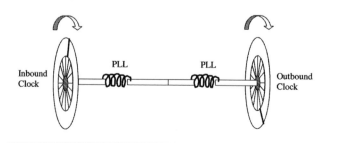

FIGURE 12.35: Two PLLs in Series

set of wheels the spring is chosen that ensures the greatest amount of buffering for the maximum tolerance in the driving wheel. In effect, though, the right wheel is actually slaved to the left wheel through an extra long spring, as in Figure 12.35.

The relationship between the starting clock and the ending clock is now brought into question. It is very possible at this point for the two clocks to fall out of sync with each other even though neither clock is out of sync with the "middle" clock. The same can occur if multiple pieces of digital audio equipment are connected so that the clock goes "through" each box on its way to the next box. Not only is the clock subjected to a lot more transmission induced jitter because of the additional connections and cabling involved, but it also is more prone to falling completely out of sync with the master clock, causing dropouts or audible "pops" and "clicks" in the audio handled by that piece of equipment.

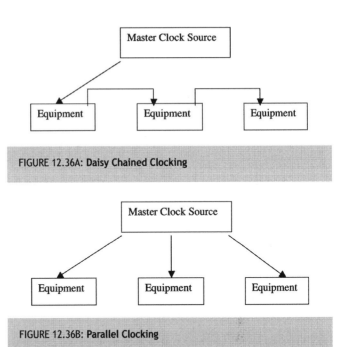

FIGURE 12.36A: Daisy Chained Clocking

FIGURE 12.36B: Parallel Clocking

For this reason, "daisy chaining" wordclock signals, or connecting each box to the next in a series is less desirable and more prone to clock related problems than connecting each piece of equipment to a master clock directly. See Figure 12.36.

Akin to daisy chaining wordclock is "T'ing off" or "Y'ing" wordclock between equipment. Either of these methods utilizes a type of connector that splits the wordclock signal in two directions so that two boxes can be clocked to the master clock without inducing the intermediate PLL into the chain. The supposed advantage to T'ing off a wordclock signal is that the integrity of wordclock signals can deteriorate when being passed through multiple PLLs. When a wordclock signal enters a piece of equipment it almost always goes into the PLL first. The output of the PLL not only feeds the internal circuitry, but also feeds the wordclock output on the back of the box, which then feeds any additional pieces of equipment in the studio. Upon entering the next box the wordclock signal undergoes an additional stage of PLL. As discussed above, this can increase jitter problems.

By T'ing a wordclock signal, the wordclock gets to the next pieces of equipment without going through additional PLL stages. The problem with this method is that the signal is simply split, decreasing the amplitude of the wordclock

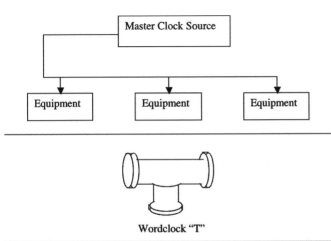

Wordclock "T"

FIGURE 12.37: T'ing Clocks

signal by 6dB and potentially adding impedance problems by feeding multiple boxes with one signal. An example can be seen in Figure 12.37.

The best method of providing clock to all items in a studio is to connect all devices to a master clock using a dedicated cable for each item. In lieu of connecting each box to a master clock, a word clock distribution amplifier can be used which properly splits the wordclock signal while amplifying each resulting leg in order to give the cleanest signal to each device. Because the converters are the only place where jitter causes an audible deterioration of sonic transparency, most converter manufacturers put stable and high quality clocks in their equipment. Most A/D and D/A converters, however, only have one wordclock output, so either daisy chaining or using a distribution amplifier may become necessary for the best quality clocking with other devices.

Having said this, if only one piece of equipment in a studio is used for conversion (such as an eight channel A/D and D/A converter all in one box in a small, project studio) then high quality distribution is completely unnecessary. Even if a dozen other digital devices are used in the studio including digital recorders, effects processors, mixers, digital audio tape machines and more, strict, low jitter clocking may be completely irrelevant since the converters are the only component audibly affected by timing inconsistencies. Many engineers are unnecessarily concerned that, after traversing the length of all of the digital equipment, by the time the digital data gets to the D/A converter for conversion back to analog audio, the timing of the data is inconsistent and will reproduced as such. Fortunately, D/A converters have a small buffer in them of a sample's worth of data so that as the data hits the converter it is held until the *next* clock pulse and is not converted as it enters the converter.

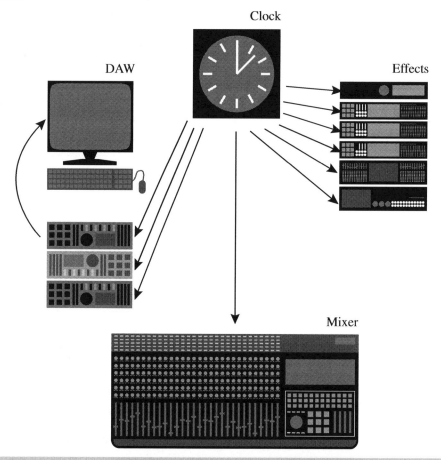

FIGURE 12.38: A Large Studio Utilizing a Master Clock

In a digital studio with multiple devices that handle conversion, such as a series of stand-alone analog to digital converters, a digital mixer with converters, a CD burner with a D/A converter for a headphone output, a digital mixer with analog inputs and outputs for effects sends and returns and maybe even a digital microphone or a pair of digital speakers, disseminating high integrity clock signals to each becomes difficult. The last items in the chain are likely to suffer so that the sound quality in the fourth outboard analog to digital converter box will not sound as good as the first. In these situations either a distribution amplifier or a high quality, dedicated master clock is appropriate. An example of a large studio design can be found in Figure 12.38.

Devices that function exclusively as clock generators are common in larger studios as a way of reducing clock transmission problems to the multitude of digital equipment used. Such clocks often also serve as distribution amplifiers providing multiple wordclock outputs as well as other clock formats such as superclock or video reference clocks. Dedicated master clocks often have very high quality clock generation methods in them using NCOs or OCXOs. In many cases the use of a dedicated master clock can also improve the A/D and D/A conversion in a less complex studio simply because the clock generation in a master clock is of significantly higher quality than budget quality A/D and D/A converters' clocks. In some cases an outboard, dedicated master clock can outperform an onboard crystal even though the outboard clock must get divided down to 44.1kHz, transmitted through a wire, and upsampled back to 256x using a PLL inside the converter. This can be true even though the crystal clock in the converter generates at the 256x frequently inherently and need not go through additional down and upsampling stages before being put to use at the converter chip.

Many engineers have made an excessive issue out of the lengths of cable used for clock transmission when a master clock or distribution amplifier is used. While it is true that shorter cable lengths reduce high frequency loss and thus provide better reproduction of the square wave pulses used for clocking, there is no need in a studio to have all wordclock cables the same length. The concern stems from the notion that clock pulses might not all arrive at the same time between all devices, somehow causing irregular timing errors as data is transmitted between devices. Any digital device, however, buffers the data as it comes in so that slight timing variations do not cause gross timing errors between digitally interfaced boxes. Another oft-heard concern is that two analog to digital converters both synchronized to the same master clock but with different length cables will not end up sampling at precisely the same time. If the data coming off of each of these boxes is mixed together the results would theoretically have phase irregularities. This, also, is not a valid concern because the speed of electricity through copper wires is approximately 500,000,000 feet per second, so that even if an extra 1000 ft (308 meters) of cable was used to clock the second converter, the samples would only be taken .000002 seconds apart from each other, which is not enough of an offset to cause any audible problems. Further, we must remember that wordclock only carries pulses indicating the passing of time, and does not actually "tell the time." If clock pulse number two gets to a device at the same time that clock pulse number one gets to a different device then each device will still sample at the same times. Even though it would take exaggeratingly long cable lengths to accomplish this, it is a reminder that not every box needs to clock at the exact same time but merely needs to have the same semblance and sensing of the "passing of time." Either way, word clock cable lengths should always be minimized, but matching lengths between various items is unnecessary.

CONCLUSION

The various issues involved with the proper clocking of digital audio equipment are clearly extensive. Many studio owners find the proper implementation of clock sources and cabling in the studio to be more of an art than a science because of a lack of understanding of the science involved. Armed with the information contained within this chapter, determining the best clocking method in a studio should be easier and the results should be more conclusive. Listening to various permutations of studio clocking, combined with understanding why such solutions may or may not work well, is an excellent way of determining the most audibly transparent clocking scheme for a digital audio system.

Part Three

Signal Processing

Chapter Thirteen

Introduction to Signal Processing

So far we have discussed what sound is, how it is created, and how we hear it. We also discussed how audio can be transferred between air pressure waves and electrical voltages. By converting the waves to electrical voltages we provide a method to transmit sound more effectively than through air pressure. Electricity is more effective than air for transferring sound for a multitude of reasons, including that it is faster and does not suffer nearly as much from the energy dissipating over distance like sound waves transferred through the air. We then discussed that any method of transmission, however, is prone to change (distortion and filtering) and the addition of random variations (noise) over time. By turning the acoustical air pressure changes to digital numbers we provide a method for perfect transmission of audio within a given dynamic range and a given frequency range. We have also discussed, however, that the process of changing sound pressure wave information to digital, numerical information can cause errors of its own. The preceding chapters have highlighted ways in which these errors are minimized.

We also discussed ways to record sound that also involves transferring the changes in air pressure to other media, such as changes in the height of vinyl or wax on a disk, or changes in magnetism on tape. We discussed that these methods are also inherently imperfect, as changes happen to the material during this transfer.

The advantages of using digital methods to record audio are not restricted to the transmission or the recording of the sound. The vast majority of audio undergoes some form of processing, often to "improve" the audio. Any audio transmitted through a telephone line, radio, or telephone undergoes processing to improve the clarity of the audio. Most audio distributed in consumer formats undergoes vast amounts of audio processing to help improve the audible appeal of the recordings. Many times audio processing is done in order to create a particular sonic event that did not actually occur and was thus not capable of being "recorded." In these situations, the sonic event is created using audio processing, examples including the use of synthesizers.

In reality, only four types of processing can be done: frequency processing, amplitude processing, phase processing, and dynamic range processing. Since these are the only actual characteristics of waveforms, these are the only changes that can occur. In a more practical sense, many types of audio processing normally used combine multiple of these basic types of effect.

Some of the types of audio processing that are often used are as follows:

• *Mixing of multiple audio signals together*

• *Filtering the material to enhance or attenuate certain frequencies present (frequency, phase, and amplitude processing)*

• *Compressing or expanding the dynamic range of the audio (dynamic range processing)*

• *Compressing or expanding the time needed in which the audio occurs (frequency and phase processing)*

• *Gating (amplitude processing)*

• *Changing the frequency content of the audio (frequency and amplitude processing)*

• *Delaying when the audio plays (phase processing)*

• *Changing the amplitude of the audio (amplitude processing)*

Oftentimes multiple types of processing are done simultaneously. Echoes and delays, for example, involve both temporarily delaying the signal and then mixing it back in with the original signal. Room simulation (reverb) involves echoes combined with low pass filters and sometimes pitch processing as well.

The methods used for various types of processing have sacrifices. For example, the method used for analog filtering inherently causes "group delay," or the shifting of phase of the frequency spectrum by varying amounts.

The methods used for analog processing are also limited to the capabilities and creative engineering of electronic components. In some situations the electrical energy is converted to another type of energy to do the processing. Some compressors, for example, convert the electrical signal to light by using the voltage of the signal to power a light bulb in their processing. This "optical" compressor uses a light sensor and the response time between the creation of light at the light bulb and the response to the light at the sensor to affect the signal. Some reverb processors convert the electrical signal back to acoustical energy in order to provide the most natural sounding reverberation to add to the signal. This is done using a traditional speaker placed in an acoustical space and a microphone used to capture the results and turn them back into electrical energy. Any time the signal is transferred from one type of energy to another (such as electrical to light, or electrical to acoustical, or acoustical to electrical, etc.) the signal inherently experiences some degree of change because of restrictions imposed by the laws of physics.

Similar to the problems created by transferring the electrical energy to another form of energy, some types of processing can only be accomplished if the signal can be re-recorded. Long echoes or delays, reversing of signals for effect, time compression or expansion, pitch shifting, and more all require that the signal be actually recorded as an intermediate step. By utilizing any of these types of processing the signal is subjected to all of the problems inherent in analog recording in Chapter Seven. If recording the signal is to be avoided all analog processing is limited as to what can be done in "real time."

In addition to this, however, any distance that a signal travels through cable or any electronic or other component that it passes through affects the signal in some capacity or another. Every electronic component has a certain amount of noise that it generates, has a certain amount of group delay that it causes, and is subject to manufacturing tolerances and manufacturing quality. There are tradeoffs with any piece of electronic equipment wherein certain aspects of its function are sacrificed by others. Besides increased noise, group delay, and manufacturing tolerance error, analog components also suffer in terms of the distortion they cause due to a property referred to as "linearity."

LINEARITY

The fact that a *digital* process can use mathematical certainty to do its processing means that digital processing is capable of having complete amplitude "linearity." In this sense, linearity refers to a system in which the

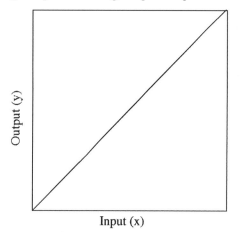

level of the output is directly proportional to the level of the input, exactly like our discussion of linearity in Chapter Ten. Linear processes involve directly proportional input levels to output levels. If no processing is done in a perfectly linear system then the level of the input would be exactly the same as the level of output. A graph of this would have a diagonal line from the lower left corner to the upper right corner on the graph. On a graph like this, wherein the x-axis represents the input level and the y-axis represents the output level, y would equal x, precisely. For any given input level there is an output level that is directly proportional and consistent across the entire range of input level possibilities. A basic linearity plot is given in Figure 13.1.

FIGURE 13.1: Linearity *(y=x)*

The most obvious type of *process* that is linear is that of a simple volume control (gain). If the amplitude lev-

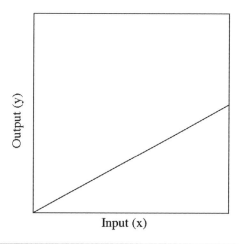

FIGURE 13.2: Other Linear Graphs *(y=2x, y=1/2x)*

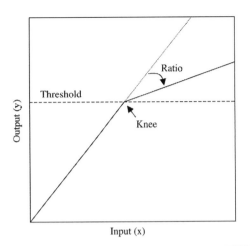

FIGURE 13.3: Compressor Linearity

An audio compressor is not linear. The ratio tells the amount of non-linearity it has, the threshold is the amplitude at which it becomes non-linear, and the "knee" is the specific point at which the transition occurs between linear and non-linear.

el is decreased by 6dB then the amplitude is changed at all input amplitude levels. This means that, regardless of the input level, the output level is changed by exactly 6dB. Since 6dB is equal to a reduction in the amplitude by half, the graph would represent this by showing a more shallow line, but the line would still be a straight line, and thus volume changes are still a 'line'ar process. The same is true if a signal is increased in amplitude by 6dB across its entire amplitude range. The input level vs. output level graph still shows a straight line, though the angle of the line is steeper (Figure 13.2).

A linear amplitude process does not necessarily leave the frequency content unaffected, nor does it have to leave the phase content unaffected. It also does not, however, *inherently* affect the frequency content, though many linear amplitude processes do actually affect the frequency content. An equalizer (a filter), for example, is considered a linear amplitude process, because the output amplitude can be consistent in relation to the input amplitude throughout the entire amplitude spectrum. Reverb processing is also considered linear, as the amplitude of the reverb that gets added is directly proportional to the amplitude level that is put in to the system.

In a non-linear system, the level of the output of the system does not change at the same rate as the level of the input. This would inherently be true in a compressor, where this is done intentionally. In a compressor, as the amplitude entering gets larger the amplitude exiting gets larger up to the threshold amplitude. Above the threshold, the level of the output is reduced at a ratio that may be 2:1, 3:1, or more. A graph of the effect of a compressor is given in Figure 13.3.

The effect of the compressor can be easily seen on a waveform as well. The waveform in Figure 13.4 shows a sine wave of a given frequency. As the amplitude of the signal going in to the compressor exceeds the given threshold the amplitude is "compressed."

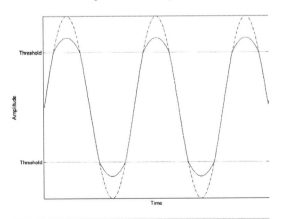

FIGURE 13.4: A Compressed Sine Wave

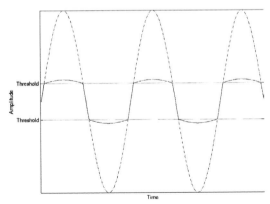

FIGURE 13.5: A Heavily Compressed Sine Wave

A sine wave that becomes heavily compressed takes the shape of a square wave.

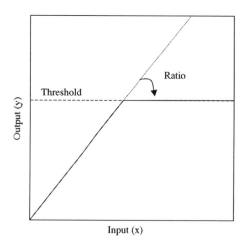

FIGURE 13.6A: **Limiter Linearity**

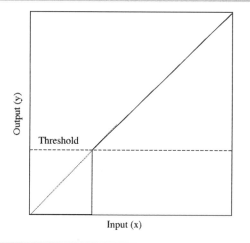

FIGURE 13.6B: **Gate (Downward Expander) Linearity**

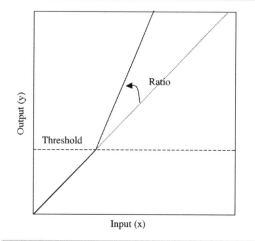

FIGURE 13.6C: **Upward Expander Linearity**

One of the consequences of a non-linear system is a change in frequency content of the waveform. Since the signal entering the system undergoes a change in its "shape" a change in the frequency content inherently results. This can be noticed very clearly under situations with extreme compression (limiting) because in such situations a sine wave is turned into a square wave at the threshold, and a square wave represents a drastic change in content from a sine wave. An example is given in figure 13.5.

While the phase of the waveforms does not necessarily undergo any change in a non-linear system, by mere definition any non-linear system causes a change in amplitude of signals entering the system as well as a change in frequency content. This does not necessarily include all signals entering the system, as the non-linearity does not have to cover the entire amplitude range, but all non-linear systems have some range of the amplitude wherein the input level is not directly proportional to the output level. Processes that are inherently non-linear are compression, expansion, gating and limiting (Figure 13.6).

The frequency content change in any non-linear system is often called "nonlinear distortion" though it comprises two types of distortion: "harmonic" and "inter-modulation distortion." The "harmonic" distortion is easy to visualize based on our understanding of square waves. We know that all square waves are comprised of the odd harmonics of a fundamental. We also know that as a sine wave is distorted more and more with non-linear processing (such as limiting) it becomes more and more resemblant of a square wave. By heavily limiting a sine wave we induce more harmonic overtones (as opposed to inharmonic overtones). As the system becomes more linear, the overtones have less amplitude and the harmonic distortion is therefore reduced.

The inter-modulation distortion caused by non-linear systems is slightly more complicated and involves a trigonometric analysis to adequately explain, which is beyond the intended scope of this book. In effect, however, if a waveform representing two frequencies is put through a non-linear system, additional harmonic information results. This harmonic content includes the difference frequency and the addition frequency of any combination of waveforms present.

In other words, if a 100Hz and a 150Hz waveform are put through a non-linear system, what comes out the

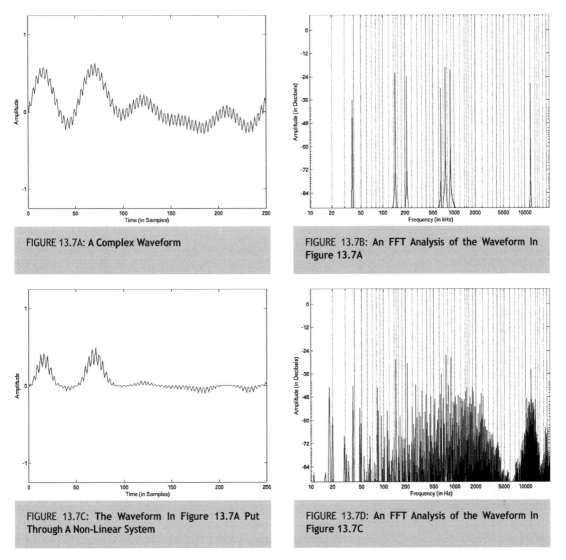

FIGURE 13.7A: A Complex Waveform

FIGURE 13.7B: An FFT Analysis of the Waveform In Figure 13.7A

FIGURE 13.7C: The Waveform In Figure 13.7A Put Through A Non-Linear System

FIGURE 13.7D: An FFT Analysis of the Waveform In Figure 13.7C

other side contains both 100Hz and 150Hz, the two original tones. In addition to this, however, are 50Hz and 250Hz, the result of the subtraction and addition of 100Hz and 150Hz. In addition to this will be the odd order harmonic distortion of both of the two original tones, including 300Hz, 500Hz, 700Hz, etc., and 450Hz, 750Hz, 1050Hz, etc.. See Figure 13.7.

Note that a non-linear system adds distortion only when the amplitude is in the range in which it is non-linear. A perfect compressor, for example, would not add any distortion when the amplitude of the signal entering it was lower than the threshold applied.

For the mathematically minded, the formula for a linear process can be given as:

$$y = Ax + B$$

where A and B are both constant coefficients, x is the input level amplitude and y is the output level amplitude. Any other formula for y, derived from x, yields a non-linear process. This includes the following formulas and the subsequent graphs in Figure 13.8.

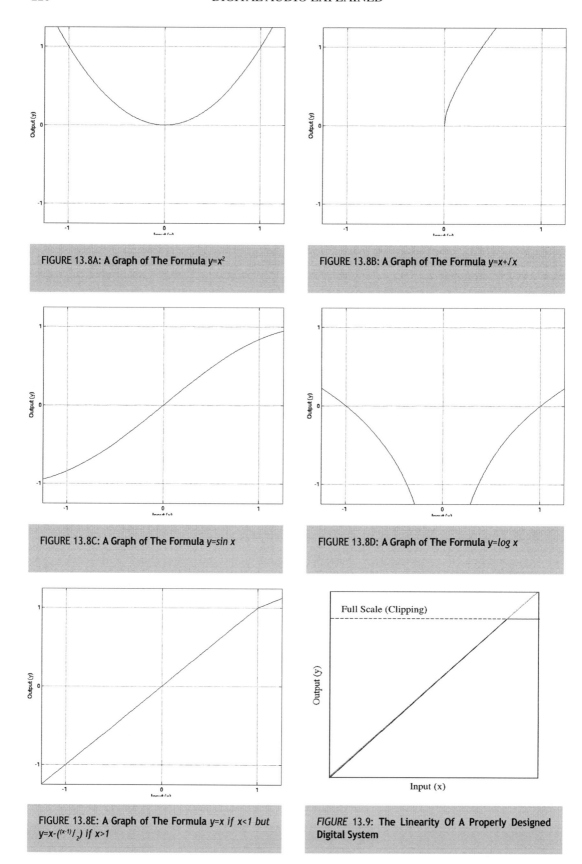

FIGURE 13.8A: A Graph of The Formula $y=x^2$

FIGURE 13.8B: A Graph of The Formula $y=x+\sqrt{x}$

FIGURE 13.8C: A Graph of The Formula $y=\sin x$

FIGURE 13.8D: A Graph of The Formula $y=\log x$

FIGURE 13.8E: A Graph of The Formula $y=x$ if $x<1$ but $y=x-\left(\frac{(x-1)}{2}\right)$ if $x>1$

FIGURE 13.9: The Linearity Of A Properly Designed Digital System

$$y=x^2$$

$$y=x+\sqrt{x}$$

$$y=\sin x$$

$$y=\log x$$

$$y=x \text{ if } x<1 \text{ but } y=x-\left(\frac{(x-1)}{2}\right) \text{ if } x>1$$

We can see that this discussion of linearity relates to our conversation on the "non-linearity" in A/D converters and the distortion that is caused by it. As the input level in an A/D converter changes, any non-linearity causes the output level to be slightly different because of the tolerances in the resistors and other analog components contained within it.

Any non-linear system inherently has some level of distortion, though it is difficult to draw conclusions about exactly how much distortion is present without thorough analysis of the system. All analog systems are actually non-linear to a certain degree. Analog components such as resistors and capacitors are non-linear, wire is a non-linear electrical conductor to some degree, air is a non-linear transmitter to some degree, the human ear is non-linear to some degree, and, as we have already determined, the lack of precision in analog components makes analog to digital and digital to analog converters subject to some degree of non-linearity.

Because every analog component and every method of analog transmission is non-linear, every analog processing system adds distortion. Not always is this distortion undesirable. The non-linearity in tube components is well documented and understood, and the distortion, being mostly harmonic in content, is used to generate a certain, pleasing effect in many pieces of equipment. Tube amplifiers in microphones, microphone amplifiers, guitar amplifiers, and other pieces of analog equipment are often sought after specifically because of the non-linearity that they provide. As discussed above, any form of "dynamics" processing, such as compression and expansion, are non-linear processes that are used specifically because of the effect they provide. Some recording engineers purport to like the sound of certain instruments when recorded onto analog, magnetic tape. The non-linearity of the analog tape medium provides a certain, formulaic compression and distortion that is desired on instruments that have very wide dynamic ranges. Each of these is an example of non-linearity used as an effect.

Digital systems, due to the fact that the signal is completely numerically represented and the processing is done mathematically, are capable of being completely linear and are therefore capable of avoiding distortion. A digital system, such as a piece of software in a computer, is capable of passing the numerical values without any change at all, or with a change that is completely linear. There are, however, a few caveats to this statement.

First, digital systems can be made to be non-linear by either intentional or unintentional means. Some processes, such as dynamics processes, can be done in the digital realm, and are therefore examples of intentional non-linear digital processes.

Second, the converters are capable of being non-linear, but the internal processing need not be. During the time in which the signal is digitally represented it is possible to process it in various ways and completely avoid non-linear distortion.

Finally, digital systems are only linear within the amplitude range that they are specified as being able to handle. Once the amplitude of digital processing exceeds the tolerable amplitude of the system (full scale) it becomes non-linear. Clipping is not only a concern during the conversion stages to and from analog, but is also a concern during processing stages. If the amplitude of the waveform increases until it can no longer be represented within the binary code allowed then it clips and distorts in a non-linear fashion. The input level vs. output level graph of a digital processing system would look like that in Figure 13.9.

Digital systems that do not utilize non-linear processing are inherently linear throughout their entire allowable range but become non-linear if that amplitude range is exceeded.

SUMMARY OF ANALOG VS. DIGITAL PROCESSING

Because any electrical component, any signal transmission, and any conversion from one type of energy to any other is inherently imperfect per the laws of physics, analog processing is always subject to error and imperfections.

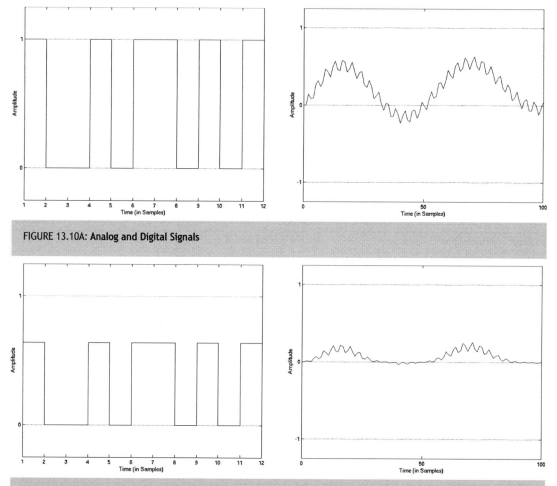

FIGURE 13.10A: Analog and Digital Signals

FIGURE 13.10B: The Waveforms in Figure 13.10A After Distortion is Added

The digital signal, while distorted, still represents the same numerical values and thus provides 100% accurate data transmission. The analog signal, on the other hand, does not represent the same signal after enduring the same distortion.

Once the signal has been converted to digital values, however, processing can be done in the digital realm without the problems that are present when processing is done in the analog realm. Even simple amplification of signals can be done flawlessly in the digital realm yet is subject to error resulting in noise and distortion in the analog realm. Taking a 1V electrical signal and making it a 2V electrical signal cannot be done perfectly in the analog realm, and it is arguable whether or not it can even be done audibly transparently. Any amplifier inherently adds some amount of inter-modulation distortion, some amount of harmonic distortion, some amount of noise, and causes some amount of group delay. In the digital realm, however, changing a "1" to a "2" is as simple as math, and any of the non-linearity or other errors of the analog components that do the processing have no effect upon the result unless the signal undergoes enough change to be indistinguishable from another binary value. In other words, large amounts of distortion and noise can be added to a digital system without changing the numerical values represented in the binary pulses; they only create a problem if a binary code gets so heavily distorted that it gets changed accidentally – a rare occurrence indicative of broken equipment. An example of the difference in distortion of analog versus digital signals is shown in Figure 13.10.

Because of all of these reasons there are many benefits to processing signals digitally as opposed to processing them through analog means. Further, any process that can happen in the analog world can be formulaically calculated. This means that anything that can happen in the analog realm can be represented by numbers and mathematical formulas that can then be applied in the digital realm. Doing so can get very mathematically complex as we will discover in future chapters, but any analog process can be recreated digitally with enough math. This basic concept is worthy of repeating. Anything that can happen in the analog realm can be represented by mathematical formulas that can be applied in the digital realm.

In order to more fully comprehend this it might be appropriate to consider that digital data is capable of representing all possible waveforms that can exist with the frequency and dynamic range bounds that befit the system. For example, 44.1kS/s, 24-bit data is capable of representing any possible waveform that the human ear can hear. An audible waveform cannot exist that cannot be accurately described with a 44.1kS/s, 24-bit sampling system. Therefore, any analog process that would alter said signal in such a way as to create another waveform that is also audible can *also* be represented by the same digital system. Since we know that the original waveform and the processed waveform can both be represented digitally, the only challenge is to find out what mathematical process can transform the original waveform into the processed waveform. The question no longer becomes whether or not it can be done, but rather which specific mathematical formula yields the desired results. One might say that a given analog processor might create frequency material above 22.05kHz, but because the human ear cannot hear this information, keeping that frequency content present is unnecessary, thus that material can be filtered. When it is filtered and the results are band-limited to the range of the human ear, the signal can be represented by the same sampling system as the original waveform. Therefore there exists a mathematical relationship between the original and the processed signals, and that relationship is determinable.

Respecting the fact that analog processing can be perfectly replaced by digital signal processing without loss to the signal quality (pending the quality of the math incorporated) and also respecting the various less-than-desirable consequences that can accompany keeping the signal in the analog realm, there are several advantages to processing signals digitally.

Chapter Fourteen

Introduction to Digital Signal Processing

Digital Signal Processing (DSP) is the backbone of most audio systems from the musical greeting card to the most sophisticated recording studios. In this chapter we will demystify what actually happens inside a digital signal processor.

Processing signals digitally requires taking the electrical pulses representing binary codes and using an electronic circuit that is capable of doing math to them to get different results. All of these circuits are simple electronic components such as those already discussed in previous chapters: comparators, integrators, gates, resistors, capacitors, and more. The basic building blocks of digital processing systems are gates.

A gate is an electronic component that allows signal to pass only if a certain condition is met. The simplest form of gate can be represented by a light switch that allows electricity to pass through it when the condition is met that the switch is turned on (Figure14.1).

Previously we have discussed gates that require the condition to be met that the amplitude of the electronic signal be above a certain threshold. If the amplitude is above a certain threshold then the gate is opened, allowing the signal to pass through. Even this simplest form of gate is commonly used in audio mixing. When the amplitude of a signal such as a snare drum exceeds a certain threshold the gate opens, allowing the signal to pass through. In this way the ambient noise is not allowed to pass through and the audio channel is only opened when an actual note plays. A gate such as this, designed to inhibit noise from playing between notes is called a "noise gate."

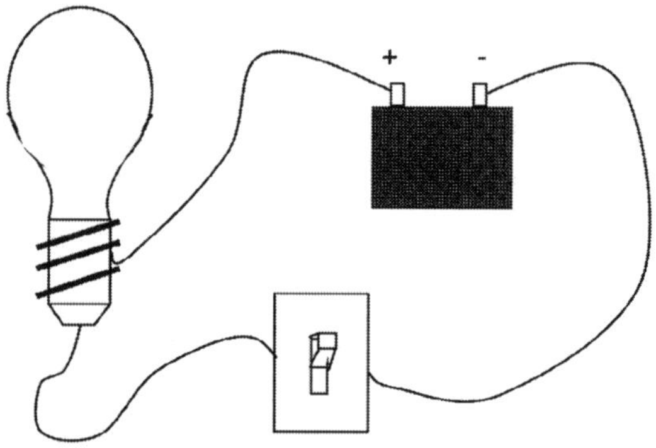

FIGURE 14.1: A Simple Electronic Gate (Switch) Circuit

Gates can be made to open if other conditions are met. Two specific types of gates used in digital audio are called AND gates and OR gates. Both types of gates are dependent upon at least two signals being fed into them. An AND gate opens if the signal coming from each input exceeds a certain amplitude. An OR gate opens if the signal coming from *either* input exceeds a certain amplitude. It is important to understand that neither of these types of gates acts as a summing amplifier, adding the two voltages together from either input. These gates only put out a fixed voltage, depending on the state of the input signals.

We can think of AND gates as making the statement, "if *this* AND *that* are true then put out a certain value." An example would be "if it is morning AND you are tired then have a cup of coffee." The implication here is that you would not have a cup of coffee if only it is either morning or you are tired. You are only to have a cup of coffee if both conditions are met. An AND gate as an electronic circuit represents the statement, "if this bit is a '1' AND that bit is a '1' then put out a '1.'" The implication being that in any other situations the gate puts out a '0.'

If an AND gate has two inputs and is closed if the inputs are less than .5V, and if 1V binary signals are sent to it then there can be four different combinations of signals that enter it. If we identify the two incoming signals as A and B then the four possible combinations of bits entering the AND gate are as follows:

A=0V B=0V (both of the signals coming in have a "0" value)

A=1V B=0V (the signal coming in on the "A" wire has a "1" and the "B" wire has a "0")

A=0V B=1V

A=1V B=1V

Only the fourth possibility, where both signals yield "1," allows the gate to open, and a "1" is emitted from the gate. The functionality of an AND gate is shown in Figure 14.2.

Another type of gate is called an "OR" gate, where the gate opens if *either* of the input signals exceed the threshold. An example would be the statement, "if either the phone is ringing OR you want to call someone then pick up the phone." Obviously, if both conditions are met then the phone gets picked up as well. An OR gate in electronics represents the statement "if this bit OR that bit is a '1' then put out a '1.'" The implication, again, is that it defaults to '0' otherwise. OR gates can be used with two or more signals. Again, if two signals are used then any of the values where a "1" was present on either the A signal or the B signal would open the gate, so the gate would emit a "1" value in all of the situations described above except for the one where A=0V and B=0V. The functionality of an OR gate is shown in Figure 14.3.

We have already discussed inverters, but for the sake of review, an inverter is a type of gate that emits a voltage when a signal below the threshold is presented, and emits no voltage when a signal above the threshold is presented to it. Since binary values are all either 0s or 1s, an inverter would put out 1V when it is fed 0V (representing a binary "0") and would put out 0V when it is fed a 1V signal (representing a digital "1.") An inverter is only fed a single signal and can also be called a "NOT" gate,

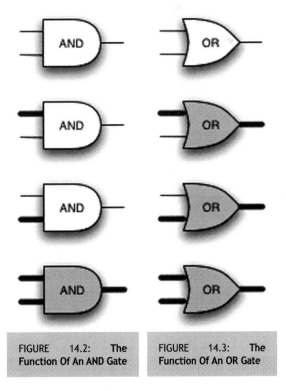

FIGURE 14.2: The Function Of An AND Gate

FIGURE 14.3: The Function Of An OR Gate

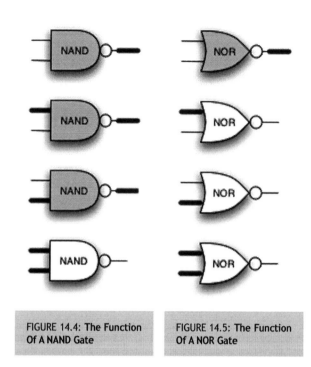

FIGURE 14.4: The Function Of A NAND Gate

FIGURE 14.5: The Function Of A NOR Gate

as the inverter emits a signal only when a signal does "not" enter it.

Another type of gate used in digital circuitry is a NAND gate, which is simply an AND gate with an inverter on the output. A NAND gate will do precisely the opposite of an AND gate because the inverter flips the output values such that the NAND gate puts out a 1 value in all situations *except* if all of the input values are 1s. Only if all of the input values are 1s does it send out a 0 value. A NAND gate might be thought of to represent the statement, "if the lights are off AND the door is closed then do NOT come over." The implication is that in any other situation, such as if only one of those conditions is met, there is an invitation to come over. In electronics a NAND gate represents the statement, "if this bit is a '1' AND that gate is a '1' then do NOT send out a '1.' Otherwise send out a '1.'" The functionality of a NAND gate is shown in Figure 14.4.

Finally, there is a NOR gate that is an OR gate with an inverter on the output. A NOR gate puts out a 1 value only if all values entering it on all lines are a 0. If any value entering it is a 1 then it emits a 0 value. An analogy would be, "if the stop light is yellow OR the stop light is red then DO NOT go through the intersection, otherwise do." In binary it is to say, "if this bit is '1' OR that bit is '1' then DO NOT put out a '1,' otherwise do." The functionality of a NOR gate is shown in Figure 14.5.

The symbols shown in Figure 14.6 are used to denote the five different types of gates used in digital circuitry. These gates (with the exception of the NOT gate) all have two inputs. They can be made with more inputs, however, though the functionality of a three-input or more-input gate remains the same.

Using these basic gate types we will be able to construct electronic circuitry that is capable of solving the most complicated mathematical algorithms. We need to determine how, using these basic electronic building blocks, simple addition of binary values can occur.

The first step is to take the digital words entering the system and send each "bit" into a separate physical input in an electronic circuit. Each bit will go into a separate capacitor – a device that will hold the charge long enough for the circuit to complete its function. If we want to do addition then the first digital word enters, followed by the second digital word, each bit in each word going into a separate capacitor that holds the charge (or lack of a charge) from each bit. For the sake of simplicity we will start with a one bit system, so that each digital word has one bit. In case both bits are "1s", however, the output of the system will necessarily yield two bits.

We will refer to the first digital word as word "A" and the second digital word as word "B." We want a system wherein the A and B voltages are fed into a series of gates that compare the two and emit a "0" if they are both negative and emit

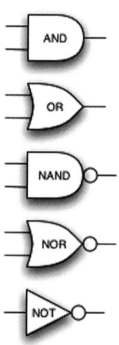

FIGURE 14.6: Symbols For Various Electronic Gates

a "1" if only one of them is positive. If both are positive then we want the gate to emit a "0," but we want, somehow, for a "1" to get emitted as the leftmost bit, but in all other cases we want for this bit to be a zero. The circuit shown in Figure 14.7 would accomplish this. There are many ways of accomplishing the same results using simple gates, but this one works as efficiently as any other design.

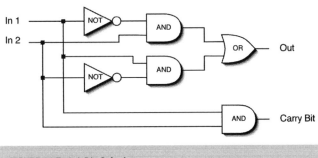

FIGURE 14.7: A 1-Bit Calculator

We can observe that indeed this circuit would properly add any combination of two 1-bit numbers together properly, as shown in Figure 14.8.

A 2-bit calculator would inherently be more complicated because the "carryover" bit from the right bit needs to be factored in to the calculation for the left bit. The output of a 2-bit system will necessarily be three bits in case a bit is carried over from the math in the other two columns. The circuit in Figure 14.9 would serve to properly add together any two digit numbers.

Figure 14.10 demonstrates that indeed several different addition problems yield proper answers when using this 2-bit "calculator" design.

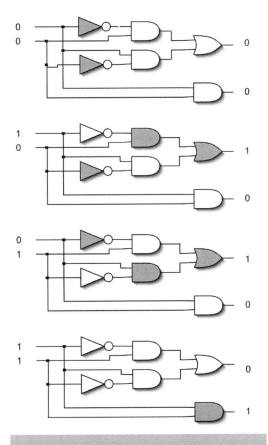

FIGURE 14.8: The Function Of The 1-Bit Calculator

Once a 2-bit calculator has been designed the circuit can be repeated for any number of bits required simply by duplicating the portion of the calculator circuit that determines the MSB and the middle.

If more than two *addends* (numbers) need to be added together there are two ways of doing it. The easiest way to solve the addition problem for multiple addends is to add two of them together, producing a binary sum from the "gate array." The sum from the first addition would be fed back into the front of the gate array as a new addend and the additional addend would be added to it. This process could be repeated for any number of addends so long as the eventual sum did not exceed the number of bits that the gate array was designed to handle.

Another way to solve addition problems for multiple addends would be to design a more complex gate array that had multiple binary inputs. A complex gate array can be constructed that can sum together any number of addends, and if the circuit designed is commonly going to be used for summing together multiple addends then the solution using more complex gate arrays may be faster, though not as simple to design and less efficient if smaller numbers of addends ever need to be summed together.

Addition can be easily done using a simple series of electronic gates. Now that we understand how to de-

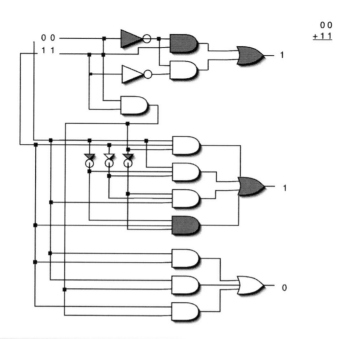

sign a circuit that will add two numbers together we need to figure out how to do any other math problems that the digital circuitry will need to handle in order to do comprehensive digital processing.

SUBTRACTION

We studied two's complement math in Chapter Eight and discussed that it is a method of notating binary numbers that makes subtraction easier for computers. If two's complement notation is used then subtraction can be done using the same addition circuit we just devised. All that we need to do is first turn the number to be subtracted (the "subtrahend") into a two's complement number and we can then use our previous circuit design and simply add the two's complement notated subtrahend to the *minuend* using normal addition. To turn the subtrahend into a two's complement number we need to use a circuit that will accomplish two things: first, flip all of its bits, and second, add a single "1" to the LSB. A circuit that flips all of the bits is as simple as a series of inverters, one for each bit. The subtrahend is fed, bit by bit, into a series of inverters that flips the value of each bit.

Once all of the bits have been flipped the result can then be put into our already-designed calculator and the number "1" can be added to it at the LSB. At this point we have a two's complement to the original number and thus have made it into a "subtrahend." Now this subtrahend and the original minuend can be fed into the calculator again, but this time added to each other to produce the appropriate and correct subtraction result.

If the subtrahend is already a negative number then it will need to be turned into a positive number before the "addition" occurs. For example, -6 - -3 is the same as –6 + 3. Rather than do a subtraction of a negative number we instead do an addition of a positive number. A negative number in two's compliment is made positive by first "adding a –1" (subtracting 1) and then flipping all of the bits using inverters. Then the number can be added to the minuend, completing the subtraction process.

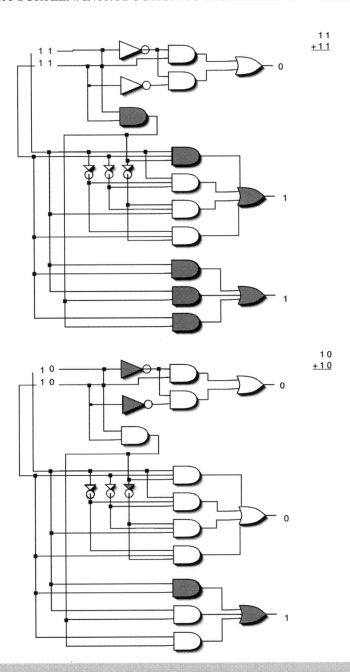

FIGURE 14.10: Various Addition Problems Done With A 2-Bit Calculator

Subtraction using binary numbers requires the same circuits as addition problems because of two's complement notation systems described earlier.

MULTIPLICATION

Multiplication of numbers is done precisely the same as it is done in long form decimal math. In decimal math we refer to the parts of a multiplication problem as the multiplicand, the multiplier, and the product. The multiplicand is the top number, the number that is to be multiplied. The multiplier is the bottom number, the number of times that the multiplicand is to be multiplied. The product is the result.

In school we are taught to multiply each bit in the multiplicand by the rightmost bit (the LSB) of the multiplier. If the value of any of the multiplication of two bits yields a number greater than "9" then the "tens place" number is carried over and added to the result of the next bit in the multiplicand multiplied times the same bit in the multiplier. After all of the bits in the multiplicand have been multiplied times the LSB then the process is repeated using the next bit to the left in the multiplier. Because that bit represents a value ten times greater than the LSB, the ensuing results of the bit multiplications are shifted one decimal place to the left. When the multiplicand has been multiplied times each separate bit in the multiplier and each set of results have been shifted by one decimal place then the results are added together.

$$\begin{array}{r}
{\scriptstyle 1\ \ 2}\\
{\scriptstyle 1}\\
3162\ \textit{multiplicand}\\
\times\ 43\ \textit{multiplier}\\
\hline
{\scriptstyle 1\ 1}\\
9486\ \textit{the result of the multiplicand multiplied times the LSB (3)}\\
\end{array}$$

12548   the result of the multiplicand multiplied times the next bit to
             the left in the multiplier (4) and shifted to the left.
             An implied "0" fills the leftmost bit.
135966 product – the sum of each step of the multiplication.

Multiplication can be done in exactly the same way in binary, but because the largest number used is "1" there will not be any "carry bits" in the first part of the multiplication. The final stage, the summing, can still have carry bits as multiple values of "1" can be added to each other, producing a carry over to the next binary column. In the first stage, however, where the multiplicand is multiplied by each bit in the multiplier, the only values that can be used are 0 and 1, so the only possible results from any bit to bit multiplication are 0 and 1, and no carryover bit will be used.

1011   multiplicand – equivalent to the number eleven in decimal

x 101   multiplier – equivalent to the number five in decimal

1011   the result of the multiplicand times the LSB (1)
   1
0000   the result of the multiplicand multiplied times the next bit
            to the left in the multiplier (0) and shifted to the left
            one bit place
+1011   the result of the multiplicand multiplied times the MSB of
            the multiplier
            (1) and shifted to the left on additional bit place
110111 the product, equivalent to the number fifty five in decimal

Whenever the multiplicand is multiplied by a bit in the multiplier, the result can only be one of two possible numbers: either the multiplicand itself or zero. For that matter, the math can be significantly reduced in processes. Rather than going through the step of actually multiplying each bit in the multiplicand by each bit in the multiplier we can simply observe whether or not the bit in question in the multiplier is a 1 or a 0 and then either write the multiplicand down or write a 0 down. The work might be more visually obvious if we did the math in a grid instead, where along the left side was the multiplier and along the top was the multiplicand. An example is given in Figure 14.11.

We can see at this point that because of the fact that binary numbers only consist of 1 and 0, multiplying binary numbers requires no multiplication at all. It merely requires adding the multiplicand to itself, shifting it a bit or more left every time. We can do multiplication of binary numbers by observing the multiplier and then adding.

Multiplier		Multiplicand→	1	0	1	1
1		1	1	0	1	1
0		0	0	0	0	
1	1	0	1	1		
Answer →	1	1	0	1	1	1

FIGURE 14.11: **Multiplication of 1011 x 101 (In Binary)**

Is the LSB in the multiplier a 1? If so we start our addition with the multiplicand. If not we put a 0 in the LSB and go to the next bit to the left in the multiplier. Is it a 1? If so we add the multiplicand, shifted a place to the left. We keep adding the multiplicand to itself, shifting it a bit every time for every 1 in the multiplier and an additional bit for every 0. After every subsequent addition the result is fed back into the gate array for the next addition. Multiplication takes (at most) as many addition stages as the number of bits in the multiplier.

Multiplication in this fashion is not done using two's complement math. It is instead done using what is called "sign and magnitude" math, where the first bit represents the sign (+ or -) and the remaining bits represent the magnitude, or the actual number. In sign and magnitude notation the number 1 would be represented as 0001 and the number –1 would be represented as 1001 where the last three bits represent the magnitude. In sign and magnitude notation the only difference between a positive number and its negative equivalent is the value of the first bit.

Multiplication requires that any two's complement number first be converted to sign and magnitude, though in the end, if the product is negative, the product can be reconverted to two's complement. Both stages are simple and are similar to the method described above used in subtraction.

In multiplication the sign is determined by the sign of the multiplicand and the multiplier. If each is positive or each is negative then the result is positive. If one is positive and one is negative then the result is negative. Since the MSBs in both the multiplicand and the multiplier represent the sign, determining the sign of the product is simple and can be done with simple addition. The two sign bits can be added together and if the result is a "0" then the product is positive. If the result is "1" then the product is a negative. If each of the sign bits is "0" then the result will obviously be "0." If each of the sign bits are "1" then the result will be "10." The carry bit is ignored and only the LSB is of concern, which is a "0," and the sign of the product is therefore positive. If one of the sign bits is a "1" and the other sign bit is a "0" then the result will be a "1" and the product will be negative.

It is evident at this point that multiplication can easily be done using only creative addition, utilizing the shifting of bits for each subsequent stage. The same gate array used for addition can be used for multiplication problems with some clever implementation.

DIVISION

The parts of a division problem are called the dividend, the divisor, the quotient, and the remainder. The dividend is the part from which the divisor is divided. The quotient is the result of the division. If the divisor does not divide evenly into the dividend then a portion remains undivided and is called the "remainder." Division of decimal numbers mostly involves multiplication and subtraction. The multiplication part is due to the fact that division is the opposite of multiplication, so we use multiplication within the process. The way we are taught to divide longhand involves multiplying the divisor enough times to fit within the most significant bits of the dividend. When the number of times that the divisor can fit into the most significant bits of the dividend has been determined that number is written down in the quotient. The product of the divisor and the quotient is then subtracted from the dividend to leave a remainder. The next bit to the left within the dividend is then "dropped down" and added to the remainder and this number is treated as the new dividend. The process is repeated until either the entire division problem is solved or a remainder is left unaccounted for within the quotient.

$$
\begin{array}{r}
3 \\
\hline
72\,\lvert\,23847 \\
216 \\
\hline
22
\end{array}
$$

divisor ... quotient / dividend

quotient

dividend

the quotient is multiplied times the divisor and subtracted from the dividend

the remainder is the result of the subtraction. The next bit to the right in the dividend is then "dropped down" to the remainder and the process repeated until either the remainder is zero and there are no remaining significant digits in the dividend, or until the quotient is deemed accurate enough.

The same process is done with binary division except that the only possible bit values in the quotient are 1 and 0. This means that, once again, multiplication is not necessary. Either the bit put in the quotient is a 1 and the divisor is then subtracted from the dividend's most significant bits, or the bit put in the quotient is a 0 and the divisor is not subtracted, but rather another bit is "dropped down" from the dividend and the process is repeated.

More simply, we could start with the most significant bit in the dividend and try to subtract the divisor from it. If the divisor is larger than the MSB of the dividend so that the subtraction yields a negative number then a 0 is put in the quotient at that point and the process is repeated adding the next bit to the right in the dividend. If the divisor is larger than the two most significant bits then the process is repeated. Once the divisor is smaller than the bits in the dividend a 1 is put in the quotient and the divisor is subtracted. The remaining bits are pulled down and the process is repeated, constantly comparing the divisor to as many bits are necessary in the dividend and if the divisor is larger a 0 is put up and another bit in the dividend is used. If the divisor is smaller then a 1 is put up and the divisor is subtracted.

To better understand we can look at an actual binary division problem and see how it works. We will divide binary versions of five into two hundred fifteen and see how it comes up with the result.

$$
101\,\overline{)\,11010111}
$$

First we subtract the divisor from the most significant bit in the dividend. If the result is greater than zero then we will put a 1 as the MSB of the quotient. In this situation 101 is larger than the MSB in the dividend of 1, so we put a 0 in the quotient for the most significant bit.

$$
\begin{array}{r}
0 \\
\hline
1\,1010111 \\
-101 \\
\hline
-100
\end{array}
$$

The process is then repeated but we use two bits of the dividend instead of only the first. Again the divisor is larger, so again a 0 is placed in the quotient.

$$
\begin{array}{r}
00 \\
\hline
11\,010111 \\
-101 \\
\hline
-\ 10
\end{array}
$$

The process is then repeated using the three leftmost bits in the dividend, and this time the difference between the divisor and the dividends is a positive number (the number "1," actually), so a 1 is placed in the quotient.

$$
\begin{array}{r}
001 \underline{} \\
110\mathit{10111} \\
\underline{-101} \\
1
\end{array}
$$

The remaining bits are then dropped down from the dividend and the process is repeated using this new dividend to establish the remainder of the quotient.

$$
\begin{array}{r}
001\underline{} \\
110 \\
\underline{-101} \\
110\mathit{111} \quad \mathit{new\ dividend}
\end{array}
$$

The complete, long-form math would look something like this:

$$
\begin{array}{r}
00101011 \\
11010111 \quad \mathit{original\ dividend} \\
110\mathit{10111} \\
\underline{-101} \\
110\mathit{111} \\
\underline{-101} \\
111\mathit{1} \\
\underline{-101} \\
101 \\
\underline{-101} \\
0
\end{array}
$$

The quotient is 00101011, or forty-three, which is indeed two hundred fifteen divided by five.

The process can actually be further refined to not have any subtraction, but instead substituting two's complement values for the divisor wherever subtraction is done. Instead of subtracting –101 and determining if the result is negative we could instead think of it as *adding* 1011 and simply observing the leftmost bit of the difference whenever subtraction is done. If the MSB of the difference is a 1 then the difference is negative and a zero is put in the quotient. If the MSB of the difference is a 0 then the difference is positive and a 1 is put in the quotient.

Further refinement would have the gate array configured so that as soon as each new dividend is determined, the new dividend is fed back into the front of the gate array, replacing the original dividend. This way a simple two-input gate array would be able to do complete, long form division. The number of steps necessary to solve the division problem using a simple, two-input gate array is the same as the number of bits in the dividend. With these refinements a long-form division problem might look like the example that follows on the next page.

This process continues, shifting the dividend to the left and adding the divisor to it until the division problem is completed. The signs in division problems can work the same as the signs in multiplication problems: if the sign bit for both the dividend and the divisor are the same then the sign for the quotient is positive, otherwise it is negative.

Division, just like multiplication, is capable of being done simply using addition. The numbers are added, bits are shifted, the gate array is fed information from the previous part of the problem and the cycle continues. In this way division (as with multiplication, subtraction and addition) can be handled by simple gate arrays that can only add binary values together. Gate arrays can be optimized for certain types of addition as discussed above. All math problems, however, stem from either one of or a combination of addition, subtraction, multiplication and division. High level trigonometry, multiple variable calculus, statistics, mathematical analysis, complex geometry, and all forms of mathematics are based entirely on simple, 2nd grade math skills. Since all of these can be done on simple arrays of electronic gates that only do addition, any complex mathematical problem can be solved on digital systems such as these.

11010111	*original dividend*
+1011	
1100	*the difference starts with a 1 so a 0 is put in the quotient. The result is ignored because a 0 was put in the quotient, the divisor is fed back into the gate array, shifted one place to the left, and the problem starts again.*
0	*current quotient*
11010111	*current dividend, shifted one bit to the left*
+1011	*the divisor*
1110	*the difference starts with a 1 so a 0 is put in the quotient. The result is ignored because a 0 was put in the quotient, the divisor is fed back into the gate array, shifted one place to the left, and the problem starts again.*
00	*current quotient*
11010111	*current dividend, shifted another bit to the left*
+1011	*the divisor*
0001	*the difference starts with a 0 so a 1 is put in the quotient. The remaining bits from the dividend are dropped down, creating a new dividend. That new dividend is then put back into the gate array as the new dividend and shifted one place to the left.*
001	*current quotient*
00110111	*current dividend, (new dividend) shifted one bit to the left*
+1011	*the divisor*
1110	*the difference starts with a 1 so a 0 is put in the quotient. The result is ignored because a 0 was put in the quotient, the divisor is fed back into the gate array, shifted one place to the left, and the problem starts again.*

CURRENT IMPLEMENTATION

Modern digital "adders" are composed of electronic components that can be made of silicon and put onto microchips called "integrated circuits," or "ICs." Each gate array capable of doing addition is called an "Arithmetic Logic Unit," or "ALU." Modern silicon microchips can house millions of individual gates. Since the circuits use simple electronic devices, the amount of time it takes for a single process to happen is very fast. Current computers use microchips that can handle billions of mathematical operations per second, making digital signal processing affordable and widely available. Digital signal processing can be done on small microchips that only handle a specific function and have a specially designed gate array that handles a specific set of needs. Other microchips are designed for a broad range of applications and the gate arrays within them are designed to be flexible enough to use in many different applications. Some manufacturers of digital signal processing equipment have specific microchips made with specific adders that provide a way of processing digital audio that is unique to a particular process that they provide. Having custom made microchips, however, is expensive. Many manufacturers use readily available processing ICs from manufacturers such as Motorola.

Audio processing manufacturers look for a microchip that handles the digital data in the way that is most conducive to the processing that they need to do. Since most audio is recorded with 24 bits to provide a large dynamic range, manufacturers look for processing ICs that accept 24-bit data, for example. A manufacturer might also look at how many digital words can be stored in on-chip temporary memory banks ("registers") at one time and how much "parallel processing," or multiple math problems it can do at the same time. Audio manufacturers also look at how the data is treated while on the microchip, how efficiently it can handle the data that needs to be processed, whether the chip is designed in a way that provides the greatest benefit for the type of processing that audio requires.

By far, the most common microchips used in the audio industry are those made by Motorola and IBM (used in Apple computers), Intel, and AMD. Most processing that is currently done in the modern recording studio is done by a personal computer, though in the past much of the processing was done in stand-alone "external" processors. Due to economies of scale, the personal computer generally provides the greatest amount of processing power for the money. In a computer the main microchip that handles the majority of the processing is called the Central Processing Unit, or "CPU." These processors are often also called "General Purpose Processors," or "GPPs." Currently designed computer GPPs are designed to handle very broad applications and in many respects outperform much of audio's processing requirements. This has made it easy for audio processing manufacturers to provide audio processing capabilities to digital audio studios.

One trade-off of using GPPs is that their primary performance gains are made at the expense of latency (delay) by using high clock speeds combined with extensive parallel processing and multiple levels of memory (temporary storage). Unlike audio-specific DSPs that produce their results very quickly, GPPs are designed to process large blocks of data at a time, but with significant delays. For example a simple process coded on a GPP might take scores of clock cycles whereas it may only take a few clock cycles on a more basic DSP designed specifically for the task at hand.

FLOATING-POINT PROCESSING

We have so far discussed only the methods used for doing math to fixed-point numbers. Floating-point math is done much the same as fixed-point math on a processor called FPU, or "Floating-point Processor." In theory, a 32-bit floating-point number wherein the first 8 bits are the exponent can represent a range of numbers that are 256 columns apart. For example, the largest number that can be represented might be:

1 1111 1111 1111 1111 1111 1111 x $2^{1111\ 1111}$ or 33,554,432 x 2^{255}

Written out in fixed-point notation this number would be:

*1111111111111111111111111100000000000000000000000000000000000000000
00000000000000000000000000000000000000000000000000000000000000000000
00000000000000000000000000000000000000000000000000000000000000000000
00000000000000000000000000000000000000000000000000000000000000000000
00000000000000000000000000000000000000000000000*

On this scale, the smallest number that could be represented using the same 32-bit floating-point notation would be:

1 0000 0000 0000 0000 0000 0000 x $2^{0000\ 0000}$ or 256

Written out in fixed-point this number would be:

1 0000 0000 0000 0000 0000 0000

The difference between the largest and the smallest number that are capable of being represented is so large that no math problem needed currently by the human race requires math that is accurately computed to the scale of magnitude provided by most floating-point systems if they had enough accuracy. For this reason the math is significantly reduced to only what is necessary. In order to demonstrate this easier we will use a 7-bit floating-point system wherein the first three bits are the exponent and the remaining four bits are the mantissa. For ease of visualization there will be no negative numbers. The range of numbers in our 7-bit system extends from 000 0000 to 111 1111. As we discussed in Chapter Eight, a 4-bit mantissa actually represents five bits, the most significant bit is always implied to be a "1." The numbers represented really represent the range of 10000 to 11111 x 2^{111}. In fixed-point notation this would be written out as follows:

10000 to 111110000000

We can think of this as covering the range from 16 to 3968, thought not every number can be counted. For example, 2049 can not be counted because it would be 100000000001, which cannot be represented accurately if the mantissa only has five bits.

If, however, we determine that accuracy of numbers out to the LSB column is unnecessary and that we only need five bits of accuracy then the calculator would not have to be able to add twelve columns of numbers together. We could, for example, design a calculator that only adds five columns of numbers together. The rest could be truncated before the addition occurs. For example, if 1011000000000 is added to the number 11101000 then the addition would be set up as follows:

1011000000000

+   11101000

To avoid having to design processors that handle more bits than the precision that is actually needed, the math problem is truncated so that only the five most significant bits are used from each number and the rest are discarded. The math problem now looks as follows:

10110xxxxxxx

+   xxxxxxx

The result is obviously 10110 x 2^7, or 10110 x 2^{111} in binary, or, in raw floating-point notation, 111 10110.

In floating-point processing units, or "FPUs," the math is performed using the same types of gate arrays that are used in fixed-point math but the bits are "shifted" into their proper places, based on the exponents before the process starts. If an insufficient number of bit places are available in the gate array for the complete set of bits for one of the addends then the excess bits are removed.

If the excess bits are simply lopped off (truncated) then the results are likely to be inaccurate. A simple example of why this is can be visually demonstrated with the following addition problem:

$$
\begin{array}{r}
1011\ 0011 \\
1011 \\
1001 \\
0011 \\
1010 \\
+\quad\quad 1111 \\
\end{array}
$$

If the last four bits are all removed from the problem before the problem starts then the result will be 1011 x 2^{100}. If the last four bits are added in, however, then the result of the problem is really 1110 x 2^{100}. These two numbers are very different, thus truncating the excess bits before doing the math leads to inaccuracy.

Another approach might be to round the excess bits. If the excess bits start with a 1 then the "insignificant bits" are rounded up and a "1" is added to the last bit that remains. If the value of the excess bits starts with a 0 then the bits are merely truncated. In the addition problem above, the math would go as follows:

1011 0011   *last four digits start with a 0, so they are truncated*

1011   *last four digits start with a 1, so the number is rewritten as 1 0000*

1001   *last four digits start with a 1, so the number is rewritten as 1 0000*

0011   *last four digits start with a 0, so the number is ignored*

1010   *last four digits start with a 1, so the number is rewritten as 1 0000*

+   *1111*   *last four digits start with a 1, so the number is rewritten as 1 0000*

This problem can now be rewritten as follows:

$$
\begin{array}{r}
1011\ 0000 \\
1\ 0000 \\
1\ 0000 \\
0000 \\
1\ 0000 \\
+\quad\quad 1\ 0000 \\
\end{array}
$$

The result of the addition is now 1111×2^{100}, which is also not correct. Even though we only need four bits of accuracy in our end result, and even though we are trying to conserve processing power and not use excess amounts, the bits deemed "insignificant" are proving to have a significant effect on our results. FPUs have a specific way of dealing with these excess numbers that we will address in a later chapter.

The advantage of floating-point math is that it can handle much larger and smaller numbers than fixed-point math can. The disadvantage of fixed-point math is that it is inefficient to use such large numbers with which to do math. Doing completely accurate addition with 32-bit floating-point numbers might require a gate array that accepts 256 bits for every number added. Compromises are made to allow this range of numbers to be used. Most 32-bit floating-point processors actually keep the bit depth inside the processor larger than the 25-bit mantissa requires. Many times, a 64-bit or an 80-bit system is used internally so that the errors due to the floating-point range do not accumulate and cause gross miscalculations. A 64-bit system is called a "double-precision" system in that twice the precision is allowed over the 32-bit numbers it accepts and processes. An 80-bit system uses what is called a "double-extended-precision" protocol, wherein 64 bits are the mantissa, 15 bits are the exponent, and 1 bit is the sign bit.

NUMBER OF BITS FOR COMPUTATION

Certain laws of mathematics fall in to play in regards to the calculation of numerical problems. When any type of math is applied to any two numbers the resultant number (the sum, difference, product, or quotient) might be larger than the original addend. If two numbers are added the result can be as large as one digit greater than the largest number. If (in decimal notation) a single digit number is added to a single digit number the result can be anywhere between 0 and 18. If we want to ensure that we represent the sum of the two numbers accurately, regardless of the addends used, we would need to have two decimal places available for the result. If we did this math problem on a calculator that only had one digit available on the screen and we tried to add 6 and 7 the number displayed on the screen could not be correct. Any time two numbers are added the system that adds them must be able to represent an additional decimal place if the answer is to be accurate. The same is true with binary notation. If two 8-bit numbers are added the result can be up to nine bits long. Any adder used to add two 8-bit numbers must have up to nine bits in its output for the result to be correct. Since subtraction is really just addition using negative numbers the same applies to subtraction problems.

To determine the number of bits needed to represent multiplication products, the number of bits in both the multiplicand and the multiplier are added together. An 8-bit number times an 8-bit number can yield a number up to sixteen bits long. This holds true whether the bits are in front of, across, or behind the decimal point, and holds true whether the multiplicand or multiplier are positive or negative. For example:

$$64.137$$
$$\underline{x \qquad -.991}$$
$$-63.559767$$

The product is eight digits long, the result of a five-digit number and a three-digit number multiplied together, regardless of the placement of the decimal points in the multiplicand and the multiplier.

Division problems have no fixed number of bits beyond which the quotient cannot extend. This is because not all division problems solve to a finite number, whereas all addition, subtraction and multiplication numbers do. The simple division problem of $1 \div 3$ yields a quotient that extends ad infinitum.

If math is to be done to digital audio for the sake of digital audio processing then the numbers are assuredly going to "grow" in size. Oftentimes the processing required involves doing some math to a number, then doing some more, then doing some more, etc. There are several stages where intermediate values are calculated before they undergo further processing. Each stage of arithmetic done to a number will allow the number to grow larger. The size of the end result is determined by how large the number was to start with (how many bits), what type of math was being done to it, how many bits the numbers being added (subtracted, etc.) to it were, and how many stages of processing there were. As we saw with floating-point math, reducing the size of the number (the number of bits) requires careful consideration. Reducing the number of bits by truncating or rounding will almost assuredly result in incorrect values. For this reason, most *processing* is done within a digital signal processor with many more bits (more bit depth) than the original number or the resultant value needs to be.

In audio we want to feed our digital signal processor as many bits as equates to the dynamic range we captured. Feeding the digital signal processor any more bits than the overall dynamic range of our audio is unnecessary and excessive. For a review of the relationship between bits and dynamic range, see Chapter Five.

For similar reasons, we do not need the processor to provide, as a final product, any more bits than are necessary under the same pretext. This does not negate, however, that while the audio is processed the digital signal processor needs to have as many bits as are required with which to calculate the various types of processing that are to be done. For this reason, most digital signal processors that handle 24-bit digital audio actually maintain 48 bits within the processor while the computations are completed. Once the computations are complete and the final product is ready to be released it is reduced to 24 bits. With 32-bit floating-point processors, the internal math is also done with very high precision. Some computers currently do the processing internally with 80 bits of precision. Many use at least 64-bit registers with which to temporarily store the data during intermittent stages.

For the past twenty pages we have not discussed audio at all in light of needing to understand how digital processing is done. While the explanation only barely grazes the surface of the immense amount of knowledge to be gained in the field of digital processing and computer sciences, it gives us the idea that digital signal processing can be done efficiently and quickly, and that with the immense and ever growing processing power available from computers and other digital processing systems the capabilities of digital signal processing appear to have no bounds.

Chapter Fifteen

The Last Bit

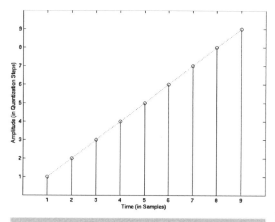

FIGURE 15.1: A Digital Test Signal

Over the most recent pages we have discussed how the precision of numerical arithmetic is maintained. An obvious question is why we are so concerned with minor errors in the digital audio processing. The answer was given in Chapter Thirteen. We remember that one of the most consequential advantages of digital signal processing over analog signal processing is that digital signal processing can be completely linear, thus avoiding the introduction of distortion components into the signal. In order to ensure that the results of the digital audio system are linear, the math needs to be done accurately. If the math is rounded to a value with less precision prematurely then the compounding effects of that will create non-linearity. A simple example of this can be demonstrated as follows.

The following digital audio signal (represented in the decimal system) is digitally sampled: 1, 2, 3, 4, 5, 6, 7, 8, 9 and is shown in Figure 15.1.

We then feed this digital signal into a processor that multiplies the "data stream" by .8 and then multiplies it by .8 again. Then it divides it by .8 and divides it by .8 again and the result should be what we started with, each value output by this processor should be the same as the value going in. In order to demonstrate the flaws of truncating the word length we will make this processor truncate to 1-bit (digit) after each process. Any numbers behind the decimal point are simply removed and only whole exponents remain in the "register" for the next part of the process. The processing on our simple signal goes as follows:

1 x .8 = .8 (truncated to 0) 0 x .8 = 0 0 ÷ .8 = 0 0 ÷ .8 = 0

2 x .8 = 1.6 (truncated to 1) 1 x .8 = .8 (truncated to 0) 0 ÷ .8 = 0 0 ÷ .8 = 0

3 x .8 = 2.4 (truncated to 2) 2 x .8 = 1.6 (truncated to 1) 1 ÷ .8 = 1.25 (truncated to 1) 1÷ .8 = 1.25 (truncated to 1) = 1

4 x .8 = 3.2 (truncated to 3) 3 x .8 = 2.4 (truncated to 2) 2 ÷ .8 = 2.5 (truncated to 2) 2 ÷ .8 = 2.5 (truncated to 2) = 2

The remainder would be calculated the same way:

5, processed, equals 3

6, processed, equals 3

7, processed, equals 6

8, processed, equals 6

9, processed, equals 7

The result can be graphed on a linearity plot, just as we did in Chapter Thirteen. The input values, one through nine, go across the x-axis. The output values from the processing go up the y-axis. This plot is given in Figure 15.2.

We know that this particular process should be completely linear. That is that the output levels should be exactly the same as the input levels because the process cancelled itself out (any number x .8 then ÷.8 equals the original number). The graph, however, is clearly not linear. Since any non-linearity causes harmonic and inter-modulation distortion (as discussed in Chapter Thirteen) the result of this processing yields distortion in the output signal. Clearly the truncating of the extra bits during the processing can yield distortion of the signal.

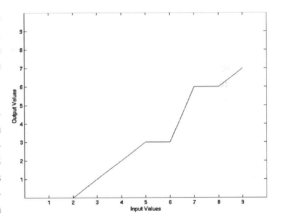

FIGURE 15.2: The Signal in Figure 15.1 Multiplied By .8

We can instead do the same process but round (instead of truncate) the extra bits to the nearest value. If the numbers behind the decimal are equal to or larger than .5 we round up and if they are less than .5 we round down. The math for this processor doing the same process as above looks as follows:

1 x .8 = .8 (rounded to 1) 1 x .8 = .8 (rounded to 1) 1 ÷ .8 = 1.25 (rounded to 1)
1 ÷ .8 = 1.25 (rounded to 1) = 1

2 x .8 = 1.6 (rounded to 2) 2 x .8 = 1.6 (rounded to 2) 2 ÷ .8 = 2.5 (rounded to 3)
3 ÷ .8 = 3.75 (rounded to 4) = 4

3 x .8 = 2.4 (rounded to 2) 2 x .8 = 1.6 (rounded to 2) 2 ÷ .8 = 2.5 (rounded to 3)
3 ÷ .8 = 3.75 (rounded to 4) = 4

4 x .8 = 3.2 (rounded to 3) 3 x .8 = 2.4 (rounded to 2) 2 ÷ .8 = 2.5 (rounded to 3)
3 ÷ .8 = 3.75 (rounded to 4) = 4

The remainder of the values calculate as follows:

5, processed, equals 5

6, processed, equals 6

7, processed, equals 8

8, processed, equals 8

9, processed, equals 10

If we plot the linearity of the same process using round-ing (using the values calculated above) the linearity plot is given in Figure 15.3.

Clearly this plot also does not show a linear result. We, once again, have processed the data using simple math but have managed to add distortion to the sig-nal through the processing means. We know that this simple process can be done in such a way as to produce linear results because the math should cancel itself out. If no rounding and no truncating are done at any inter-mediate stage and the full bit depth of all of the values is maintained throughout the process (as we discussed in Chapter Fourteen) then the result will clearly pro-duce accurate, linear results.

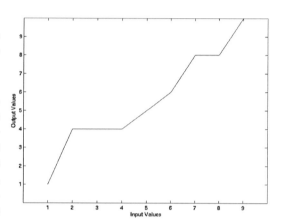

FIGURE 15.3: **The Data in Figure 15.2 Using Rounding instead of Truncation**

1 x .8 = .8 x .8 = .64 ÷ .8 = .8 ÷ .8 = 1

2 x .8 = 1.6 x .8 = 1.28 ÷ .8 = 1.6 ÷ .8 = 2

3 x .8 = 2.4 x .8 = 1.92 ÷ .8 = 2.4 ÷ .8 = 3

4 x .8 = 3.2 x .8 = 2.56 ÷ .8 = 3.2 ÷ .8 = 4

5, processed, equals 5, and all of the other values equal themselves after the processing is done. The linearity plot of the process, done without rounding or truncating is given in Figure 15.4.

These examples are extreme for the sake of example, but it is clear that truncation or rounding of bits causes distortion. The effect of this type of distortion over a longer period of time becomes very obvious. Above we created a waveform that was a simple, diagonal line lasting nine samples (1, 2, 3, 4, 5, 6, 7, 8, 9). If we now create a sinusoidal waveform (or a close approximation) and digitally sample it using those same nine values we would come up with the waveform shown in Figure 15.5.

The spectrograph analysis of this waveform (Figure 15.6) yields a predictable result: a sine wave at a particular frequency with a relatively high amount of error due to the quantization error from only having nine quantization steps. We remember that Chapter Nine tells us that the fewer the quantization steps the higher the quantization error in relation to our overall signal level.

If we take this digitized sine wave and run it through the same process we did above (x8 x8 ÷8 ÷8) then we should theoretically get the same sine wave that we started with and the spectrograph plot of the result will be the same. If, however, we truncate the values to 1 digit after every processing stage then the resultant values, after the processing, will suffer the same as they did in the test sample above. Whenever the amplitude of the waveform is 2, for example, it becomes 0 after the process. Whenever the amplitude of the waveform is 8 it becomes a 6 after the processing, and so on. The waveform that results from this processing would have very systematic errors, where every time the waveform yields a given amplitude the processing alters the resultant amplitude the same way. This fits, precisely, the definition of non-linearity: the input values do not have a linear correspondence with the output values. The sinusoidal waveform will have undergone severe distortion after the processing is complete if truncation is used after every processing stage. This can be seen in Figure 15.7.

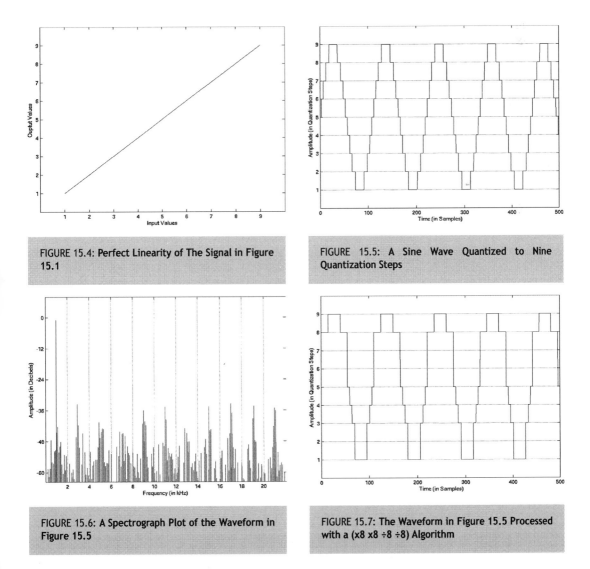

FIGURE 15.4: Perfect Linearity of The Signal in Figure 15.1

FIGURE 15.5: A Sine Wave Quantized to Nine Quantization Steps

FIGURE 15.6: A Spectrograph Plot of the Waveform in Figure 15.5

FIGURE 15.7: The Waveform in Figure 15.5 Processed with a (x8 x8 ÷8 ÷8) Algorithm

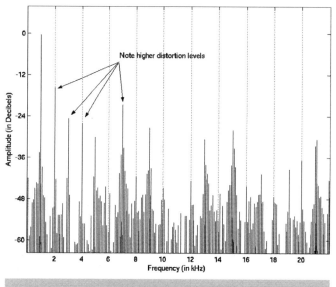

FIGURE 15.8: A Spectrograph Plot of the Waveform in Figure 15.7

The spectrograph plot of this waveform (Figure 15.8) yields what could be expected: harmonic and inter-modulation distortion due to the non-linear processing.

Clearly, truncating the "least significant" digits (bits) during the processing stages results in non-linear processing, precisely what we were trying to avoid by using digital signal processing. We can do the same exercise using rounding instead. We have already determined the non-linear results from processing each of the quantization values (1 thru 9) so we only have to plug those values in for the values that represent the actual sine wave. The "rounded" version of the processed sine wave is given in Figure 15.9.

Again we can clearly tell that this waveform has been heavily distorted with systematic alterations that are completely dependent upon the input amplitude. Any time a given amplitude is put in to the system, the wrong amplitude is put out; any time another amplitude is put in a completely different wrong amplitude is put out. This non-linear processing again yields a spectrograph plot that shows the original content and the original noise floor but with a bevy of distortion content at various audible frequencies that clearly affects the audible character of the sine wave. See Figure 15.10.

Somehow we would like to be able to do completely linear processing in the digital environment. One solution might be to simply not reduce the "bit depth" or number of digits used to represent a signal at all. Every time we do math to a signal we would simply let the size of the number grow, thus allowing ourselves perfect linearity. This solution, while certainly a valid way to avoid non-linearity in our digital signal processing, is impractical when we become aware of the amount of processing that gets done and the size to which the number grow. Digital values would easily be hundreds, if not thousands of bits long, which is not only impractical

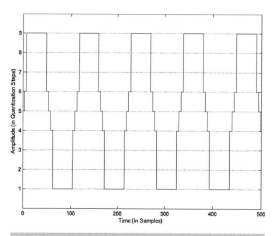

FIGURE 15.9: The Data in Figure 15.7 Using Rounding Instead of Truncation

to deal with but is unnecessary since *most* of those bits give us detail that is well below the noise floor and is therefore completely inaudible. We already know from our comprehensive work in preceding chapters that any more than 24 bits to represent a number is completely overkill and totally unnecessary. Certainly we have no need to represent digital signals with hundreds of bits during intermediate processing stages.

Further, at *some* point we will have to get our material down to a reasonable bit depth such as 16 or 24 bits for eventual distribution of the material (such as compact disc or DVD) or conversion back to analog. Currently, digital to analog converters, knowing that they need to only cover the audible dynamic range of the ear, are not designed to accept digital words that are larger than 24 bits in length. Even if we did allow the processing to increase the bit depth of our digital words to unnec-

essarily long lengths, eventually we will
have to reduce the bit depth back to 16
or 24 bits for distribution. The problems
with truncation and rounding do not go
away just because we only do it once
(at the very end) as opposed to at every intermediate processing stage. Even
one truncation back to 24 bits, or one
rounding back to 24 bits will suddenly
relegate the entire process to being non-
linear and will ensure the introduction of
distortion into our signal.

We can demonstrate this again through
our sine wave with nine quantization
steps. If we take that one sine wave and
do a single process to it and then convert
it back to 1 digit (bit) then we can see the
damage that can be done even through
only truncating once and not at each intermediate process along the way. Let us
take our sine wave above and lower its
amplitude by twenty percent. The logical
way to do this is to multiply each sample
by .8. If we are able to do this completely linearly then our spectrograph of the
waveform will have changed in only one
way: the amplitude of the peak on the
graph will drop by twenty percent in relation to the noise floor, as is shown in
Figure 15.11.

We already know from our reading in
Chapter Nine that these nine quantization steps should be perfectly capable
of representing this new waveform.
We know this because the only thing
that changes about this waveform is the
content of the waveform that is *above*
the noise floor, and any aspect of this
waveform that is above the noise floor,
or within the potential dynamic range of

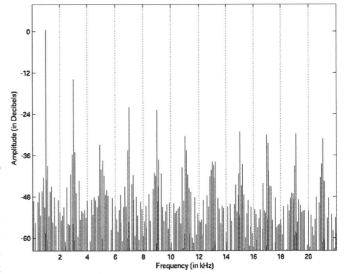

FIGURE 15.10: A Spectrograph Plot of the Waveform in Figure 15.9

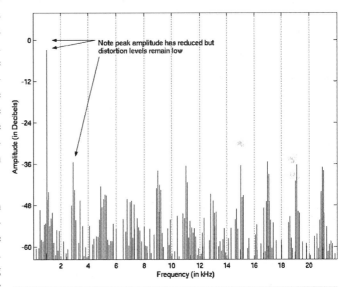

FIGURE 15.11: A Spectrograph Plot of a Perfectly Linear Amplitude Reduction of the Waveform in Figure 15.5

the quantization steps used is perfectly capable of being represented. Therefore we already know, concretely, that this new waveform that we would like to create – the waveform that is the original waveform with its amplitude lowered twenty percent – can accurately be created through digital signal processing, and that the result can be represented with a series of numbers that are each only one digit.

In fact, we can easily demonstrate that it can be done by creating the waveform that we would like to generate, and then sampling it. Figure 15.12 shows the waveform we would like to create and the samples that would represent it.

The spectrograph of this waveform, shown in Figure 15.13, clearly matches the plot shown in Figure 15.11, indicating that 1 digit is capable of representing this new, reduced amplitude version of the original sine wave.

Now that we know that this waveform can indeed be created we can analyze how to generate this waveform through digital signal processing. Theoretically, all we need to do is multiply each of the values by .8, as we discussed above. When we are done, however, we will end up with more than one digit in our resultant values:

1 x .8 = .8

2 x .8 = 1.6

3 x .8 = 2.4

4 x .8 = 3.2

5 x .8 = 4

6 x .8 = 4.8

7 x .8 = 5.6

8 x .8 = 6.4

9 x .8 = 7.2

If we truncate off the digit behind the decimal place then our values, after processing, are as follows:

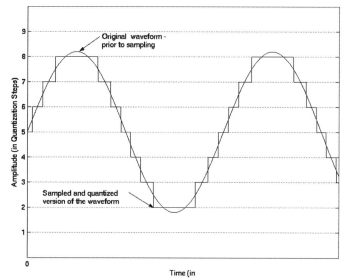

FIGURE 15.12A: The Sine Wave Reduced in Amplitude 20% and Sampled

Input value	Output
1	*0*
2	*1*
3	*2*
4	*3*
5	*4*
6	*4*
7	*5*
8	*6*
9	*7*

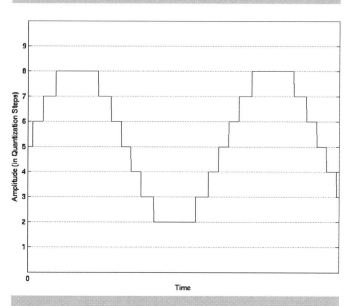

FIGURE 15.12B: The Resulting Data from the Sampling in Figure 15.12A

We can already tell that this will not result in linear processing. The linearity plot clearly does not show a straight, diagonal line from lower left to upper right, as given in Figure 15.14.

Sure enough, when we process our sine wave with this process we end up with a sine wave that is reduced in amplitude by twenty percent, but the spectrograph plot shows us a clear indication of distortion present in our signal (Figure 15.15 and 15.16).

Since we know that a single digit is capable of representing our sine wave without distortion, and since this method of multiplying and then truncating clearly did not accomplish these results, there must be another way of accomplishing this processing. Without going through the entire exercise, it is probably evident that rounding the values will also not get us our linear results.

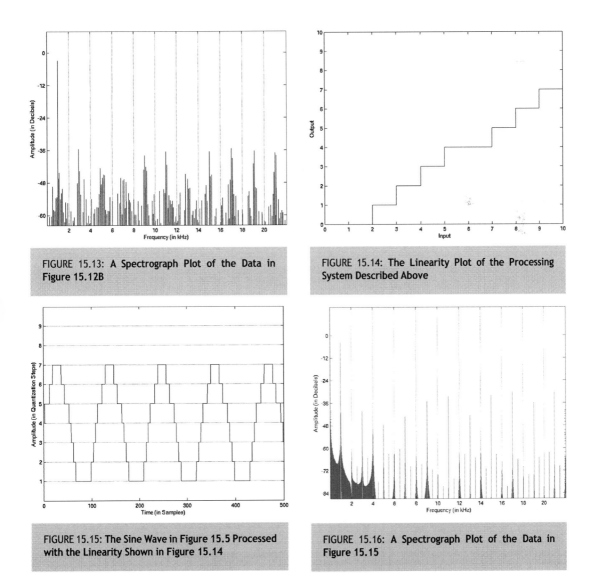

FIGURE 15.13: A Spectrograph Plot of the Data in Figure 15.12B

FIGURE 15.14: The Linearity Plot of the Processing System Described Above

FIGURE 15.15: The Sine Wave in Figure 15.5 Processed with the Linearity Shown in Figure 15.14

FIGURE 15.16: A Spectrograph Plot of the Data in Figure 15.15

INTRODUCTION TO DITHER

The problem with the processing we have attempted is that we really want the waveform amplitude to exist somewhere *between* two quantization steps. By assigning it to one or the other quantization steps we are creating a non-linear process, because every time the amplitude lands on that quantization step at a sampling point we know that the waveform is going to be changed a very predictable amount. This predictability means that the change to the signal is "correlated" to the signal, meaning that the alterations to the signal are completely dependent upon the signal. If the amplitude of the signal never hits a particular quantization step at a sampling point that specific alteration to the waveform never occurs. This "correlation" between the errors and the signal itself is what causes the system to be non-linear. The non-linearity is what causes distortion, as we covered extensively in Chapter Thirteen. The solution is to "decorrelate" the processing errors from the signal itself so that the processing can again become linear.

Let us look for a moment at the specific processing we have discussed above: reducing the sine wave by 20%. We concluded that any time the sine wave amplitude landed on a value of "6" at a sampling point that it should become an amplitude of "4.8." The number "4.8" is not capable of being represented with only one digit (the number "4" or the number "5"). We cannot get the number "4.8" to be represented by the number "4" or the number "5" all the time because the system becomes non linear. We can, however, get it to switch *between* the two values over the course of the waveform. On one occasion the processed value for "6" would be "4" and on another occasion the processed value for "6" would be "5." We could theoretically just switch it every other time. Every other time the value for "6" comes up our processor spits out the number "4" and every other time it spits out the number "5."

One problem with this approach is that the long-term average for an input value of "6" would actually be "4.5." Though this is much closer to getting us the linear result of "4.8" that we were looking for, this approach still causes the processing to be non-linear, though to a lesser degree. This problem can be solved by alternating between "4" and "5" so that 80% of the time an input amplitude of "6" results in an output amplitude of "5" and the other 20% of the time an input amplitude of "6" results in an output amplitude of "4." We could arrange this simply so that as the input value "6" shows up the first four times it becomes a "5" and the next time it becomes a "4." This way, the long-term average of an input value of "6" is actually "4.8" – precisely where we want it to be for the process to be completely linear!

This approach, however, causes another problem. Even though the signal is now linear in that, on average, an amplitude of "4.8" is represented as "4.8," the "error" is still correlated to the signal. If, exactly every fifth

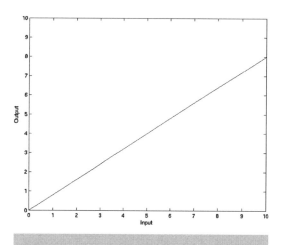

FIGURE 15.17: **The Linearity Chart From the Process Described Above**

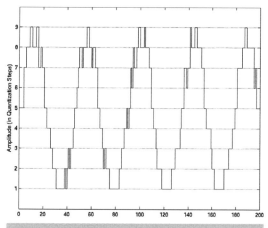

FIGURE 15.18: **The Sine Wave Shown in Figure 15.5 Processed with the Linearity Shown in Figure 15.17**

time that the input amplitude happens to be a "6" the output undergoes a certain, predictable, statistically determinable variation then the quantization error resulting is still correlated to the signal entering the processor. Even though the overall average represents the proper value, the method of accomplishing this provides "neat" and "mathematically regular" errors that still result in distortion being added to the signal.

We can actually see this take effect using our sine wave above. If we take each value of the output amplitude after the processing and vary the amplitude between the nearest two quantization steps using the proper ratios then we can redraw our waveform and analyze the effect.

1 x .8 = .8 Four times out of five it will result in a value of 1. Every fifth time the input amplitude of 1 is hit the amplitude put out will be 0.

2 x .8 = 1.6 Three times out of five it will result in a value of 2. Then the next two times the input amplitude of 2 is hit the amplitude put out will be 1

3 x .8 = 2.4 Three times out of five it will result in a value of 2. Then the next two times the input amplitude of 3 is hit the amplitude put out will be 3

4 x .8 = 3.2 Four times out of five it will result in a value of 3. Every fifth time the input amplitude of 4 is hit the amplitude put out will be 4.

5 x .8 = 4 Every time the input amplitude is 5 the output amplitude will be 4. The remaining values for the additional input amplitudes can be quickly and easily determined.

If we look at a linearity chart of our new process we can see that, over a long-term average, this process works, as Figure 15.17 shows.

The waveform that results is shown in Figure 15.18.

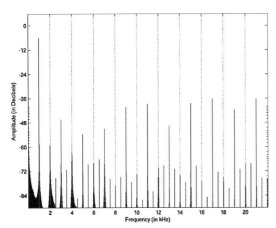

FIGURE 15.19: A Spectrograph Plot of the Data in Figure 15.18

The spectrograph of this waveform, however, yields that distortion still exists. Small amounts of harmonic and inter-modulation distortion still exist above the noise floor. See Figure 15.19.

The method used for solving this problem involves *randomly* changing the output amplitude instead of methodically and determinably changing it. Previously we were adding specific quantization error to the signal to get the average output amplitude for a particular input amplitude. Instead we add this quantization error in a random fashion. Statistically, four times out of five an input amplitude of "6" will yield an output amplitude of a "5," but *when* this happens to occur is completely random. This way the quantization error is no longer directly related to, or correlated to, the signal itself, but is instead randomized. The end result is a linearity plot that, on average, is completely linear, and a signal that has absolutely no distortion.

Let us look for a moment at what we have actually done over the course of this process. We have really just added quantization error to our signal. That quantization error, however, randomly changes values. We learned many chapters ago what random quantization error is: it is white noise. In other words in order to make our system linear and remove any distortion, we had to add a random signal (noise) that allowed the opportunity for the error to become random, thus turning the error into noise. By adding noise we made the system linear and removed the distortion.

At first the concept of adding noise to reduce distortion may seem counterintuitive, but perhaps it would help to explain the origination of the concept of dither comes. In the 1940s the British naval air fleet was having problems with its navigation systems. The navigation systems were large mechanisms full of cranks and gears and cogs. Everything in these systems was quite primitive, similar to an old grandfather's clock. Apparently a problem arose in that these cogs would chatter and stick and not move very smoothly and were therefore very difficult to calibrate. These problems seemed to go away when the airplanes were in the air. It was determined that the vibrations from the airplane engines were in effect "lubricating" the cogs and gears and they were working more properly – predictably. This "noise" added to the system (of the vibrations from the engines) helped the accuracy of the system by removing the opportunity for the gears to stick. The result was that the British installed small motors on all of their navigation systems just to help vibrate the mechanisms on the ground for calibration. "Dither" is a British colloquialism for "vibration" or "oscillation." The motors that they added to vibrate the navigation systems added "dither" to help rigid mechanisms operate more fluidly, or "linearly."

In audio we add additional noise, or "dither" to help digital systems operate more "fluidly," or linearly.

THE APPLICATION OF DITHER

In order to randomize the dither for audio and ensure that the quantization error causes the bits to "toggle" at the appropriate ratio between the bit above and the bit below, a specific process is used. For now we will continue to discuss this in terms of the sine wave we have been discussing above.

A stream of random numbers is generated between -1 and +1. The numbers can be any value between -1 and 1, the "depth" of the number does not need to be any greater than the depth of the number of digits we wish to remove. If we only round off one decimal place then the random numbers would only be one digit long, such that for this example the random numbers will be -1, -.9, -.8, ... 0,...-.8, .9, 1. The random numbers will be generated using what is called "triangular probability weighting." We can remember from Chapter Five that naturally occurring white noise uses Gaussian probability. For dither we will use triangular probability noise such that the greatest chance is that the random number will be a 0 and the random number has the least chance of being a -1 or a +1. The probability of any particular number being chosen is triangular in its determinability.

We can think of "rectangular probability" as providing an equal chance that any number will be chosen. With rectangular probability there is an equal chance of pulling the number .8 as 0 or -.2. Rectangular probability can be simulated with a simple, six-sided die. As the die is rolled there is an equal chance of it landing on any side. If two dice are rolled, however, the sum of the values shown has a much greater chance of being a 7 than a 2 or a 12. The weighting of the probability is triangular and can be visually observed to be so in Figure 15.20.

A "Triangular Probability Density Function" generated set of numbers is created ranging from -1 to +1 with the greatest probability that any individual value is a 0 and the lowest chance that any individual value is -1 or +1. If we plot these random numbers on a timeline as samples we can see that the signal they generate is random and very similar to naturally occurring white noise (Figure 15.21).

This noise signal is then added to the original waveform using simple addition. If the amplitude of the signal is 4.8 then, after the noise gets added to it, the signal will end up somewhere between 3.8 and 5.8, with triangular probability that it ends up right at 4.8, as we see in Figure 15.22.

After the noise has been added the results can be rounded to the number of bits intended. The result is that some of the values will equal 4, most will equal 5, and a few will equal 6, but all of them will average out to 4.8. The net effect of adding this noise is that all non-linearity is removed from the processing and the noise floor is raised because noise has been added to the signal. Triangular probability dither with an amplitude of 2 (-1 to +1) adds 3dB of noise to the signal. Though the noise floor is raised by 3dB in this process, the distortion components are removed, so the net audible effect is that the dynamic range improves and the "perceived noise floor" is reduced.

An intriguing thing happens if, instead of rounding after adding dither, we truncate the signal to the nearest value. This means that with the range of amplitudes of our test signal above (3.8 to 5.8), the results would be mostly 4s with several 5s and very few 3s. The result of this is that the signal averages to 4.3 instead of 4.8. In fact, if truncating is used, the amplitude lowers by exactly .5. An input amplitude of 5 would yield an output average of 4.5, etc. This still yields a linear signal, though the entire signal shifts, or "biases" by an amplitude of .5. Since truncating is slightly easier for a digital signal processor to do than rounding, an alternative to dither as described above (generating random numbers from −1 to +1, adding them to the signal and then rounding them to the nearest whole number value) involves generating random numbers from −.5 to 1.5, adding them to the signal, and then truncating to the nearest whole number value. The results will be the same.

Oftentimes, however, digital programmers take an even easier route and generate their random dither with values from 0 to 2, centered on 1. After the noise is added they then truncate the signals to the nearest values. They generate random numbers from 0 to 2 to make it easier to add the dither to the original signal (no subtraction is needed). This *biases* the signal up an entire quantization step. After the noise is added, however, the signal is truncated and shifted back down a half quantization step. In the end, this method does bias the entire signal up by an amplitude of .5, but the system is still linear and the net consequence of this is considered insignificant in practical applications.

We can now process our original sine wave in Figure 15.5 with accuracy. We multiply all of the values by .8 and then add "Triangular Probability Density Function" (TPDF) dither to them. The noise floor is slightly raised, but the process is completely linear and devoid of distortion. The result is shown in Figure 15.23.

When we look at the spectrograph of this sine wave we can see that the noise floor is slightly raised in relation to the signal, but that the distortion components are completely removed. By doing so, the material "sounds" much better. The noise floor sounds lower to our ears because the quantization error has been randomized and turned into true noise instead of distortion (Figure 15.24).

THE IMPORTANCE OF DITHER

Dither is a mandatory and required part of proper digital processing. Digital systems simply do not work properly without it. Our discussion of the dynamic range captured by specific numbers of quantization steps in Chapter Nine changes if we do not adhere to proper processing, including the proper use of dither.

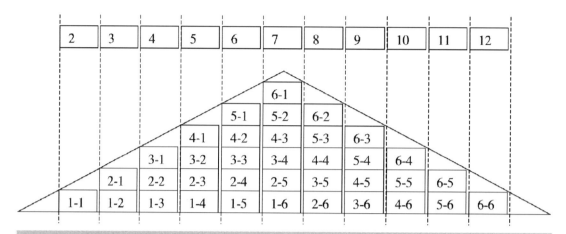

FIGURE 15.20: The Rolling Probability of Two 6-Sided Dice

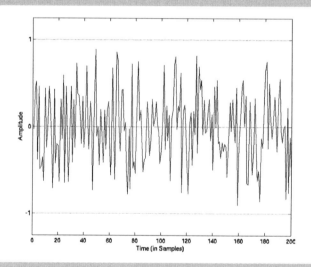

FIGURE 15.21: Randomly Generated Noise

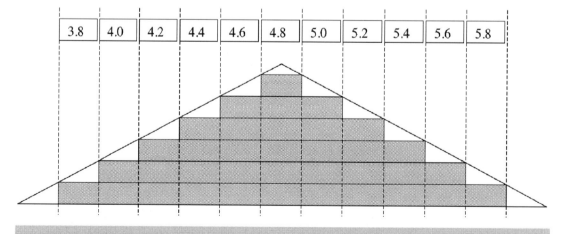

FIGURE 15.22: Triangular Probability Distribution of Values Between 3.8 and 5.8

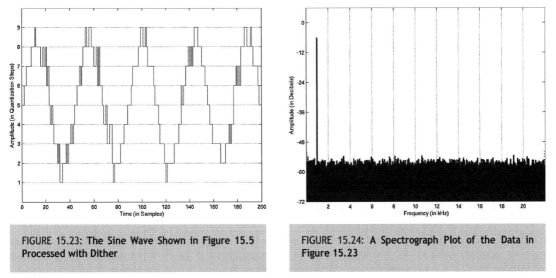

FIGURE 15.23: The Sine Wave Shown in Figure 15.5 Processed with Dither

FIGURE 15.24: A Spectrograph Plot of the Data in Figure 15.23

In our discussion in Chapter Nine we logically demonstrated that digital sampling does not remove any part of a waveform. The entirety of a waveform is still preserved through the sampling process though some of it ends up below the noise floor. While counterintuitive to our definitions, it is sometimes said that "digital audio provides *infinite* dynamic range, though most of it is below the noise floor." At first this sentence does not make sense, but the essence of it is logical: *all* of the signal is still there, even gyrations well below the noise floor. Any systematic air pressure changes at all are still captured in digital audio systems but most of them end up below the noise floor and most of *those* are masked enough that the human auditory system cannot discern them. While for the sake of auditory hearing the dynamic range is limited, the capabilities of digital audio are not, and a digital audio system truly exhibits infinite detail, though much of it is masked by the noise.

If dither is not used and truncation or rounding are to decrease bit depth instead then that essence gets lost and the dynamic range is subsequently limited. If we had a stream of values that represent a waveform well below the required dynamic range of a system we still want those values to be represented in the digital system. The following is a string of values wherein the numbers behind the decimal point can be removed. These numbers represent a very low level sine wave present in a signal.

...4.000175	...4.000011	...4.000197
...4.000199	...4.000008	...4.000180
...4.000155	...4.000067	...4.000108
...4.000075	...4.000148	*etc.*

The sine wave that these values represent can be seen in Figure 15.25.

If the values are truncated or rounded to the 1s place (the "4," in this example) the entire waveform hidden below the least significant bit will be lost and the entire signal will become a string of "4s." If dither is applied, however, such that a random number between −1.000000 and +1.000000 with triangular probability is added then over the long term the small oscillation well below the noise floor will have a very small effect on the resultant data, and thus will have a small effect over the resultant waveform. Over millions of samples, a tendency would exist in the pattern of the least significant bit such that the very low level oscillation, well below the noise floor, could be picked out and visually or mathematically discerned, even if it was below the threshold of audibility. Over a long enough period of time the repeating pattern could be seen. Obviously, if the oscillation happened, not in the 4th, 5th, and 6th bits behind the decimal point, but in the first few bits, the difference would be much more noticeable and potentially even audible depending on how far below the noise floor it ended up being.

When truncation is used to reduce bit depth, the information behind the decimal point (the eventual least significant bit) has no effect at all upon the result. When dither is used to reduce bit depth the information behind the decimal point has a dramatic effect on the signal, though the further out the decimal place the less significance it has. Only when dither is used does the entire signal, well into the noise floor, get maintained and still represented.

For these reasons dither is also used in analog to digital converters. A small amount of noise is added to the signal because the bit depth is reduced from a high amount to a lower amount. In analog to digital converters the bit depth is essentially lowered from an infinitely high number of quantization steps (analog) to only 24 or 16 bits worth. In order to maintain linearity some noise must be added to the process. Fortunately this is already inherently done by the many producers of noise in the analog circuitry prior to the converter process itself, so that no manufacturer needs to add any *extra* noise. If analog components were not so noisy, however, manufacturers would have to add random noise to the signal prior to the conversion in order to maintain the linearity of the converter circuit.

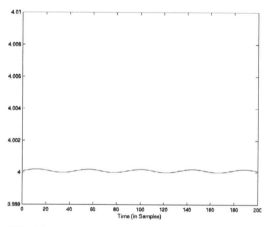

FIGURE 15.25: The Waveform Represented By the Data Above

We hinted at this issue in Chapter Nine when we discussed that the amplitude of the noise must be high enough to decorrelate the quantization error in the sampling process. We also discussed that there was a minimum amount of noise that must be present in the process if the error is to be completely decorrelated. That paragraph in Chapter Nine provides a precursor to this chapter in that it clearly shows us that any time quantization is to happen involving a reduction in the statistical resolution of the amplitude of the waveform, noise must be present at a high enough amplitude so as to decorrelate the results, much as we have identified in this chapter. The noise necessary to do so at the converter stage is no different than the noise necessary to do so at any other bit reduction stages.

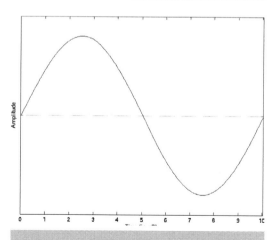

FIGURE 15.26: A 24 Bit 100Hz Sine Wave Sampled At 44.1kS/s

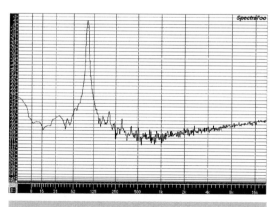

FIGURE 15.27: The Spectrograph of the Waveform in Figure 15.26

PRACTICAL EXAMPLES

So far, for visual aid, we have been discussing dither in terms of the decimal system. The knowledge is easily transported to the binary numerical system. If 24-bit data is to be reduced to 16-bit data then the process is the same:

1101 1001 0100 0110 *1011 0100*

Represents a binary word that is 24 bits long that we want to reduce to only 16 bits. It might be easiest to think of the decimal point, in this situation, as being after the 16th bit:

1101 1001 0100 0110.*1011 0100*

Using one of the techniques discussed previously, we generate a random number between zero and two, or between 00.0000 0000 and 10.0000 0000 (binary), but with triangular probability, centered on the chance of pulling the number 1 (or 01.0000 0000). We then add this random number to the original value. We pull the random number, say, 00.1111 0010 (equivalent to about .8) and add it to our waveform:

1101 1001 0100 0110.*1011 0100*

+ _____ 00.*1111 0010*

1101 1001 0100 0111.*1010 0110*

We then remove the last eight bits (in italics) and we have a dithered 16-bit signal. Notice that this time the dither, in combination with our original signal, caused the LSB to change in the resulting, 16-bit word. Other times it would not have, but the probability that it will or will not have is completely based on the value of the last 8 bits of the original word.

The benefits of dither become clear when looking at real world examples. Figure 15.26 shows a 100Hz sine wave recorded at relatively low level in a 24-bit system. Because we are using 24 bits, the noise floor is so low as to not be visually discernable. Figure 15.26 represents 441 samples of the waveform.

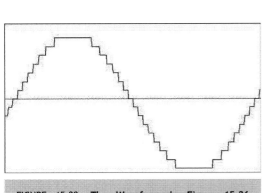

FIGURE 15.28: The Waveform in Figure 15.26 Truncated to 16 Bits

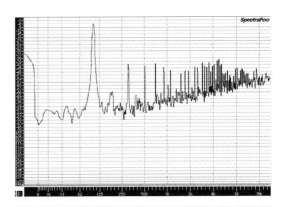

FIGURE 15.29: The Spectrograph of the Waveform in Figure 15.28

The spectrograph of this waveform is given in Figure 15.27. We can see that the waveform indeed represents 100Hz.

If the waveform is truncated to 16 bits (Figure 15.28) the quantization error becomes notably obvious but the quantization error does not represent random noise. It represents distortion of the sine wave, which adds (non) harmonic content.

The spectrograph plot of this waveform (Figure 15.29) clearly shows that additional frequencies representing distortion have been added to the waveform.

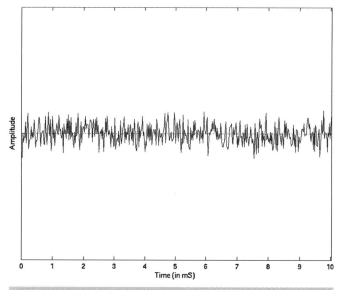

FIGURE 15.30: TPDF Dither Noise

The dither that we add to the waveform has an amplitude of two of the eventual quantization steps and is TPDF dither, as is shown in Figure 15.30.

The dither is then added to the original waveform, prior to the reduction in bit depth, as shown in Figure 15.31.

The values are then truncated to 16 bits. We notice that there are very few quantization steps available, just like in Figure 15.28, except that the waveform does not systematically move between the steps, but rather does so in a more random fashion because of the dither noise that was added. The result is shown in Figure 15.32

The resultant waveform is a 16-bit waveform without distortion, but, by definition, with a reduced dynamic range, as is given in Figure 15.33.

When the spectrographs of the truncated and dithered waveforms are laid on top of each other we can clearly see that the dithered waveform has a noise floor that is 3dB higher, but that the distortion components in the truncated waveform have a higher amplitude. The dithered version is more accurate and more audibly appealing than the truncated version. Figure 15.34 shows the spectrograph plot of the truncated and the dithered versions of the waveform.

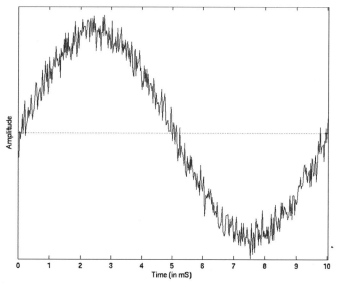

FIGURE 15.31: TPDF Dither Noise Added to the Waveform in Figure 15.26

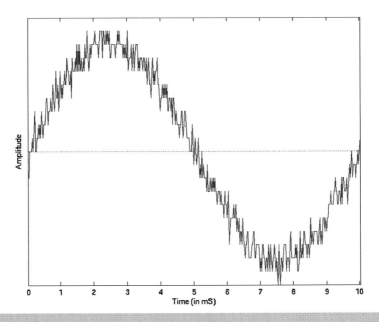

FIGURE 15.32: **The Waveform in Figure 15.31 Truncated to 16 Bits**

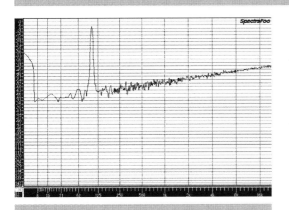

FIGURE 15.33: **The Spectrograph of the Waveform in Figure 15.32**

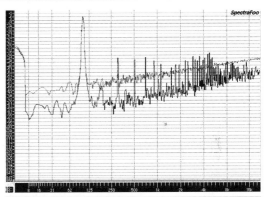

FIGURE 15.34: **Figures 15.29 and 15.33 Shown Simultaneously**

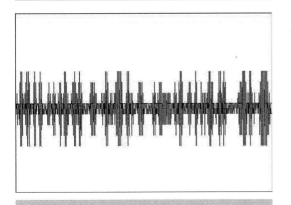

FIGURE 15.35A: **Apogee's UV22 Dither**

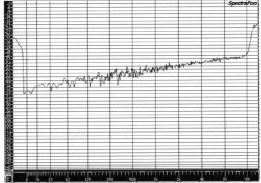

FIGURE 15.35B: **The Spectrograph of Apogee's UV22 Dither**

COLORED DITHER

Since dither raises the noise floor of material, various methods of making dither noise less audibly noticeable have been developed. Many of these methods are based on the simple fact presented in Chapter Six that the ear is more sensitive to low-level noise at specific frequencies and less sensitive to low-level noise at other frequencies. If dither noise can be implemented that still has the same amount of overall noise power and still represents a peak amplitude of at least 2 quantization steps (2 LSB) but has noise content that is more present in the areas where the human ear is less sensitive then the noise floor would be *perceived* as being lower while still avoiding any distortion.

The methods used vary, but most simply involve generating TPDF dither and then filtering it to conform to a specific frequency curve. Several manufacturers have developed dither varieties that serve to provide options to audio engineers to use during the final dithering stage, when the bit depth of audio is typically reduced from 24 bits to 16 bits to distribute to consumers. One converter manufacturer, Apogee, has developed a patented dither algorithm called UV22 (or, more recently, UV22HR) that works using this premise. As seen in Figure 15.35, most of the dither noise is above 20kHz, above the human hearing range. The noise from 20kHz to 22kHz is very high in overall amplitude, but the noise below 20kHz is low enough to be below the noise floor of the digital system. The overall noise amplitude across the entire range from 0Hz to 22kHz, however, is still the same.

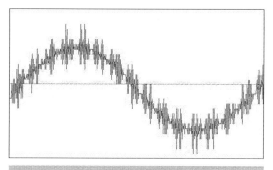

FIGURE 15.36: The Waveform in Figure 15.26 with UV22 Added

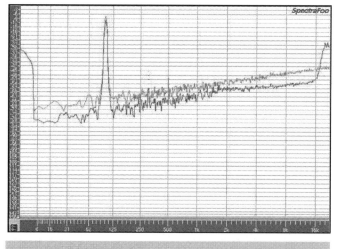

FIGURE 15.37: Spectrograph Plots of TPDF Dither VS. UV22 Dither

If UV22 were to be added to our sine wave above and truncated the results would look slightly different than the results from TPDF dither, as demonstrated in Figure 15.36.

The results, however, do yield a lower noise floor than TPDF dither throughout the audible range, even though the overall amplitude of the noise throughout the *Nyquist frequency range* (up to 22.05kHz) is the same as TPDF white noise dither. Figure 15.37 shows spectrograph plots of our signal with UV22 added versus the same signal with TPDF white noise dither added.

Several other types of this "colored" dither are available on the market. Many manufacturers that develop digital audio software and hardware have developed some form of "less audible than TPDF" colored dither. Careful listening tests at low levels can help the audio engineer determine the most appropriate type for their work.

Colored dither, however, has its consequences. The noise generated by colored dither, being not white, is subject to change through any digital processing. As digital processing of various forms occurs, the noise floor can "spread out" and the noise can "bleed" outside of its preferred range. When this occurs the previously-out-of-audible-band   noise can start to bleed in to the audible range and become noticeable. Because the overall peak amplitude of the noise needs to be higher (because the range with which to spread the 3dB of overall noise is smaller), when the colored dither does start to bleed it can be more noticeable than if TPDF, white noise dither were used instead.

Further, as multiple stages of processing occur and the bit depth is reduced after each stage, dither must be added. If dither is used at these stages the amplitude of the dither noise adds and increases in level. If the dither noise is colored such that it should be less noticeable, but adds up over multiple passes, the noise can become much more noticeable than if TPDF, white noise dither was used throughout. This is demonstrated in Figure 15.38.

The conclusion to be drawn is that colored dither can effectively be used to reduce the bit depth, but *should only be used at the final processing stage*. Colored dither and truncation to lower bit depths is the very last process that any signal should undergo prior to listening or pressing a CD or DVD or other distributable means. If *any* digital processing is still to happen, from EQ to compression to simple level changes, then colored dither should not be used and TPDF, white noise dither should be used to have the least audible effect.

Some manufacturers of equipment provide two options for dither. One option is often TPDF, white noise dither and the other is some sort of filtered or colored dither. If the piece of equipment is used in the middle of a signal path, such as on an effects insert, then the dither is used to get from the internal processing bit depth of, perhaps, 48 bits to 24 bits to get back in to the audio system. In this situation the bit depth is reduced so dither must be used and TPDF dither is the correct choice. If that piece of equipment, however, is used as the final stage of processing on the way to a CD burner then the dither is used to get from the internal processing bit depth of, perhaps, 48 bits to 16 bits to put on the CD. As this is the last processing stage before the disk is burned, the most appropriate dither choice would be the colored dither.

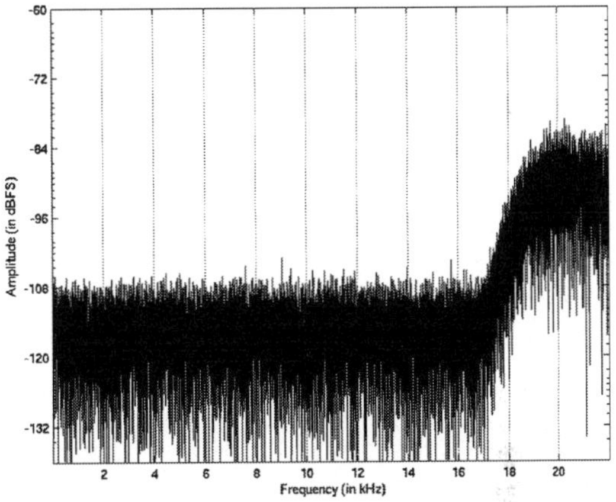

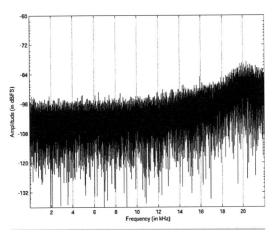

FIGURE 15.38A: A Spectrograph Plot of "Colored" Dither

FIGURE 15.38B: A Spectrograph Plot of "Colored" Dither After Several Consecutive Uses"

NOISE SHAPING

It is important to think of an analog signal as simply a signal with infinite bit depth and an infinite sample rate. When we "sample" analog signals we are simply sampling them *less frequently* than they are already sampled. When we sample analog signals we are also *reducing the bit depth* of the original material as well. Therefore, the need for dither applies equally to the initial sampling stage as it does at any bit reduction stage, as we have discussed many times, now. A bit reduction stage can just as easily be thought of as a "resampling" stage at the same sample rate but a lower bit depth than the original.

In Chapter Eleven we discussed a method used for changing the quantization error during the initial sampling process. This method was called "noise shaping" and involved feeding the quantization error back to the next sample to create a high pass filter. The quantization error yielded from each sample was added to the next sample prior to truncation. By feeding back multiple previous samples with varying ratios (half of the error from the last sample plus a quarter of the sample before that, etc.) one can change the shape of the resulting error.

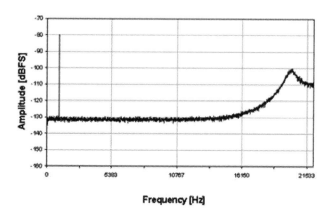

1kHz Sine at -80dB (44.1kHz) with POW-R 1

This very method can be used in the bit reduction stages as well. Rather than simply adding TPDF generated white noise dither to the signal, or even a colored dither such as Apogee's UV22, one can add a noise shaping process that takes the quantization error and "shapes" it to conform to a desired frequency response. The methodology is the same: as truncation is done to one sample, the error yielded is fed backward and added to the next sample prior to its truncation. This very simple method filters the error signal so that it has more high frequency content than low frequency content, much like the desired effect of UV22 – pushing the error signal above 20kHz so that it cannot be heard. Simply pushing the error signal above 20kHz, however, is not necessarily the most optimal solution to the problem. Taking a cue from our discussion on colored dither on previous pages, shaping the noise so that it follows more closely the contour of the human ear's threshold of hearing helps to extend the dynamic range of the material. By using a more complex feedback loop, involving controlled and mathematically computed ratios between how many samples' errors are put into the feedback loop and how much of each of the appropriate samples' errors are used, we can "shape" the frequency content of the error so that it results in an error signal that is well below the threshold of hearing for any reasonable amplitude at which the audio will be played.

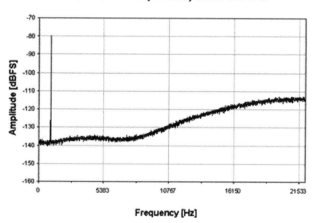

1kHz Sine at -80dB (44.1kHz) with POW-R 2

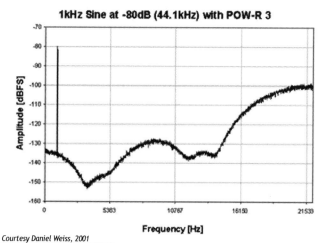

1kHz Sine at -80dB (44.1kHz) with POW-R 3

Courtesy Daniel Weiss, 2001

FIGURE 15.39: Spectrograph Plots of the Various POW-r Noise Floors

One such example of this type of noise shaping is an algorithm called POW-r, which comes in three different varieties (shown in Figure 15.39). The difference between the three different varieties is the amount and the ratios of the feeding back done. The most complex of the POW-r algorithms can allow for up to 150dB of dynamic range in a 16-bit signal at certain frequencies. This is done by filtering the error signal such that at the frequencies the ear is most sensitive to the error gets so heavily filtered as to leave an extended dynamic range in those frequency ranges.

An observant reader will notice that the term "filtering the error signal" has been used as opposed to "filtering the noise." This is because the error signal is most decidedly *not* noise. As we discussed in Chapter Eleven, the error signal is correlated to the waveform and is therefore actually a *distortion* signal as opposed to a noise signal. Calling the filtering and shaping of this error "*noise* shaping" is a misnomer unto itself, as we know by now that the error is distortion, so filtering and shaping of this distortion is really "*distortion* shaping." Even though complex math is done that feeds the quantization error backward, adding this signal to the next sample, what is added to the next sample is not "noise" because it is correlated to the signal. Even if we take half of the error from the last sample, a quarter of the error from the sample before that, an eighth of the error from the sample before that, and commensurate amounts of the error from the previous dozen samples and add all of those errors to the next sample prior to truncating it, what gets added is not random and is not noise. What gets added is correlated, to some extent, to the signal itself, and is therefore distortion. This point bears great significance with respect to an upcoming chapter on future technologies and is worth thoroughly comprehending; it is even worth reviewing Chapter Eleven if necessary.

If a perfect sine wave at exactly one quarter the sample frequency is fed into a sampling system, the sample values will repeat ad infinitum, as see in Figure 15.40.

If the error from each of the samples is fed backward, even in a complex arrangement that feeds them backward with complex organization between them, at some point the values are going to repeat and the sample values are thus going to repeat as well. This does not yield "noise" but rather yields a repeating, cyclical waveform added to the sine wave. This is therefore not random noise, but is rather distortion. Further, if a sine wave was sampled at one eighth the sample frequency and the same feedback algorithm was used, the repeating, cyclical waveform added would be different. Therefore, the added tones are correlated to the signal and specifically qualify as distortion. Because the waveform is notably cyclic, this example makes it easy to visualize how the feedback loop adds (and then filters) the distortion. Any waveform, regardless of how cyclic it is, however, is subject to the distortion generated through this process.

While feeding back the error by itself will allow a reshaping of the distortion so that it is less offensive and exists at lower levels, the results still yield a "floor" in the recording that is dependant and correlated to the signal itself, albeit removed by a healthy dose of filtering. A method is therefore used to completely decorrelate this floor from the signal, making it indeed a "noise floor" instead of a distortion signal. Random, TPDF, white noise is added, but it is added in the feedback loop. The noise is not added directly to the signal as it is when dither is applied, but is rather added to the error signal that is fed backward from previous samples. By adding random noise to the feedback loop, the error signal that is added is decorrelated (if enough noise is added) from the original signal such that the result is indeed a filtered (shaped) noise floor rather than a distortion floor, thus the name "noise shaping" is apropos.

Noise shaping is decidedly different than dither, though noise shaping as a bit reduction process *requires* that dither be added to it to prevent distortion from resulting, just the same as dither is added to any signal prior to truncating. Due to the filtering used by the noise

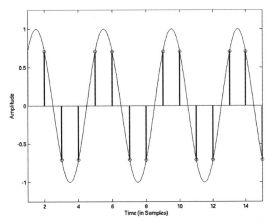

FIGURE 15.40: A 12kHz Sine Wave Sampled At 48kS/s

shaping process, it is capable of having a significantly lower noise floor and creating much greater dynamic range than colored dither can yield. Noise shaping still suffers from the same consequences, however, in that it can only be used in the final processing stage. By adding noise shaping in earlier processing stages when further digital signal processing is still yet to happen, the careful shaping of the noise floor can easily be compromised as the noise signal bleeds into frequency ranges that it was specifically filtered away from.

POW-r type 3, for example, plays off of the Fletcher-Munson equal loudness contour curves and pushes the noise away from the threshold of hearing at all frequencies when the signal is turned up a reasonable amount. If a POW-r type 3 processed 16-bit signal is turned up to typical listening levels (85dB SPL RMS, for example) the noise floor yielded by the bit-reduction process is lower than the threshold of hearing across the entire frequency band and should therefore be inaudible. If additional processing is done to the signal, however, some of the delicately shaped noise that was pushed outside of the frequency ranges where we are most sensitive can "bleed" into those specific ranges where we can hear it. For this reason, noise shaping should only be done during the final bit reduction stage.

It is also worth noting that when listening to bit reduction algorithms one should listen to them at the amplitude with which they are intended to be reproduced. If POW-r type 3 noise shaping is amplified to levels at which it is not intended to be played, for example, it can no longer play off of the threshold of hearing as indicated by the equal loudness contour curves. The ear's sensitivity to different frequencies changes at different amplitudes, so amplifying the bit reduction signal for the sake of comparison can counter the intended results of the algorithm. To listen to what UV22, POW-r, Sony's "Super Bit Mapping" (another noise shaping system) or any other bit reduction scheme will sound like, one must make sure they listen to the bit reduction scheme at the amplitude with which it is intended to be played back with any given signal. By turning up a test signal 60dB so that one can really hear what the shape of the noise sounds like one negates the specific benefits that noise reduction algorithm may have.

IMPLEMENTATION OF DITHER

The implementation of dither sounds relatively simple for a DSP processor: generate a random number, add it to the current value, truncate off the least significant bits. In practice, however, this is much more difficult than it might at first appear. The randomness of the dither is absolutely critical. The ear is remarkably acute when it comes to noticing cyclic oscillations, even over lengthy periods of time. If the dither is to be effective and not cause audible distortion the noise must be completely random. If the noise is correlated to the signal in any way the system becomes non-linear and distortion results.

Further, over the course of a digital system the number of digital processes a signal undergoes is very high. In most systems the digital words are increased for the sake of accurate processing and then reduced to more reasonable rates after the process is complete. A digital mixer with twenty four tracks and an EQ and compressor on each track would typically have dither implemented after each EQ, after each compressor, and may undergo bit depth changes after any other process such as gain control, panning, and the summing of the tracks to each other. Dither would also get implemented after any submixes, (such as aux sends) and after any digital effects that are used during the mixing process. An all-digital system like this might have many dozen (or even hundreds) of places that dither has to get implemented simultaneously. None of the random numbers that are generated for any dither at any point can be related to the dither used at any other point in the mixer. Not only can the same random number sequence not be used at any two places at once within the mixer, but also any random number sequence must be totally removed and unassociated from any other sequence used elsewhere in the system. If one track uses a set of random numbers that get used on another track later in time the noise generated can become audible in its repetition. Also, if the dither used on the left track is similar to the dither used on the right track the effect becomes increasingly noticeable.

Implementing proper dither in digital equipment or digital software is much easier said than done. Many manufacturers do not implement dither internally at all during their bit depth reduction from the processing bit depth. One digital mixer manufacturer used approximately 150 high speed digital signal processing chips just for the generation of random numbers for the many places that dither was needed throughout the mixer, exceeding the combined processing power of several personal desktop computers.

CONCLUSION

The proper generation and implementation of dither is one of the most significant and untapped areas in digital audio processing. Many studies have demonstrated that the sonic degradation of digital audio effects, mixers, or other systems has been shown to lie in the simple treatment of the supposed "least significant" bit.

Chapter Sixteen

Digital Mixing

We have now discussed how digital signals can be processed using electronic components and how the numbers need to be treated in order to yield linear results. With these understandings we can now start to determine how a digital mixer can be made with all of the functionality of an analog mixer but without the disadvantages of non-linear processing, excess noise, and added distortion.

The function of a digital mixer is really divided into three parts: changing the amplitude of signals, splitting signals, and summing signals. In an analog mixer, the signals are physically routed around the mixer to the various places where these functions occur using electrical circuit board traces and jumper or ribbon cables. In a digital mixer, they are often graphically displayed as though they happen this way, but internally the processing all happens on as little as one microchip. In this chapter we will analyze how digital processing is capable of performing the three functions of a mixer without the degradation of analog mixers.

AMPLITUDE ADJUSTMENT

The amplitude of a digital signal is defined by the sampling quantization steps. Adjusting the amplitude of a digital signal is as simple as adjusting the amplitude of all of the sampling points and adjusting them all the same percentage. We can prove this to ourselves by refreshing our understanding of audio in the first part of this book. We know that, by definition, if we take two identical signals and add them together we generate a waveform wherein the amplitude at each, infinitely small point is twice as large as the two, initial, individual waveforms. We also know that doubling the amplitude of a waveform yields an increase in the amplitude by 6dB. If we cut the amplitude of each point along the waveform in half we reduce the signal by 6dB. Notice that this is not the same as adding a fixed amount (such as 100 quantization steps) to every point along the waveform. Amplitude adjustment is handled by multiplying every point in a waveform by the same number. If this is done then neither the frequency content, nor the phase, nor any other aspect of the waveform changes. Even the dynamic range of a waveform does not change if the amplitude changes – the noise, as well as the rest of the waveform all gets reduced proportionally, so the difference in level between the peak and the quietest discernable level remains constant.

To change the amplitude of a digital waveform the only process that needs to occur is a multiplying of every sampled value by a specific number. In this way, digital amplitude adjustment can be done perfectly: without any flaws, distortion, or signal changes. To increase a signal by 6dB each sample needs to be multiplied times "2." To decrease a signal by 6dB each sample needs to be multiplied times ".5." To fully attenuate a signal, or apply maximum "gain reduction," or "attenuation," we multiply each sample times "0." If we know the amount of amplitude change we want in terms of decibels then, using a simple formula, we can calculate the number to multiply every sample by in order to yield that amount of change. The number to which we multiply the signal in order to perform a gain adjustment is called a "coefficient." To determine the coefficient "K" from a desired change in amplitude:

$$K = 10^{(change\ in\ dB/20)}$$

This formula is used to derive the coefficient for amplitude change. If we want to attenuate the signal by 6dB (change of –6 inserted into the formula) then we use the coefficient, ".5," as established above. In Chapter Fifteen, the example in which we multiplied every sample in a sine wave by ".8" was an example of attenuating a signal. ".8" Is a coefficient. The amount of attenuation that ".8" is equivalent to can be determined using a variation on the formula given above:

$$Change\ in\ dB = 20\ log\ (^1/_K)$$

A coefficient of ".8" is equivalent to an amplitude reduction of ~1.94dB.

A mixer has several different places where amplitude adjustment is done. The main track faders, the aux sends and returns, and the master fader are all places where signals are amplified or attenuated. In each of these places the digital signal passing through gets multiplied times a coefficient that is based on the setting of the fader or potentiometer assigned to that function in the mixer. In digital mixers the fader is "virtual" in that signal does not actually pass through it as in an analog mixer. The position of the fader or potentiometer is measured and determines the coefficient by which the signal passing through that part of the mixer gets multiplied. Many faders and potentiometers in digital mixers represent a range of steps that is determined by a particular number of bits. An 8-bit fader, for example, has 256 different potential positions. A 10-bit fader has 1024 potential positions.

Most faders cover the range from infinite attenuation to something like +6dB, wherein 0dB means that the coefficient is "1," such that the signal is unchanged (any input value times "1" equals no change). If an 8-bit fader is used there are 256 different coefficients between "0" and "2," representing the entire range of amplitude control. When a fader is moved, the coefficient changes over time such that some values get multiplied by a certain coefficient but as the fader moves, later samples are multiplied by differing coefficients. If the coefficients change abruptly such that there is an abrupt change between the coefficient value for some samples, but the next samples are all multiplied by a different coefficient, then distortion is generated. In Chapter Three we discussed that very rapid changes in amplitude necessitate the presence of high frequency content and that an audible "click" can be heard when the amplitude of a waveform changes fast enough. If there are only 256 potential coefficients then almost any time an amplitude change is necessitated, low-level, audible "clicks" would be heard as the fader moves through the various coefficients. The series of audible "clicks" is called "zipper noise," and is an undesirable side effect of poorly designed digital mixers.

In order to avoid zipper noise, many digital mixer manufacturers, while only using an 8-bit fader, provide as many as 8 million coefficient values. Though the fader itself might skip from a value of -6dB to –12dB instantaneously, the coefficients used slowly sweep through a broad range of perhaps hundreds of values. Manufacturers of digital consoles want the amplitude control to be fast enough to be quick and flexible, but slow enough to avoid an audible amount of distortion. The math used to pick appropriate coefficient values is simple digital processing, akin to digital sampling.

As the fader moves, it is filtered and then digitally sampled. The software does not allow the coefficients to change as dramatically as the fader can change, so the fader movements are run through a digital low pass filter that slows the movement of the fader's effect. On a physical mixing board this is not as important as it is in

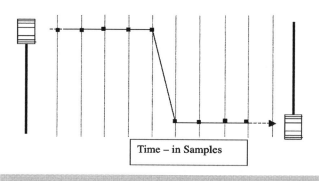

FIGURE 16.1: Potential Fader Movement For A Software Digital Fader

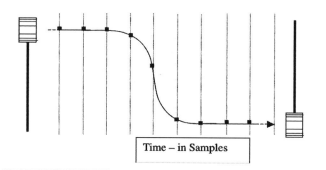

FIGURE 16.2: Desired Fader Movement For A Digital Fader

a software-based mixer. This is because the physical faders on a digital mixing board are inherently limited by physical constraints, such as the speed with which one can move them. It inherently takes some amount of time to move between positions and the coefficients can therefore be derived from the already-slowed physical action of the faders. In a software-based mixer, however, the fader can move much faster than a fader on a physical mixer can move. In a software-based mixer the fader can "snap" between positions instantaneously (Figure 16.1).

As the fader's movement passes through the low pass filter, the fader's effect is quantized to the nearest coefficient value, which is much more precise than the range of the fader's movement (Figure 16.2). There are many more intermittent values that a fader will pass through then values that a fader can "land" on.

By handling amplitude gain and attenuation in this way, the manufacturers provide a digital mixer that performs more "fluidly," causing less distortion and a function that is identical to the smooth, analog movement of an analog fader or potentiometer. The math described above happens wherever on a mixer an amplitude adjustment needs to be implemented

Manufacturers do not always use the same math for all of the points on a mixer where amplitude adjustment is done. One manufacturer indicated that the track faders use 21-bit coefficients (two million steps) but the master fader uses a more precise 23-bit coefficient.

After the sample values are multiplied times whatever coefficient is deemed appropriate for those samples, the word size of the sample becomes inherently larger, per our discussion in Chapter Fourteen. A 24-bit sample multiplied times a 21-bit coefficient yields an up-to 45-bit sample. What happens with this sample depends on the implementation of the mixer. Some mixers keep it as 48-bit data at this point until future processing is done. Other mixers dither it to 24 or 32 bits after each processing stage.

SPLITTING OF SIGNALS

In analog mixers splitting a signal between two different destinations is a tricky work of electronic engineering. Impedance changes cause non-linearity whenever a signal is routed to two different places at the same time. In digital mixing routing the same signal to two different destinations is completely linear and error free. A digital signal can simply be duplicated and go through two different virtual paths at the same time. When a digital signal goes through a channel on a digital mixing board, turning up or down one of the aux send knobs on that channel simply will not have any effect on the signal that travels through the rest of that mixer channel.

The panning knob is an example of a function that both splits the signal to two destinations and provides amplitude adjustment at the same time. Panning is done by splitting the channel into two different destinations. Depending on the position of the panning potentiometer (pan pot) the signal moves to the left or the right channels by multiplying each new channel by related coefficients. If the signal is panned all the way to the left, the "left signal" gets multiplied by a coefficient of 1 and the right channel gets multiplied by a coefficient of 0. In this way, the signal passes to the left channel of the master fader (or other destination) at full amplitude and to the right channel with no amplitude, causing a complete shift in the data to the left. When the pan pot is positioned in the center, each channel is multiplied times a coefficient of .5 so that the combined effect is that the signal is routed to both the left and the right at fifty percent amplitude for a total, combined amplitude of unity, or the level that entered the pan pot function. Material panned in the center often sounds louder because the sound coming out of each speaker causes an increase in sound pressure level over situations where a signal is panned to one side or another. Analog mixers often compensate for this by attenuating the signal a small amount when the signal is panned dead center. Some digital mixers use these "pan laws" so that when the signal is panned in the center the signal is attenuated some number of dB (often 3dB) in the same way in which analog boards work.

For any other position of the pan pot, coefficients are derived for the left and the right channels that are inverses of each other. As the pan pot is rotated to the left, the left coefficient gets larger inversely to the right coefficient getting smaller and vice versa. The movement of the pan pot would, just like any amplitude controller, have to be low pass filtered to prevent the pan pot from producing non-linear, distorted results. The coefficients for the left and right are then dithered and quantized to appropriate coefficient values, identically to the method used for fader controls described above.

SUMMING SIGNALS

Summing signals is another area in which digital mixers can easily excel over their analog predecessors. Summing digital signals together is as simple as adding the values together, sample by sample. Having said this, there are unique details for both fixed-point and floating-point mixers when it comes to the summing of signals together. Each has its own idiosyncrasies.

Fixed-point digital mixers take the digital signals from various sources and combine them together. The most common application of this in a digital mixer regards the summing of all of the track channels together, though the summing of various aux sends together before running them to an aux bus has the same issues. The bit depth coming off of each channel is likely to be large, though this depends on the manufacturer's design. In many cases a 32-bit or 48-bit number is emitted from each track and these sample values are all summed together. A problem occurs in that any 48-bit number at full scale (all 1s) plus any other number causes the processor to "overflow," or exceed its maximum value. For this reason the digital processor is generally designed to handle larger than 48-bit numbers. In many digital processors a 56-bit or larger "accumulator" is used. This means that, even though the data entering and leaving the process is 48 bits, within the processor math up to 56 bits can be handled.

If a digital mixer has a 56-bit accumulator and sums together signals coming from tracks that are all 48-bit then odds are not likely that overloading will occur. If two tracks each had 48-bit numbers that were full scale then it would take 49 bits to represent the result. If we added two more tracks to that, both of which were full scale we would have a 50-bit result. Each time we double the signal by doubling the amount of tracks we add one more bit, so 8 tracks, summed together, would take 51 bits. It would take more than 256 tracks summed together, each of which is putting out maximum amplitude (full scale) at the same time before the accumulator would overload and "clip." Because this is not likely in any practical environment, current DSP chips are perfectly capable of fulfilling any current summing requirements without distortion.

Once the summing is done and a 56-bit result remains, the master fader is implemented. The master fader adjusts the level of the overall mix while it is in the 56-bit accumulator. Depending on the position of the master fader a final coefficient is multiplied times the signal to bring the mix up to the required overall amplitude for monitoring or pressing to a distributable media.

Once the 56-bit signal has been summed and multiplied times the master fader coefficient, the "mix" has to be reduced to 24 bits (or 16 bits) for monitoring and distribution. There are two ways of doing this: the first method involves simply dithering off the last, say, 32 bits so that only the 24 most significant bits remain, as follows:

These bits remain   *These bits are dithered off*

1001 0101 1011 1111 1011 1010 0110 0101 0100 0000 1101 0010 1101 1111

This method has its drawbacks. Most signals that get summed will never utilize all 56 bits in the accumulator. Most signals that get summed may never utilize even 48 bits, and of those tracks, most will not reach their peak amplitude at the same time. The majority of the time the summing of the digital channels will not require more than perhaps 50 bits. This means that, if only 50 bits are used and the last 32 are truncated off, our signal is reduced to only 18 bits, lowering its dynamic range.

These bits remain   *These bits are dithered off*

0000 0010 0101 1011 1111 1011 1010 0110 0101 0100 0000 1101 0010 1101 1111

Note that the first 6 bits of those that remain are unused. Since each bit represents 6dB, the peak amplitude of the remaining signal is very quiet, around −36dB FS. In order to keep this signal hot enough to comfortably put onto a medium for distribution we would need to give 36dB of gain to the signal by multiplying every sample by a coefficient of around 63. This could also be achieved by shifting the entire signal to the left 6 bits. In order to use this type of system the master fader would have to have a tremendously large gain range so that it could accommodate all signals that get mixed. A digital mixer with a master fader that covered the range of −60dB to +60dB, for example, would work just fine but would not mirror the typical design of the analog mixing board that it is trying to replace.

The more common method involves "biasing" the system so that the few most significant bits that are rarely used are considered "overflow" and eliminated. Since the average mix only uses (on this particular mixer design) 49 bits or so, if we just eliminate the first 7 bits then our remaining bits are at a decent, hot level. For this system the first several bits are simply removed and if any bits in that range are actually in use then the signal is considered above the maximum amplitude of the mixer and the remaining bits are all toggled to 1s to represent full scale.

Our 24 remaining bits   *These bits are dithered off*

0000 00 **1001 0110 1111 1110 1110 1001** 1001 0101 0000 0011 0100 1011 0111 11

If the signal does not get up to a full 49 bits of amplitude then some gain will be required at the master fader to raise the amplitude to full level before finishing. If the signal exceeds the 49th bit then the signal is out of range and the master fader will have to be reduced to get the entire signal within the 49 allowed bits. After the signal is within the proper range the last bits are dithered off leaving a 24-bit signal.

Some DSP chips have limitations in their ability to perform an entire mix on one DSP chip. In these situations multiple DSP chips are generally used. One chip might handle the panning and track fader coefficient generation and application for, say, 32 tracks, as well as the summing of the tracks together. A second chip might handle all of that for 32 more tracks. The results of each are sent to a third chip where they are combined and the master fader coefficient is applied and final dithering is handled. An example is given in Figure 16.3.

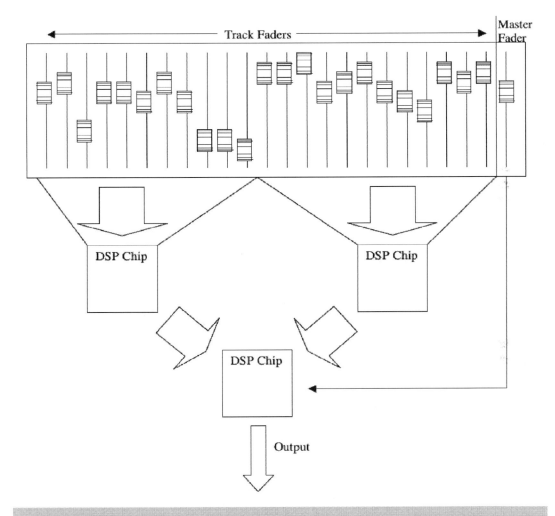

FIGURE 16.3: A Large Mix Spread Across Multiple DSP Chips

A final note is that any aux busses essentially function as a complete mixer. If several tracks send a bit of signal to an aux bus for processing elsewhere, the bussed signals from each track are summed in exactly the same way as the track fader signals are summed together for the master output.

Floating-point mixers operate in much the same way as fixed-point notation mixers. The signals are multiplied times coefficients for each of the gain and attenuation stages and the results of them are then summed. One difference that can occur in a floating-point mixer is that the results can change slightly depending on the order in which the tracks are summed depending on the range of the values. If the following numbers are summed, the way in which they are summed can change the net result:

0110 0010 x 2^0

1101 1011 x 2^{-8}

1110 0001 x 2^{-9}.

To turn these values into fixed-point numbers we add a 1 to the beginning and then shift them based on the value of the exponents, as follows:

10110 0010 0000 0000 0   (The 0s on the end are implied)

00000 0001 1101 1011 0

00000 0000 1111 0000 1

To sum them together, simple addition is done and the resultant value in this situation would be 1011 0010 0110 0101 11, or (1)0110 0100 x 2^0 in floating-point notation. We know, however, that floating-point processors are not designed to add the entire range of values that they can represent (per our discussion on floating-point processors in Chapter Fourteen), so some number of bits on the right are removed in the processor. In our example above we can demonstrate the issue if the processor could only sum 9 bits together. The remaining 9 bits are removed in some way. Oftentimes the math processors are only designed to add two numbers at a time, and each subsequent number is added to the sum of the two. If the numbers above were to be added in a floating-point system the process used would be as follows:

0110 0010 x 2^0

+   1101 1011 x 2^{-8}

Since the two numbers do not fit into the same bit range the first number (the larger number) establishes the range that the processor will use for the addition process. The second number is then shifted the appropriate number of bits to the right and whichever bits do not fit into the equation are removed through dithering. For the sake of this demonstration we will assume that the random dither value is 0 in all situations and the results get rounded. Now the math is as follows:

10110 0010

+   00000 0010   (The last bit two bits rounded up from …1 1 to …10 0)

10110 0100

Then the next value is added to the result:

10110 0100

+   00000 0001   (The last bit was rounded up from …1 to …1 0)

10110 0101

The result is 0110 0101 x 2^0. If, however, the track signals were summed together in reverse order, the result would be different:

$1101\ 1011\ x\ 2^{-8}$

$+\quad 1110\ 0001\ x\ 2^{-9}$

The top number (the larger number) establishes the range for the processor. The math looks as follows:

$1\ 1101\ 1011\ x\ 2^{-8}$

$+\quad 0\ 1111\ 0000\ x\ 2^{-8}$

$10\ 1100\ 1011\ x\ 2^{-7}$ *(The remaining 1 will get removed to keep this only 9 bits)*

This number is then added to the first number in our series:

$0110\ 0101\ x\ 2^{-7}$

$+\quad 0110\ 0010\ x\ 2^{0}$

The numbers are then shifted in bits to get the numbers to align, and the remaining bits are removed using the dithering we discussed above.

$00000\ 0110$ *(The last bits were rounded from …101 1 to …110)*

$+\quad 10110\ 0010$

$10110\ 0010\ or\ (1)0110\ 0010\ x\ 2^{0}$

The value generated when doing the math in reverse order is different than when we did the math in forwards order (10110 0*010* vs. 10110 0*101*). This is because the values are dithered much more frequently than in fixed-point notation. In fixed-point notation there is a risk of an overload if too many numbers are added together. This is not likely in floating-point notation. Consequentially, however, the values are continually reduced to only significant digits and this process can cause the math to be less accurate (if there are multiple answers to the same math problem then clearly at least one of the values is not correct). Since these errors are not random, but are instead signal based, these problems can lead to distortion. Fortunately, however, most manufacturers of floating-point processors (such as Intel, Apple, AMD, and other computer chip manufacturers) design the chips to be able to handle a significant amount of digits before excess values are removed. Current chip implementations allow up to 80 digits to represent a floating-point number, limiting the amount of bit reductions that occur and relegating any distortion to well below the noise floor level of the audio system.

Once the sum of all of the tracks is obtained there are two methods that can be used for determining the value that is emitted as the final 24-bit (fixed-point) result. The first method works much like our biased fixed-point system: a particular range of 24 bits is defined as the range for output. The series of 32-bit floating-point numbers is turned in to a series of 24-bit fixed-point numbers by means of dithering with a particular range of 24 bits being the acceptable range. Perhaps, within the entire range of 256 bits that a 32-bit floating-point number can represent, bits number 40 through 63 are determined to be the range that is used for output values. If this is the case then the final result from summing all of the tracks will have to again get multiplied times a gain coefficient to put the complete mix within that range of numbers without exceeding the 40th bit.

Another method that has been used simply takes the 24 most significant bits in the result and converts the 32-bit number to 24 bits based on the largest number in the mix. If the largest number in the mix reaches all the way to the 1st bit or only reaches as high as the 67th bit, the output level will be the same without the use of a master fader. If this method is used then the system will have to either review the mix ahead of time to conclude what the largest value that will result will be, or simply estimate the range that the final result will fit in and fine tune with a master fader from the range that it estimates is correct.

CONCLUSION

Since a mixer is merely the result of changing the amplitude of signals, summing signals, and splitting signals, and since each of these processes can be done without error, digital mixers are capable of being perfect in regards to the human ear's audibility. Designing a perfect digital mixer such as this is not necessarily easy to do, nor computationally inexpensive. The amount of processes that happen, combined with the amount of stages of dither required, is very large and many digital mixers, whether computer based or using a "stand alone," external processor, have continued to be refined over the years as the computational power available has increased and become more efficient and accurate.

There is little question that digital mixers are inherently capable of being more accurate than analog mixers. There is also little doubting that digital mixers are capable of being more flexible than analog mixers. In some situations, however, analog mixers are preferred over currently available implementations of digital mixers specifically *because* of their inaccuracy. Analog mixers, as audibly "defective" as they are, can be made to be non-linear in a way that many engineers find audibly appealing. If the distortion caused by non-linear processing is harmonic in content then the frequencies that are added fit into the musical scale in a way that can complement the fundamental frequency. The result is that analog processing can be considered more "musical" even though it is not more accurate.

This is not to say that digital processing (such as digital mixing) cannot be made in such a way as to generate the same types of harmonic distortion that analog mixers tend to generate. It is only to say that, to date, no

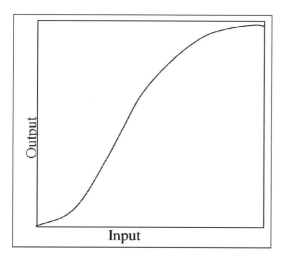
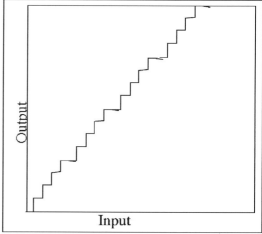

FIGURE 16.4: Analog Mixer vs. Poorly Implemented Digital Mixer Linearity Graphs

manufacturers have attempted to do so because the aim of digital mixers has been to provide complete mathematical accuracy over intentional (but "musical" sounding) harmonic distortion.

This is also not to say that digital mixers are all designed as perfectly as they can be, nor that digital mixers are all designed without added distortion. Generally speaking, however, the distortion that results from digital implementation errors is less audibly appealing than analog mixer distortion. This is because the non-linearity in analog mixers, when plotted, follows a smooth and consistent "curve," whereas errors in the implementation of digital mixers cause a less smooth linearity curve, resulting in less audibly appealing distortion. See Figure 16.4.

In the following two chapters we will discuss digital filters and digital dynamics processors (non-linear processors). Since two of the greatest ways in which analog mixers are different than digital mixers are in the inherent filtering that the components involved provide and the non-linearity that they have, understanding how digital filters and digital dynamics processors are created can explain how it is very possible for this type of processing to be built in to a digital mixing circuit. If implemented well, a digital mixer can be made to sound like any analog mixer made simply by adding mathematical algorithms to the digital mixer that provide the same types of filtering, noise, and non-linearity that is a part of any given analog mixer.

Chapter Seventeen

Digital Filters

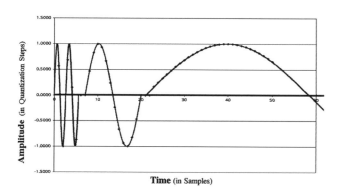

FIGURE 17.1: A Waveform with High, Mid, and Low Frequencies

A simple observation can be made of digital sampling systems in that lower frequency waveforms have less amplitude change from sample to sample than high frequency waveforms. As the low frequency waveforms take a long time to go from any point to any other point (such as from zero to peak), the greatest variance between two subsequent sample points for a low frequency waveform is very small. For higher frequencies, the difference in values between any two samples is much higher. For example, a full scale (maximum amplitude) waveform of one quarter the sample frequency might have a sample at zero followed by a sample at the maximum value. This is not possible with a lower frequency wave. For a lower frequency waveform it takes much longer for the values to get from zero to the maximum value.

Therefore, as a general rule, the higher the frequency the greater the difference in values between subsequent samples. While it is theoretically possible for two subsequent values to be at the same amplitude with a high frequency waveform, the average variation between all samples will be less than the same average variation for a low frequency waveform.

Since high frequency waveforms have greater variance between samples than low frequency waveforms, setting up a system wherein every sample is averaged together with the previous sample affects high frequency waveforms more than it does low frequency waveforms. The overriding premise behind digital filters is that averaging the inbound samples with previous samples creates a predictable change to the frequency content of the data, thus, a filter. The effect of this is easy to see on a very basic example. Notice in Figure 17.1 that we have a waveform that has both high frequency and low frequency content. If we simply take every sample and average it with the sample before it we notice that the high frequency information gets attenuated by means of the mathematical reality that drastic changes in amplitude are reduced. Large changes in amplitude cannot exist if the two samples that have such wide differences are averaged together. The averaging of two drastically variant sample amplitudes causes the output difference to be only half as drastic, as in Figure 17.3.

Notice, however, that low frequencies pass through without as much attenuation. This is because averaging one sample with one that is nearly at the same amplitude causes the output sample to be nearly the same (if not precisely the same) amplitude as the sample amplitudes that went in. This is, in effect, a simple low pass filter: the low frequencies are allowed to "pass" through wherein the high frequencies are attenuated.

We see that this simple averaging of one sample with the sample before it yields a very simple low pass filter.

To make this discussion easier, we should establish certain numerical conventions. "x" Will always signify the inbound sample and "y" will always signify the outbound sample. If we have no processing involved at all then y=x. We can read this more intuitively as, "the outbound sample always equals the inbound sample". Obviously when discussing filters this situation will rarely occur. When we apply filters, most of the time y will not equal x.

Sample #	Inbound Sample Value (From Figure 17.1)	Formula Average current sample and previous sample together.	Outbound Sample Value (See Figure 17.3)
1	.00	(.00 + .00) / 2	.00
2	.56	(.00 + .56) / 2	.28
3	-1.0	(.56 + -1.0) / 2	-.22
4	.68	(-1.0 + .68) / 2	-.16
5	.15	(.68 + .15) / 2	.415
6	-.87	(.15 + -.87) / 2	-.36
7	.00	(-.87 + .00) / 2	-.435
8	.00	(.00 + .00) / 2	.00
9	.46	(.00 + .46) / 2	.23
10	.82	(.46 + .82) / 2	.64
etc.			

FIGURE 17.2: Creation of Data on Figure 17.3 from Data on Figure 17.1

To continue with our establishing of numerical conventions, a pair of parenthesis such as () indicates which specific sample value we are speaking about. For example, $x_{(1)}$ would be, "the value of the first inbound sample." $y_{(5)}$ would be, "the value of the fifth outbound sample."

Because we do not often know which sample numbers we are actually dealing with (and in order to keep our formulas a bit universal) we will most often refer to the current sample value as (n). Therefore $x_{(n)}$ can be rephrased in English, "the value of the current inbound sample". When we want to discuss a sample other than the current one we will refer to it in reference to the current one such as $y_{(n-2)}$. This would be, "the value of the outbound sample 2 samples ago." The very next value would have been $y_{(n-1)}$, followed by $y_{(n)}$, or the current sample. If we want to talk about future outbound samples we will refer to them as $y_{(n+3)}$, etc. Most often we will refer to past samples.

Back to the example we had at the top of the page where we took every sample and averaged it with the sample before it we would have had the following formula:

$$y_{(n)} = \frac{[\, x_{(n)} + x_{(n-1)}\,]}{2}$$

This formula can be rephrased in English, "the current outbound sample is equivalent to the values of the current inbound sample plus the inbound sample before it, summed together and divided by two." This is indeed the appropriate formula for averaging the most recent two samples together.

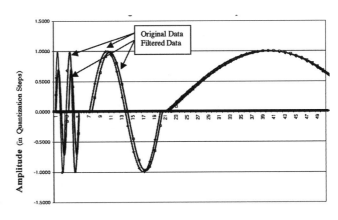

FIGURE 17.3: The Waveform in Figure 17.1 Filtered with a Simple Low Pass Filter

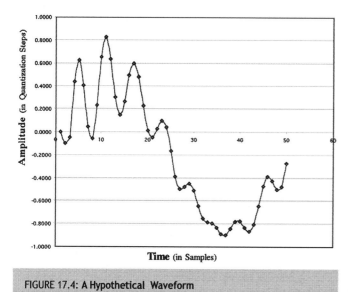

FIGURE 17.4: A Hypothetical Waveform

A revised way of writing this example and one that we will be using more consistently throughout this chapter is:

$$y_{(n)} = .5\, x_{(n)} + .5\, x_{(n-1)}$$

The English way of saying this would be, "the current outbound sample is equivalent to half of the current sample plus half of the sample before it." One will note that this yields the same result as the prior example.

We can take a series of samples (Figure 17.4) and plug them into that formula and examine the results that come out the other side, as is given in Figure 17.5. The results are given in Figure 17.6.

We can visually discern that, indeed, the high frequency content has been attenuated, but a Fourier Transform more accurately indicates this to us in Plot 17.7.

A mathematical analysis would yield several properties about this digital filter. First, we can ascertain the exact function of the filter, per the frequency response curve of this filter, as is graphed in Figure 17.8.

Secondly, this filter inherently yields a delay on the signal. In this particular filter, the delay is 1/2 sample. This means that waveforms that pass through this filter will come out the other side 1/2 sample later. For a visual proof of this, observe the waveforms in Plot 17.6. Notice the location in time of the first peak of the filtered version with respect to the same peak in the original waveform. The peak occurs 1/2 sample later.

As a minor sidebar, let us look at what would happen if we *subtract* the previous sample from the current sample instead of added them together. The formula for this would be:

$$y_{(n)} = x_{(n)} - x_{(n-1)}$$

Instead of, "the outbound sample is equivalent to the most recent two samples added together and divided by two," this formula would be, "the outbound sample is equivalent to the difference between the most recent two samples."

Looking at our same sets of sample data from Figure 17.4, the new sample values would be those given in Figure 17.9. The graph of this is given in Figure 17.10.

We see that this becomes a high pass filter. The difference between a high pass filter and a low pass filter is whether the

Sample #	Inbound Sample Value (From Figure 17.5)	Formula $y(n)=.5\,x(n) + .5\,x(n-1)$	Outbound Sample Value (See Figure 17.6)
1	.00	(.5 x .00) + (.5 x .00)	.00
2	-.10	(.5 x -.10) + (.5 x .00)	-.05
3	-.05	(.5 x -.05) + (.5 x -.10)	-.075
4	.44	(.5 x .44) + (.5 x -.05)	.195
5	.63	(.5 x .63) + (.5 x .44)	.535
6	.41	(.5 x .41) + (.5 x .63)	.52
7	.05	(.5 x .05) + (.5 x .41)	.23
8	-.06	(.5 x -.06) + (.5 x .05)	-.005
9	.23	(.5 x .23) + (.5 x -.06)	.085
10	.65	(.5 x .63) + (.5 x .23)	.43
etc.			

FIGURE 17.5: First Ten Values of Sample Data For Further Analysis

previous inbound sample is added to or subtracted from the current inbound sample. For the sake of this chapter we will not be discussing high pass filters for two reasons. First, the majority of areas where the understanding of digital filters is pertinent for understanding digital audio are low pass and not high pass filters. This includes A/D conversion, D/A conversion, sample rate conversion, and filters used to simulate the natural effects of high frequency attenuation in analog transmission. Second, the difference between the two types of filters is merely whether we average samples together or measure the difference between them. Once one understands low pass filters it is relatively easy to port that knowledge over to high pass filters.

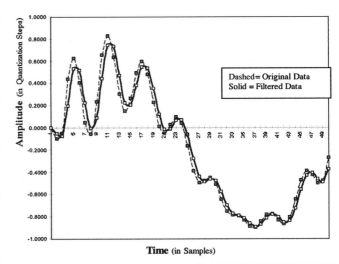

FIGURE 17.6: The Waveform in Figure 17.5 Filtered With a $y_{(n)} = .5 \, x_{(n)} + .5 \, x_{(n-1)}$ Filter

Regarding low pass filters, we have so far looked at taking two samples and averaging them together. Next we determine what would happen if we average three samples together. This formula would look as follows:

$$y_{(n)} = .33 \, x_{(n)} + .33 \, x_{(n-1)} + .33 \, x_{(n-2)}$$

Or, "the current outbound sample is equal to one third of the current inbound sample plus a third of the value of the inbound sample before that plus a third of the value of the inbound sample before that one." Or, "the current outbound sample is equivalent to the average of the most recent three inbound sample values."

In order to understand the effect of this filter it is important to recognize that our previous example was really a notch filter, completely notching (attenuating) at the Nyquist frequency. Since there is no material in a digital system above the Nyquist frequency this acts as a simple low pass filter.

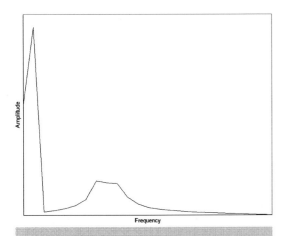

FIGURE 17.7A: Fourier Transform of the Waveform in Figure 17.5

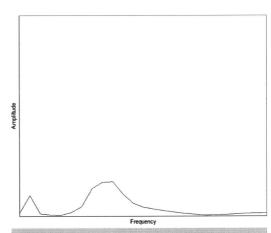

FIGURE 17.7B: Fourier Transform of the Waveform in Figure 17.6

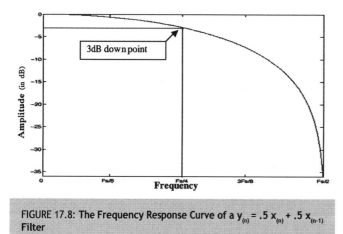

The effect of this three-sample filter is a filter with the same shape as the two-sample average filter, but lower in frequency. It functions as a notch filter at one third of the sample frequency instead of half of the sample frequency. It is still, in effect, a low pass filter because it is not a symmetrical notch filter – it attenuates more above the center frequency than below. A plot of the frequency response of this filter is found in Figure 17.13.

Plugging in some values yields the following sample data, starting from our same set of inbound sample data from Figure 17.4. Figure 17.11 shows the mathematical process for the implementation of this filter. The graph of this is given in Figure 17.12

Let us go back for a moment to our examples where we used the following formula:

$$y_{(n)} = .5\, x_{(n)} + .5\, x_{(n-1)}$$

Let us explore for a moment slightly modifying this formula to the following:

$$y_{(n)} = .8\, x_{(n)} + .2\, x_{(n-1)}$$

Notice that this is the same as the previous formula in that we are averaging the current inbound sample with the previous sample, but in this formula we have heavily weighted the "effect" of the current sample. This means that the effect of the filter will not be nearly as steep because drastic differences in sample values can still occur but will get slightly attenuated by averaging them with the samples before, though disproportionately. We could say that, "the outbound sample is equivalent to the current inbound sample averaged with the previous inbound sample, but with 4/5 weighting going to the current inbound sample."

The graph of this with the data in Figure 17.4 yields the waveform in Figure 17.14.

Sample #	Inbound Sample Value (From Figure 17.5)	Formula y(n) = x(n) - x(n-1)	Outbound Sample Value (See Figure 17.10)
1	.00	(.00 - .00)	.00
2	-.10	(-.10 - .00)	-.10
3	-.05	(-.05 - -.10)	.05
4	.44	(.44 - -.05)	.49
5	.63	(.63 - .44)	.19
6	.41	(.41 - .63)	-.22
7	.05	(.05 - .41)	-.36
8	-.06	(-.06 - .05)	-.11
9	.23	(.23 - -.06)	.31
10	.65	(.63 - .23)	.40
etc.			

FIGURE 17.9: Data from Figure 17.4 Processed with the Filter y$_{(n)}$ = x$_{(n)}$ - x$_{(n-1)}$

Just as in our discussions of amplitude changes in digital mixers, the ".8" and ".2" are called "coefficients," and are the values that we multiply the samples by. In a filter such as this we are, in effect, summing digital signals with amplitude changes just like with a digital mixer. The effect of the particular coefficients in the example above is that we are no longer really "averaging" samples together, per se. We are now "weighted averaging" samples together. "Weighted averaging" simply refers to the fact that each value does not have the same effect on the result, but rather that different samples have more effect than others on the results of the averaging.

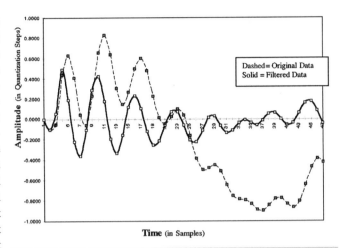

FIGURE 17.10: The Waveform in Figure 17.5 Filtered with a $y_{(n)} = x_{(n)} - x_{(n-1)}$ Filter

GETTING TO IIR FILTERS

We have now discussed two different changes to our basic formula that can have a drastic effect upon our basic formula. First, we can change the number of samples that we are going to use in our "averaging" of samples to change the frequency of the filter with respect to the sample frequency. Second, we can change the coefficients, thus giving certain samples some weighting as to the result and changing the slope of the filter. Combining these two variables we notice that creating a more desirable filter likely requires the use of many samples, all of which are weighted differently. Using more samples provides us with the ability to have great control over the frequency of the filter while tempering the effect of each sample by using coefficients in front of each sample. For example, if A, B, C, D, and E represent different coefficients, then

$$y_{(n)} = A\,x_{(n)} + B\,x_{(n-1)} + C\,x_{(n-2)} + D\,x_{(n-3)} + E\,x_{(n-4)}$$

would give us a very flexible filter design wherein the filter could be shallow

Sample #	Inbound Sample Value (From Figure 17.5)	Formula $y(n) = .33\ x(n) + .33\ x(n-1) + .33\ x(n-2)$	Outbound Sample Value (See Figure 17.12)
1	.00	(.33 x .00) + (.33 x .00) + (.33 x .00)	.0000
2	-.10	(.33 x -.10) + (.33 x .00) + (.33 x .00)	-.0330
3	-.05	(.33 x -.05) + (.33 x -.10) + (.33 x .00)	-.0495
4	.44	(.33 x .44) + (.33 x -.05) + (.33 x -.10)	.0957
5	.63	(.33 x .63) + (.33 x .44) + (.33 x -.05)	.3366
6	.41	(.33 x .41) + (.33 x .63) + (.33 x .44)	.4884
7	.05	(.33 x .05) + (.33 x .41) + (.33 x .63)	.3597
8	-.06	(.33 x -.06) + (.33 x .05) + (.33 x .41)	.1320
9	.23	(.33 x .23) + (.33 x -.06) + (.33 x .05)	.0726
10	.65	(.33 x .65) + (.33 x .23) + (.33 x -.06)	.2706
etc.			

FIGURE 17.11: Data from Figure 17.4 processed with the Filter $y_{(n)} = .33\ x_{(n)} + .33\ x_{(n-1)} + .33\ x_{(n-2)}$

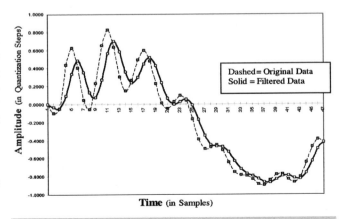

FIGURE 17.12: The Waveform in Figure 17.5 Filtered with a $y_{(n)} = .33\ x_{(n)} + .33\ x_{(n-1)} + .33\ x_{(n-2)}$ Filter

or steep and at the frequency desired, all of which could ultimately be controlled by changing the values of the coefficients.

For that matter, the most flexible filter would really be:

$$y_{(n)} = A\, x_{(n)} + B\, x_{(n-1)} + C\, x_{(n-2)} \ldots + ?\, x_{(n-n)}$$

This filter could be rephrased, "the outbound sample is equivalent to the average of the current inbound sample, the one before it, and all of the inbound samples before that back to the very first sample."

The problem with using this formula is that the amount of math that needs to be done in order to calculate the outbound sample value will increase as the number of samples in our data stream continues to grow. At a sample rate of 44.1kS/s there are 44,100 numbers to add together to figure out the sample value that happens at the end of the first second. Think of how many numbers will have to be added for each sample that occurs five minutes into a recording!

The way that this is dealt with is by using the following formula instead:

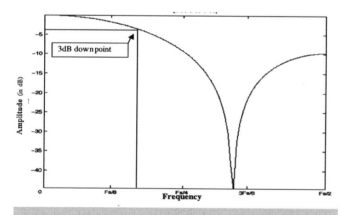

FIGURE 17.13: The Frequency Response Curve of a $y_{(n)} = .33\, x_{(n)} + .33\, x_{(n-1)} + .33\, x_{(n-2)}$ Filter

$$y_{(n)} = A\, x_{(n)} + B\, y_{(n-1)}$$

Note that the value following the B coefficient is y instead of x, or the outbound sampled instead of the inbound sample. This could be restated, "the current outbound sample is equivalent to the weighted average of the current *inbound* sample and the previous *outbound* sample." This is called a "recursive" filter in that the previous outbound sample "re-occurs" in the formula for the next sample.

For the sake of example, let us use the simple formula:

$$y_{(n)} = .5\, x_{(n)} + .5\, y_{(n-1)}$$

In this example we are truly averaging (not weighted averaging) the current inbound sample with the previous outbound sample. Let us look at the effect of this filter on our sample data from Figure 17.4, given in Figure 17.15 and 17.16.

Notice that the first outbound sample is .00 because the previous outbound sample is assumed to be zero. The outbound sample is therefore half of the in-

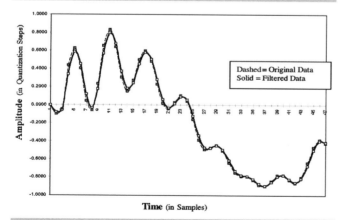

FIGURE 17.14: The Waveform in Figure 17.5 Filtered with a $y_{(n)} = .8\, x_{(n)} + .2\, x_{(n-1)}$ Filter

bound sample. For the second outbound sample we end up taking half of the first *outbound* sample, which was half of the first *inbound* sample. Notice here that the first sample has an effect on both the first outbound sample AND the second outbound sample, but that its "effect" is diminishing. By the time we get to the second outbound sample the effect of the first inbound sample is only one quarter (half of one half). At this point we really could simply rewrite this as:

$$y_{(2)} = .5 \, x_{(2)} + .25 \, x_{(1)}$$

Or, "the second outbound sample is equal to half of the *second* inbound sample plus one quarter of the *first* inbound sample."

If we want to calculate the value of the third outbound sample we would take:

$$y_{(3)} = .5 \, x_{(3)} + .5 \, y_{(2)}$$

And since we have spelled out above what $y_{(2)}$ equals, we can plug that in as follows:

$$y_{(3)} = .5 \, x_{(2)} + .5 \, [\, .5 \, x_{(2)} + .25 \, x_{(1)} \,]$$

or

$$y_{(3)} = .5 \, x_{(2)} + .25 \, x_{(2)} + .125 \, x_{(1)}$$

Sample #	Inbound Sample Value (From Figure 17.5)	Formula y(n)=.5 x(n) + .5 y(n-1)	Outbound Sample Value (See Figure 17.16)
1	.00	(.5 x .00) + (.5 x .00)	.00
2	-.10	(.5 x -.10) + (.5 x .00)	-.05
3	-.05	(.5 x -.05) + (.5 x -.05)	-.05
4	.44	(.5 x .44) + (.5 x -.05)	.195
5	.63	(.5 x .63) + (.5 x .195)	.4125
6	.41	(.5 x .41) + (.5 x .4125)	.4113
7	.05	(.5 x .05) + (.5 x .4113)	.2306
8	-.06	(.5 x -.06) + (.5 x .2306)	.0853
9	.23	(.5 x .23) + (.5 x .0853)	.1577
10	.65	(.5 x .63) + (.5 x .1577)	.4038
etc.			

FIGURE 17.15: Data from Figure 17.5 Processed with the filter $y_{(n)} = .5 \, x_{(n)} + .5 \, y_{(n-1)}$

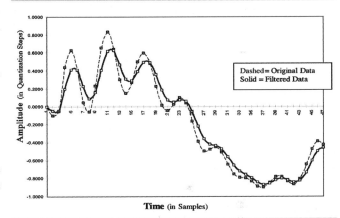

FIGURE 17.16: The Waveform in Figure 17.5 Filtered with a $y_{(n)} = .5 \, x_{(n)} + .5 \, y_{(n-1)}$ Filter

We can see that the value of the first inbound sample still has a bearing on the output of the third sample, but with decreasing effect. One would notice that the effect of this is essentially the same as with Figure 17.16 above, where we average ALL of the samples together, but with more weighting on the most recent inbound samples and decreasing weighting on inbound samples from long ago. With a recursive filter such as this one, each inbound sample has an effect on an infinite number of outbound samples in the future, but with decreasing significance. This type of filter is called an "infinite impulse response" filter, or an IIR filter. The formula for a single pole, low pass IIR filter (6dB roll-off per octave) is indeed:

$$y_{(n)} = A \, x_{(n)} + B \, y_{(n-1)}$$

We have already discussed that the more averaging that is done the steeper we can make the filter. While the above formula incorporates a bit of ALL previous samples in it to determine the value of a single outbound sample, it only uses two pieces of data (the inbound sample and the last outbound sample) to calculate it. This can still allow fairly drastic movement from sample point to sample point that, while flexibly controlled to be effective at a certain frequency, can still only be as steep as 6dB per octave. Creating a 12dB per octave filter utilizes 3 numbers averaged together, and the following formula is used:

$$y_{(n)} = A\,x_{(n)} + B\,y_{(n-1)} + C\,y_{(n-2)}$$

Or, "the outbound sample is equivalent to a weighted averaging of the current *inbound* sample, the previous *outbound* sample, and the *outbound* sample before that." This formula is precisely the one that is used for the creation of IIR low pass filters in our industry. Filters that need a greater than 12dB per octave slope simply utilize two of these filters run sequentially where the data goes through one filter and then through another identical filter in series. Any steepness of filter at any frequency can be created simply by utilizing multiple two pole filters, and any frequency of the filter below or even above the Nyquist frequency can be the focal point of the filter.

At this point we should probably expound upon some additional terminology. With low pass and high pass filters there are three different "bands". The "pass-band" is the area that we are not attenuating. With a 1kHz low pass filter the pass-band would be 1kHz and below. The "stop-band" is the area that we are attenuating. On this filter the stop-band would obviously be the range above 1kHz. The "transition band" is the range in which the filter is transitioning between the pass-band and the stop-band. On a 1kHz 1 pole filter (6dB per octave) in which we want 60dB of attenuation, the transition band is 10 octaves long (60dB of attenuation divided by 6dB per octave takes 10 octaves to be fully attenuated). In this situation the "stop-band" is really not above 1kHz, but is actually the range in which the fully desired attenuation (60dB) is achieved. For this sample filter, that would be 1024kHz and up (the 10th octave of 1kHz). The transition band would be 1kHz to 1024kHz

Sample #	Inbound Sample Value (From Figure 17.5)	Formula $y(n)=.5\,x(n) + .25\,y(n-1) - .25\,y(n-2)$	Outbound Sample Value (See Figure 17.18)
1	.00	(.5 x .00) + (.25 x .000) - (.25 x .000)	.00
2	-.10	(.5 x -.10) + (.25 x .000) - (.25 x .000)	-.05
3	-.05	(.5 x -.05) + (.25 x -.050) - (.25 x .000)	-.037
4	.44	(.5 x .44) + (.25 x -.037) - (.25 x -.050)	.223
5	.63	(.5 x .63) + (.25 x .223) - (.25 x -.037)	.380
6	.41	(.5 x .41) + (.25 x .380) - (.25 x .223)	.244
7	.05	(.5 x .05) + (.25 x .244) - (.25 x .380)	-.009
8	-.06	(.5 x -.06) + (.25 x -.009) - (.25 x .244)	-.093
9	.23	(.5 x .23) + (.25 x -.093) - (.25 x -.009)	.094
10	.65	(.5 x .65) + (.25 x .094) - (.25 x -.093)	.372

FIGURE 17.17: Data from Figure 17.4 Processed with the Filter y(n) = .5 x$_{(n)}$ + .25 y$_{(n-1)}$ - .25 y$_{(n-2)}$

ISSUES WITH IIR FILTERS

Looking back at our recursive IIR filter, one property of IIR filters that closely relates to filter design in the analog world is that they are not phase-linear. In other words they have phase "issues". This is reflective of a property in filters and other processing called "group delay". Group delay is the latency of the signal getting through the process, but is most often used in relation to different frequencies getting through that process. Some frequencies make it through some processes faster than other frequencies,

Sample #	Inbound Sample Value (From Figure 17.17)	Formula $y(n)=.5\,x(n) + .25\,y(n-1) - .25\,y(n-2)$	Outbound Sample Value
1	.372	(.5 x .372) + (.25 x .000) - (.25 x .000)	.186
2	.094	(.5 x .094) + (.25 x .186) - (.25 x .000)	.093
3	-.093	(.5 x -.093) + (.25 x .093) - (.25 x .186)	-.070
4	-.009	(.5 x -.009) + (.25 x -.070) - (.25 x .093)	.045
5	.244	(.5 x .244) + (.25 x .045) - (.25 x -.070)	.128
6	.380	(.5 x .380) + (.25 x .128) - (.25 x .045)	.233
7	.223	(.5 x .223) + (.25 x .233) - (.25 x .128)	.138
8	-.037	(.5 x -.037) + (.25 x .138) - (.25 x .233)	-.042
9	-.050	(.5 x -.050) + (.25 x -.042) - (.25 x .138)	-.070
10	.00	(.5 x .000) + (.25 x -.070) - (.25 x -.042)	-.007

FIGURE 17.18: Data from Figure 17.17 Processed in reverse order with the Filter y$_{(n)}$ = .5 x$_{(n)}$ + .25 y$_{(n-1)}$ - .25 y$_{(n-2)}$

and this is what causes filters to have their reputation of altering the phase of the signal. This alteration happens increasingly as we get toward the transition band. It is said that *all* filters have this effect, but this is definitely not the case. In order to eliminate this, however, the filter must be symmetrical. This means that the signal has to run through the formula once normally and then through the formula again backwards. By doing this, any phase shift imparted onto particular frequencies in the signal is nullified as the data runs through the filter again in reverse order. If a filter causes any 1kHz content in the waveform to be shifted 90° forward in phase, then running the signal through the same filter backwards would cause a 90° phase shift backward, nullifying the phase shift entirely. For example, if we have ten samples going into the following formula:

$$y_{(n)} = .5\,x_{(n)} + .25\,y_{(n-1)} - .25\,y_{(n-2)}$$

and our ten samples are labeled $x_{(1)}$ through $x_{(10)}$. First we would run our 10 samples in as follows:

$$y_{(1)} = .5\,x_{(1)} + 0 - 0$$

$$y_{(2)} = .5\,x_{(2)} + .25\,y_{(1)} \text{ which is also } .5\,x_{(2)} + .125\,x_{(1)}$$

$$y_{(3)} = .5\,x_{(3)} + .25\,y_{(2)} - .25\,y_{(1)} \text{ which is also } .5\,x_{(3)} + .125\,x_{(2)} - .09375\,x_{(1)}$$

etc.

For the sake of example we will use the first 10 samples from Figure 17.4, and we will only compute 10 output samples (since this is an IIR filter it will theoretically go on forever, but we will stop the processing after the tenth outbound sample is produced). See Figure 17.17.

Then the entire signal is run through the same filter in reverse order, so that:

$$y_{(1)} = .5\,x_{(10)} + 0 - 0$$

$$y_{(2)} = .5\,x_{(9)} + .25\,y_{(10)} \text{ which is also } .5\,x_{(9)} + .125\,x_{(10)}$$

$$y_{(3)} = .5\,x_{(8)} + .25\,y_{(9)} - .25\,y_{(10)} \text{ which is also } .5\,x_{(8)} + .125\,x_{(9)} - .09375\,x_{(10)}$$

etc.

The result is given in Figure 17.18.

The attenuation that the filter provides does not change based on which direction the data is run through the filter - the filter functions the same and has the same effect, but by running the data through the opposite direction the phase shifting happens backwards and the effects of the filter are essentially doubled. If the data is run through the same filter twice, once forward and once backward, then the result will be no phase shifting at all across the entire frequency spectrum.

There is a problem with this, however. In our example above we only had 10 samples at the start. It would be very easy to calculate new data from our 10 samples run through our filter and then do the same process in reverse, followed by adding the results together. In the practical world, however, a "data stream" goes on for much longer than 10 samples. In a 3-minute piece of digital audio sampled at 44.1kHz there would be 7,938,000 samples to run through in each direction before ANY output sample could be released. This would require an "off-line" process, or one that was most definitely non-realtime. After all, in order to put out sample #1 we

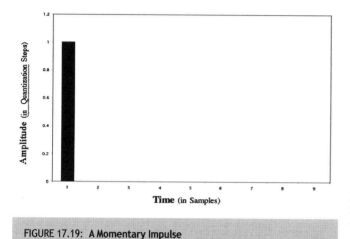

FIGURE 17.19: A Momentary Impulse

have to know what sample #7,938,000 is in order to calculate the forwards and backwards results of this filter. Therefore, while it would be possible to create a linear phase IIR filter in non-realtime, doing so in real-time is nearly impossible. This would also mean that the majority of the situations where filters are needed, such as oversampled A/D converters, would not be capable of having linear phase results. Further, as phase shift in the pass-band is directly related to the steepness of the filter, the very steep filters needed in the downsampling portion of A/D converters, for example, would create an unacceptable amount of phase-shifting. At 44.1kS/s sampling rates where we want to have our transition band only be from 20kHz to 22.05kHz and we want everything above 22.05kHz to be attenuated greater than 144dB (for 24-bit audio) we would need something like a 1000 pole filter, which would have tremendous phase shift problems in the pass-band.

There is, however, a way to create linear phase digital filters.

GETTING TO FIR FILTERS

In order to understand how we create linear phase filters we need to look at how IIR filters work from a different approach:

First we must go back to the beginning and look at IIR filters as adhering to the following formula:

$$y_{(n)} = A\,x_{(n)} + B\,x_{(n-1)} + C\,x_{(n-2)} + D\,x_{(n-3)} + E\,x_{(n-4)} \ldots ?\,x_{(n-n)}$$

An IIR filter can be represented in this fashion, but only if we know how many samples we are dealing with and if we do the process in non-realtime. One can recall that we do not often know how many samples we are dealing with in a data stream, so we make the actual formula reflect this lengthy formula by using previous *output* values instead of only using *inbound* sample values. As a refresher, let us look at a five-sample data stream and a very simple filter. Our five sample data stream will be represented as $x_{(1)}$ through $x_{(5)}$. Our filter will be:

$$y_{(n)} = .5\,x_{(n)} + .5\,y_{(n-1)}$$

Let us figure out the longhand formulas for the outbound samples:

$$y_{(1)} = .5\,x_{(1)} + 0$$

$$y_{(2)} = .5\,x_{(2)} + .25\,x_{(1)}$$

$$y_{(3)} = .5\,x_{(3)} + .25\,x_{(2)} + .125\,x_{(1)}$$

$$y_{(4)} = .5\,x_{(4)} + .25\,x_{(3)} + .125\,x_{(2)} + .0625\,x_{(1)}$$

$$y_{(5)} = .5\,x_{(5)} + .25\,x_{(4)} + .125\,x_{(3)} + .0625\,x_{(2)} + .03125\,x_{(1)}$$

$$y_{(6)} = .25\,x_{(5)} + .125\,x_{(4)} + .0625\,x_{(3)} + .03125\,x_{(2)} + .015625\,x_{(1)}$$

$$y_{(7)} = .5 \text{ of } y_{(6)}, \text{ etc. etc. etc.}$$

Notice that by the time we get to $y_{(5)}$ we truly do have this formula:

$$y_{(n)} = A\,x_{(n)} + B\,x_{(n-1)} + C\,x_{(n-2)} + D\,x_{(n-3)} + E\,x_{(n-4)}$$

Wherein A=.5, B=.25, C=.125, D=.0625, E=.03125

Since we have only five inbound samples we really *could* replace our filter formula with the lengthy non-recursive one above so that we never use a previous outbound sample value to calculate the next one. It is also easy to see, though, that using more sample values means much longer formulas. An infinite number of samples requires an infinitely long formula.

To look at it another way, let us take a hypothetical situation where we have a momentary impulse and we look at how that momentary impulse is treated by the filter and what effect that filter has on that momentary impulse over time. To simulate this we make the first sample equal to 1 and all other samples equal to 0 (Figure 17.19).

Another way that we can find out the coefficients that could make a non-recursive filter (only inbound sample points) from a recursive filter is to run the momentary impulse through the recursive filter and observe the results. In Figure 17.20 below, the results from this pass of the impulse through the filter $y_{(n)} = .5\,x_{(n)} + .5\,y_{(n-1)}$ are as follows:

$$y_{(1)} = .5$$

$$y_{(2)} = .25$$

$$y_{(3)} = .125$$

$$y_{(4)} = .0625$$

$$y_{(5)} = .03125$$

etc.

This exercise shows us the effect of one sample over time, and the weight that that sample has on future output values. This tells us that by the fifth sample this filter only has a weighting of .03125. This tells us that a filter could be made using these as the first five coefficients and it would have the same results as the IIR filter - at least for the first five samples of the IIR filter. Again, it also shows us that the more coefficients we use the closer it gets to the actual results of the IIR filter with which we started.

We can see that the outbound data stream will continue on forever as the output values get closer and closer to zero. This also means that the effect of the first sample wears off over time, but will also not ever reach

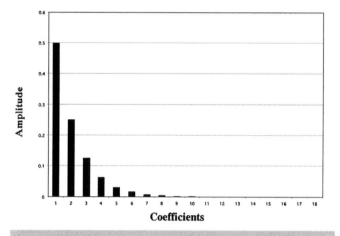

FIGURE 17.20: Momentary Impulse Run Through the Filter $y_{(n)} = .5 x_{(n)} + .5 y_{(n-1)}$

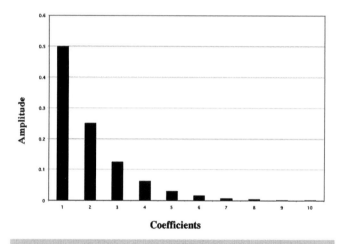

FIGURE 17.21: The First 10 Coefficients Yielded From the Filter $y_{(n)} = .5 x_{(n)} + .5 y_{(n-1)}$

zero. With the example formula above, by the time we get out several hundred samples the effect of the first sample value is going to be nearly moot, and depending upon rounding errors in our formulas it very well *could* be moot. If we accept this notion then we can stop making recursive filters and we can instead make *non*-recursive filters, such that $y_{(n)}$ will only ever equal various coefficients multiplied times $x_{(n-?)}$. If we do this then the filter only looks back a fixed number of samples to come up with its result, but no more than that.

For instance, if we say that with the formula that we used above: $y(n) = .5 x(n) + .5 y_{(n-1)}$, that by the time we get eleven samples out the first sample is effectively irrelevant for our purposes then we can decide to rewrite this formula as the following:

$$y_{(n)} = A x_{(n)} + B x_{(n-1)} + C x_{(n-2)} + D x_{(n-3)} + E x_{(n-4)} \dots J x_{(n-10)}$$

That is the end of the formula (Figure 17.21). This is no longer a formula that is looking infinitely far back to generate a sample value. It is now only looks back ten samples. Said another way, any inbound sample no longer affects an infinite number of samples into the future with decreasing weighting. Now each sample only affects the next ten samples with decreasing weighting. This is no longer an "Infinite Impulse Response" filter as we are no longer affecting an infinite number of samples, but is now referred to as a "*Finite* Impulse Response" filter (FIR). An impulse put into this filter will produce a response that lasts only ten samples. It has a finite length. An impulse put into the IIR filter will produce a response that continues to decay indefinitely. Thus the "impulse response" of that filter is infinite.

Our original problem was that we were trying to create a filter that had a finite length so that we could run our data into it forwards and backwards without having to wait for the entire waveform to pass through it first. Since this filter is of finite duration we can now run the data through the filter both forwards and backwards to create a "linear phase filter". The easiest way to do this process, however, is to make the *filter* go forwards and backwards and just let the data go through in one direction. Let us make our example a little easier to manage. Let us take an FIR filter that "weighted averages" the last three samples, as follows:

$$y_{(n)} = A x_{(n)} + B x_{(n-1)} + C x_{(n-2)}$$

In order to make a single "linear phase" filter we have to figure out what would happen if we ran the information through this filter forwards and then backwards. In order to do that we could run our impulse through the filter, then take the results and run them through the filter again backwards. Looking at the three values above it is easy to see that if we ran our impulse through the filter above the result would be precisely the samples in the filter above. Then, if we take the result and run it through the same filter backwards we would have a linear phase version of this filter. This is how we create a linear phase filter: we take the filter coefficients of two identical filters and run them through themselves backwards.

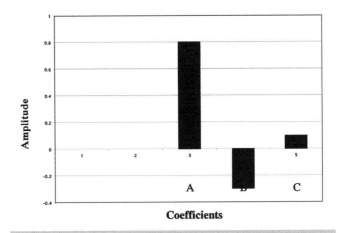

FIGURE 17.22: A Hypothetical Three-Coefficient FIR Filter

In the example above, the first outbound sample would equal (C x A), or the last sample times the first sample. The second outbound sample would equal (C x B) + (B x A). Figure 17.23 shows how a linear phase version of the filter in Figure 17.22 is realized. Figure 17.24 yields the resulting coefficients

Notice, though, that this means that we are no longer averaging the current sample with the past two samples. We are now averaging the current sample with the past two samples *and* the *next* two samples. This means that this becomes a sort of a "look ahead" and "look behind" filter in that it requires previous samples and future samples in order to properly calculate the outbound sample. This also means that this type of filter has inherent latency equivalent to nearly half of the length of the filter. In our example above we do not calculate the output until two samples later such that this FIR filter has an actual latency of 2 samples. The latency for

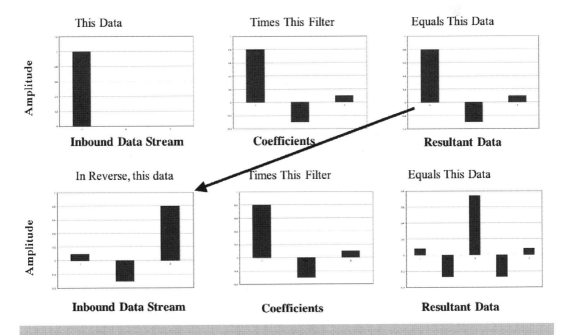

FIGURE 17.23: The Creation of a Linear Phase Filter from the Data in Figure 17.22

a linear phase FIR filter will always be 1/2 of a sample less than half the number of coefficients. For example, a 13 coefficient linear phase FIR filter has a latency of 6 samples. An 8 coefficient linear phase FIR filter has a latency of 3 1/2 samples.

Having done this, though, we have successfully created a filter such that the data essentially goes through once and becomes phase shifted, but then goes through again backwards and becomes phase shifted back the other way so that the data has no phase shift and is therefore "phase linear".

Conventionally, the filter is written without future samples as follows:

$$y_{(n)} = C\, x_{(n)} + B\, x_{(n-1)}\, A\, x_{(n-2)} + B\, x_{(n-3)} + C\, x_{(n-4)}$$

Not all FIR filters are linear phase filters. FIR filters can be constructed non-symmetrically, much like the inherent nature of an IIR filter. They can also be constructed anti-symmetrically such that half of it is the opposite "polarity" of the other half, such as Figure 17.25 represents.

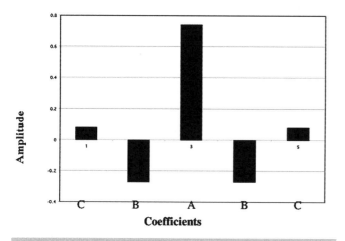

FIGURE 17.24: A Linear Phase Version of the Filter in Figure 17.22

FIR filters are most useful in our industry, however, in that they can be easily made to pass data without any phase shift. There are many other uses for FIR filters in our industry besides just those where complete phase linearity is required.

ISSUES WITH FIR FILTERS

There are complications with FIR filters, however. Looking at IIR filters again for a moment we can see that the formula:

$$y_{(n)} = A\, x_{(n)} + B\, y_{(n-1)} + C\, y_{(n-2)}$$

only requires that the digital signal processor do three multiplication functions and then add three numbers together: coefficient "A" times the current sample, coefficient "B" times the previous outbound sample, and coefficient "C" times the previous outbound sample to that. Then the three results get added together. This very simple mathematical formula looks infinitely far back in time to calculate its results.

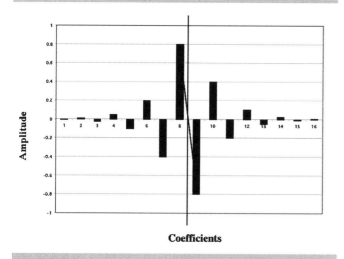

FIGURE 17.25: An Example of an Anti-Symmetrical FIR Filter

With an FIR filter that looks, say, 100 samples back in time to do its formula, that means 100 separate coefficients are used, meaning 100 separate multiplication stages followed by the addition of the 100 results together. This yields three problems.

First, the accuracy of the coefficients is limited to the number of bits we allow for them. If we use 8-bit coefficients then the coefficients are limited to basically representing 256 possible steps. For very accurate numbers such as -.00784256 there would have to be significant dithering of the coefficient values if we only allowed 8-bit coefficients. For this reason we need very lengthy coefficients, but this requires greater amounts of processing and more sophisticated digital signal processors to calculate the results. Regardless of how many bits are allowed for the coefficients, at some point the coefficient value is going to have to be dithered, limiting its accuracy. In IIR filters this is not as significant an issue because the math is somewhat "automatically" done by using the previous outbound sample rather than calculating all of the coefficients back 100 samples individually. Additionally, the summing of 100 large numbers together requires further powerful processors. Having said this, the calculation of the appropriate coefficients is actually more crucial with an IIR filter because of its recursive nature. Any errors that exist in a coefficient of an IIR filter manifest themselves ad infinitum as the incorrect value continues to cycle around for further processing.

Second, making a small change in the filter means recalculating ALL of the coefficient values. In an IIR filter, a change in the frequency of the filter or the slope of the filter is essentially reduced to changing one of the three coefficients (or perhaps all three). In an FIR filter a small change that would be equivalent to changing one of the coefficients in an IIR filter by even a slight amount yields needing to recalculate all 100 coefficients. Using FIR filters in A/D converters or sample rate converters, on the other hand, is easily implementable because the coefficient values can be permanently built into the microchip's internal memory (ROM) for the specific process and never need to be changed.

Another complication with FIR filters is in establishing how many "taps" (previous samples) are necessary. Again, with an IIR filter every sample infinitely back in time has an effect on the outbound sample, but with decreasing importance. With an FIR filter we have to essentially decide how many samples are truly important and only use that many taps. Depending on the slope of the filter more taps will be required. The more taps the more accurate and flexible the results and the lower the frequency capable of being the focal point of the filter, but the longer the latency and the greater the opportunity for coefficient rounding errors. Wherever that point is, we essentially have to "truncate" the filter's effect. It really is desirable to select the coefficients appropriately and only use as many as are necessary to avoid the errors discussed above, but in doing so the truncation point of the filter may occur long before the coefficients are close to zero. An example of this can be seen in Figure 17.26

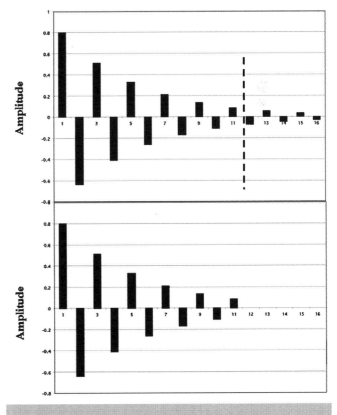

FIGURE 17.26: A Demonstration of Coefficient Truncation

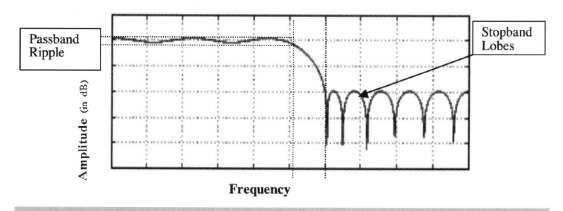

FIGURE 17.27: Demonstrations of Stopband Lobes and Passband Ripple

At the point that this truncation happens there are several ways to handle the transition. One way would simply be to truncate the end of the filter and allow the filter coefficients to never fully recede to zero. The effect of this is a very steep filter capability, but artifacts are created in the form of "lobes" in the stop-band, such that the attenuation level in the stop-band is not as was previously calculated. See the example in Figure 17.27.

Because of the effect of stop-band lobes it is generally desirable to "force" the filter's coefficients to actually get to zero through a process called "windowing." There are several algorithms used for windowing, including Kaiser, Hann, Hamming, and others. These are mathematical formulas to "treat" the last of the coefficients such that the FIR filter's coefficients do smoothly get to zero, simulating the IIR filter's coefficients getting to zero in an infinite amount of time. The different formulas all have a balance between the steepness of the filter and the size of the lobes in the stop-band. A simple truncation of the filter without the use of any of the above techniques is called a "rectangular window." A visible representation of the effect of windowing is shown in Figure 17.28.

Another side-effect of overly-shortened FIR filters that is often talked about is "pass-band ripple", a sort of undesirable effect that is audible in the pass-band such that some frequencies are slightly attenuated in the pass-band causing a form of "ripple" in the frequency plot. See an exaggerated example of pass-band ripple in Figure 17.27. Pass-band ripple is mostly a byproduct of the method that is used to calculate the coefficients in most filters and can be minimized or decreased completely if appropriate steps in filter design are used.

Pass-band ripple and stop-band lobes are both byproducts of mathematically altering an IIR filter in order to create an FIR filter. It is important that any mathematically created "error" in the filter's response ends up inaudible, either well below the noise floor of the audio, outside the frequency range for human hearing, or in any other way that is identifiable to the human auditory system.

"RINGING"

Much talk in the audio industry has regarded the "ringing" that follows the main lobe in any filter design and precedes any linear phase filter design. Any transient put into a filter yields some frequency content that follows the initial lobe of energy and tails out over time. On a linear phase filter, some of that energy bleeds out in advance of the main lobe. On any waveform other than a transient, the energy still follows the end of the waveform, though at lower amplitudes and not quite as obviously as with a transient. The existence of the "ringing" out of the energy is a byproduct of band-limiting the waveform. As we discussed in Chapter Four, any waveform that contains only one frequency must inherently last forever. If the waveform ever comes to a stop it inherently indicates additional frequency content. The more abrupt the stop the more high frequency content is created.

In order to create a waveform that contains no high frequency content, for example, a filter must be put in place that slowly brings the waveform to an infinitely low amplitude. If it changes amplitude abruptly then too much high frequency content is created. Therefore, any waveform that is band-limited must treat any transient by bleeding the transient's frequencies out over time. This "ringing" out of that extra content after a transient is merely the manifestation of band-limiting the transient. Any device that functions as a filter does this, including the human ear, a microphone, a speaker, and more. Certain characteristics can be ascertained about the "ringing" in low pass filters, however.

First, the frequencies in the ringing are the inverse of the frequencies in the transition band of the filter. For example, for a filter with a stop-band at 4kHz and with a pass-band ending at 2kHz, the transition band is from 2kHz to 4kHz. The frequency content of the ringing in the low pass filter is from 2kHz to 4kHz with more of it at 4kHz than at 2kHz. Second, the narrower the transition band the longer the ringing. Theoretically, on an IIR filter the ringing goes on forever at very low amplitudes, but on an FIR filter, the steeper the filter the longer the ringing. Shortening the ringing inherently changes the characteristics of the filter by changing the frequency content of the filter, and thus the frequency content of the waveform that it affects. A steep filter inherently must last a long time because it takes that long to slowly bleed out frequencies that are in the transition band without automatically generating very closely related frequency content that is outside the transition band and in the stop band.

It should be clear that the "ringing" is not an inherent weakness of filter design and implementation, but it is rather an inherent characteristic of any waveform that is band-limited. The Fourier Transform of a filtered waveform indicates that, although a given waveform has become lengthened in time by filtering it, its frequency content and phase content (at least in a linear phase design) reflects a band-limited version of the waveform.

DIGITAL FILTER PRACTICE AND APPLICATIONS

IIR and FIR filters are the backbone of a significant amount of digital signal processing. The synopsis given above on digital filter design is only intended to skim the surface of how they are generated and some practical considerations for the most common filter design methods. There are a few applications that we need to discuss in slightly more detail that may further help to clarify the differences and the practical uses of IIR and FIR digital filters.

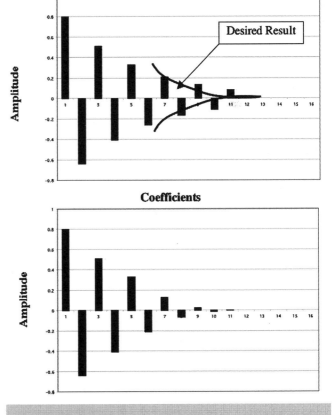

FIGURE 17.28: A Demonstration of Windowing

EQUALIZATION

Digital EQs in the form of computer software or dedicated, external processors use almost exclusively IIR filters. There are currently only a handful of DSP EQ algorithms for the audio industry that have any form of FIR filters in them as processing tools, and in these situations they are almost exclusively fixed-setting low pass or high pass filters that have almost no variable parameters. In every other situation, however, when a user alters a setting on their EQ (or digital crossover or multi-band compressor, etc.) they are essentially telling the processor to calculate a few new coefficients to change the effect of the IIR filter in use. The difference in frequency, cut/boost, Q, or shape of the filter (shelf, bell, cut, etc.) is controlled by the alterations of very few coefficients. Digital EQs that use IIR filters, in turn, use little computational power and have an inconsequential amount of overall processing delay.

ANALOG TO DIGITAL CONVERTERS

Analog to digital and digital to analog converters use FIR filters almost exclusively for the anti-aliasing and reconstruction filters. Per our discussions in Chapters Ten and Eleven, most digital sampling and analog reconstruction is done at very high sample frequencies and then filtered and decimated to the eventual sample frequency to be used for either storage or transmission. By using a digital filter for the anti-aliasing filter, the filter can be designed to allow the range below 20kHz to pass unaffected while attenuating at and above the Nyquist frequency enough that any aliasing is below the noise floor. For a 24-bit converter, the frequency spectrum above the Nyquist frequency needs to be attenuated at least 144dB. Filters never *completely* attenuate frequency ranges. Filters are designed rather to *attenuate* frequency ranges more than a needed amount.

It is acceptable for an anti-aliasing filter to allow aliasing to occur so long as the aliased frequencies end up below the dynamic range of human audibility (25dB or so below the noise floor). An analog to digital converter needs to have an anti-aliasing filter that attenuates more than the dynamic range at and above the Nyquist frequency while not affecting the audible range (the frequency range below 20kHz) in either phase or in frequency gain or attenuation. A digital filter is perfectly capable of accomplishing this. There is not a limit to how steep (how narrow of a "Q") a digital filter can be and still have linear phase. The steeper a digital filter the more "taps" it requires, providing for two tradeoffs: a longer delay before the signal is emitted, and thus more processing power is required to compute all of the additional values. An anti-aliasing filter that is phase-linear, allows the full frequency response below 20kHz to be unaffected, and attenuates more than 144dB for frequencies at and above 22.05kHz (the Nyquist frequency for 44.1kS/s sampling rates) requires a lot of taps and takes more processing power than an anti-aliasing filter that does not need to be as steep, such as an anti-aliasing filter for 96kS/s sampling rates. While it is possible to design filters that are inaudible and transparent for perfect 44.1kS/s sampling, the higher Nyquist frequency in 96kS/s sampling systems obviously provide manufacturers the ability to have less steep filters, requiring shorter (and less precisely designed) filters. Most anti-aliasing filters used in converters using higher sample frequencies do not have as steep a roll-off, rather the extra frequency range between the audible range and the Nyquist frequency is used to make the filter less steep and therefore require fewer taps, less computation, and less latency between the signal entering and the signal emitted from the filter.

We can further make an observation about 1-bit converters. A 1-bit data stream that is processed by an FIR filter undergoes a significant amount of mathematical multiplication and addition. It is these mathematical processes that "create" the additional quantization steps, providing for 24 bits to be emitted by the converter. We know from our understanding of Chapter Eleven that 1-bit converters sample at very high sample rates of 64x or 128x base rate. The 2.8224MHz 1-bit signals represent the frequency range from 0Hz to 1.144MHz but with a very high noise floor throughout most of that range. The range from 20Hz to 20kHz has a noise floor of approximately −120dB FS, so if the range above 20kHz is filtered out and the sample frequency is reduced then the audible range requires more quantization steps to maintain the 120dB dynamic range. It is the math used in the filters that "creates" these additional quantization steps. Figure 17.29 is a waveform and the 1-bit representation of that waveform. When that waveform is filtered to remove all of the noise we can see that the quantization steps needed to represent that waveform necessarily change. Once the range has been band-limited to only the audible range the material can be re-sampled at the base rate sample frequency of 44.1kS/s and the entire waveform is represented. In this example the 1-bit, 64x data stream is effectively converted to a 24 bit, 1x data stream, and the audible range is completely unaffected.

Oftentimes in A/D converters, multiple filters are used in series. The reason is that it has been theoretically demonstrated that the calculation requirements can be reduced to their minimum if multiple stages of filtering are used instead of one, long filter. For this reason the work is done by a series of small filters. The data may pass through a series of 10-tap filters serially that effectively filter the material from 2.8224MS/s down to 96kS/s. The material then passes through a larger filter - perhaps 100 taps - that performs the critical stage of filtering the material down to its desired final state.

Sometimes a type of FIR filter called a "Canonical Integer Coefficient filter", or CIC, is used. This type of filter utilizes only whole number integer coefficients that are powers of 2, such as 2, 4, 8, and 16. An FIR filter using only these values as coefficients can significantly ease the processing load on the CPU because

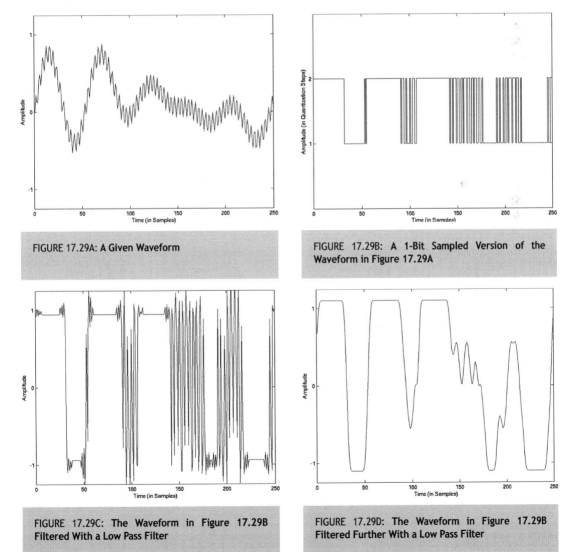

FIGURE 17.29A: A Given Waveform

FIGURE 17.29B: A 1-Bit Sampled Version of the Waveform in Figure 17.29A

FIGURE 17.29C: The Waveform in Figure 17.29B Filtered With a Low Pass Filter

FIGURE 17.29D: The Waveform in Figure 17.29B Filtered Further With a Low Pass Filter

no multiplication has to happen. Instead, the 24-bit sample values simply get shifted to the right or the left: a multiplication of a binary number times "2" simply adds a zero on the right (times "4" adds two zeros, etc.). The beginning stages in the complex downsampling process in an A/D converter can be achieved using DSP friendly CICs, though the results would be inadequate if not passed through a larger, more accurate, final FIR filter. CICs, because of the rounding of the coefficients, provide less than ideal filter slopes. For early stages of downsampling this is acceptable (Figure 17.30), though filters with more precision must be used for the final stage in order to prevent pass-band ripple and other forms of distortion.

The digital "decimating" downsampling filters used by most A/D converter (and the reconstruction filters used by most D/A converter) manufacturers are designed and built into the microchips provided by the converter manufacturer (such as AKM, Burr-Brown, Analog Devices, or Crystal Semiconductor). Due to the cost of the DSP power involved in designing highly accurate and audibly transparent downsampling filters, many of the converter chip manufacturers trade off some level of accuracy in their filters for cost, trying to find a middle ground per the market demand. A few converter manufacturers, dissatisfied with the corners cut in the designs of these filters and the expenses spared to put these filters onto the converter chips that come from the manufacturers, are known to take the data off of the converter chip while the data has not undergone the final, critical downsampling stage. These converter manufacturers supply their own DSP chips that are used exclusively for the final decimation process using tremendously more DSP power and consequently more accurate filters. This type of processing is often done on more expensive A/D and D/A converters because of the additional research and development expense and the additional processing power required.

Digital to analog converters use lowpass, linear phase FIR filters to eliminate the effects of the "stair step waveforms" created by digital sampling. When oversampling D/A converters are used, the material is upsampled to many times the sample rate and FIR filters filter out high frequency information thus smoothing out the "stair stepped" sample data without allowing digital "images" or high frequency noise into the signal. For this reason, the reconstruction filters used in digital to analog converters are sometimes called "anti-imaging filters." Without anti-imaging filters the distortion present in the stair-stepped waveforms provides "images" of the audible range at harmonic intervals. See Figure 17.31.

The process of oversampling is exactly the opposite of decimating - additional sample values are inserted into the material and the result is then filtered until those new values are positioned, amplitudinally, where they accurately represent the original waveform. In a 16x oversampling D/A converter, fifteen additional samples are placed between every two sampling points. A complete description of the upsampling process will be explored in Chapter Eighteen.

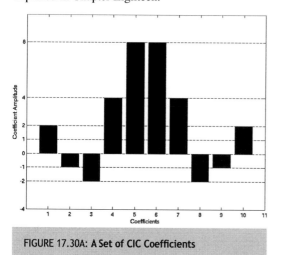

FIGURE 17.30A: A Set of CIC Coefficients

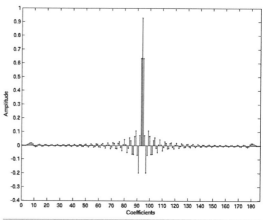

FIGURE 17.30B: The Set of Coefficients for a More Accurate Filter Used to Filter From 88.2kS/s to 44.1kS/s

Some people are concerned about the "ringing" that is a side-effect of the low pass filters needed to handle the very steep transition bands required for 44.1kS/s sampling systems. Per the discussion earlier in this chapter, the frequency content of the "ringing" is contained entirely within the transition band of the filter. Therefore, if the transition band of the filter starts above the human range of audibility then the "ringing" of the transients put through the filter is entirely above the range of audibility, whether the ringing is in advance of the main energy lobe (as in a linear phase design) or it is behind the energy lobe (as in an IIR design). Either way, the ringing is inaudible on these filters if the transition band is entirely inaudible unto itself.

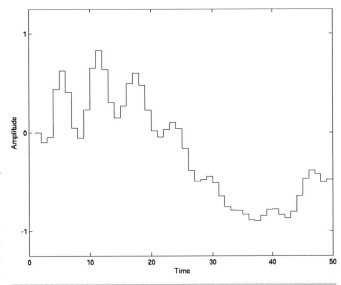

FIGURE 17.31A: **The Waveform in Figure 17.5 Unfiltered**

SAMPLE RATE CONVERTERS

Sample Rate Converters (SRCs) use FIR filters as well. There are two types of sample rate converters. Synchronous SRCs simply take the data coming in and convert it using a certain fixed ratio to the new sample rate for the output. Asynchronous SRCs (per our discussion in Chapter Twelve) upsample the material to a very high rate and then, using an unrelated clock, new sampling is done of the data stream and the nearest sample to the new clock pulse is taken as a new sample. Conceptually, both sample rate conversion circuits are similarly designed and simple to understand. Practically, each is challenging to audibly transparently design.

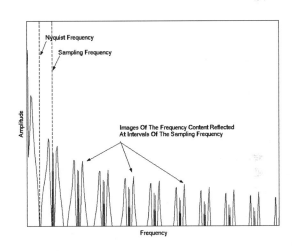

FIGURE 17.31B: **The Frequency Content of the Waveform in Figure 17.5**

There is a mathematically determinable ratio between any two sample rates: between 44.1kHz and 48kHz the ratio is 147 to 160. All that need be done to convert the data from one rate to the other synchronously is upsample the data the appropriate amount using FIR filters to remove the necessary amount of quantization distortion, then downsample or "decimate" the data back down using the appropriate sample rate, also using an FIR filter (or series of FIR filters). There will be a temporary new sampling rate of the lowest common multiple of the two original sampling rates (as well as a new temporary Nyquist frequency). For sample rate conversions from or to 44.1kS/s and 48kS/s the temporary new sample rate is 7.056MS/s. The temporary Nyquist frequency is 3.528MHz. For example, going from 48kS/s to 44.1kS/s one would add 146 sampling points between each pair of existing points. Then the material is filtered using linear phase FIR filters to eliminate all of the quantization noise between 24kHz and 3.528MHz. At this point we have a series of sample data that has a sample rate of 7.056MS/s but is band-limited to no greater than 24kHz. The material is then decimated using FIR filters to get it to 44.1kS/s, which involves removing 159 of every 160 samples. While this is done, however, a new series of FIR filters must be used because the new Nyquist frequency of 22.05kHz is lower than the original Nyquist frequency of 24kHz.

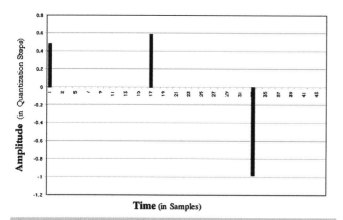

FIGURE 17.32A: Sample Data To Be Upsampled

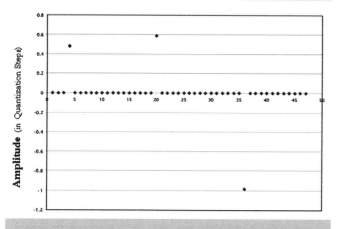

FIGURE 17.32B: Sample Data from 17.32A is Upsampled to 16f_s

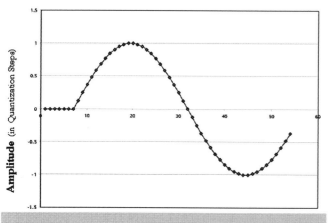

FIGURE 17.32C: Sample Data from 17.32A is Upsampled and Filtered to 16f_s

The basic formula here is to add new sampling data then filter it. Then filter it again and remove some sample data. The process is shown in Figure 17.32.

Asynchrononous sample rate converters work in a similar capacity, but once the material has been upsampled, the downsampling process is essentially done with an unrelated analog to digital converter (though it does not sample analog but rather very high rate digital values). The effect is that the downsampling process does not necessarily happen with a perfect, mathematically determinable ratio to the upsampling process. A conversion between 48kS/s and 44.1kS/s might have 159 out of every 160 of the upsampled values removed on average, but depending on the relationship of the clocks in the two halves of the circuit, the downsampling circuit may take every 159th sample on some occasions and every 160th sample on other occasions. It is for this reason that clock stability affects asynchronous sample rate converters – it affects how accurately the proper samples are pulled. As we discussed in Chapter Eleven, asynchronous sample rate converters are just as prone to clock related errors as A/D and D/A converters.

Asynchronous sample rate converters are required, however, when a digital device clocking independently needs to be interfaced with a system clocking either to a different clock or an entirely different clock rate. Any piece of equipment that accepts digital information and claims to "reclock" it to a different clock is doing an asynchronous sample rate conversion, and any jitter in either of the clocks involved in that process can affect the results. Synchronous sample rate conversion can be done whenever the process does not need to happen in real-time. A piece of computer software can do synchronous sample rate conversion completely off-line. We can think of the computer piece of software as taking a given number of samples and converting them to a different number of samples. When the material is played back at a proportional clock rate, the resultant audio will sound the same.

Sample rate converters are as conceptually simple as: the implementation of the filters used in the D/A conversion process followed by the filters used in the A/D conversion process. It is therefore possible to design sample rate converters that are as audibly transparent (for synchronous designs, asynchronous designs are subject to clock stability) as A/D and D/A converters can be. The quality of a synchronous SRC is completely dependant upon the quality of the implementation of the FIR filters used in their design.

REVERB SIMULATION

Reverb boxes and software have traditionally been based on IIR filters. Properties of acoustical spaces and acoustical surfaces are analyzed, and algorithms (mathematical formulas) are generated that denote the effect of the sound in that acoustical space.

In acoustical spaces a sound emitted from a source radiates in every direction to some capacity. A listener standing at a point in the room will hear the direct sound but will also hear the sound that emanates off of the side of the source after it reflects off of a surface. Since sound travels at a constant speed, and since the direct path for the sound to travel is shorter than the sound reflecting off of a surface, the latter will arrive to the listener later and will be mixed in with the direct sound and heard as a combination of the two. This is shown in Figure 17.33.

The direct sound (indicated by the large arrow) travels a more direct path and gets to the ear sooner than the indirect, or reflected sounds, which arrive later depending on how far a distance they have to travel. In this diagram reflections A and B will arrive at the listener slightly later than the direct sound, reflection C will arrive shortly thereafter, and reflection D will arrive much later.

Not only are there "reflection points" in a room where the sound wave reflects off of a wall and gets to the listener, but there are also "secondary reflection points" where the sound bounces off of two walls before getting to the listener. Sound that undergoes two reflections takes even longer to get to the listener than sound that only undergoes one reflection, thus it arrives at the ear even later before being mixed in with the direct sound (Figure 17.34).

We can already see that there are also tertiary and more reflection points, going on ad infinitum. Since sound that travels longer distances loses amplitude (per our discussion in Part One of this book) the sound that reflects off of the surfaces and takes longer to arrive at the listener also arrives with less amplitude than the direct sound. As a general rule, the more reflections, the less amplitude each has, such that sound that reflects twice often has less amplitude than sound that only

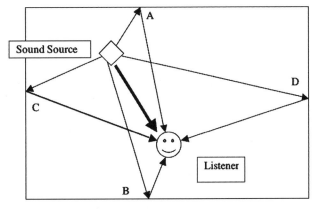

FIGURE 17.33: The Reflections In A Room

reflects once, though differing room shapes and where the sound source and the listener are located in the room can affect this.

Depending on the construction of the materials in a room, each time the sound bounces off of any wall in the room certain frequencies can be attenuated. If a room is covered in a material that attenuates high frequencies (such as thin acoustical foam), then any time the sound reflects off of any wall some high frequency energy is attenuated. Different materials affect the absorption versus the reflection of the sound in different ways.

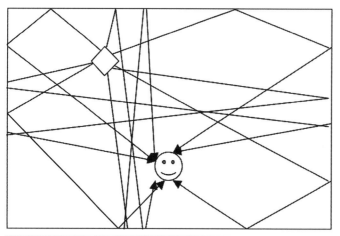

FIGURE 17.34: The Secondary Reflections In A Room

The simplest way to design a digital reverb simulator involves a series of delays. A sample is fed directly to the output, but some of the signal is delayed depending on the distance to the surfaces in the room. If there is only one reflection point in the room such that sound gets to the listener directly and after only one reflection, then the reverb can be designed with a single, simple delay. A circuit that represents this is given in Figure 17.35.

The distance from the listener and the source from the surface can be controlled by how much delay there is. As the delay gets longer the amplitude of the reflected sound is supposed to get proportionally lower, so our delay circuit would actually have an amplitude attenuation stage involved. To make the surface sound further away, the amplitude of the delayed signal is reduced and the length of time of the delay is increased. A single-surface reverb simulator can be seen in Figure 17.36.

We can change the texture of the surface by filtering the delayed sound. If the surface is made of a hard material then almost no attenuation will occur. If the surface is made of acoustical foam, for example, then high frequencies are attenuated. The thickness of the foam affects the frequencies that are affected. A filter can be put in place in the delayed line to simulate different surface textures. A modified reverb circuit complete with a filter simulating the acoustical nature of the reflective surface is given in Figure 17.37.

This signal path is capable of accurately reproducing the reverberation that occurs

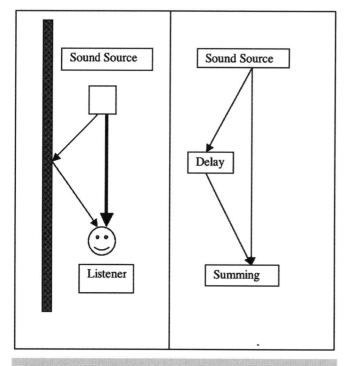

FIGURE 17.35: The Reflections Off Of A Single Surface

The reverberation off of a single surface can be roughly simulated by putting some of the signal through a delay, simulating the delay that sound undergoes when reflecting off of surfaces in acoustical spaces.

in an environment with a single reflection point. The digital simulation of this requires the following digital signal processes: splitting the signal, delaying one signal (storing the samples temporarily), a gain coefficient, an IIR filter, and then mixing the delayed signal back with the direct path. A change in the amount of delay, amount of the coefficient, or the settings in the IIR filter will change the sound of the "room."

If we want a room with two surfaces then things get more complicated. We have to start with two delay circuits, each representing one surface. The various characteristics of each surface can be changed independently of each other by changing a few variables in the digital signal processing equations, as shown in Figures 17.38 and 17.39.

A complication occurs in that by introducing a second surface, secondary reflection points are introduced. We now have to account for the fact that sound reflects off of the first surface and onto the second surface and then to the listener. The easiest way to simulate this is to take some of the output of the first delay line and feed it into the beginning of the second delay line. This simulates sound reflecting off of one surface and being fed into the next. Since the sound has to actually *propagate* from one surface to the next, a delay has to be put in the signal path from delay line to delay line, along with an additional amplitude attenuation circuit and an additional filter. The length of time of the delay and the amount of amplitude attenuation are directly related to the distance between the two surfaces, as shown in Figure 17.40.

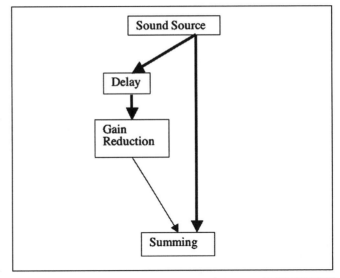

FIGURE 17.36: A Reverb Simulation of a Single Surface

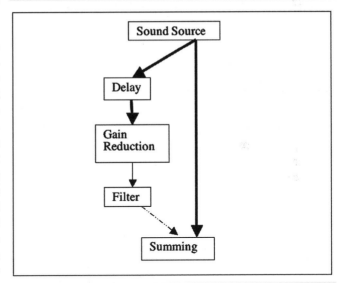

FIGURE 17.37: A Reverb Simulation of a Single, More Realistic Surface

We can clearly see that as the room becomes more complicated and has more surfaces the amount of delay lines increases significantly. A simulation of a typical six-sided room (four walls plus ceiling and floor) would have a digital processor configured something like the one in Figure 17.41.

The system actually gets more complicated than indicated because the distances traveled from wall to wall change depending on the angles of incidence (the angle from which the sound comes). The delay used to simulate sound bouncing off of the first wall and getting to the listener is slightly different than the delay used to simulate sound bouncing off of the first wall and going to the second wall and getting to the listener. See Figure 17.42.

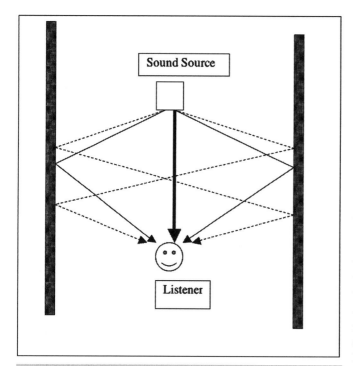

FIGURE 17.38: The Reflections Off Of Two Surfaces

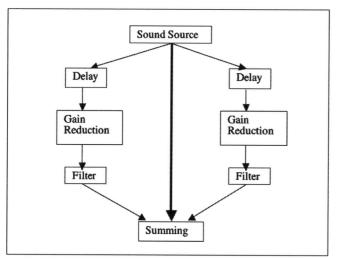

FIGURE 17.39: A Two-Surface Reverb Simulator

The reverberation off of two surfaces can be roughly simulated by putting some of the signal through two different circuits, each comprising of a delay, a gain reduction circuit, and a filter that simulates the absorptive characteristics of the surfaces.

Since this reverb *simulator* is meant to simulate a room and is not meant to perfectly *reproduce* a room, various shortcuts may be used to decrease necessary processing requirements. When this system is analyzed closely it becomes obvious that the entire system is recursive – that is that the signal leaving any process is not only fed to the output, but is recycled back to the input of the system for further calculations. This entire system is, in effect, an infinite impulse response system in that an impulse fed into the system never completely dissipates in amplitude. This system will theoretically continue to attenuate, filter, and delay the signal indefinitely, though in a digital system the bit depth affects this. A digital reverb simulator is, by definition then, an IIR filter. The system is a filter even if no traditional low pass or high pass filters are used in the process. In other words, even if we pull the filters out of every signal path and pretend that all of the surfaces are perfectly reflective and none of them absorb any sound at all, the *system* itself is a filter. Because the system does not attenuate any frequencies this type of filter is called an "all pass filter."

Digital reverb simulators are traditionally all pass filters comprised of delays, gain coefficients and low pass filters. The entire system is a lengthy IIR filter unto itself.

SAMPLING REVERBS

The easiest way to get a digital reverb simulator to sound like a real, particular room is to use an FIR filter design instead of an IIR filter design. The digital reverb algorithms that do this are called either "sampling reverbs" or "convolution reverbs." These reverbs take samples of actual acoustic spaces and create FIR filter algorithms that mirror the reverberation in those acoustic spaces. If a single impulse of acoustical energy is played into one of those rooms a sample can be taken of the room's response to the impulse. This "impulse response" of the room can then be used as a set of filter coefficients for a lengthy FIR filter. "Lengthy" is an understatement, and an understanding of this will explain to some degree why sampling reverbs have historically been expensive to manufacture. The set of coefficients for a small reverb sample for a room is shown in Figure 17.43.

Previously we observed filter algorithms that looked at 100 or 200 samples and discussed the necessary processing demands and the problems with adding the numbers for such lengthy FIR filters. For a reverb sample that lasts five seconds, the amount of samples generated (and thus the number of taps used for the FIR filter) is 44,100 (for 44.1kS/s sample rates) x 5 seconds, or 220,500. This means that 220,500 multiplications of a coefficient times a sample value coming in, followed by the addition of those 220,500 results, are necessary in order to generate a single outbound sample. The formula for the output of a single sample would look as follows:

$$y_{(n)} = A\,x_{(n)} + B\,x_{(n-1)} + C\,x_{(n-2)} + \ldots\, ?\ x_{(n-220,500)}$$

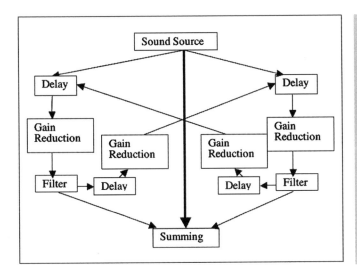

FIGURE 17.40: A Two-Surface Reverb Simulator

To do a more accurate reverb simulator one must incorporate feedback loops to simulate additional reflection points. This happens by taking some of the output off of each of the signal paths and "feeding it back" into the circuit that simulates the opposite wall. In so doing, however, an additional delay and gain reduction must be added between the circuits to simulate the distance the sound travels between the two walls and the attenuation of the signal as it does so.

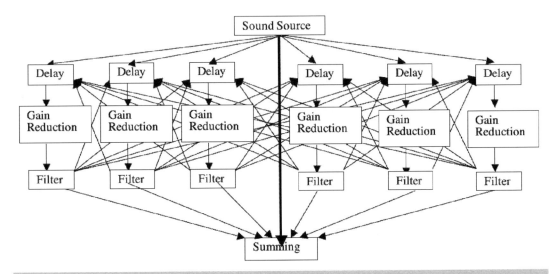

FIGURE 17.41: A Six-Surface Reverb Simulator

The above represents a simplified arrangement of a reverb simulator, neglecting the delays and gain reduction stages in each of the 25 feedback loops for the sake of the ease of viewing.

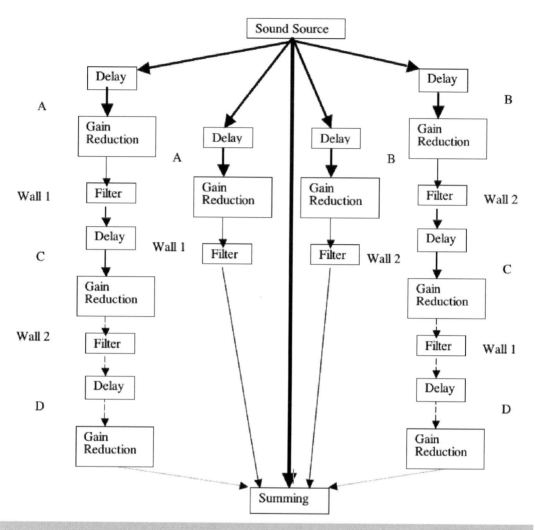

FIGURE 17.42: A Corrected Two-Surface Reverb Simulator

A more accurate reverb simulator shows how sound actually travels between the two walls, accounting for the fact that secondary reflections do not have the same delays nor the same gain reductions as primary reflections. The center two circuits show the primary reflections with the delay and gain marked "A" representing sound traveling to the first wall and the delay and gain marked "B" representing sound traveling to the second wall. The filters represent the absorptive characteristics of the walls. The delay and gain marked "C" represent the sound traveling to the opposite walls, thus the secondary reflection. The delay and gain marked "D" represent the sound traveling to the listener off of the respective walls.

Not only does this require an inordinate amount of DSP power, but it is also difficult to do at all with today's DSP chips. While the math involved in this type of reverb box is much simpler (conceptually) than the acoustical and mathematical models "created" for traditional, IIR based reverb simulators, the implementation is still very difficult to accomplish because of the inordinate amount of brute-force, simple math that needs to happen concurrently. The math is further compounded when stereo processors or surround processors are used.

The term "convolution reverb" comes from the mathematical function of "convolving" which simply refers to the math involved in an FIR algorithm. The values representing the filter algorithm are *convolved* with the values representing the sample. This is accomplished by multiplying each value of the signal with each value of the filter and adding them all together as shown in Figure 17.44.

This is precisely the process used in convolution reverbs: the sample of the room is convolved with the sample of the audio passing through it. The convolution of the two is identical to what would happen if the audio were played in that room and recorded in that room the same way that the digital sample was taken of the room. We can think of every sample in a piece of audio as being an impulse of varying amplitudes. By convolving each sample (or impulse) with the impulse response of the room and then adding the results together sequentially we get a mathematically accurate model of what would happen if music itself were played in that room.

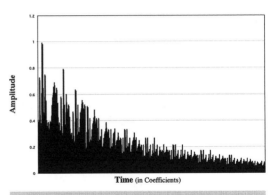

FIGURE 17.43: A Set of Coefficients for a Small Reverb Sample

Convolution (or "sampling") reverbs do not use FIR filtering algorithms in order to become phase linear (as they are not phase linear), but rather because there is not a predictable, neat, orderly, simple, mathematically identifiable relationship between all of the coefficients. If there were then an IIR filter would work fine, but every sample of the sampled acoustical space would have to be somehow relatable to the previous samples in a fashion likened to a formula such as $y_{(n)} = A$ $x_{(n-1)}$ or $x_{(n-1)}^2$ or something consistent that could be held to be true for any sample at all in relation to the previous samples. Since this does not seem to be the case with real acoustic spaces (though it is fine for simulated "ideal" acoustic spaces) we need to take each coefficient on its own and thereby create a very long FIR filter instead, which does yield a nearly unwieldy amount of data to process.

The samples of the rooms are generated by feeding them an impulse, and the sound that results is called the "impulse response" of the room. It is this impulse response that is used during the convolution process. The impulse can be generated from various means. Some engineers use a pistol shot from a starter pistol. Some use the sound of a balloon popping. In either situation the sound that results is not a true impulse, but has a complex frequency spectrum. The impulses, therefore, also have a frequency spectrum – one that relates to the sound of the pistol or the balloon. Therefore, prior to using the impulse response from the room, the sample is "prepared" by filtering the result to create a neutral sounding impulse as opposed to one with frequency weighting in particular spectrums.

Another method used for sampling rooms involves feeding a frequency sweep through a speaker and playing it into the room. The frequency sweep spans the entire audible range, from 20Hz to 20kHz. The resultant sound needs to then have the sweep itself removed so all that is left is the impulse of the room. This is done through a process called "deconvolution" which is the reverse of convolution. *Convolution* takes the two pieces of data and creates a third. In the case of reverbs, convolution takes the data of the audio material and the data of the room and *creates* the sound of the audio being played into the room. *Deconvolution* takes the resultant sound (the frequency sweep being played into the room) and, using one of the sets of data used to create it (the frequency sweep used), determines the other set of data (the impulse response of the room). Starting with a sine wave sweep played through very linear speakers and then deconvolving the result to determine the impulse response of the room is the most accurate method for determining the impulse response of a room.

A variation on the sampling reverb is currently being used that employs Fourier Transforms to drastically reduce the amount of processing power required to calculate sampling reverbs. A mathematical principle tells us that the convolution of two samples is equal to the Fourier Transforms of each number multiplied together and then transformed back to the frequency domain. This means that, instead of doing brute-force multiplication and addition of hundreds of thousands of samples in order to apply an acoustic space to a signal, instead the Fourier Transform of the audio and the Fourier Transform of the impulse response of the room can be generated and the two can be multiplied by each other. See Figure 17.45.

When the resulting waveform is then transformed back to the frequency domain (as we covered in Chapter Three) the result will be identical to convolving the two sets of data with each other. The advantage of doing this math instead of brute force convolution is that, for very large numbers, it takes less math to derive the Fourier Transform of numbers then it does to do convolution. For smaller numbers (such as the filters used for analog to digital converters) it takes less processing power to do the convolution then it does to generate the Fourier Transforms of each number. The math produces the same results either way.

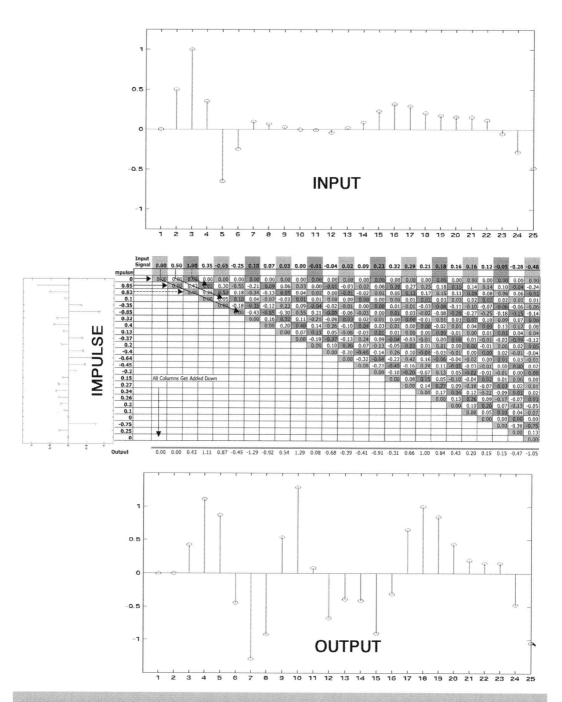

FIGURE 17.44: A Visual Representation of Convolution

If a sampling reverb algorithm uses the Fourier Transform method to derive its results then it would not be called a "convolution reverb," though the results would be the same. This is primarily a semantics issue, as with digital signal processing, "convolution based reverb" is a general term that includes the Fourier Transform method of doing the math. To date, most of the sampling reverb equipment in the audio industry has been convolution based, though with the increasing power and reliance on the personal computer to do signal processing, Fourier Transform based sampling reverbs are gaining popularity.

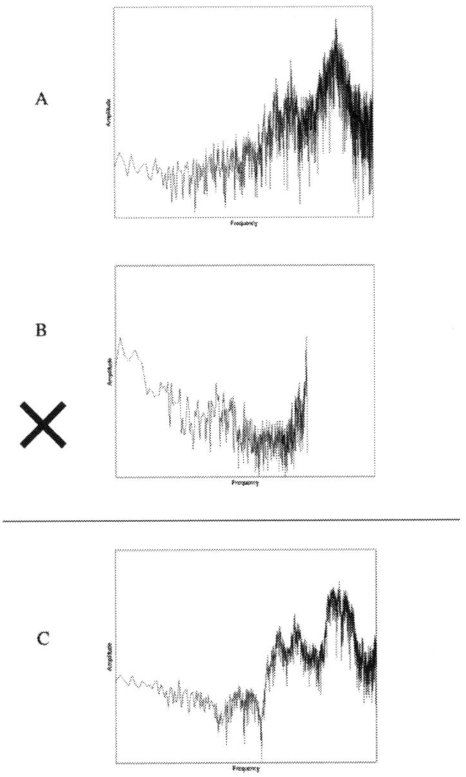

Convolution or Fourier based processing may become a common effect in music to come. Even as new as this type of processing is, various engineers are experimenting with using impulse responses from non-acoustic spaces to generate interesting digital effects. The impulse response of the soundboard of an acoustical piano or the top of an acoustical guitar can be used. The simple sound of the plucking of a string, convolved with either of these impulses responses, sounds like a piano or an acoustic guitar. Other possibilities involve taking the impulse response from a signal chain, such as a guitar amplifier, or a telephone, or even other effects processors such as traditional reverb simulators for processing. Nearly any signal path can have an impulse put into it and can be sampled and have that sample used for convolution based effects.

A further adaptation of this technology has some engineers taking digital samples that are not the impulse response of anything in particular and using those for convolution based effects. An example involves taking a digital sample of a thunderclap, or a sample of a

FIGURE 17.45: The Multiplication of Two Fourier Transforms

When the waveforms of two Fourier Transforms are multiplied the result is the same as convolving the waveforms with each other. In this example, the multiplication of the sound wave (A) to the Fourier Transform of the impulse response of the room (B) is the same as convolving one with the other (C).

dripping water faucet, or the sample of a rainstick, and using one of those as the "impulse response" of some hypothetical "acoustic space." A further creative derivation of this type of effect involves taking a musical phrase and using it to convolve with another musical phrase that was at the same, or a closely related tempo. The types of effects that can be derived from this type of digital processing are relatively new and the market for this is largely unexplored.

Convolution is dependent upon the idea that a particular device or room has a specific impulse response. This means that when an impulse is fed into a device (an impulse being an infinitely short burst of energy that contains all frequencies) the device produces a result that has a fixed frequency spectrum. Regardless of the amplitude of the impulse, the same frequency content is released, though at a proportionate amplitude to the impulse. Not all devices function in this way. A non-linear processor, for example, yields different frequency content depending on the amplitude of the impulse. If the impulse amplitude exceeds the threshold for the compressor, for example, then the compressor yields distortion, which is to say that it releases different frequency content. Because of this, any non-linear device or environment cannot be used as the basis for convolution processing as we have discussed it thus far.

Recently, however, a company has released a technology that allows them to sample the impulse response of a non-linear device at several different amplitudes. Then, depending on what the amplitude of the inbound signal in the audio is, the appropriate impulse response can be chosen for the convolution. In order to simulate a non-linear device in this manner, hundreds of thousands of amplitude steps may be necessary to sample in order to reproduce the audio in a manner that is acceptable for the human ear's discernability. This process has been dubbed "dynamic convolution" and is now available in the audio industry, bringing the sound of convolution to non-linear devices.

CONCLUSION

This chapter has only loosely covered some of the various issues that go into the design and implementation of digital filters. Clearly, the actual design of these processes is very involved and highly mathematically related. The digital filter is, however, the backbone of a vast amount of digital signal processing.

NOTES:

Chapter Eighteen

Dynamics Processing

In the audio industry, dynamics processing specifically refers to processing that is designed to be non-linear, per our discussion on linearity in Chapter Thirteen. Dynamics processes can be broken into two major categories: compression and expansion. Compression is the reduction of dynamic range, indicated by a linearity plot that becomes shallower. Expansion is the increase of dynamic range, indicated on a linearity plot by a line that becomes steeper. Examples are given in Figure 18.1.

All forms of dynamics processing are rooted in either compression or expansion or a combination of the two. Limiting and de-essing are both dynamics processes that are based on compression of waveforms. Gating is an example of a process that is based on the expansion of waveforms.

A compressor starts to compress when the signal exceeds a particular threshold. When the signal has enough amplitude that it exceeds that threshold, the compressor generally compresses at a given and established ratio, such as 2:1 or 3:1. The compression circuit has two major components: the reader and the effector. The reader "reads" the amplitude of the incoming signal to establish the amount of compression that is necessary. In the

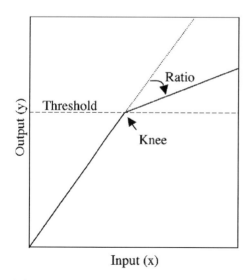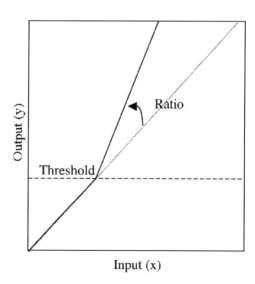

FIGURE 18.1: Compressor and Expander Linearity Curves

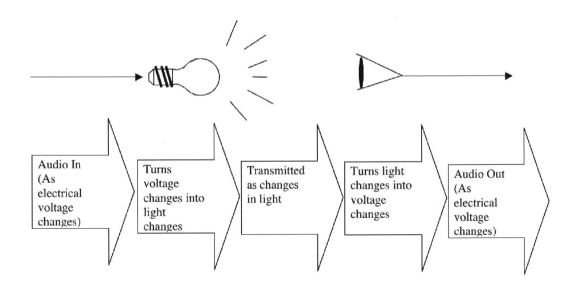

FIGURE 18.2: An Electrical-Optical Compressor Circuit

analog domain this can be done with voltage-controlled amplifiers that change their amplitude depending on the amplitude that enters them. An older approach involves what is essentially a light bulb and a photo-sensor. The signal is split in two – half of it goes through the compressor to be processed and the other half powers the light bulb. As the voltage to the light bulb increases (as the signal increases) the bulb gets brighter. If the bulb gets bright enough to trigger the photo-sensor then the circuit is designed to attenuate the output signal by a certain amount. Adjusting the threshold setting on the compressor adjusts the sensitivity of the photo-sensor. This circuit flowchart is shown in Figure 18.2.

This example of a traditional compressor highlights the two parts of a typical compressor and how the signal is split into two different signal paths: one that measures the amplitude of the signal and the other that processes the signal and sends it to the output.

A digital compressor works in much the same way. The digital signal enters the compressor and splits in two. One copy of the signal is used for determining the amplitude of the signal. The other half of the signal is then processed. The processing of the signal is no more complicated than simple amplitude changes as described in Chapter Sixteen: the signal is multiplied times a coefficient. If the signal level is below the threshold then the coefficient is 1 because the signal entering the compressor is identical to the signal that exits the compressor. If the signal level exceeds the threshold then the value of the coefficient is changed.

The changing of the coefficient is not as simple as a fader control as in Chapter Sixteen. Understanding it may be easier in decimal rather than binary numbers. If the signal has a range of 100 and the compressor is set to compress at a 2:1 ratio if the threshold of 50 is exceeded then any time the amplitude is at or below 50 the value gets multiplied times 1. If the compressor exceeds 50 then the amplitude might get multiplied times a coefficient of .5? This would not work properly. As soon as the amplitude of the signal hit 51 then the output value would drop suddenly to 25.5. The linearity plot of this compressor would look like the in Figure 18.3.

If a compressor has a 2:1 ratio it means that every signal that is above the threshold gets compressed by half of its *increase over the threshold*. Therefore, if the signal hits a value of 51 we want the compressor to decrease it to only 50.5 (half of the difference between the input amplitude and the threshold amplitude). The formula that we actually want to use measures the difference between the input amplitude and the threshold amplitude, divides it by two, and then adds it back to the threshold amplitude. If y is the outbound sample and x is the inbound sample then the formula for our 2:1 compressor would look as follows:

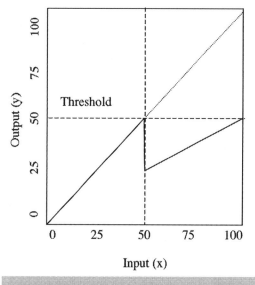

FIGURE 18.3: The Linearity Plot For A *y=x if x<50, y=.5x if x>50* Compressor

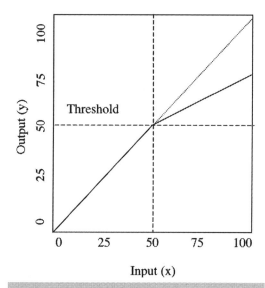

FIGURE 18.4: The Linearity Plot For A *y=x if x<50, y=.5x + 25 if x>50* Compressor

If x>50 then y = .5 (x-50) + 50

Or y = .5x + 25

In general, if R is the compressor ratio and T is the threshold amplitude, then y = (1/R)x + .5(T)

If this formula is used then the compressor's linearity chart would look like that shown in Figure 18.4.

This method is merely the easiest way to calculate the amount of attenuation. The result when the input amplitude is 51 is the same as simply multiplying the input amplitude by a coefficient of approximately .99. This coefficient changes, however, depending upon the amplitude of the input signal. For example, an input amplitude of 52 would need a coefficient of approximately .98, an input amplitude of 80 would need a coefficient of .8125, and an input amplitude of 100 would need a coefficient of .75. The coefficients change for each input amplitude. Clearly, the above formula is simpler because the math involved does not change and a consistent formula can be used for each input amplitude above the threshold.

This compressor has what is referred to as a "hard knee" in that compression starts immediately after the threshold is exceeded and the compression is at full effect immediately. This type of compressor has a very audible effect that is often used on instruments with fast at-

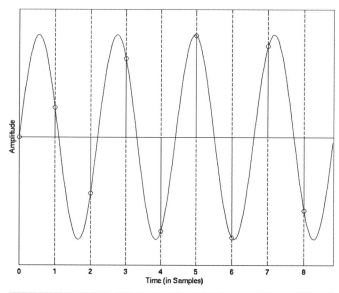

FIGURE 18.5: A Portion Of a 20kHz Sampled Sine Wave (at 44.1kS/s)

tack times such as snare drums. It can be disturbing, however, on more delicate sources such as classical instruments. Many compressors use what is referred to as a "soft knee" in order to avoid the audible effect caused as the signal crosses the threshold. If a soft knee is used then the coefficients do gradually change until the compressor is at full effect. Regardless of whether or not the compressor is hard knee or soft knee, has fast or slow attack times, or uses other controls like hysteresis (a different threshold for attack than for release in a compressor), the action of a compressor is no different than a gain coefficient being multiplied by the signal which changes over time, much like "riding a fader" on a mixer.

The other half of the compressor might be slightly more complex. Theoretically all that need be done is determine if the amplitude of a sample exceeds a certain value and have the coefficients change accordingly. In reality this type of compression may be common, but is not an accurate way of applying compression.

We know that a 20kHz sine wave can be accurately captured with 44.1kS/s sample rates per our discussion in Chapter Nine. We also know from that discussion that the entire waveform would be captured, including the amplitude, phase, frequency, and dynamic range, even if only 2.x samples are taken per waveform cycle. We know that this works because the reconstruction and anti-aliasing filters cause the waveform to be reconstructed with complete accuracy, even though only 2.x samples are taken in the time of a complete cycle.

This means that a 20kHz sine wave can be captured with the samples taken very near the zero crossing. This causes the amplitude of the waveform represented by the sampling points to be very high, even though the amplitude of the samples themselves are relatively low.

If a compressor is put on the waveform shown in Figure 18.5 and a threshold is applied at half of the amplitude of the signal then this signal should undergo compression. If, however, the compressor gauged whether or not the amplitude was exceeded based on the amplitude of the samples then this waveform would not undergo proper compression. If our 20kHz waveform were drawn out long enough we would see that eventually the samples exceed the threshold, but this goes in cycles. Sometimes the samples exceed the threshold and sometimes they do not, but this occurs in a repeating cycle. This occurs far more often in high frequency

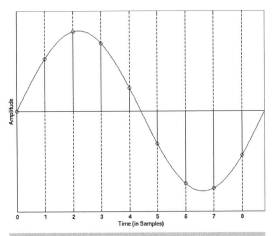

FIGURE 18.6A: A Portion Of a 5kHz Sampled Sine Wave (at 44.1kS/s)

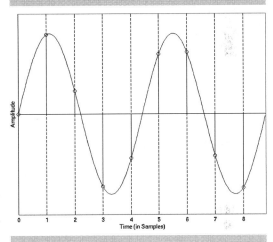

FIGURE 18.6B: A Portion Of a 10kHz Sampled Sine Wave (at 44.1kS/s)

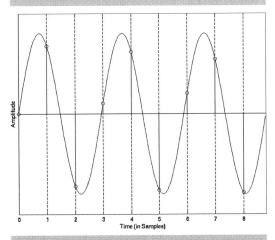

FIGURE 18.6C: A Portion Of a 15kHz Sampled Sine Wave (at 44.1kS/s)

waveforms, as the lower the frequency the more likely that a *sample* exceeds the threshold if the amplitude of the *overall waveform* exceeds the threshold.

The rate at which the high sampling frequencies' samples do and do not exceed the threshold changes as the frequencies increase. A 10kHz waveform exceeds the threshold twice as often as a 20kHz waveform. A 5kHz waveform exceeds the threshold twice as often as a 10kHz waveform, as shown in Figure 18.6.

If the compressor compresses only when the sample amplitudes exceed the threshold then these waveforms undergo "oscillating" compression. The oscillations are inversely proportional to the frequency of the waveform and are heard as an additional tone audibly present at the rate of the oscillations. As the threshold increases in amplitude the oscillations change.

Clearly, this is not a phenomenon we would like an ideal compressor to exhibit. A solution for this is upsampling the "reader" half of the compressor so that a more thorough rendition of the waveform is represented. If the material is upsampled to a high enough sample rate then the complete waveform can be analyzed to determine whether or not the threshold is exceeded. As soon as the "reader" notices that the amplitude exceeds the threshold then it engages the compressor to change coefficients. Even if the amplitude exceeds the threshold *between samples*, the compressor would engage so that the next sample would be affected an appropriate amount.

In these situations (which are most situations in which compressors are applied) the compressor should be engaged even though the amplitude of the waveform *at the time of the samples* does not exceed the threshold. By upsampling the reader portion of the waveform (per the methodology described in Chapter Eighteen) the compressor can be made to work more accurately, avoiding the modulation artifacts described earlier.

Most compressors are designed with an "attack" and "release" time parameter, so that the compressor does not disengage once the amplitude of the signal drops below the threshold (since this happens every cycle). Instead, a release function is used so that the compressor only disengages after the threshold has not been passed in some amount of time. Since high frequency waveforms change amplitude very quickly, the com-

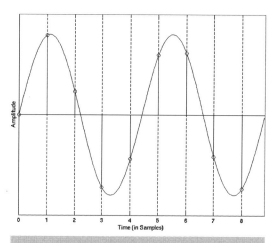

FIGURE 18.7A: An Oversampled 20kHz Sine Wave (at 44.1kS/s)

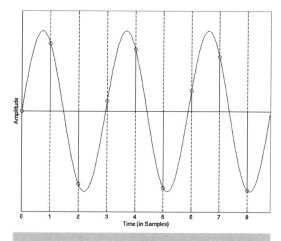

FIGURE 18.7B: A Sampled 20kHz Sine Wave (at 44.1kS/s)

A compressor that utilizes the oversampled sine wave as the gauge for its compression system will yield more accurate results, as any time the sine wave exceeds the threshold the compression circuit is re-engaged.

pressor does not normally disengage until the threshold has not been reached over several consecutive cycles (Figure 18.7).

A comprehensive discussion about expanders should not be necessary because the function is the same but the coefficients get larger instead of smaller as the signal exceeds the threshold. Certainly, complicated dynamics processors can be made that use both compression and expansion to create a linearity curve that has an "S" shape, so that between two thresholds the signal expands, but beyond the second threshold the signal compresses. The processing used in any of these situations is the same as the processing described above with regards to compressors.

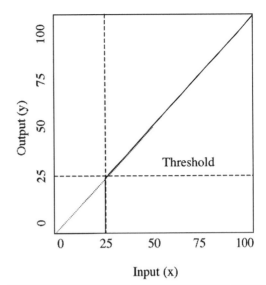

FIGURE 18.8: The Linearity Plot For A y=x if x>25, y=0 if x<25 Gate

A gate is merely a dynamics processor wherein the amplitude is compressed with an infinite ratio *until* it exceeds a threshold. Once the signal exceeds the threshold the signal is allowed to pass unaffected. The formula for a gate that has a threshold of, say, "25" would be as follows:

If x<25 y = 0x

If x>25 y = 1x

This gate's linearity curve is shown in Figure 18.8.

A limiter is a dynamics device that has a threshold set for infinite compression so that no signal can exceed the threshold. If the threshold is set to, say, "75" then any signal entering that exceeds 75 has an output of 75. The formula for this limiter would be as follows:

If x<75 y = x

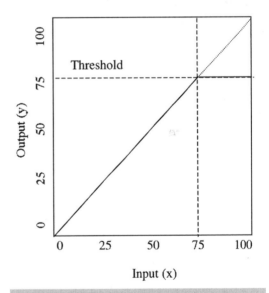

FIGURE 18.9: The Linearity Plot For A y=x if x<75, y=75 if x<75 Limiter

If x>75 y = 0 (x-75) + 75 per our formula for compressors, or, more simply,

y = 75

This limiter's linearity curve is shown in Figure 18.9.

We can easily see that in the situations of gates and of limiters the reader needs to be upsampled so that the signal can be processed accordingly. If, in a gate, the amplitude of the samples never exceeds the threshold, even though the amplitude of the signal *represented* by the samples does, then the gate will simply not work and will not open when it is supposed to. If, in a limiter, the amplitude of the samples never exceeds the threshold, even though the amplitude of the signal *represented* by the samples does, then the limiter will not work

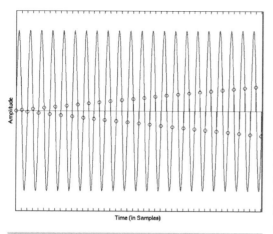

FIGURE 18.10: A Portion Of a 22kHz Sampled Sine Wave (at 44.1kS/s)

and signal will be allowed to pass wherein the signal represented by the samples exceeds the threshold.

One principle that we can derive of our knowledge of sampling, however, is that at some point, *almost* any waveform at any frequency below the Nyquist frequency and an amplitude at or above the threshold will eventually have samples reach the amplitude of any given threshold. Even a sine wave at 22kHz (in a 44.1kHz sampling system) will eventually have its samples exceed any given threshold if the threshold is lower than the amplitude of the sine wave represented by those sampling points. Figure 18.10 indicates that even with high frequency sine waves, the amplitude of the samples eventually reaches the same amplitude as the signal itself.

Most dynamics processors have an "attack" control so that the processor does not fully engage for a period of time after the threshold has been exceeded. Theoretically this principle could be used to alleviate the need for upsampling the reader. After all, if the sampling points will *eventually* exceed the threshold then this only simulates a slow attack time on the compressor. The problem with this approach is twofold. First, sine waves at *some* frequencies can exist without ever exceeding a threshold. For example, an 11.025kHz waveform is well below the Nyquist frequency for 44.1kS/s sample rates. Since, however, the sample rate is an even multiple of the sine wave frequency, the sample points will never change their amplitude over the course of a waveform, as displayed in Figure 18.11.

If the threshold of this waveform is above the amplitude of the samples then the waveform will never be affected by the dynamics processing, despite the fact that the waveform exceeds the threshold. Second, the fact that the dynamics process "simulates" a slow attack time makes the process less flexible than it would be if the waveform was upsampled by the reader and implemented properly. Generally speaking, on certain applications of gates and limiters no attack time is used, so the process itself simulating a slow attack time through inadequate math makes the dynamics processor work inaccurately.

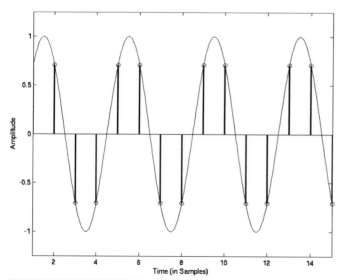

FIGURE 18.11: A Portion Of a 11.025kHz Sampled Sine Wave (at 44.1kS/s, 45° Out Of Phase)

UPSAMPLING

Our discussion on linearity in Chapter Thirteen tells us that any nonlinear process adds distortion. One of the types of distortion is harmonic distortion, which yields overtones above the original waveform.

In Chapter Nine we discussed that clipping causes harmonic distortion above the Nyquist frequency. Since the digital system cannot recreate any frequency content above the Nyquist frequency, the harmonic distortion is aliased back into the audible range and becomes audible.

If a waveform is digitally limited due to dynamics processing, the same waveform shape is created as would be generated if clipping were to occur at the analog to digital converter. Clipping that occurs due to the sampling point amplitude exceeding full scale is merely a very effective form of a limiter, per our discussion on limiters on the previous page: the signal passes unaffected until it reaches a particular amplitude (full scale). Any signal above that amplitude that enters the system is emitted at the threshold amplitude (full scale). If a digital limiter is used as a process then the same results will occur as occur during clipping at a converter: harmonic distortion is created above the Nyquist frequency, but because that harmonic material cannot be recreated by the digital to analog converters it is aliased back into the audible range.

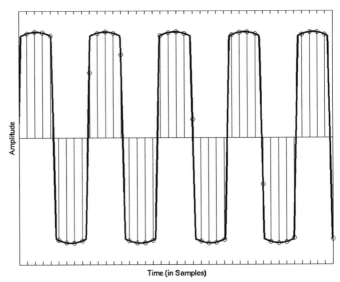

FIGURE 18.12: A Heavily Limited 5kHz Sine Wave

A digital limiter is not the only dynamics processor that creates harmonic distortion above the Nyquist frequency. By mere definition, all dynamics processing does, though some dynamics do not create harmonics that are above the Nyquist frequency and at an amplitude that is capable of being heard or causing audible aliasing distortion. In order to alleviate the aliasing caused by dynamics processing, some manufacturers of dynamics processing software do the processing at higher sample frequencies and then filter out the distortion that is generated that is above the "legal" frequency range (i.e. above the Nyquist frequency).

For a severe example, consider a 5kHz sine wave that is limited enough that it becomes a square(ish) wave, as shown in Figure 18.12.

Since this waveform is square we know that it is the sum of all odd order harmonics of 5kHz, such that it contains 15kHz, 25kHz, 35kHz, 45kHz, etc. frequency content. Once this square wave is created, the frequencies that it represents are established, though a 44.1kS/s system can only reproduce the 15kHz component as the rest are above the Nyquist frequency. Instead, the 35kHz and higher components are aliased back into the "legal" range of frequencies, and when this waveform is recreated at the digital to analog converter it will be recreated with the aliased frequencies in it. The 25kHz component will be recreated as 19.1kHz. The 35kHz component will be recreated as 9.1kHz, etc. As we discussed in Chapter Nine, this distortion is no longer harmonic distortion but is rather *in*harmonic distortion. A more accurate solution would leave only the 5kHz component and the 15kHz component in the waveform and would remove the rest of the frequencies so that they do not cause aliasing.

The most efficient way of doing this is to upsample the material to a high sample frequency before the processing is done. If the material is upsampled to, say, 8x the base rate of 44.1kS/s then the new Nyquist frequency is 176.4kHz. The 5kHz waveform can then be limited and all of the harmonics up to and including 175kHz (the 35th harmonic) can be fully created without aliasing. Then the results can be downsampled back to the base rate, removing all of the harmonic content created by the limiting process with the anti-aliasing filters used in the downsampling process (per the methodology described in Chapter Seventeen). What remains would be a waveform with 5kHz and 15kHz frequencies, but no harmonic content higher than the Nyquist frequency, and thus no aliasing back into the audible range. The 5kHz and 15kHz frequencies will sound "natural" to our ears because these are the frequencies that we would hear if a 5kHz were to be limited in an analog environment – our ears would filter out the 25kHz and higher harmonics just like the converters do. All that our ears *should* hear are the 5kHz and 15kHz harmonics, per our discussion on the audibility of square waves in Chapter Six. Upsampling and downsampling the dynamics process more accurately reflects what happens in the natural world and the analog environment.

Upsampling the various dynamics processes is a debated discussion in the audio manufacturing community. Some manufacturers point out that severe aliasing as described above is only caused by situations wherein the dynamics processing is so severe as to not be readily used in audio mixing environments. Regardless, if the greatest amount of flexibility is desired from the dynamics process then running the process at higher sample rates (followed by downsampling and filtering the results) is the obvious method to provide the desired results. While very few manufacturers currently provide upsampling dynamics processors, systems that inherently operate at higher sample frequencies (such as 96kS/s or higher) are less prone to dynamics induced aliasing because the harmonics do not start to alias until they are much higher in frequency.

Processes that are linear do not benefit from higher sample rate processing. Linear processes include, as described prior, reverb simulators, equalizers, gain changing, and many other effects. Certainly a manufacturer can develop a specific algorithm for an equalizer that benefits from high sample rate processing, but in principle (and inherently) no benefit exists. Some processes actually suffer when higher than necessary sample rate processing is used.

NOISE REDUCTION

The most common process used to reduce the sound of unwanted noise in recordings uses dynamics processing as described above while taking advantage of the masking in the human auditory system. The typical method for reducing unwanted, low-level noise is as follows:

The noise itself is sampled with no desired material playing. A Fourier Transform is done on the noise, indicating which frequencies of noise are present. The noise is then divided into frequency bands and a threshold is established for each band. The threshold is placed just above the amplitude of the noise within that band.

As the material is played into the processor a Fourier Transform is done on the signal. If the signal within any of the pre-configured frequency bands does not exceed the threshold then that frequency band is gated and no signal is allowed to pass within that band. Any frequency band wherein the signal exceeds the band's threshold allows all signal in that band to pass. Whatever is left is then transformed back to the time domain using the

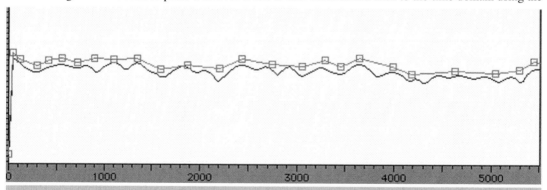

FIGURE 18.13: The Frequency Bands In A Noise Reduction Algorithm

inverse Fourier Transform. The new signal contains all of the frequency content from the frequency bands where the threshold was exceeded, but contains no frequency information in the bands in which the threshold was not exceeded. An example, using the noise from Figure 18.13, is given in Figure 18.14.

Note that between about 1kHz and 2kHz and then between about 4kHz and 5kHz the signal fell below the pre-determined threshold and was thus gated away. The remainder of the signal was above the threshold. The waveform, upon reconstruction, will contain only the frequencies wherein the signal was above the threshold.

The premise, here, is that frequency content will only exceed the threshold within any given band if the content is louder than the noise, and is therefore "real" signal. If the threshold in a given band is not exceeded then it is not "real" signal, only contains noise, and thus can be removed. If the signal in a given band exceeds the threshold then it is allowed to pass, noise and all. Since the ear masks signals of very near frequencies, the noise will not be heard in light of the louder, more noticeable "real" signal in that band.

Because of the method used, this type of noise reduction is most effective when used with low level, constant, unchanging noise. If this type of noise is used then the thresholds can be very precisely determined.

Crucial to this type of processing is that the noise sample must be accurately taken. Further, increasing the number of frequency bands used allows the masking to be more effective, as the effect of masking is reduced as the frequency content of signals is further removed from the stronger tone.

Often, noise shaping processors are thought of as a way to increase the dynamic range of audio signals. In reality the entire noise spectrum is allowed to pass in each band that the "real" signal is present within. Therefore, whenever signal is present, noise is present as well, though the human auditory system does not hear it this way.

CONCLUSION

Dynamics processing in the digital domain is conceptually simple. It is conceptually no more complicated than applying dynamically changing gain coefficients to the signal. In reality, several considerations need to be taken into regard to prevent undesirable effects from entering the signal. The proper use of upsampling dynamics algorithms accompanies the other considerations previously discussed, such as dithering the results properly and ensuring that radical changes in level do not create audible distortion. In general, dynamics processors are amongst the easiest to design, yet many such processes available on the market still suffer from various forms of unwanted distortion.

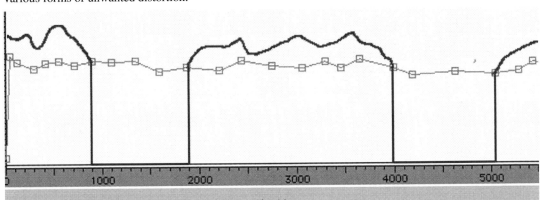

FIGURE 18.14: A Signal Presented To A Noise Reduction Algorithm

Chapter Nineteen

Pitch and Time Based Effects

So far, in regards to digital signal processing, we have discussed digital filters, methods of changing the amplitude of waveforms, dynamics processing, reverb simulators and other effects. The last major category of effects processing is pitch and time based effects including pitch shifting, time compression and time expansion.

Pitch and time based effects are all effects that are not capable of being effectively done in the analog domain. Pitch (frequency) and time are invariably intertwined, as simply changing the time that it takes for a recording to play inherently changes the frequencies that play back. This relationship has been experienced by anyone that has fast-forwarded a cassette tape when it was still playing and heard the frequency content increase proportionally to the decrease in the amount of time that it took for the material to play. The relationship is easy to observe. If a waveform is played back in half the time then the frequencies of each waveform take only half as long to complete a cycle, thus an increase in frequency content, or the "pitch" of the recording (Figure 19.1).

If the pitch of recorded material is to be changed without changing the time of the recording then the waveform necessarily has to change. If, for example, a 100Hz sine wave is played for one second then it will complete 100 cycles. If the waveform is pitched up to 200Hz and is desired to last for the same amount of time (one second) then it requires 200 cycles. By itself this does not pose a problem, because all that need be

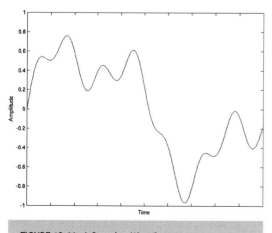

FIGURE 19.1A: A Complex Waveform

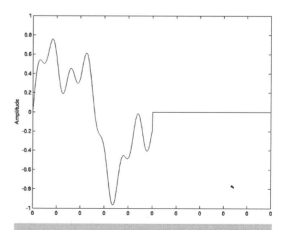

FIGURE 19.1B: The Waveform In Figure 19.1 Played In Half The Time

done is cut the time in half that it takes to play the waveform and then play the material twice consecutively, as shown in Figure 19.2.

If, however, the goal is to pitch shift a complex, non-repeating waveform then this form of processing is insufficient. If the waveform to be pitch shifted is a complex waveform consisting of a single cycle of a 100Hz sine wave in addition to a single cycle of a 200Hz sine wave then the resultant waveform should contain two cycles of 200Hz and two cycles of 400Hz, meaning that the signal would last the same amount of time as the original but the frequencies will be twice as high. This equates to raising the pitch of the waveform one octave and the waveform would last the same amount of time, and would represent a shift of the frequency content without changing the time in which it plays. This can be seen in Figure 19.3.

The original waveform and the new waveform look very different, but we know that they sound the same, though one octave apart. The fundamental frequency lasts for 1/100th of a second and the second harmonic lasts for 1/200th of a second and they are added to each other. The situation becomes more complex when more harmonics are added to the waveform. It quickly becomes obvious that the waveform cannot be processed simply by modifying the waveform through changing the time scale or repeating the waveform cyclically.

The only way that this process can accurately be done is if the waveform is divided into several small parts, each part is pitch shifted, and then each part is added back together. We can only pitch shift the waveform in this manner if we know all of the frequencies that are present at all times that they are present and at what amplitudes they are present at those times. If we do this then we can theoretically simply pitch shift all of the waveforms independently and sum them all together. For example, the waveform in Figure 19.4 can be divided into several parts.

Once we have broken the waveform apart into the frequency content that composes it we can double the frequencies of each component within the waveform. This is shown in Figure 19.5. Note that the resultant waveform is not merely the same as a doubling of the initial waveform – the second half of the waveform in Figure 19.5 is not the same as the first half.

The result is a waveform that lasts the same amount of time but has been pitch shifted up exactly one octave.

Fortunately, we already have a tool that we are familiar with that has the capability of breaking a waveform into its compositional components. This tool is the Fourier Transform and we studied it in Chapter Three. The Fourier Transform of a waveform tells us all of the information we need to know about the waveform: the frequencies present, the times that those frequencies occur (the phase of the frequencies) and the amplitude of

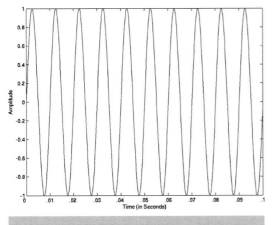

FIGURE 19.2A: A 100Hz Sine Wave Over One Second

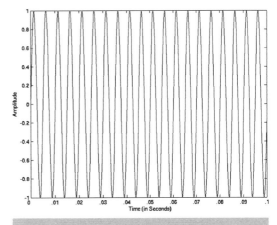

FIGURE 19.2B: A 200Hz Sine Wave Over One Second

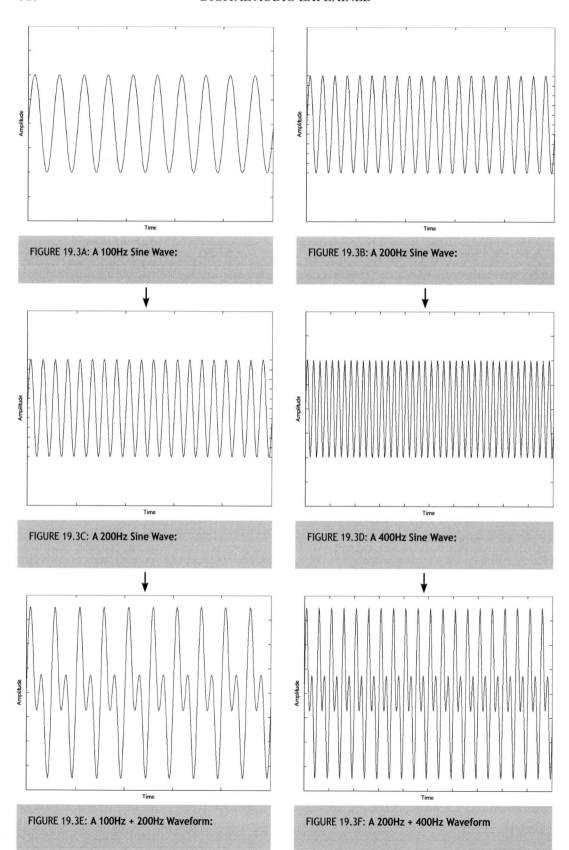

FIGURE 19.3A: **A 100Hz Sine Wave:**

FIGURE 19.3B: **A 200Hz Sine Wave:**

FIGURE 19.3C: **A 200Hz Sine Wave:**

FIGURE 19.3D: **A 400Hz Sine Wave:**

FIGURE 19.3E: **A 100Hz + 200Hz Waveform:**

FIGURE 19.3F: **A 200Hz + 400Hz Waveform**

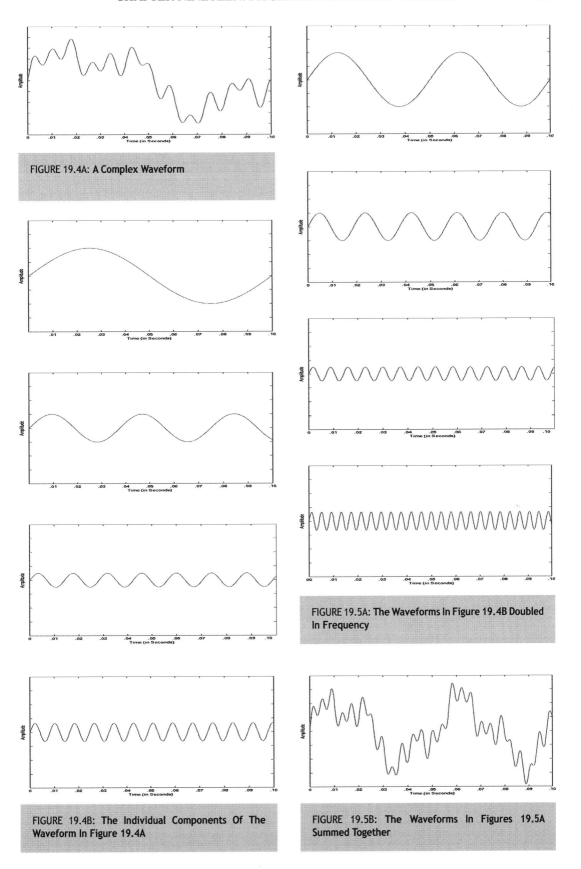

FIGURE 19.4A: A Complex Waveform

FIGURE 19.4B: The Individual Components Of The Waveform In Figure 19.4A

FIGURE 19.5A: The Waveforms In Figure 19.4B Doubled In Frequency

FIGURE 19.5B: The Waveforms In Figures 19.5A Summed Together

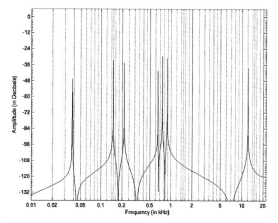

FIGURE 19.6: The Spectrograph Plot Of A Waveform

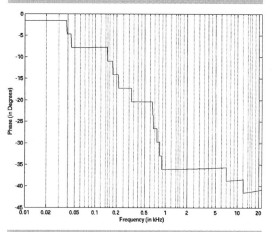

FIGURE 19.7: The Phase Plot Of The Waveform In Figure 19.6

those frequencies when they occur. Visually displaying, or plotting the Fourier Transform of a waveform, is difficult because it contains a lot of information to display in one graph. Typically the Fourier Transform is only displayed showing the frequency content versus the amplitude of that content. This is visually displayed on a spectrograph plot, as given in Figure 19.6.

As we discussed in Chapter Three, however, a spectrograph plot only presents half of the information that a Fourier Transform gives us. Just looking at a spectrograph plot does not give us any idea of *when* certain frequencies occurred in relation to each other; it only tells us the total amount of energy present at each frequency. There are many different ways that waveforms can be created that represent the same spectrograph plot, but lasting different amounts of time. It is important to remember that a Fourier Transform yields a mathematical function and that only half of the function is the spectrograph plot. The other half of the function is the phase plot, which tells us exactly when the various frequencies are present. A phase plot of a waveform is shown in Figure 19.7.

The two plots put together fully represent the full Fourier Transform of a given waveform. Once the two plots are put together we can see that we have essentially determined the information needed to do pitch processing. Upon looking at the spectrograph plot of a given waveform we can determine which frequencies are present and at what amplitude. By then shifting all of the frequencies up one octave (doubling them) we can effectively create the Fourier Transform of the waveform we would like to produce. Once the new Fourier Transform is complete, the inverse Fourier Transform can be applied to transform the waveform back to the time domain. The result yields the pitch-shifted version of the waveform in question. The method, then, for doing pitch processing without affecting time is as follows:

1. Calculate the Fourier Transform of a waveform

2. Shift the frequency content within the Fourier Transform

3. Calculate the inverse Fourier Transform of the resulting data

When this is complete the resulting waveform will be pitch shifted the desired amount. An example of this process is shown in Figure 19.8

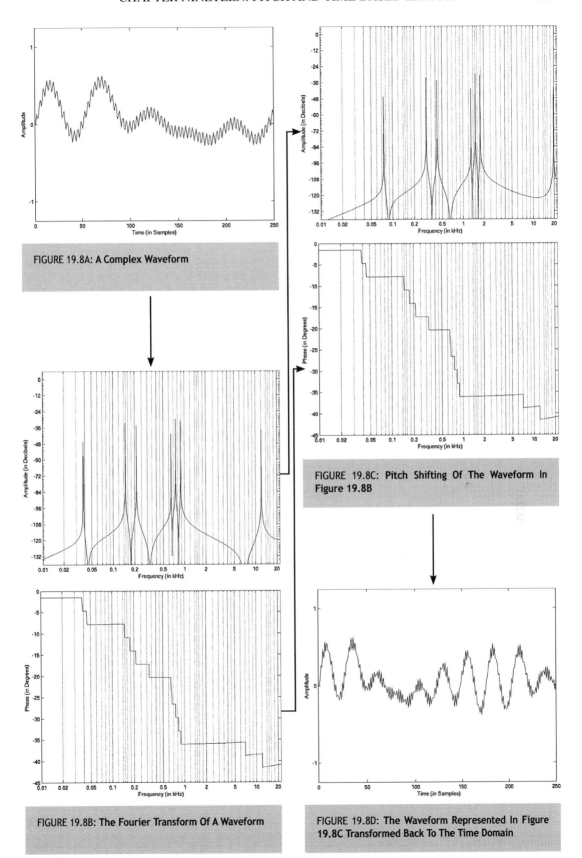

FIGURE 19.8A: A Complex Waveform

FIGURE 19.8B: The Fourier Transform Of A Waveform

FIGURE 19.8C: Pitch Shifting Of The Waveform In Figure 19.8B

FIGURE 19.8D: The Waveform Represented In Figure 19.8C Transformed Back To The Time Domain

ISSUES WITH PITCH SHIFTING

Not all applications that require pitch shifting require that the entire frequency range is shifted the same amount. Most applications that require pitch shifting actually require that different parts of the frequency spectrum are treated differently. Pitch shifting of human voices, for example, cannot be done adequately through the simple means described above.

"Formants" in the human voice are frequencies generated when sound created by the vocal chord movements resonates through the vocal tract. These frequencies are determined by the size and the shape of the pharynx. As the vocal chords resonate, the sound waves travel through the vocal tract. Depending on the size and shape of the vocal tract, different frequencies are amplitude modulated with the vocal chords in much the same way that speaking through a tube enhances the frequency content of the voice. The frequencies, or "formants" can be altered by changing the shape of the mouth or the size of the throat (by pushing the larynx down or lifting the upper palette). Some formants cannot be changed, however, such as the formants generated by the shape of the sinuses. These formants are unique to every person and it is the distinctive formants that are present that make each of our individual voices identifiable to each other.

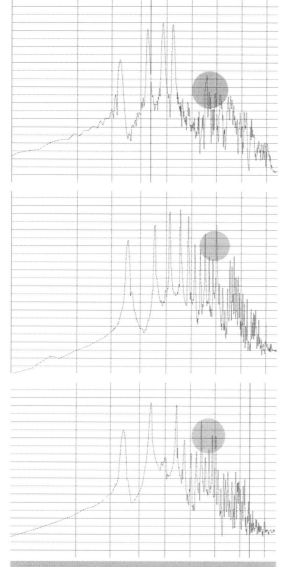

Figure 19.9 shows spectrograph plots of three different pitches sung by the same person. Note that the formants do not change in frequency when the singer sings different fundamental notes. The amplitude does change because the notes the singer creates also have overtones at those frequencies, which add to the formants. The frequencies of those formants, however, does not change while the rest of the frequencies in the spectrograph do.

If a pitch shift process is done in the manner described above then the formants also shift in frequency, and when the inverse Fourier Transform is applied the result will represent a pitch shift, but will be accompanied by an apparent change in the person that sang the note. If, for example, the note from a woman singing is pitch shifted upwards then the voice tract will sound smaller and more childlike. If the note is pitch shifted downwards then the voice tract will sound longer and the results will sound more masculine.

In order to pitch shift the human voice without having the character of the voice change precipitously, the formants present have to be analyzed and preserved throughout the pitch shifting process. This involves pitch shifting some of the frequencies while leaving the formant frequencies unaffected.

FIGURE 19.9: Spectrograph Plots Of Three Notes Sung By The Same Singer

The formants are identified in the three spectrograph plots above.

Some processors allow the frequency of the formants to be shifted independently of the fundamental frequencies performed. In this way, an individual note can be changed without changing the identifiable characteristic of the voice singing it, or the voice of the person can be changed without changing the notes sung.

It is not only the human voice that has formants. Any device that has a shape has a formant. In Chapter Two we discussed the "perfect drumhead," and identified that it can generate very specific sine waves. In reality, any drumhead is attached to a drum, and certain characteristics of the size and shape and build of the drum, combined with the build of the head itself, cause a drum to produce the same types of amplitude modulated frequencies as the human voice. These characteristics of the drum give each drum a unique sound. The same holds true with a piano, a trumpet, or any other musical instrument. Every device that resonates in the real world has a given set of formants based on its shape, size, and build. Most "formant preserving" processors are designed to handle the unique and very identifiable formants in the human voice. Since the formants produced by each instrument are vastly different, the algorithms that perform formant preserving pitch shifting may be inadequate at producing audibly indiscernible pitch shifting of other acoustical devices.

Most pitch processing happens in "real time," or "on the fly." The calculations are done as the material is fed into the system, give or take a bit of processing "latency" that delays the results by some amount. We know that the Fourier Transform of a waveform takes the entire length of the waveform to fully calculate. If the Fourier Transform of an entire waveform is to be used then the process requires that the entire waveform is played into the processor before the analysis can be done. To avoid this, a "Short Time Fourier Transform" (STFT) is done on small sections of the audio. The STFT looks at sections of, perhaps, 1000 samples and does a Fourier Transform on each set of 1000 samples, processing the pitch shifting of each set individually. This process is shown in Figure 19.10.

Much like our FIR filters in Chapter Seventeen, STFT portions intersect and the intersections of the portions are "windowed" to avoid inaccurate Fourier analysis and thus inaccurate results from the processing. If long enough sections are used and the windowing is done properly the results from using STFT analysis to do real time pitch processing can be inaudible.

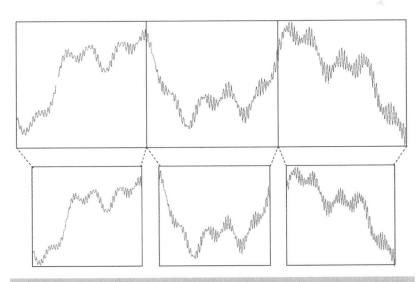

FIGURE 19.10: A Complex Waveform Divided Into Segments

TIME COMPRESSION AND EXPANSION

Very closely related to the effect of pitch shifting is the effect of altering time, also called, "time compression," or "time expansion." The concept is to make something occur in less or more time but with the same frequency content. This effect is identifiably used in radio advertising to give all of the "fine print" of an advertiser's claims in as little time as possible. The recording is done with the performer talking at normal speed and the recording is then "sped up" without changing the sound of the voice.

A crude form of time compression is used in radio broadcasts to make the songs played take less time, allowing more time for advertisements. This method involves simply increasing the speed of the digital clocks used for the playback. If material recorded at 44.1kS/s is played back 1% faster, or at ~44.5kS/s then the length of each song can be reduced by 1%, leaving more time for advertisers. Unfortunately, simply speeding up the rate of playback necessarily changes the pitch of the material, as we discussed earlier in this chapter.

Another method used in radio applications for reducing the time it takes to play some material works more efficiently on syndicated talk shows, where pauses between dialog can be removed and the rest of the material can be "pushed together." While this method does not change the pitch of the recording, it is only effective in spoken voice and similar recordings. Clearly, with musical content, removing dead space between notes would destroy the timing of the music, if there were any truly "dead space" between the notes.

A more appropriate method simply involves speeding up or slowing down the playback rate. While this inherently causes a pitch shift of the material, we can then use our knowledge on pitch shifting to put the material back to its original frequency content. If, for example, a piece of music is to be time expanded by 100%, so that it takes twice as long for the event to happen, but with the frequency content remaining the same, then the following steps can be undertaken:

First we slow the material down by playing it back at half the sample rate. Because the sample rate for the system is fixed, this can be accomplished by first upsampling the material to twice the sample rate and then playing it back at normal speed. For example, if the material to be affected is 100 samples long at 44.1kS/s then we want the material to last for 200 samples. In order to do this we upsample the material to 88.2kS/s, using appropriate filtering as discussed in Chapter Seventeen. When this is done the material contains the same frequency content but uses twice as many samples. When this material is then played back at 44.1kS/s it will take twice as long to play the material but the pitch of the material will have dropped by fifty percent (one octave).

Shifting the pitch back into place is easy to accomplish and has already been explained. We calculate the Fourier Transform of the results. We follow this with a shift of the entire frequency spectrum up one octave in the frequency domain. Finally, we calculate the inverse Fourier Transform of the results and are left with material that takes twice as long to play but has the same frequency content as the original material.

This method of doing time compression and expansion requires many steps. A less complicated method of doing this process removes the first step from the equation. Instead, the Fourier Transform of the waveform is calculated first. The Fourier Transform not only contains the analysis of frequency versus amplitude as we see on the spectrograph plot, but it also has the oft-ignored phase plot. The time compression can be handled simply by affecting the phase plot of the transform. The scale of the phase plot can simply be changed to represent more or less time while the spectrograph plot of the Fourier Transform remains the same. Once this is complete, the inverse Fourier Transform will recreate the waveform with no frequency changes, but the time scale will have been affected the desired amount. An example of this is shown in Figure 19.11. Note that the spectrograph plot in Figures 19.11B and C are the same, but the phase plot has shifted slightly. It is this shift in the phase plot that accounts for the time expansion of Figure 19.11A into the waveform in Figure 19.11D. Notice again that the waveform is not simply doubled in time. The second half of the waveform is different from the first half, though the frequency content is the same.

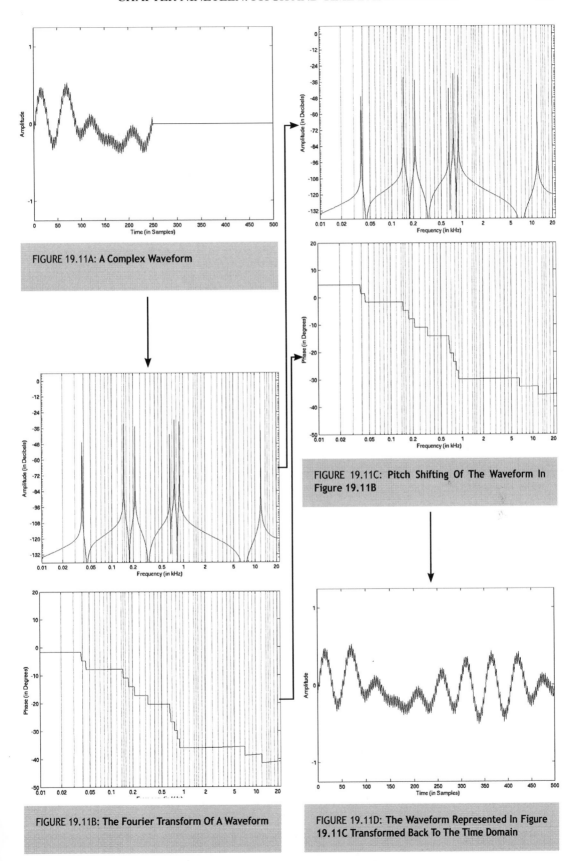

FIGURE 19.11A: A Complex Waveform

FIGURE 19.11B: The Fourier Transform Of A Waveform

FIGURE 19.11C: Pitch Shifting Of The Waveform In Figure 19.11B

FIGURE 19.11D: The Waveform Represented In Figure 19.11C Transformed Back To The Time Domain

CONCLUSION

The methods shown above for performing pitch and time processing are simplistic and conceptual. Clearly, the math involved in such analysis is complex and the results can vary in terms of the quality produced. Such processing is entirely unique to the digital realm, as neither form of processing can be done with any accuracy using exclusively analog based equipment.

While other forms of signal processing can be done, the methods shown in the past four chapters clearly cover the basis and the concepts behind the vast majority of digital signal processing used in the audio industry. Nearly every digital process used stems from one or more of the many digital processes we have covered:

- *Splitting signals and processing them separately by duplicating the data stream*

- *Summing signals together using point-to-point addition*

- *Changing the amplitude of the signal by multiplying each sample by a coefficient*

- *Filtering the signal by using infinite, recursive feedback loops*

- *Filtering the signal by using finite length filter impulse responses and convolving them with the original samples*

- *Filtering the signal by using finite length impulse responses and simulating the convolution of them with the original samples by adding together the Fourier Transforms of each*

- *Affecting the dynamic range of a signal by automating the gain coefficients based on the amplitude of the signal*

- *Changing the frequency content of a signal by calculating the Fourier Transform of a waveform, affecting the Fourier Transform, and then transforming it back to the time domain*

- *Changing the time it takes for a waveform to play by calculating the Fourier Transform of a waveform, affecting the Fourier Transform, and then transforming it back to the time domain*

NOTES:

Part Four

Other Digital Systems

Chapter Twenty

DSD

HISTORY

The digital audio industry has long been waiting for the next digital revolution to occur. Over the course of this book we have covered many aspects of digital audio technology that have improved over time (and some that are still improving). Because of the less than desirable implementation of the various technologies used in digital equipment over the past several decades, many recording engineers, audiophiles, record labels and mastering engineers have been waiting for some technology to come along that would more consistently provide the results that digital recording, transmission, and processing is capable of achieving.

Since 1981, for example, when the compact disc was formally released and the consumer market started to listen to and purchase digital recordings and the studio industry started to record with digital audio equipment, many major advancements have occurred. Analog to digital and digital to analog converters have undergone a complete overhaul many times over, starting with oversampling converters in the 1980s, continuing through 1-bit converters in the 1990s, and most recently culminating in low-bit, multi-bit modulators in only the year 2000. All of the converters that use oversampling, including 1-bit and low-bit, multi-bit modulators, require digital filters. Such digital filters require processing power, which has continued to become more available at more reasonable prices with more capabilities throughout the years. Many changes have also been made to the processing power available inside digital audio processors such as digital mixers and digital effects processors. While digital audio is capable of accurately reproducing audio per the specifications we identified in Chapter Six, much of the equipment used has fallen short of these needs over the years due to manufacturing costs and market demand.

For this reason, many people have been anticipating a new, "better sounding" digital environment and delivery format to replace the 44.1kS/s sample rate used in digital audio systems and the 16-bit delivery format used by the compact disc. This market desire erroneously anticipates that using higher sample frequencies or more bits in the delivery format would *necessarily* improve the sonic accuracy of the initial sampling, the processing, and the reproduction. Many equipment manufacturers have played into this market misunderstanding by providing equipment with higher sample frequency capabilities and various explanations (often based on false pretense or cynically fabricated) of why these products might produce more audibly-accurate results. For many years the audio market has been convinced that simply increasing the sample frequency would inherently provide more accurate results. In light of this, there has been anticipation for many years that a new delivery format would be released that would end the life of the compact disc as a delivery format. For a long time it was theorized that any new format would use 88.2kS/s sample rates so that material that had already been mastered at 44.1kS/s could easily be upsampled to the new rate using a single, high quality, low pass, digital filter and upsampling stage.

Along with an increase in sample rate, many people theorized that a new delivery format would have greater bit depths. This stems from the history of converters and the fact that early converter designs had very erratic low-level non-linearity and high noise floors. Though the 16-bit converters could *theoretically* capture and reproduce a dynamic range of 96dB, in practice many of the best early converters did not exceed a dynamic range of even as much as 85dB. Even at that level, the distortion from the non-linearity was very high. It was correctly surmised at the time that a fix to this problem would be a larger bit depth so that people reproducing their audio at home could reproduce the majority of the audio above the noise floor and the non-linear range of their converters. People desired this especially when the playback was done at very loud listening levels (at low levels the raised noise floor and the distortion components in converters end up below the noise floor in the room the music was played in, and thus ends up inaudible). For many years people have theorized that any new delivery format would be 24-bit and provide 144dB of theoretical dynamic range, but with a hope that at least 96dB of that dynamic range would be relatively linear.

In 1988 Sony records bought CBS/Columbia records, and with that purchase came the entire tape archive of all of the great historical recordings from both record labels. Magnetic tape erodes with time and use and can never be completely accurately duplicated. Digital media, however, can endure many copies without degradation to the material. Since digital recording was capable of audibly perfect playback (pending the quality of the implementation of the converters), the executives at Sony wanted to convert the entirety of the CBS/Columbia archives to digital data. Sony did not want to have to pull the tapes out of their archives every time that a new release of older recordings was warranted in a new collection or in a new format.

Sony wanted to convert the entire library to digital audio but did not know when, or if, a new digital delivery format would be released. They were not sure if said new delivery format would be 16-bit, 20-bit, 24-bit, or some other bit depth. They also did not know if a new format would be at 44.1kS/s or 88.2kS/s sampling rates. Not wanting to archive all of their recordings using the delivery format at the time and then not have their library meet the consumer demands that any new format might bring, they came up with a new archival format with which to store this library.

In the 1990s nearly all analog to digital and digital to analog converters used 1-bit delta sigma modulators to do their conversion. As we remember from Chapter Eleven, the 1-bit converter uses a delta sigma modulator to generate a very high sample rate, 1-bit signal that has very low noise in the audible range. The sample frequency of the modulator is an even multiple of the eventual sample rate of the audio, and the material is converted to the lower sample rate by filtering out all of the content above the eventual Nyquist frequency and decimating it down to the lower rate. The deeper bit depth (more quantization steps) are "created" by the filters' removal of the high frequency noise, leaving waveform shapes that more accurately represent the audio waveforms we hear. From a 1-bit modulator sampling at a rate of 2.8224MS/s, a 16-bit or 24-bit (or other bit depth) output can be generated at any number of sample frequencies including 44.1kS/s and 88.2kS/s. Sony decided to archive their entire library using the unfiltered feed, straight from the 1-bit modulators. By doing so, they would have an archive from which would (in theory) be flexible enough to create any seemingly viable sample data. While the sampling method of using delta sigma modulators had already been in use for some time, the concept of *archiving* the data at this higher rate was new. This archiving format was called "Direct Stream Digital," or "DSD."

Originally developed as an archival format, it soon became obvious that the material could be played directly out a D/A converter without using any filtering. When DSD material was played, completely bypassing all filtering in the A/D and D/A stages, the result was found to be very appealing. Soon, Sony started marketing DSD as a potential new delivery medium. A partnership with Phillips soon ensued and an eventual delivery medium called "SACD," or "Super Audio Compact Disc" was developed as a co-venture between the two manufacturers.

DSD VERSUS PCM

All digital recording prior to DSD used the conventional approach provided by Nyquist and his contemporaries of recording at slightly over double the frequency of the highest sample frequency needed to be captured and at a bit depth commensurate with the desired dynamic range of the recording. These recordings used binary PCM digital encoding to store the data. A standardized name had not been applied to this method of digital recording over the seventy-plus years that it had been in use, perhaps because it was the only digital recording method in use.

DSD also uses binary PCM coding to record audio, though the method used is not what would be termed a "conventional" approach. Delta sigma modulators and DSD use very high sample rates at very low bit depths to produce a result that provides the necessary dynamic range in the audible frequency spectrum, though the (overall) dynamic range is very low. The recordings still use PCM coding per our discussion in Chapter Eight, in that a "1" is represented as a pulse and a "0" is represented as no-pulse. The system is still binary in that numbers are represented in the binary coding method described in Chapter Eight. For these reasons, DSD (1-bit, 2.8224MS/s) is as binary and as PCM as 16-bit, 44.1kS/s sampling formats. To call only one of these systems "PCM" is a misnomer as both of them are clearly PCM. Regardless, the audio market has lent itself great confusion upon the advent of DSD by now calling traditional, low sample rate, high bit depth digital recordings "PCM" and referring to high sample rate, low bit depth recordings as something other than "PCM." The implication here is that DSD is not a digital signal derived in the same method as more traditional PCM methods, and that the bits represent something different than they do in PCM methods, which is not correct. Several trade publications have even insinuated that DSD uses delta modulators (a completely different recording method than using delta *sigma* modulators), which it does not.

For the purposes of clarity we will refer to 1-bit recording methods as DSD, per Sony's coining of the term, and high bit, low frequency, traditional digital recording methods as PCM, though we need to be clear that *each* system is clearly a "PCM system." It is important to keep this clear. 16 or 24-bit recordings at any sample rate such as 44.1kS/s, 48kS/s, 96kS/s, or 192kS/s will all be referred to as PCM systems only because, over the seventy years of implementation, no other term has been coined to accurately and uniquely describe them in a way that accurately distinguishes them from DSD type, high frequency, low bit depth systems.

The question really becomes "what is the difference in audio quality between PCM and DSD?" Or, more to the point, "what is the benefit of DSD recording?" The only known, quantifiable benefit to DSD recording is that digital filters are not used to convert the material to, for instance, 16-bit, 44.1kS/s PCM recordings and then used again to convert the material back to DSD for output. Since most analog to digital and digital to analog converters use some form of delta sigma modulators at high sample rates to do the sampling, using DSD simply keeps that material at the high sample rate without filtering it and decimating it down to 44.1kS/s for processing and delivery. If filters are used in the DSD to PCM conversion process (as in most A/D and D/A converters built since 1990) that cause an audible characteristic to the audio (such as attenuation in the audible range, the increase of distortion or noise, or the allowance of some amount of aliasing into the audio spectrum) then removing those filters would provide for more accurate audio reproduction. DSD processing can benefit because the processing is all done at very high sampling rates, so the distortion that can be generated from non-linear, PCM processes will not end up aliasing back into the audible range as we discussed can happen in Chapter Eighteen.

ISSUES WITH DSD

As DSD was originally designed to be a form of archiving and was not intended to be a final delivery format, there are some issues regarding its use as a final delivery method.

NOISE

The first issue is the high amount of noise that is present in any DSD signal. 1-Bit delta sigma modulator converters used for analog to digital conversion were originally intended to have their resultant data filtered to yield PCM data. Without that filtering the very high amount of noise at higher frequencies that is present due to the noise shaping is left as a part of the signal. Most of this noise is above the audible spectrum and is therefore theoretically not of concern. There really is not a need to filter that high frequency material out

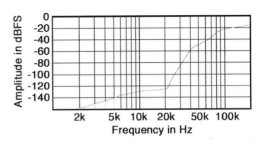

FIGURE 20.1: **The Noise Floor of DSD Systems**

externally because the ear will do it naturally, leaving only the material in the audible range to be used by the ear.

Unfortunately, this is not necessarily the case in entirety. The high amounts of "noise shaped noise" in the 70kHz to 100kHz range can cause irregularities in speakers and amplifiers used for playback equipment. Playback equipment is inherently analog and analog components are all non-linear and add distortion. By putting large amounts of high frequency information into speakers and amplifiers that are not designed to play that material, distortion components can be generated in the lower frequency ranges such as in the audible range. Further, as speakers attempt to play high frequency information at very high amplitudes above their intended range they can heat up due to friction, causing a change in the performance of the speaker often manifesting itself as a damping of its response. Surely these problems are not the fault of the DSD system itself, but they are a problem with the playback equipment upon being fed material that has such high frequency content present at high amplitudes. Until the playback equipment used for audio purposes is designed for the type of signal that DSD puts out, however, DSD playback will invariably cause some amount of distortion in playback systems.

The solution for this, per Sony's recommendation, is the placement of an analog, low pass filter *after* the signal is converted back to analog to filter out the extreme high frequency range and therefore removing much of the noise that is of concern. By doing so the amount of noise above the performance range of playback equipment is limited, allowing for less distorted playback of the results. Several manufacturers of DSD converters are implementing analog low pass filters (similar to the digital low pass filters used in PCM recordings) in order to remove the unwanted noise. Since the filters are analog, however, the transition band must be wider and the filter must be placed high enough above the audible range that the phase shift caused by the filter does not audibly affect the material in the audible range.

Figure 20.1 shows the noise floor of a typical DSD converter. The noise shaping clearly removes much of the noise from the audible range and pushes it outside of the audible range, creating the quickly-rising slope of noise above 20kHz. In traditional PCM systems this noise is created after the very gentle analog anti-aliasing filter in the A/D converter. Then the filters used in decimation remove all of this noise so that nothing remains above 20kHz, including the fast-rising noise floor. In DSD systems the noise remains unless a gentle analog filter is put in the circuit after the conversion back to analog, and that filter assuredly has an effect on the phase of the content in the audible range.

This problem is further mitigated in PCM converters because recent converters use multi-bit converters and therefore have less-steep noise shaping – if more bits are in use then the dynamic range increases and less noise shaping is needed. Finally, DSD systems inherently have this noise present during all processing stages. As we discussed in Chapter 15, noise content can "bleed" outside of its range during processing, so some of this noise in DSD may end up in the audible range. Because this noise is filtered out prior to working with traditional PCM, this is not a problem with PCM systems.

HIGH FREQUENCY CONTENT

There is some feeling in the audio community that information above 20kHz should be recorded in performances. Without validating this concept we can analyze whether or not DSD is an appropriate method with which to record such material. Based on our discussion of the high level of high frequency noise above 20kHz that is present in DSD signals it is clear that DSD would not be an appropriate format for recording material above 20kHz. The dynamic range of the frequency spectrum above 20kHz is drastically reduced as the noise shaping takes effect. Further, the implementation of a low pass filter in playback devices to reduce this high frequency noise level would not only provide phase distortion in this range (as discussed above), but would also attenuate the very material that was deemed necessary to record.

As a system to record information above 20kHz, DSD is not as viable as higher sample frequency PCM systems such as 192kS/s recorders that have a linear phase frequency response up to approximately 96kHz and greater than 110dB of dynamic range throughout the frequency spectrum.

Further analysis on all high sample rate systems including DSD and high sample rate PCM systems will be covered in the following chapter.

PROCESSING

DSD processing uses the exact same algorithm types that PCM processing does, specifically because DSD systems are represented through the same binary PCM code, and that code represents the same type of sample data that it does in "PCM" systems. Filters are implemented in the same way; pitch effects are implemented in the same way; gain changes are implemented the same, etc. Because of this, several problems and issues arise with DSD.

First, the processing required for a DSD signal is significantly more intense than the processing required for a PCM signal. We know from our study of filters in Chapter Seventeen that each output sample is the result of a mathematical formula (y = some derivation of x). We know that implementing an amplitude change requires the multiplication of each inbound sample times a coefficient ($y = A x$). In PCM recordings at 44.1kS/s, these formulas have to be computed 44,100 times per second. In DSD recordings these formulas have to be computed 2,822,400 times per second, requiring 64 times the processing power of 44.1kS/s PCM recordings. Because of this, adequate processing of DSD recordings is still under development. Some DSD systems actually decimate the audio to high frequency, traditional "PCM" data in order to process the data, specifically in order to conserve processing power. Many feel that decimating the DSD data to, say, 8-bit, 384kS/s data for the sake of processing sacrifices the intent of the system. Others observe that there should be no disadvantage to doing so if the filters in the decimation process can be kept audibly transparent – which should be possible at said rates. By decimating the system for processing, significant amounts of processing power are saved.

Further, the processing of DSD becomes complicated because, as we know from Chapter Fourteen, any digital processing inherently yields more bits than were initially presented. Processing a 1-bit system will necessarily turn it into a more-bit system. For example, if 20-bit gain coefficients are used to alter the amplitude of a signal in DSD, the resulting math will yield 20-bit values. Somehow these 20 bit values need to be reconciled back to a 1-bit paradigm (two quantization steps) since 1-bit is the eventual delivery format. We know that we cannot round or truncate the data back to 1-bit because it will yield erroneous and non-linear results. We also know, however, that we cannot dither the data back to 1-bit, because properly implemented dither necessary to decorrelate the error from the signal requires TPDF dither at an amplitude of *two quantization steps*, and a system that only provides one quantization step cannot have two quantization steps worth of noise in it. Even if dither *could* be applied to the signal to get it back to 1-bit from the 20 bits yielded from processing, dither noise is white. White dither noise at an overall amplitude of –6dB FS would have an amplitude of -24dB FS in the audible range, per our discussion in Chapter Eleven. This would reduce the dynamic range in the audible spectrum to only 24dB. Clearly dither cannot be used to get our signals back to 1-bit after processing stages.

One solution to this problem has been the introduction of a new *working* format of DSD called DSD-wide. DSD-wide uses 8 bits instead of 1, though still at the 2.8224MS/s rate. This allows dither to be used at intermediate processing stages, and the dither that is applied can be appropriate and effective. DSD-wide is not a delivery medium, but is only an intermediate medium used in DSD processors for transmitting the data from one processor to another and for temporary storage of DSD signals.

Not all DSD processing is done with the DSD-wide format. Further, at some point DSD-wide signals of 8 bits will have to be turned in to DSD signals of 1-bit, and truncation, rounding, nor dither are appropriate ways of doing so. The appropriate method for doing so is the same way that a 1-bit, noise shaped signal was generated from analog to start with: using a delta sigma modulator. To convert processed 1-bit signals or 8-bit DSD-wide signals back to 1-bit DSD signals for delivery, the signal has to go through a digital delta sigma modulator that functions precisely like the ones described in Chapter Eleven, using feedback of the quantization error to "shape" the noise.

Converting DSD signals to DSD-wide signals does not require such processing, just as converting 16-bit PCM data to 24-bit PCM data does not take complex processing. All that is required is the addition of a number of 0s on the end of each digital word. It is the conversion from more bits to fewer bits that requires the additional processing in order to prevent error and non-linearity or excess noise.

Therefore, whether signals are processed and then immediately turned into 1-bit data, or signals are processed and maintained as 8-bit data for further processing before being returned to 1-bit data, the conversion back to 1-bit data requires putting the data through a digital delta sigma modulator. This process is significantly more involved than simply adding dither and truncating off the remaining bits. For example, we can explore the process we described above wherein a 1-bit signal is multiplied times a 20-bit gain coefficient will yield 20-bit data, necessarily. At the end of the process the signal must undergo delta sigma modulation to return it to 1-bit material. The digital delta sigma modulator functions by adding the quantization error from previous samples to the current sample using appropriate ratios of previous samples in order to filter the quantization error. This process is much more involved than simply adding dither. The result is that the simple gain change requires *far more than* 64 times the processing power to complete, as the bit reduction stage at the end that returns the data to 1-bit actually requires more digital signal processing than the gain change itself.

The sample rate conversion of DSD signals to other sample rates (such as 128x if that is deemed appropriate for some form of processing) is done in precisely the same method that sample rate conversion of PCM signals is done, per our discussion in Chapter Seventeen. The signal has to be filtered and upsampled or filtered and downsampled. Of course, any filters create long digital wordlengths that have to be subsequently treated using the methods described above to reduce them in order to either DSD-wide or DSD for further processing.

CONVERTERS

At the time of the introduction of DSD, the 1-bit delta sigma modulator was the best A/D converter available on the market, providing better linearity than SAR A/D converters and R-2R ladder D/A converters. The DSD format was thusly based on the 1-bit converters that were in use, and the dynamic range of those converters is limited to the dynamic range capable from a 1-bit converter. Since the introduction of the 1-bit converter, however, the multi-bit modulator was introduced. This new type of converter increased the dynamic range capabilities of analog to digital and digital to analog converters.

Multi-bit modulators do not lend themselves easily to producing 1-bit outputs. Therefore, many DSD systems use an older conversion technology that is not capable of the same dynamic range that more modern PCM systems are capable of.

This issue may be of consequence in live recording situations where large dynamic ranges are desired to provide adequate headroom and avoid clipping. In playback situations, such as consumer playback decks, even 1-bit modulators with 106dB of dynamic range far exceed the dynamic range required for accurate audio reproduction.

DISTORTION

Potentially, the largest issue with DSD, however, is that it inherently has distortion byproducts in it. We remember from our discussion on noise shaping in Chapter Fifteen that noise shaping requires that dither be present in the feedback loop in order to decorrelate the quantization errors from the signal. We discussed that simply feeding back the error from one sample and adding it to the next sample does not substitute for the use of dither. Even adding a little error from the previous, say, nine samples (as in the implementation of POW-r) does not adequately decorrelate the quantization error from the signal itself. If the signal is not decorrelated from the quantization error then distortion will result, as we have reviewed several times.

The only adequate method for decorrelating the signal from the quantization error is to add random noise of high enough amplitude to either the signal directly or to the feedback loop. With only a 1-bit system and a 1-bit feedback loop it is simply mathematically impossible to add noise with two bits worth of amplitude to the signal path or to the feedback loop. This means that 1-bit systems as described in Chapter Eleven suffer from inevitable distortion, especially noticeable with low level, constant tones. The "noise shaping" done by 1-bit systems is not actually noise shaping as we discussed in Chapter Eleven, but is actually *distortion*-shaping because the error, or the "noise floor" is correlated to the signal. It was with this in mind that multi-bit converters were developed, and such converters do successfully decorrelate the quantization error from the signal because enough bits are in use that proper, random noise can be added in the delta sigma modulator's feedback loop.

Sony, however, had already formalized the DSD format and its ensuing SACD delivery format before the low-bit multi-bit converter had been invented and first presented to the scholastic community at large in 1999. Because of this, the DSD and SACD formats as currently exist are relegated to having higher distortion levels and the possibility that, in certain circumstances, those distortion components can become audibly noticeable on common playback material.

REASONS THAT DSD MAY SUCCEED

Regardless of the various issues described above, there are several reasons why DSD may succeed as a delivery method.

SOUND QUALITY

The sound quality has been reported by many to exceed the sound quality of traditional PCM recordings. Rugged tests of traditional PCM versus DSD are difficult to accomplish in a scientific fashion for various reasons stemming from particular details about the specific delivery format (SACD) for DSD material. To date no scientifically controlled study has been published comparing the sonic qualities of the two recording methods. Several factors make such a study difficult. One possible explanation for a perceived difference between PCM and DSD recordings is the effect that the high frequency noise in DSD can have on generating distortion components and damping high frequencies in playback devices. Such effects *could* be described as "sounding more analog," a term sometimes used to describe the differences perceived in DSD systems.

Further, DSD systems do not have digital low pass filters in them. Many playback systems for PCM recordings (including some very expensive ones) do not have *audibly transparent* low pass filters in them. If PCM systems have filters that affect the sound then any DSD converter could sound better with regards to the effected frequencies.

If a PCM system is played back using optimal converters, such as the low-bit multi-bit converters described in Chapter Eleven, then it will almost inevitably sound different than a DSD system that uses the inferior 1-bit converter that has higher distortion byproducts. Almost all PCM converters designed since the year 2000 utilize multi-bit converter circuits. This only helps to explain why the systems would sound *different* and does not explain why people might prefer DSD to PCM.

Finally, material that is released on DSD systems needs to be re-mastered specifically for that purpose. The re-mastering process for DSD almost inevitably guarantees differences between DSD and traditional PCM versions of the same material. One specific way in which this can happen has to do with compression. The "scarlet book" (the authoritative code on the burning of SACD disks) limits the amount of compression that can be added to a signal when the signal has a high amplitude in order to prevent what is called "modulator overload," or the equivalent of "clipping" in a 1-bit converter. As a result, many DSD disks do not contain signals that have been as heavily compressed as compact disks or DVDs have. The result can be a more "open," "airy" sound on the SACDs, akin to the characteristics people ascribe to DSD. A comparison between this less-compressed material on an SACD and the more-compressed material on traditional PCM systems can lead one to the conclusion that DSD sounds "better" than traditional PCM, though this leads to a tenuous conclusion based on implementation and choices made by mastering engineers as opposed to inherent characteristics between the two systems.

In short, there are multiple reasons that DSD *can* sound different than PCM, but without the ability for the average consumer to do a fair test between the two, conjecture and innuendo are very likely to dominate the press with regards to sound quality. If this is the case then it is very possible for "sound quality" to be a predominant reason that DSD may be successful, whether it "sounds better" or not. Even if there is a difference between the two in a certain implementation, however, that may be all that is required for DSD to be successful. Even if the compact disc of a particular song was mastered differently, at a different time, with different converters, different amounts of compression, and a different mastering engineer than the "equivalent" SACD of the same performance, the mass public may not care whether or not one of them is inherently *capable* of being better. The mass public may only care that "in a particular situation, with a particular piece of material, on a particular machine, the SACD sounded better" and regardless of how unscientific that is, it may be all that need be known for that consumer to decide to subscribe to the SACD/DSD format.

EXPENSE

Since DSD systems do not use digital low pass filters that have to sound transparent, the DSP power required at the converters is reduced. This means that home playback systems can use less expensive D/A converters, resulting in the ability to make DSD playback equipment less expensive than equivalent PCM playback equipment.

The expense for the consumer should not be confused with the expense for the digital audio engineer who will need to pay a tremendous amount more money in order to implement the more than 64 times the processing power (over 44.1kS/s systems) that is required to perform any task in the digital audio environment. The consumer, however, is often thought of as the driving force in the audio market because "consumers" account for practically anyone that purchases music. Professional digital audio engineers are a very small market in comparison to the consumer market. A lowering of the price on the consumer end (that subsequently necessitates an increase in the price by the professional) can help the SACD format succeed.

RECORD LABEL SUPPORT

Several record labels are producing material in DSD (on SACD) for three reasons. First, with a more standardized D/A converter on the consumer side, the record labels can be more assured that the end user hears the audio as close to how it was heard in the recording studio as possible. By removing the need for a digital reconstruction filter on the consumer's playback equipment, the record labels are removing one more way in which the consumer's experience might not be the same as the experience in the recording studio where the converters may be designed well enough that the reconstruction filters become inaudible.

Second, record labels are in support of the DSD format because the proliferation of recorded material right now makes it difficult to have a disk on the shelves that stands out from the rest of the material a consumer might consider buying. By investing in a DSD recording system and an SACD mastering system, a record label can once again stand out as being unique and have the perceived value of being more professional.

Finally, and perhaps most importantly, the SACD delivery format for the DSD recording method has a very well encrypted copy protection scheme within it that helps prevent unwanted digital copies of material being made and distributed, especially in foreign countries. Record labels are likely to readily adopt any system that helps prevent them from losing money to illegal copies and illegal distribution.

CONCLUSION

Originally designed as an archival method for lack of knowing what the future format would be, Sony has attempted to make DSD the future format of choice. There are many characteristics of DSD that have appeal to many people. Conversely, the academics and scholars of the theory of digital audio have had difficulty with DSD from an accuracy and efficiency perspective.

DSD is sure to be one of the most hotly debated subjects of the audio community at large. Clearly, much of the information about DSD is not widely understood, lending to rampant, market wide dissemination of misinformation and conjecture.

The larger question about emerging formats such as DSD, is "what is wrong with the current format?" Throughout this book that question has been largely answered. In the following chapter we will discuss this question, potentially bringing more light upon the viability of future formats.

NOTES:

Part Five

The Practical Application of Understanding Digital Audio

Chapter Twenty One

The Myths of Digital Audio

Throughout this book we have discussed the finer details of how and why digital audio actually works. At this point we will discuss and discredit, as promised in the preface, seven of the major myths of the audio industry with substantiation borrowed from the last several hundred pages of explanation included herein. To the reader who has not read the entire book, the following points may seem full of holes and incomplete analysis. It really takes this entire book's worth of writing and reading to comprehensively substantiate the following. This is merely a summary combining many of the major topics covered within, with simplified explanations of each.

MYTH NUMBER ONE: HIGHER SAMPLE RATE RECORDINGS INHERENTLY SOUND BETTER THAN LOWER SAMPLE RATE RECORDINGS, ALL THINGS BEING EQUAL

False. This topic probably holds the largest amount of marketing hype, preying on the simple, intuitive conclusion drawn by the majority of people that more equals better.

"HEARING ABOVE 20KHZ"

First, we cannot hear above 20kHz. We established why this is in Chapter Six. We cannot hear above 20kHz. We cannot hear *the effect* of anything above 20kHz. We cannot hear inter-modulation distortion or beat frequencies caused by material above 20kHz being mixed with material in our hearing range. The only way that we can hear the *effect* of material over 20kHz is if it is aliased *back into the hearing range*, or if it is combined with other frequencies in a non-linear environment, creating artificial tones *within our hearing range* that we can hear. In none of these situations are we actually hearing the material above 20kHz. In these situations we are hearing a change in frequency content below 20kHz.

People have suggested that we can "perceive" air pressure changes above 20kHz even if we cannot hear them. It has been pointed out that light, for example, oscillates at a frequency above 20kHz. This, however, is a poor analogy. Light is not comprised of waves of changes in air pressure but is rather comprised of waves of electromagnetic radiation. No documented study has shown that the human body can detect air pressure changes above 20kHz, though one major study has indicated that it cannot. The Oohashi study out of Japan, as presented to the American Physiological Society and the Audio Engineering Society, has demonstrated that under scientifically controlled conditions not a single person in the study was capable of recognizing the presence of harmonic material above 20kHz in a recording.

To date there are, however, three known ways that the body physiologically reacts to sound waves above 20kHz, though in each situation not a single test participant was able to identify that their body was experiencing such a physiological reaction. The first known way again speaks to the Oohashi study out of Japan. In that study, participants yielded different brain wave activity after being hooked up to an alpha-electroencephalogram (Alpha EEG). Certainly it would have been possible for a participant to have looked at his brain wave chart and determined, based on his brain's activity, that his body must have been experiencing frequency content above 20kHz. It would be a stretch to call the looking back at scientific data the "perceiving" of the presence of high frequency information.

The second known physiological change the body can undergo in the presence of sound waves above 20kHz is the transmission of high frequency material through bone conduction. Studies have shown that high frequency material, above the human range, can result in audible detection when a metal rod is applied to the skull and high frequency material is directly applied to it. Specifically, speech recognition amongst the hearing impaired has been shown to improve in these conditions. Unfortunately, however, the signal levels necessary to accomplish this have to be tremendously high and applied directly to the skull. The high frequency material *itself* is not audible, but lower frequency vibrations *in the audible range* are conducted through the bones to the inner ear where they result in fluid vibrations in the audible range that can be heard. For people that are not hearing impaired, however, the material that gets to the ear from bone conduction is so low in relation to the material that gets to the inner ear through the traditional means that it is nearly entirely masked. When the masking effect of this low level transmission is combined with the fact that people do not often listen to music through the conduction of metal rods attached to their heads, the viability that this bone-conduction method of transmitting audio to the brain actually allows the ability to discern material above 20kHz is simply not substantiated. This, in combination with the fact that the Oohashi study mentioned above did not yield a single participant that was capable of discerning the presence of material through this method.

Finally, high frequency sound waves can physically maim the body in extreme situations. This phenomenon is used in the medical industry as a type of non-invasive surgery. Human corneas are currently being reshaped using high frequency sound waves, for example. While this, too, is a physiological change that the body undergoes in the presence of high frequency sound waves, a person should not expect to see any better after listening to music with frequency content above 20kHz. Sonar welding systems currently used in plastics can burn the skin or even a hole right through a person's hand. Not only are the signal levels used in these situations so high as to be laughable when discussing the playback of digital music, but the ability to perceive that one's hand is being burned is likely not the type of "perception" of material above 20kHz that people discuss as a benefit to recording at higher sampling frequencies.

There are many ways of quickly running incomplete tests and drawing inaccurate conclusions about the ability to perceive sound waves above 20kHz aided by inaccurate playback equipment that induces beat tones into the audible range. To date, no properly conducted study has indicated that sound waves above 20kHz are perceivable at all to the human.

Because of this, the supposed major benefit of recording material above 44.1kS/s is moot. There is not an audible benefit to capturing the material above 20kHz in a recording in any way. This is actually one of the ways that analog mixers cause degradation to the signal. If two speakers are placed on a stage, one of which plays a 15kHz tone and the other of which plays a 25kHz tone we know that we would only hear the 15kHz tone. The 25kHz tone would not be audible, and the 10kHz "beat frequency" would not be audible on account that the higher tone was inaudible. If the air is allowed to mix the two sounds then the result is that only the 15kHz tone is audible.

If the material is recorded using a microphone in front of each speaker and the recording is done in a digital environment at a sample rate of 44.1kS/s then the 15kHz tone would be recorded and the 25kHz tone would not. If the material is then mixed digitally only the 15kHz tone will be present, just as the ear should hear it.

If the tones are recorded, however, with higher sample frequencies then both the 15kHz and the 25kHz tone will be recorded. If the two channels are then mixed in (or passed through) an analog environment (such as an amplifier) that has some degree of non-linearity then the beat frequency of 10kHz *will* be created, and when the recording is played back the 10kHz tone will be available to be heard. This is an inaccurate reproduction of the original material with respect to the ear. In any natural environment the 10kHz sub-tone would not have been audibly present.

By recording higher frequencies than the ear can hear we create the possibility that the analog equipment in the signal path will create unnatural and inaccurate results. This very effect is often blamed for tests in which square waves at 15kHz are said to sound different than sine waves at 15kHz. We already know that the human ear cannot hear the difference between a square wave and a sine wave, each with a fundamental of 15kHz, as the first overtone of the square wave is at 45kHz, well above the hearing range. If a difference can be heard it can often be identified to be the creation of harmonic material *within* the hearing range because of nonlinearity and distortion in the playback equipment upon attempting to recreate high frequency waveforms. (This, and the fact that a square wave and a sine wave of equal amplitude have different amplitudes of the 15kHz fundamental, resulting in the square wave version sounding louder than the sine wave version by a few decibels.) Since any analog component is non-linear, recording material that should have no effect on audibility only provides the possibility that distortion may be added within the audible range, thereby affecting the accuracy of the playback of the recorded material.

THE CONVERTERS

Several tests have been done that have indicated that recordings done at higher sample frequencies have sounded "different" than recordings done at lower sampling frequencies. In most situations this can be attributed to the analog to digital and digital to analog converters used in the test.

We discussed the importance of the anti-aliasing and reconstruction filters in converter design, and the fact that the proper design of them is imperative to the proper function of digital circuits. If the anti-aliasing filter rolls off at too low of a frequency then the audible spectrum is affected. If the anti-aliasing filter rolls off at a frequency that is too high, or if the transition band reaches above the Nyquist frequency then aliasing will be allowed into the signal within the audible band. Per our discussion on digital filters in Chapter Eighteen, the perfect anti-aliasing filter *can* be designed to not attenuate any frequency content below 20kHz but to attenuate at least 144dB FS at all frequencies at or above 22.05kHz and not affect the phase of the frequencies in the pass band. This filter, however, is very steep and requires a tremendous number of taps and very accurate calculations for each of its respective tap values. Most filters built into the chips of A/D converters are not audibly transparent. As a testament to that fact, several manufacturers design A/D converter circuits that bypass the filters on the converter chip and replace them with very computationally expensive DSP so that the filtering process is more accurate.

The advantage to higher sample rates in this context is that the filters in the converters do not have to be as steep and can therefore be less expensive to implement. Many inexpensive converters will demonstrate a marked improvement when comparing 44.1kS/s recordings versus 96kS/s recordings, for example. This is often because the filters in the converters are not of audibly transparent quality. On higher quality (and thus more expensive) converters, the difference between 44.1kS/s recording and 96kS/s recording is indeterminable under proper testing conditions and procedures. Not to be fooled, however, even some of the most expensive converters have filters in them that are not audibly transparent. One such manufacturer provides multiple filter settings. Clearly, not all of the filter settings can be accurate. As such, at least most of their multiple settings are "flawed" by the specifications we require.

Because we know that sound waves above 20kHz are not audible, and because we know that digital filters implemented for higher sample rate recording are significantly less affecting of the audible range, a very simple test can be done to determine the quality of the filters in any analog to digital converters: record the same material through the same converters at 44.1kS/s and at 96kS/s. If there is an audible difference then most likely the converters are not audibly transparent in the 44.1kS/s setting. Clearly this is not a completely sufficient test, as the playback equipment after the converters can cause audible-range distortion when trying to reproduce frequencies outside of its specified range. As a general rule, however, it can indicate a lot about the quality of a given converter – especially on good playback equipment.

It is therefore correct that there *can* be audible differences between lower sample rate and higher sample rate recordings of band-limited material, but only insomuch as the quality of the filters in the converters varies. The notion that there is an *inherent* difference is false, as with properly designed, audibly transparent equipment, no difference will be audible.

PROCESSING BENEFITS

We have discussed that the processing of non-linear dynamics should be done at higher sample rates in order to allow the distortion frequencies above the bounds of the digital system to be removed through filtering. This does not, however, necessitate the *recording* of the material at higher sample rates. It only speaks to the *processing* of the material at higher sample rates. By the time the recording is finished, mixed, mastered and ready for delivery, there is no need to present the consumer with recordings at higher sample rates for the sake of processing. There is also not a need to record the material at those rates for the sake of processing that is to be done. During the processing stage, the material should be upsampled, processed and then downsampled. There is not a need to leave it at the higher sample rate throughout the system.

Upsampling and downsampling both require low pass filters as part of the process. The algorithm for the upsampling and downsampling filters are precisely the same as the algorithms needed for anti-aliasing and reconstruction filters. A logical conclusion is that if the converters do not often have audibly transparent filters then the processing stages, such as the implementation of compression, could not be expected to have audibly transparent filters either. It is important when working with base sample rates such as 44.1kS/s to use algorithms that perform the functions accurately and in an audibly accurate fashion including the upsampling and downsampling portions of the algorithms. Again, there is not an *inherent* benefit to recording audio with respect to any necessary processing the signal may undergo, though there can be benefits if processes are used with less than adequate implementation.

ACCURATE REPRESENTATION OF WAVEFORMS

The introduction of the digital audio workstation into the recording industry has allowed a very intuitive (but very incorrect) conclusion to be drawn from looking at waveforms on computer screens. It is easy to correctly analyze that, at 44.1kS/s sample rates, a 20kHz sine wave would only get sampled twice per waveform. A 10kHz sine wave would only get sampled four times per waveform. A 5kHz sine wave would only get sampled 8 times per waveform, etc. This leads to the conclusion that, clearly, the 10kHz waveform, for example, cannot be accurately recreated to be a 10kHz sine wave. The representation on the computer screen clearly shows a triangle wave or a square-ish waveform. Further, the amplitude of the waveform is not accurately represented

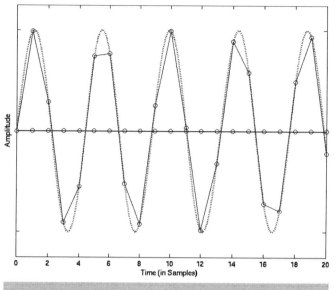

FIGURE 21.1: A Typical Representation Of 10kHz Waveform in a Computer System (at 44.1kS/s)

if the sampling points are near the zero crossing. The typical on-screen representation of sample data is shown in Figure 21.1.

The visual demonstration on the screen shows a "connect the dots" display and does not demonstrate what waveform will be created after the digital values have been put through the reconstruction filter in the digital to analog converter. A 10kHz sine wave of a given amplitude, digitally sampled at 44.1kS/s, will only be sampled four times in a single cycle. When those four samples are fed through a reconstruction filter and properly converted to analog, however, the resulting waveform will be a 10kHz waveform of precisely the same frequency, phase, and amplitude that went in to the system.

FROM WHENCE THE MYTH ORIGINATES

In the case of high sample rate recording, the myth likely stems from the fact that audible differences have been able to be heard because of poor filtering in converters. At the time that the industry started to murmur about high sample rate recording, converters used analog anti-aliasing filters instead of the process of oversampling and the incorporation of digital anti-aliasing filters. Analog filters have much worse performance than digital (linear phase) filters do because they are not phase linear. Until digital filters were used, the industry was clamoring for a way to improve the sound quality and the notion of increasing the sample frequency seemed an easy remedy.

This myth has been furthered by the intuitive (yet incorrect) deduction that "more must be better" and simple misunderstandings of many of the issues covered in this book.

Finally, manufacturers of audio equipment and industry media have aided and abetted the myth by either presenting completely incorrect information to consumers or by allowing consumers to draw incorrect conclusions.

While this myth is incorrect in its wording, it is valid to recall that many pieces of equipment are designed to fit particular budgets and the result can yield lesser quality implementation. This can lead to an audible improvement when using higher sample frequencies. There is not, however, an *inherent* difference, and when all is equal and the systems are properly designed for audible transparency there are no audible difference between different sample rates for recording.

MYTH NUMBER TWO: MORE BITS INHERENTLY SOUND BETTER THAN FEWER BITS, ALL THINGS BEING EQUAL

False. This statement is again an example of intuitive deductions based on incomplete information providing the opportunity for incorrect conclusions.

There are only four characteristics of audio waveforms: amplitude, frequency, phase, and dynamic range. In digital sampling technology there are two variables: the bit depth and the sample rate. The sample rate affects the maximum frequency that can be represented and the bit depth affects only one property of recordings: the dynamic range.

Per our discussion in Chapter Nine, the higher the bit depth the more quantization steps are available. The more quantization steps the less the quantization error. The less the quantization error the lower the quantization noise. The lower the quantization noise the lower the noise floor. The lower the noise floor the greater the dynamic range. Therefore, the more bits used, the more dynamic range, but that is the *only* property of a waveform that is affected by bit depth.

Per the formula that we derived, each "bit" provides 6dB of dynamic range in the recording system. This means that 16 bits provides a maximum capability of 96dB of dynamic range. 24 bits provides a maximum capability of 144dB of dynamic range. The number of bits needed to record a signal is completely based on the dynamic range of the material being recorded.

Further, if the material is to be played back, the number of bits needed is limited to the amplitude with which the material is to be played. If the material is to be played at a level of peak=85dB SPL then the noise level of an optimal 16-bit system will be –11dB SPL, well below the threshold of hearing. If the material is to be played at a level of peak=85dB SPL, but the white noise floor in the room it is to be played in is 45dB SPL then the maximum dynamic range that will be heard is around 40dB SPL. Even recognizing the human's ability to hear up to 25dB or so below a given white noise floor, the maximum dynamic range that will be heard (including the range below the noise floor) is only 65dB. 65dB Of dynamic range only requires 11 bits. Therefore, an 11-bit recording will sound the same in that situation as a 24-bit recording.

The only situation in which a recording that utilizes 24 bits will sound different than a recording that uses 16 bits (using the same, linear converters) is when the difference between the amplitude of the playback (in dB SPL) and the amplitude of the lowest level discernable sound that can be heard in the room (in dB SPL) is greater than the dynamic range capability of the 16-bit converter (in dB).

The only situation where using 24 bits to record with will sound different than using 16 bits to record with, assuming linear converters, is if the difference between the peak amplitude of the signal and the lowest level discernable sound in the signal (the dynamic range of the signal) is greater than the dynamic range of the 16-bit converters. Recording such signals is actually not very common, but a further benefit exists in the recording part of the signal chain in that an increase of bit depth allows for more headroom while recording in order to prevent clipping from running the signal too hot to ensure an accurate capture.

Finally, with the bit reduction algorithms (such as colored dither and noise shaping) available on the market, 16-bit delivery formats can provide up to 150dB of dynamic range in the most sensitive frequency ranges of human hearing, keeping all of the quantization error below the threshold of human hearing at all frequencies for any viable amplitude with which the signal might be played back. While there can still be viable recording situations wherein 24 bits has advantages over 16 bits (if, for no other reason, the headroom gained when recording live) only in extreme situations should a mastered 24-bit signal sound any different from a properly prepared and mastered and bit-reduced 16-bit signal.

LOSS OF "RESOLUTION"

Until now the term "resolution" has not been used in conjunction with bit depth of digital recordings in this book. Certainly, more quantization steps provides for more "statistical resolution" by mere definition. The term "resolution," however, also implies a subjective measure of quality. The phrase, "that recording didn't have a lot of 'resolution'" implies that the signal was audibly distorted. The connection between the phrase "bit depth" and the word "resolution" has led to the confusion that fewer bits leads to a reduction in sound quality. There are, however, only four characteristics of a waveform, as described above. The "resolution" of the waveform is not one of them. A change in "statistical resolution" *causes* a change in one of the characteristics in a waveform, and per our reading that area of change is the dynamic range of the waveform. If the statistical resolution of the recording provides enough dynamic range to represent a signal accurately then more quantization steps does not improve the audible quality of a recording.

FROM WHENCE THE MYTH ORIGINATES

The myth of the number of bits in a recording grows, again, out of incorrect conclusions drawn by "intuitive" but incorrect analysis. The widely held philosophy that "more is always better" assists in this deduction. This is further compounded by the observation that every increase in bit depth yields a *doubling* of the amount of quantization steps available, such that the difference between 16 bits (65,536 quantization steps) and 17 bits (131,072 quantization steps) is double. It should be clear after reading Chapter Nine, however, that the number of bits used in a recording does not need to exceed the dynamic range requirements of a signal.

This does not undermine the benefits of higher bit depth *processing* of signals. Processing should almost always be done at bit depths that are greater than the bit depth of the inbound data in order to maintain accuracy regardless of the dynamic range needed for the recording or the playing back of signals. This also does not undermine the value of 24-bit recorders. 24-bit analog to digital converters can currently achieve a dynamic range of approximately 120dB (while theoretically 144dB, approximately 24dB is lost to the inherent noise in the conversion process). There are several potential audio sources that have very wide dynamic ranges. Further, we want the dynamic range of the recording system to be larger than the largest dynamic range in the loudest source we intend to record in order to provide adequate "headroom."

This does, however, undermine the notion that greater than 16 bits is required for playback. When a recording is ready to be heard it does not need any headroom. If all 16 bits in a 16-bit recording are used then the result is only inadequate if, in an anechoic chamber with 0dB SPL of room noise, the recording is to be played back at greater than 96dB SPL, peak amplitude. In more realistic environments where the threshold of audibility is above 20dB SPL, a 16-bit recording is only inadequate if the material is played back at amplitudes that border on the threshold of pain, louder than concert levels, and at 116dB SPL. As this is entirely an unrealistic need, a playback format that uses more than 16 bits is entirely unnecessary. If the converter has a linear "transfer function" in so much as the ear can discern, then there will be no audible difference between 16-bit and 24-bit recordings when played back at low amplitudes in environments with a noise floor high enough that the dynamic range of the playback environment is less than the dynamic range of the recording.

Further, 16-bit material playing back can exceed the audible dynamic range of 16-bit material being recorded because on playback one can use noise shaping such as POW-r to effectively get 24-bit performance out of only 16 bits. Although the 16-bit playback signal never has more than 96dB of dynamic range, the noise is spread unevenly across the frequency spectrum to accommodate the contour of the threshold of hearing with respect to frequency. At the frequencies at which the ear is most sensitive, the dynamic range can be up to 150dB while at frequencies at which the ear has a very high threshold of hearing (perhaps 60dB SPL) the dynamic range can be lower. Over the entire frequency range it may provide 96dB of dynamic range, but this can be spread to provide seemingly 24-bit quality as far as the ear is concerned using only 16 bits.

MYTH NUMBER THREE: RECORDING THE SIGNAL "HOTTER" WILL YIELD BETTER RECORDING RESULTS

False. At least not true as a blanket statement.

When a signal's overall amplitude is increased, the number of quantization steps that it covers is increased. As the number of quantization steps that it covers is increased, the number of bits in use increases. We already know, however, that the number of bits required to record the signal source is defined by its dynamic range. Most recording sources do not have a dynamic range anywhere near the dynamic range that current 16-bit and 24-bit recorders provide. Current 16-bit converters (even mediocre ones) are capable of around 93dB of dynamic range. In a typical recording environment of around 20dB SPL room noise, a sound source would have to be performed at around 100dB SPL in order to exceed the dynamic range of the converters. 100dB SPL is the amplitude level of a typical rock concert.

Most recording is done with 24-bit A/D converters with around 120dB of dynamic range capabilities. The actual use of that entire range is completely beyond the scope of an audio recording. The idea behind using 24 bits is to provide some headroom, allowing the engineer the ability to turn the material down in amplitude to avoid the risk of digitally "clipping" during the recording process. We now know that if the dynamic range of, say, a vocalist, recorded with a microphone in a room is 60dB, that only 10 bits of quantization are necessary to accurately record the performance. This means that with 120dB of dynamic range potential, the signal can be turned *down* up to 60dB below the level of clipping without any sacrifice to the audio in any capacity.

THE PROPER SETTING OF RECORDING LEVELS

Microphone preamplifiers and other outboard equipment are designed to operate at certain amplitude levels. This stems from the notion that analog equipment is inherently non-linear and performs best and provides the least amount of distortion when it is operated within a certain range. The amplitude required to "clip" a typical analog to digital converter is significantly higher than the ideal operating range of a given piece of analog equipment, again, to provide necessary headroom and avoid clipping. If the equipment preceding the analog to digital converter is turned up high enough that the signal is very nearly clipping, then the equipment will operate outside of its ideal operating range, potentially allowing for distortion to enter the signal.

The A/D converters of today offer such wide dynamic range capabilities (far exceeding the need of most practical recording situations) that the level entering the converter is of little concern. Most sources can be turned down as much as 30-40dB before the dynamic range of the source exceeds the dynamic range of the number of quantization steps used.

The proper levels to use in recording applications are therefore the levels that the equipment *preceding the converters requires*. If the preamplifiers and other analog equipment preceding the converters are used properly then the signal will often be recorded in the analog to digital converter at levels never exceeding –12 to -6dB FS, depending on how the converters are calibrated. There is an incredibly wide range that the signals can be set at to be recorded with exactly the necessary precision at the analog to digital converters. There is a very narrow range in which *analog equipment* sounds best. It is therefore better to record, paying attention to the analog components' levels than those entering the converters.

FROM WHENCE THE MYTH ORIGINATES

This myth originates from the same misunderstandings and conclusions that lead to myth number two. There are, however, a few other circumstances at play with this myth.

First, early analog to digital converters had poor linearity at low levels (per our discussion of R-2R D/A converters in Chapter Ten. For this reason it was beneficial, early on, to record the material relatively hot in order to bring all of the audible dynamic range above the range of poor linearity in the analog to digital converters. Since the advent of the 1-bit delta sigma modulator converters in the early 1990s, however, low level non-linearity has not been a factor in converter design and this reason for recording signals hotter than optimal no longer applies.

Second, when delivering a *final format* for listening it is desirable to allow the music to use the entire dynamic range available. The final mixing and mastering process, therefore, is used to turn the signal up in the digital environment as hot as is possible (without clipping) in order to get the levels to utilize all 16 bits. Somehow the principles at play in this convention have been erroneously applied to *recording* levels.

Third, older 16-bit converters only had about 85dB of dynamic range available at best. There would occasionally be times that the dynamic range of the material would exceed the dynamic range of the recording method. In these situations the levels were kept hotter than is necessary today.

With today's extremely linear converters (providing 120dB of dynamic range) turning the signal up to enter the analog to digital converters fairly hot is of no benefit. Because of the myth and the tendency for recording engineers to adhere to it, the typical recording levels used in today's digital recording studio are hotter than is usually optimal. In many situations sonic improvements can be made by turning the signal going in to the converters *down* to take advantage of the optimal range of the analog equipment preceding the converters.

MYTH NUMBER FOUR: CLOCK QUALITY MAKES NO AUDIBLE DIFFERENCE IN A RECORDING STUDIO

False.

There are a vast amount of misconceptions and misunderstandings about clocks and clock qualities. Per our discussion in Chapter Twelve, however, the clock makes a phenomenally significant difference at the analog to digital, digital to analog, and asynchronous sample rate converter stages.

FROM WHENCE THE MYTH ORIGINATES

The myth that clock quality is inconsequential stems from the seemingly logical conclusion that can be drawn from just looking at numbers: if the ear cannot hear higher than 20kHz (.00005 seconds per cycle) and if the ear cannot hear phase variations greater than 1 degree at 1kHz (timing shift of .0000027 seconds) then it should not be possible to hear the effect of jitter in the magnitude of picoseconds, or .000000000001s.

The error in this line of thinking is that a waveform changes amplitude very fast, especially around the zero-crossing. If samples are taken at incorrect times, or samples are turned into voltages at incorrect times, then improper amplitude measurements can be taken. Such measurements can affect the accuracy of the sampling process. The result is an audible addition of distortion in the audio signal, the amplitude of which varies with the timing variations (the jitter).

The myth may also stem from the inability for some people to hear the differences between clocks because the clock circuitry in their converters does not allow for an improvement with the connection of an external clock. Several analog to digital converters available on the market will not be improved with the addition of a "better" quality external clocking device.

MYTH NUMBER FIVE: CLOCK QUALITY IS IMPORTANT TO EVERY BOX IN A RE-CORDING STUDIO

False.

As stated above, the "quality" of a clock, or the amount of jitter in a clock signal is only pertinent at the conversion stages. This is not to say that clocks are not "important." Clocks are very important, and many problems in a recording studio can be traced to not all of the devices being synched to the *same* clock.

As for whether the clocks have jitter induced in them or not, however, the only parts of a signal chain where this affects the audio integrity are the analog to digital, digital to analog, and asynchronous sample rate converter stages. A digital effects processor fed a digital signal will produce the exact same numerical output regardless of the stability of the clock. A digital recorder will store exactly the same information regardless of how jittery the clock is. A digital audio editor will produce the exact same results regardless of the stability of the clock. A digital mixer that is not doing any analog conversion will produce exactly the same results, regardless of any jitter in the clock.

FROM WHENCE THE MYTH ORIGINATES

This myth likely originates from the vast amount of confusion about clocking systems. Due to simply not understanding digital clocking systems, many digital studios spend vast amounts of time and energy ensuring that every device receives the very best, low jitter version of the master clock possible, sometimes going so far as cutting all of the clock cables to the same length, unnecessarily. With all of the confusion and misinformation about digital audio clocking protocols, many people are taking the overly-cautious approach and propagating the myth that every device will benefit from a low-jitter master clock. People hear that clocks are important and assume that they are equally important everywhere in a digital system, again drawing what seem to be "intuitive" results from incomplete information and analysis.

MYTH NUMBER SIX: DIGITAL RECORDING OR MIXING CAN NEVER SOUND AS GOOD AS ANALOG RECORDING OR MIXING

False

For many reasons digital recording and mixing can be more audibly accurate than analog recording or mixing.

As we covered in Chapter Seven, the accuracy of analog recording is limited to the physical limitations of the medium. The limitations of digital recording are so far removed from practical needs that they are thought of as non-existent. The greatest limitation in digital recording is actually that the signal still has to be analog at some point, and that the signal has to undergo a conversion to digital at some point. Once the signal is digital the limitations are practically non-existent.

Analog mixing requires the use of a tremendous amount of noisy and non-linear components, such that the results are bound accordingly.

FROM WHENCE THE MYTH ORIGINATES

The myths about the sound quality of analog and digital recording and mixing stem from several issues. Regarding analog recording, the mechanical and physical limitations of the system provide for a few audible characteristics that have been deemed "audibly pleasing" for many years. The most notable of these is the natural compression obtained when saturating the recording capabilities of analog tape. When saturating digital converters, on the other hand, the same type of saturation occurs, but the digital system causes the harmonic overtones to alias in a displeasing way. Further, the saturation on analog tape is not abrupt, as hitting full scale is in digital. Rather, the entire recording medium is non-linear and as the bounds of the recording medium are reached the system becomes increasingly non-linear, providing increasingly audible compression until complete saturation is achieved.

In practice, most high-end digital converters far exceed the audible recording capabilities of the very best analog recording systems. Digital systems are inherently more linear, have less distortion, have less noise, have wider dynamic range handling capabilities, and have a completely transparent frequency response in the audible range. Still, several people prefer the sound of tape recordings (with certain sources) to digital recordings. In many cases the reason is that the *inaccuracies* of the tape recording medium are desired. If this "effect" is desired and the use of said effect is determined to be "the best sounding approach," then this does not determine that analog sounds "better" than digital. All that it says is that that particular effect is the proper effect. There is, however, no effect that can be created in the analog domain that does not have mathematical determinability. As such, there is no effect that can be created in the analog domain that cannot be duplicated in the digital domain. Because of this, there is no reason that a digital recording cannot sound exactly like an analog recording if digital signal processing is added to the signal to "create" the effect of the analog recording. FIR filters, as described in Chapter Seventeen, would be one method used to create such an effect, as would dynamics processing such as that which we studied in Chapter Eighteen.

Since the "effect" of analog recording can be created digitally, there is no reason that a digital recording cannot sound exactly like an analog recording, thus the myth is incorrect. To date, however, the primary goal of digital recording manufacturers has been to design audibly transparent equipment as opposed to audibly "effected" equipment. Should a market demand for analog sounding digital converters or digital signal processing effects that make a recording sound like it was done on tape develop there is no reason that a manufacturer could not capitulate.

With regards to analog mixing, the myth stems from the fact that many digital mixers have been poorly designed, not taking into regard many of the required treatments of the numerical information. Nearly ten years since the first digital mixer became widely available, the most used digital mixer in the world still had not implemented the use of dither at the various processing stages within it where bit depth was reduced. Still today, many digital mixers are not implemented with audibly transparent accuracy. This, however, is not unique to the digital mixing domain. Most analog mixers on the market are not only nowhere near as capable as digital mixers, but are just as flawed as digital mixers in other ways.

Fortunately, in the past few years much attention has been drawn to digital mixers and the offering from manufacturers continues to improve. At this time a *very* accurate digital mixer can be purchased as a piece of software for merely hundreds of dollars, outperforming analog mixers that cost a thousand times as much, in terms of audio accuracy.

Analog mixers, like analog recorders, are inherently incapable of the dynamic range and the linearity of their digital counterparts. As such, analog mixers can impart a unique sound akin to the "effect" that analog recorders provide. Since this "sound" is mathematically determinable it can be duplicated through digital signal processing with complete accuracy. If the sound of an analog mixing console is preferred for a particular application over the completely linear, audibly transparent response of an obtainable digital mixer, the sound of the analog mixer can be digitally created, making the myth that digital mixers can never sound as good as analog mixers incorrect. To date, digital mixer manufacturers have been more interested in transparency than adding in certain types of distortion with the intention of making their mixers sound more like their analog counterparts.

MYTH NUMBER SEVEN: DSD SOUNDS BETTER THAN PCM, ALL THINGS BEING EQUAL

False.

Per our discussion in Chapter Twenty One, the statement itself is a misnomer. DSD *is* PCM in every sense of the term. Since both systems referred to inherently use binary PCM coding, we will again refer to conventional, multi-bit, low sample rate systems (up through 192kS/s) as PCM, and 1-bit, high sample rate systems (2.8224MS/s) as DSD, per Sony's coining of the term, regardless of the fact that both systems are inherently PCM based.

To speak to the myth, however, all current analog to digital converters use delta sigma modulators to convert analog to digital. The only differences between DSD and PCM is that PCM then filters the result to only contain a certain frequency spectrum and PCM converters, not bound to the 1-bit system, use an improved design that does not yield the distortion inherent in 1-bit systems. Further, all current digital to analog converters use delta sigma modulators to convert digital back to analog. The only difference between DSD and PCM in this regard is what the signal represents before it enters the modulator. When converting PCM signals the data represents a fixed frequency response, covering at least the audible range (assuming accurate filters are used).

DSD is really no more than a very high sample rate system that happens to use high enough sample rates that it does not need as large of a bit depth to represent the signal. With this in regard, the inherent difference between DSD and PCM signals is completely addressed in myth number one regarding the inherent difference in sample rates: there isn't one.

There are, however, reasons that DSD signals can be less accurate than PCM signals. Unless DSD signals are filtered, removing the tremendous amount of very high frequency "noise," this error signal can enter playback systems and cause distortion. While this is not an *inherent* difference, as playback systems could always be improved to linearly and accurately reproduce up to 1.4MHz so that DSD signals do not run the risk of causing distortion in the audible range, the solution commonly implemented is an analog filter above the audible range. If this filter has any effect in the audible range of frequencies due to phase distortion then a DSD signal could be less accurate than an equivalent PCM signal.

FROM WHENCE THE MYTH ORIGINATES

The myth about DSD primarily stems from the fact that, to date, no study has been published indicating an accurate listening test between it and PCM. This is most likely because the DSD protocol does not lend itself to direct, scientifically controlled comparison, though it does lend itself very nicely to direct, *inaccurate* comparison.

As we discussed in Chapter Twenty, converter quality, filter quality, and the difference in processing used make an accurate comparison difficult. Many people have drawn conclusions about DSD after listening to it in comparison to PCM on material that was not mastered the same and was played back on equipment that may not have been of adequate quality to compare the capabilities of PCM versus the capabilities of DSD (the filters used were audibly flawed on the PCM playback side, skewing the results of the listening test). Few will disagree that DSD *can* sound different than PCM, but to make the statement that it *inherently* sounds different is a premature conclusion as no study has been done to determine this, and no reason has been found that it would sound different if a properly controlled test were conducted. One significant advantage to DSD is that the same quality can be obtained (on the consumer side) for less money because digital signal processing can be removed from the equipment, so comparisons on inexpensive equipment with lesser quality filters can often yield a preference for DSD.

CONCLUSION

The fact that these myths permeate the audio industry shows that misinformation, misunderstanding, and mythology have a disconcerting amount of influence over the way in which audio equipment is purchased and used. Armed with the information contained within this book an audio engineer will be able to more readily discern fact from fiction and marketing hype from true benefits. The end result to the application of this knowledge will hopefully be wiser equipment purchases, better choices during the recording process, and more effective recording sessions. Further, it is the desired result of this book that the reader will be more cautious and dubious of the types of misinformation that this book has attempted to correct. The savvy audio engineer will hopefully work to understand *why* and *how* systems work in order to ensure that he or she does not simply buy into the mythology that has so much effect upon how audio is recorded and worked with in modern recording studios. Eventually these benefits will yield better sounding audio recordings, which is the primary goal of any *audio engineer*.

NOTES:

Bibliography

ADC-system on the ADMC300. Analog Devices Inc., January 2000. 29 January 2001. <http://www.analog. com/marketSolutions/motorControl/applicationCode/admc300/pdf/adc300.pdf>

A/D Converter Definition of Terms. National Semiconductor Corporation, January 2000.

"ADCs for DSP Applications." Analog Devices Data Converters Design Tools. 29 November 2001. <http:// www.analog.com/technology/dataConverters/designTools/ evaluationBoards/pdf/MixedSignal_Sect3.pdf>.

AK5394A – Super High Performance 192kHz 24-Bit $\Delta\Sigma$ ADC. Asahi Kasei Microsystems Co., Ltd. (AKM), 2002.

AKD5394A – Evaluation board Rev.B for AK5394A. Asahi Kasei Microsystems Co., Ltd. (AKM), 2002.

Aldrich, Nika. "An Explanation and Proof of the Benefit of Dither for the Audio Engineer." Cadenza Recording Papers. 12 August 2002. <http://cadenzarecording.com/papers>.

Aldrich, Nika. "The Audio Engineer's Approach to Understanding Digital Filters For the Idiot Such as Myself." Cadenza Recording Papers. 12 August 2002. <http://cadenzarecording.com/papers>.

Allen, Jont. "The Dynamics of the Human Ear." Personal Interview. 23 October, 2002.

AN10 Application Note. Crystal – A Cirrus Logic Company, 1997. 3 January 2001. < http://www.cirrus.com/ pubs/an10.pdf?DocumentID=93>

An Introduction to the Sampling Theorem. Application Note 236. National Semiconductor Corporation, January 1980.

Astrom, K.J., B. Wittenmark, and A. Rantzer. "Lecture 10: Sampling Revisited." 28 September 2002. <http:// www.control.lth.se/~kursdr/lectures/f10.pdf>.

Ball, W.W. Rouse. Excerpt. A Short Account of the History of Mathematics. 4th ed. 1908. The History of Mathematics. Ed. David R. Wilkins. Trinity College, Dublin. 9 January 2003. <http://www.maths.tcd.ie/pub/ HistMath/People/Fourier/RouseBall/RB_Fourier.html>.

Beaulieu, Norman C. "Introduction to 'Certain Topics in Telegraph Transmission Theory.'" Proceedings of the IEEE Vol. 90, No. 2 (February 2002).

Beaulieu, Norman C., Christopher C. Tan, and Mohamed Oussama Damen. "A 'Better Than' Nyquist Pulse." Department of Electrical & Computer Engineering University of Alberta. 4 July 2001. <http://www.ee.ualberta. ca/~beaulieu/online_pubs/ ncb_cct_mod_clett.pdf>.

Blackmer, David. "The World Beyond 20kHz." Earthworks Products. 9 January 2003. <http://www.earthwks. com/f_more/beyond20kHz.html>.

Boyk, James. "There's Life Above 20 Kilohertz! A Survey of Musical Instrument Spectra to 102.4kHz." 1992. 10 April 2001. <http://www.cco.caltech.edu/~boyk/spectra/spectra.htm>.

Carter, Bruce. "dB Calculator." Texas Instruments Applications. Vers. 1. 9 January 2003. <http://focus.ti.com/ download/utilities/db_calc.xls>.

Cotey, Stan. "Digital Audio Theory." Personal interview. 29 October 2002.

"dB-SPL." PTM Electronics. -9 January 2003 < HYPERLINK "http://www.ptme.com/entertainment_tech-nology/audio/reference/sound/dB-SPL.htm"   http://www.ptme.com/entertainment_technology/audio/refer-ence/sound/dB-SPL.htm >.

Downs, Rick. Analog-to-Digital Conversion. Burr-Brown Corporation, 1991.

Dunn, Julian. "Anti-alias and anti-image filtering: The benefits of 96kHz sampling rate formats for those who cannot hear above 20kHz." Digital audio papers by Julian Dunn. Nanophon. 6 January 2003. <http://www. nanophon.com/audio/antialia.pdf>.

Eastty, P., N. Bentall, G. Cook, C. Gerard, C. Sleighty, M. Smith, and P. Thorpe. "DSD-Wide. A Practical Implementation for Professional Audio." Convention Paper 5377. 110th Audio Engineering Society Conven-tion, Amsterdam, The Netherlands, 12-15 May 2001. Amsterdam, The Netherlands. Sony Pro Audio Research and Development, 2001.

Frindle, Paul. "The Measure of Audio – Are we Measuring the Right Things?" AES Spring Conference 1997. 1997.

Frindle, Paul. "Here We Go Again." Email Discussion. 5 June, 2001 – 12 June, 2001.

Frindle, Paul. "Datapaths." Email Discussion. 14 August, 2001 – 17 August, 2001.

Frindle, Paul. "FIR vs. IIR." Email Discussion. 28 November, 2001 – 29 November, 2001.

Frindle, Paul. "SNR." Email Discussion. 6 December, 2001 – 12 December, 2001.

Frindle, Paul. "How Many Taps." Email Discussion. 21 February, 2002 – 19 March, 2002.

Frindle, Paul. "Compressor and 192kHz." Email Discussion. 15 April, 2002 – 16 April, 2002.

Frindle, Paul. "SRC." Email Discussion. 2 May, 2002 – 7 May, 2002.

Frindle, Paul. "Dither." Email Discussion. 2 May, 2002 – 16 May, 2002.

Frindle, Paul. "Stopband Lobes." Email Discussion. 13 May, 2002 – 14 June, 2002.

Frindle, Paul. "What's a DEM?" Email Discussion. 25 October, 2002 - 13 November, 2002.

Frindle, Paul. "Multi-bit Modulators." Email Discussion. 6 January, 2003 – 14 January, 2003.

Frindle, Paul. "Dither v Noise shaping." Email Discussion. "20 January, 2003 – 21 January, 2003.

Fuller, Steve. Personal Interview. 10 December, 2002.

Gallager, Robert G. "Claude E. Shannon: A Retrospective on His Life, Work, and Impact." IEEE Transactions on Information Theory. Vol. 47, No. 7. (November 2001) 2681-2695.

Gambit Series POW-R – Psychoacoustically Optimized Wordlength Reduction. Switzerland: Weiss, 2000.

Katz, Bob. Mastering Audio – The Art and the Science. Burlington, MA: Focal Press, 2002.

Greene, Robert E., Mike Kuller, Paul Stubblebine, and Michael Bishop. "SACD and DVD-Audio: An In-Depth Look at the New Digital Formats, Part I." The Absolute Sound. June/July 2001.

Hansen, John H.L. "SLHS-2010 Science of Human Communication." 25 September 2001. 25 October 2001.

Harper, Douglas. "Online Etymology Dictionary." 9 January 2003. <http://www.geocities.com/etymonline>.

Harris, M.N., R. Kelly, D.A. McLeod, and Mike Story. "Effects in High Sample Rate Audio Material." dCS White Papers. 1998. 10 January 2003. <http://www.dcsltd.co.uk/papers/effects.pdf>.

Haurie, Xavier and Gordon W. Roberts. "A Design, Simulation and Synthesis Tool for Delta-Sigma-Modulator-Based Signal Sources." IEEE Symposium on Circuits and Systems, Atlanta, Georgia, May 1996. May 1996.

"Introduction to Digital Filters." Digital Filters: An Introduction. 4 March 2000. <http://www.dsptutor.freeuk.com/digfilt.pdf>.

Jorgensen, Lisa, Jon Leazenby, Kelly Crandall, and Michelle Wright. "Biographies of Mathematicians – Fourier." November 1998 – December 2000. 2 October 2002. <http://www.andrews.edu/~calkins/math/biograph/biofouri.htm>.

Katz, Eugenii. "Harry Nyquist." Biographies of Famous Electrochemists and Physicists Contributed to Understanding of Electricity. 28 September 2002. <http://www.geocities.com/bioelectrochemistry/nyquist.htm>.

Kulavik, Richard. "On Clocks." Personal Interview. 22 October, 2002.

Kulavik, Richard. "On Multi-Level and Multi-Bit Converters." Personal interview. 29 October 2002.

Kulavik, Richard. "Questions." Email Discussion. 18 November, 2002 – 22 November, 2002.

Kulavik, Richard and Robert Watson. "Digital Audio." Burr Brown Products. 12 December 2000. <http://www.web-ee.com/primers/files/DesignSem5.pdf>.

Lavry, Dan. "Understanding IIR (Infinite Impulse Response) Filters – An Intuitive Approach by Dan Lavry, dB Technologies." Lavry Engineering White Papers. 1997. 31 October 2000. <http://www.lavryengineering.com/pdfs/iir.pdf>.

Lavry, Dan. "Understanding FIR (Finite Impulse Response) Filters – An Intuitive Approach by Dan Lavry, dB Technologies." Lavry Engineering White Papers. 1997. 31 October 2000. <http://www.lavryengineering. com/pdfs/fir.pdf>.

Lavry, Dan. "On Jitter." Lavry Engineering White Papers. 1997. 31 October 2000. <http://www.lavryengineering.com/pdfs/jitter.pdf>.

Lavry, Dan. "Sampling, Oversampling, Imaging, and Aliasing – a basic tutorial by Dan Lavry, dB Technologies." Lavry Engineering White Papers. 1997. 31 October 2000. <http://www.lavryengineering.com/pdfs/sample.pdf>.

Losee, Bob. "A Discipline Independent Definition of Information." Journal of the American Society for Information Science. Vol. 48, No. 3. (1997): 254-269. 29 September 2002. <http://www.ils.unc.edu/~losee/b5/node7.html>.

Ludwig, Art. The Physics of Sound. 9 January 2003. <http://www.silcom.com/~aludwig/Physics/Main/Physics_of_sound.html>.

Meijering, Erik. "A Chronology of Interpolation From Ancient Astronomy to Modern Signal and Image Processing." Proceedings of the IEEE Vol. 90, No. 3 (March 2002): 319-342.

Mudry, Albert MD. "Inner Ear and Explosions in the History of Otology." Archives of Otolaryngology – Head & Neck Surgery. Journals of the American Medical Association. Vol. 27 No. 12. December 2001. American Medical Association. 9 January 2003. <http://archotol.ama-assn.org/issues/v127n12/ffull/olt1201-1.html>.

Neve, Rupert. Why Do Amplifiers Sound Different. Amek Systems & Controls LTD, 1999.

Nyquist, Henry. "Certain Topics in Telegraph Transmission Theory." Transactions of the AIEE Vol 47 (April 1928): 617-644.

Oohashi, Tsutomu, Emi Nishina, Manabu Honda, Yoshiharu Yonekura, Yoshitaka Fuwamoto, Norie Kawai, Tadao Maekawa, Satoshi Nakamura, Hidenao Fukuyama, and Hiroshi Shibasaki. "Inaudible High-Frequency Sounds Affect Brain Activity: Hypersonic Effect." Journal of Neurophysiology. Vol. 83 No. 6. (2000): 3548-3558.

Oohashi, Tsutomu, Emi Nishina, Yoshitaka Fuwamoto, Norie Kawai, and Hiroshi Imai. "High-Frequency Sound Above the Audible Range Affects Brain Electric Activity and Sound Perception" Convention Paper 3207. 91st Audio Engineering Society Convention, New York, 4-8 October 1991. 4-8 October 1991.

Orban, Robert. "Digital Audio: Some Myths and Realities." Orban Inc., 1999.

"OCXOs – Oven-Controlled Crystal Oscillators." Wenzel Associates, Inc.. 9 January 2003. <http://www.wenzel.com/documents/ocxo.html>.

Pohlmann, Ken C., ed. Advanced Digital Audio. Carmel, IN: SAMS, 1991.

Rabiner, Lawrence R. and Bernard Gold. Theory and Application of Digital Signal Processing. Englewood Cliffs, NJ: Prentice Hall, 1975.

"Semiconductors for Digital Audio Designer's Guide August 1997." Phillips Semiconductor. August 1997.

Shannon, Claude E. "A Mathematical Theory of Communication." Bell Systems Technical Journal Vol. 27 (July 1948): 379-423.

Shannon, Claude E. "Communication in the Presence of Noise." Proceedings of the IRE Vol. 37 (January 1949): 10-21.

Shinohara, Yoshiaki, Hitoshi Terasawa, Koichiro Ochiai, Masaya Hiraoka, Hideki Kanayama, and Toshihiko Hamasaki. "ISSCC96 / Session 14 / Sigma-Delta Converters / Paper FP 14.5." 1996 IEEE International Solid-State Circuits Conference. 9 February 1996.

Shirley, Brett. "Floating Point Processors." Personal interview. 1 December 2002.

Shockman, Paul. AND 8040/D Phase Lock Loop General Operations. ON Semiconductor.

Single-Supply 16-Bit $\Sigma\Delta$ ADC. Analog Devices, Inc., 2000. 29 November, 2001. <http://mlug.missouri.edu/ ~markrages/static/projects/AD1877_a.pdf>.

Sklar, Bernard. "Designing Digital Communications Systems." 3 January 2002. <http://www.informit.com/ content/images/art_sklar2_designing/elementLinks/art_sklar2_designing.pdf>.

Specifying A/D and D/A Converters. Application Note 156. National Semiconductor Corporation.

Sprenger, Stephan M. Stephan M. Sprenger's Audio DSP Pages. 27 November 2002. <http://www.dspdimension.com/>.

Story, Mike. "Timing Errors and Jitter." dCS White Papers. May 1998. 10 January 2003. <http://www.dcsltd. co.uk/papers/jitter.pdf>.

Story, Mike. "A Suggested Explanation For (Some of The) Audible Differences Between High Sample Rate and Conventional Sample Rate Audio Material." dCS White Papers. September 1997. 10 January 2003. <http://www.dcsltd.co.uk/papers/aes97ny.pdf>.

Story, Mike, Duncan McLeod, and Martin Reynolds. "Resolution, bits, SNR and Linearity." dCS White Papers. October 1998. 10 January 2003. <http://www.dcsltd.co.uk/papers/bits.pdf>.

Suites, Bryan H. "Frequencies of Musical Notes." Physics of Music. 9 January 2003. <http://www.phy.mtu. edu/~suits/notefreqs.html>.

Tabuena, Dennis. "FIR Paper Comments." Private Email. 27 July, 2002.

Talbot-Smith, Michael. Audio Engineer's Reference Book. Paperback ed. Oxford: Focal Press, 1998.

Travis, Chris. "Multi-Level Converters." Email Discussion. 24 October, 2002.

"Understanding VCXO's – To Avoid Overspecifying Them." MFElectronics Application Notes. 19 September 2002. <http://www.mfelectronics.com/PDFs/Press/VCXOWhitepaper.pdf>.

Unser, Michael. "Sampling – 50 Years After Shannon." Proceedings of the IEEE Vol. 88, No. 4 (April 2000): 569-587.

Vaidyanathan, P. P. "Generalizations of the Sampling Theorem: Seven Decades After Nyquist." 21 March 2001. 21 March 2001. <http://www.ee.caltech.edu/EE/Groups/dsp/students/bojan/journ/Nyquist7decades. pdf>.

Völker, Ernst-Jo, and Sabine Fischer. "Phillip Reis – From the First Telephone to the First Microphone." Convention Paper 5060. 112th Audio Engineering Society Convention, Munich, 10-13 May 2002. 11 May 2002. 9 January 2003. <http://www.aes.org/events/112/papers/q.cfm>.

Vrdoljak, Zdenko. "Nyquist's Criterion and Shannon's Law." Asynchronous Transfer Mode. 28 September 2002. <http://fly.cc.fer.hr/~zdenko/appendix/shannon.html>.

Williams, Gerald E. Digital Technology. 2nd ed. Chicago: Science Research Associates, INC., 1982.

"Writing Quality." CDRInfo. 17 June 2002. 9 January 2003. <http://www.cdrinfo.com/Sections/Articles/PrinterFriendly.asp?ArticleHeadline=Writing+Quality>.

Yost, William W. and Donald W. Nielsen. Fundamentals of Hearing. 2nd ed. Orlando: Holt, Rinehart and Winston, Inc., 1985.

Yuhas, Tony. "On Waveform Propagation." Personal interview. 1 December 2002.

Zelniker, Glenn. "Glenn – Fourier." Private email exchange. 30, October, 2002.

Zelniker, Glenn. "Fourier Analysis." Personal Interview. 29 October, 2002.

The following sources are threads from the Pro Audio Mailing List

Aldrich, Nika, Glenn Meadows, Bob Katz, et al. "Colored Dither Noise." Pro Audio Mailing List. 12 January, 2003 – 13 January, 2003.

Aldrich, Nika, John Vengrouskie, Glenn Meadows, et al. "Converters." Pro Audio Mailing List. 2 November, 2001 – 5 November, 2001.

Aldrich, Nika, Daniel Weiss, Henk ten Pierick, et al. "Decimation." Pro Audio Mailing List. 5 April, 2002 – 12 April, 2002.

Aldrich, Nika, Bob Katz, Daniel Weiss, et al. "Bit Depths – Data Transmission." Pro Audio Mailing List. 9 April, 2002 – 14 April, 2002.

Aldrich, Nika, Jim Johnston, Bob Katz, et al. "Another Theoretical Question." Pro Audio Mailing List. 18 October, 2002 – 31 October, 2002.

Aldrich, Nika, Glenn Zelniker, Christ Travis, et al. "Back to the Fundamentals." Pro Audio Mailing List. 15 February, 2002 – 4 March, 2002.

Aldrich, Nika, Glenn Meadows, Seva, et al. "Digi Sound Quality." Pro Audio Mailing List. 21 March, 2002 – 29 March, 2002.

Aldrich, Nika, Bob Katz, Glenn Zelniker, et al. "Dither v Noise shaping." Also referenced as "Dither." Pro Audio Mailing List. 15 January, 2003 – 20 January, 2003.

Aldrich, Nika, Bob Katz, John Vengrouskie, et al. "DSD Levels." Pro Audio Mailing List. 21 October, 2002 – 23 October, 2002.

Aldrich, Nika, Glenn Meadows, Michal Jurewicz, et al. "Dynamic Range of 1-bit Systems." Pro Audio Mailing List. 18 November, 2002 – 20 November, 2002.

Aldrich, Nika, David Collins, Jim Johnston, et al. "Nyquist Theory." Pro Audio Mailing List. 28 September, 2002 – 14 October, 2002.

Aldrich, Nika, Bob Katz, Dick Pierce, et al. "Question About Jitter." Pro Audio Mailing List. 17 September, 2002 – 18 September, 2002.

Aldrich, Nika, Daniel Weiss, Chris Caudle, et al. "SRC." Also referenced as "SRC – When to Dither." "SRC – and a Matter of Interpretation." Pro Audio Mailing List. 2 May, 2002 – 15 December, 2002.

Aldrich, Nika, Herbie Robinson, Charlie Richmond, et al. "The Bottom Line – 16 Bits Enough?" Also referenced as "Pro-Audio-Digest V2 #299." "Cascading Audio Devices." "The Real World." "Thresholds and Audibility." "Randomness." "Our Hearing Thresholds." Pro Audio Mailing List. 12 January, 2003 – 28 January, 2003.

Aldrich, Nika, Dick Pierce, Jim Johnston, et al. "Waveforms." Pro Audio Mailing List. 15 October, 2002 – 16 October, 2002.

Aldrich, Nika, Stephen Barncard, Chris Caudle, et al. "Why 44.1kS/s?" Pro Audio Mailing List. 24 October, 2002 – 26 October, 2002.

Aldrich, Nika, Bob Katz, Chris Caudle, et al. "Wordclock/AES Question." Pro Audio Mailing List. 24 November, 2002 – 3 December, 2002.

Aldrich, Nika, Chris Caudle, Jack Andresen, et al. "Group Delay." Pro Audio Mailing List. 9 May, 2002 – 11 May, 2002.

Banquer, Dan, Dick Pierce, Herbie Robinson, et al. "Intersample Peaking." Pro Audio Mailing List. 21 December, 2002 – 31 December, 2002.

Bishop, Michael, Herbie Robinson, Chris Travis, et al. "DSD Into Power Amps." Pro Audio Mailing List. 21 October, 2002 – 23 October, 2002.

Caudle, Chris, Herbie Robinson, Chris Travis, et al. "Optimal Filters." Pro Audio Mailing List. 22 October, 2002 – 25 October, 2002.

Caudle, Chris, Bob Katz, Nika Aldrich, et al. "PCM to DSD Comparison with dCS Elgar." Also referenced as "PCM to DSD Comparison." "Effects of Filters." "We Need a Chalkboard." "Seeking Evidence of the Pre-Echo." "PCM to DSD Test?" "Shopping Trip Tip." Pro Audio Mailing List. 11 December, 2002 – 12 January, 2003.

Eaton, Thomas, Bob Katz, Michal Jurewicz. "Sampling Frequency Thoughts." Pro Audio Mailing List. 18 February, 2002 – 21 February, 2002.

Greene, Robert, Nika Aldrich, Bob Katz, et al. "20 K Not Enough." Pro Audio Mailing List. 27 October, 2002 – 31 October, 2002.

Grimm, Eelco, Rob Poretti, Glenn Zelniker, et al. "Digital Compressor Zipper Noise." Pro Audio Mailing List. 22 January, 2002 – 23 February, 2002.

Hicks, Christopher, Ken Bogdanowicz, Nika Aldrich, et al. "Processing Power..." Also referenced as "Paper on Filters." Pro Audio Mailing List. 16 July, 2002 – 6 August, 2002.

Johnston, Jim, Russell Scott, David Rick. "CIC's." Pro Audio Mailing List. 8 May, 2002 – 9 May, 2002.

Jurewicz, Michal, Nika Aldrich, Bob Olhsson, et al. "(SACD vs. CD) vs. (DSD vs. PCM)." Pro Audio Mailing List. 11 November, 2002 – 7 January, 2003.

Jurewicz, Michal, Bob Olhsson, Nika Aldrich, et al. "Protools HD Mixer." Pro Audio Mailing List. 22 February, 2002 – 4 March, 2002.

Katz, Bob, Martin, Greg, et al. "PCM vs. DSD Math and Listening..." Pro Audio Mailing List. 23 October, 2002 – 28 October, 2002.

Katz, Bob, Chris Travis, Herbie Robinson, et al. "More on 96 Versus 44." Also referenced as "Consumer D/D." Pro Audio Mailing List. 2 March, 2002 – 7 March, 2002.

Katz, Bob, Herbie Robinson, Nika Aldrich, et al. "Another Sampling Frequency Experience." Also referenced as "DSD Recording." "DSD Location Recording." "High-Rate PCM Recording." Pro Audio Mailing List. 12 February, 2002 – 5 March, 2002.

Katz, Bob, Vincent van Haaff, Tom Scott, et al. "96K Test, Jitter and Media Issues." Pro Audio Mailing List. 12 December, 2001 – 20 December, 2001.

Katz, Bob, Julian Dunn, Kevin Gross, et al. "Calling All Oscillators." Pro Audio Mailing List. 1 November, 2001 – 7 November, 2001.

Kulavik, Richard, Chris Caudle, Bob Katz, et al. "Filters Phase Issue." Also referenced as "Gentle Filters – Was Bob's Soliloquy." "Gentle Filters." "Slow Filters." "Filters (Thread #47)." "Gentle Filters and Audibility Thresholds." "Gentle Filters – Reference Monitoring Levels." "Dither Noise." Pro Audio Mailing List. 8 January, 2003 - 23 January, 2003.

Lampen, Steve, Dan Mortensen, Nika Aldrich, et al. "Boyk's Article on High Frequencies." Pro Audio Mailing List. 19 November, 2002 – 21 November, 2002.

Lukin, Alexey, Jim Johnston, Nika Aldrich, et al. "Alias-Intermodulation Distortion & Echoes Caused By Ripples in the Pass-Band." Pro Audio Mailing List. 2 February, 2003.

Maguire, Tom, Nika Aldrich, George Massenburg, et al. "The Costly vs. Necessary Issue or Why Are You Being Cheap With My Bits?" Also referenced as "Medium Compression/dB." Pro Audio Mailing List. 19 March, 2002 – 18 April, 2002.

McDaniel, John, Michael Bishop, Greg Reierson, et al. "AES SACD Demo." Pro Audio Mailing List. 22 October, 2002 – 24 October, 2002.

Meadows, Glenn, Nika Aldrich, Chris Caudle, et al. "Another Take on the Filters Issue..." Pro Audio Mailing List. 8 January, 2003 – 11 January, 2003.

Smith, Andrew, Dick Pierce, Nika Aldrich, et al. "16/24 Bit and Dither." Pro Audio Mailing List. 11 January, 2003 – 12 January, 2003.

Puntolillo, Steve, J Silberman, Nika Aldrich, et al. "Sony's Spin on SACD." Pro Audio Mailing List. 22 November, 2002 - 25 November, 2002.

Rhoades, Michael, Bob Olhsson, Tad Rollow, et al. "Did the Sheep Stay Silent?" Pro Audio Mailing List. 18 March, 2002 – 21 March, 2002.

Richmond, Charlie, Nika Aldrich, David Collins, et al. "DSD/SACD Sampling Rate?" Pro Audio Mailing List. 13 December, 2002 – 15 December, 2002.

Shepherd, Ian, Glenn Meadows, George Massenburg, et al. "DSD Processing?" Pro Audio Mailing List. 17 November, 2002 – 19 November, 2002.

Silverman, Alan, Kurt Albershardt, Dave Davis, et al. "The PCM/DSD Fracas." Pro Audio Mailing List. 14 November, 2002 – 19 November, 2002.

Simmons, Greg, Richard Hess, Nika Aldrich, et al. "Big Mouth Strikes Again." Pro Audio Mailing List. 26 August, 2002.

Travis, Chris, Bob Katz, Michal Jurewicz. "Differences Between DSD and PCM." Pro Audio Mailing List. 23 October, 2002 – 24 October, 2002.

Weiss, Daniel, Dick Pierce, David Rick, et al. "About Dithering." Pro Audio Mailing List. 6 April, 2002 – 9 April, 2002.

Sources referred to as the "Pro Audio Mailing List" include specific information from the following contributors:

Kurt Albershardt, Nika Aldrich, Hank Alrich, Jack Andresen, Stephen Balliet, Dan Banquer, Stephen Barncard, Frederick Bashour, Thomas Bethel, Michael Bishop, Richard Black, Ken Bogdanowicz, Leslie Brooks, B.J. Buchalter, John Campbell, Chris Caudle, David Collins, Dave Davis, Hanno di Rosa, Parker Dinkins, Dan Dugan, Julian Dunn, Thomas Eaton, Jeff Evans, Hudson Fair, Goran Finnberg, Paul Frindle, Steve Fuller, Alan Garren, David Glasser, Edward Gosfield, Robert Greene, Eelco Grimm, Kevin Gross, Richard Hess, Christopher Hicks, Barry Hufker, Marvin Humphrey, Jim Johnston, David Josephson, Lou Judson, Michal Jurewicz, Bob Katz, Kelly Kay, Richard Kulavik, John La Grou, Steve Lampen, John Leary, Russell Lemon, David Lloyd, Alexey Lukin, Thomas Lund, David Martin, George Massenburg, John McDaniel, Monte McGuire, Glenn Meadows, Andy Moorer, Dan Mortensen, Bob Olhsson, Marco Olivotto, Dick Pierce, Dave Platt, Rob Poretti, K.K. Proffitt, Steve Puntolillo, Charles Repka, O.J. Rancans, Greg Reierson, Michael Rhoades, Charlie Richmond, David Rick, Michael Rivers, Herbie Robinson, Tad Rollow, Brian Roth, Martin Saleteg, David Satz, Russell Scott, Tom Scott, Seva, Ian Shepherd, Greg Simmons, J Silberman, Alan Silverman, Keith Sklower, Andrew Smith, Preston Smith, Henk ten Pierick, Guido Tent, Fred Thal, Mikael Thieme, Chris Townsend, Chris Travis, Dave Tudder, Vincent van Haaff, John Vengrouskie, Daniel Weiss, Duane Wise, Lee Wright, Andre Yew, George Yohng, and Glenn Zelniker.

Index

NOTES:

NOTES:

NOTES:

NOTES:

NOTES:

NOTES:

NOTES:

NOTES:

NOTES:

NOTES:

6490647R0

Made in the USA
Lexington, KY
24 August 2010